Allegory in Dante's
Commedia

Allegory in
Dante's *Commedia*

ROBERT HOLLANDER

PRINCETON UNIVERSITY PRESS
PRINCETON, NEW JERSEY
1969

Publication of this book has been
aided by a grant from the University Committee on
Research in the Humanities and Social
Sciences, Princeton University

This book has been composed in
Linotype Caslon Old Face

Printed in the United States of America
by Princeton University Press

*For Jean, eventually for Cornelia,
and in memory of Elizabeth.*

PREFACE

The translations contained within are mine unless otherwise noted, although work of other translators was often helpful. In the case of the *Commedia* itself, I look with gratitude in the direction of the Carlyle-Wicksteed and Sinclair translations and Grandgent's notes. I have tried for literal rendering and, whenever possible, for line-by-line equivalence with the original. In the case of the Vulgate, I have bypassed the Revised Standard Version for the modernized King James (Oxford University Press, New York, 1948).

Financial aid from the Princeton University Committee on Research in the Humanities and Social Sciences is gratefully acknowledged here; and, my thanks go also to the University's Bureau of Student Aid for making available to me the services of an undergraduate research assistant, Michael A. Bernstein, who has worked for and with me over the past three years on this and other projects. It will be no surprise to those who know his extraordinary record as a student here—an accurate reflection of his ability—that his work for me was excellent.

It is hard to strike the right note in offering thanks to one's students, especially after W. H. Auden has set such a high standard. And it is somewhat like dedicating a critical work to the memory of the author who is its subject, "without whom this work could not have been written." Despite the difficulty, I do want to take notice of the debt of gratitude I owe to many of them who made the time on the other side of the lectern go so swiftly for me. A certain number of these students will find their names duly recorded herein in response to what seemed to me original and useful insights. I hope that those others whose contributions were not of the sort that is readily recollected in a footnote will not think I am unmindful of them, for I am not.

Of the many friends and colleagues who have given to me of their time, attention, and intelligence, I single out three: Edward D. Sullivan, now Dean of the College, who has held a supervisory and encouraging role in what now amounts to a full half of my life; A. B. Giamatti, for two years my colleague and, I hope, for a long time to come my friend, who has left me the legacy of more time spent listening and then responding to my notions of Dante than I had any right to claim; and Ira O. Wade, who first made me want to spend my life with books, as I now do, and whom I can never thank enough for having done that, even at the risk of making the greater seem responsible for the lesser.

Hopewell, New Jersey
31 July 1968

CONTENTS

. . . divinum et novum vehiculum Argonautarum . . .

Cicero

In nostrae ergo animae domo *historia* fundamentum ponit, *allegoria* parietes erigit, *anagogia* tectum supponit, *tropologia* vero tam interius per affectum quam exterius per effectum boni operis, variis ornatibus depingit.

Rabanus Maurus

Non enim in somniis, sed per venam divini subsurrii, spiritu revelante et aperiente os poete, divinum hoc opus prolatum est. Unde qui eum in somniis tanta suscepisse dogmatizzant, meo videre, sompniant.

Filippo Villani

Deux erreurs: 1° prendre tout littéralement; 2° prendre tout spirituellement.

Pascal

Spot more delicious than those Gardens feign'd
Or of reviv'd *Adonis*, or renown'd
Alcinoüs, host of old *Laertes'* Son,
Or that, not Mystic, where the Sapient King
Held dalliance with his fair *Egyptian* Spouse.

Milton

La plus part des fables d'Esope ont plusieurs sens et intelligences. Ceux qui les mythologisent en choisissent quelque visage qui quadre bien à la fable; mais, pour la plus part, ce n'est que le premier visage et superficiel; il y en a d'autres plus vifs, plus essentiels et internes, ausquels ils n'ont sçeu penetrer: voylà comme j'en fay.

Montaigne

Qui ne diroit que les glosses augmentent les doubtes et l'ignorance, puis qu'il ne se voit aucun livre, soit humain, soit divin, auquel le monde s'embesongne, duquel l'interpretation face tarir la difficulté? Le centiesme commentaire le renvoye à son suivant, plus espineux et plus scabreux que le premier ne l'avoit trouvé. Quand est-il convenu entre nous: ce livre en a assez, il n'y a meshuy plus que dire?

Montaigne

Allegory in Dante's
Commedia

INTRODUCTION

THE ALLEGORICAL
PROBLEM

The subject of the following inquiry—the allegorical theory and practice of Dante's *Commedia*—is not new. Recently the entire question has tended to become focused in a single continuing controversy concerning Dante's use of the techniques of fourfold Biblical exegesis.[1] Nevertheless, it is also true that the *Divine Comedy* reflects the four major medieval theories of allegory which themselves reflect one another in complex and often puzzling ways. Insofar as they may be disentangled one from another, these four theories may be described as follows: 1) the personification allegory of a few Christian poets, especially Prudentius and Martianus Capella, which in turn is essentially similar in technique to 2) the medieval allegorical interpretation of Virgil and Ovid. These two theories, the first "creative," the second critical, are together different in nature from 3) what the grammarians and rhetoricians called *allegoria*, thus signifying the writer's command of his tropes, his rhetorical embellishment.[2] While all three of these theories show their effects

---

[1] The central presence in this controversy is that of Charles Singleton. Fuller documentation awaits a more suitable context.

[2] A nice modern restatement of this medieval theory of allegory, although its author would seem to be unaware of its nicety, is the following, found in Angus Fletcher's *Allegory: The Theory of a Symbolic Mode*, Ithaca, 1964, p. 2: "In the simplest terms, allegory says one thing and means another." (See Isidore of Seville, *Etymologiae* I, xxxvii, 22: "Allegoria est alieniloquium, aliud enim sonat, aliud intelligitur.") The "allegory of the rhetoricians" is thus capable of defining all allegory, but only at the cost of failing to distinguish among the kinds. It simplifies accurately enough, but not usefully. Such, it seems to me, frequently is the nature of D. W. Robertson's work on

3

in Dante, it is the contention of this work that of primary importance to the composition of the *Divine Comedy* is 4) the fourfold exegesis of Scripture.

As has frequently been pointed out, allegory began as a critical tool, as a way of reading, either in the Greek scholiasts' work on the text of Homer or in the textual interpretations of the Hebrew exegetical tradition.[3] These two traditions came together and became sorted out—in ways that have direct bearing on the subject of this study—in the schools of Alexandria in the first century after Christ, especially in the allegorical concord forged by Philo Judaeus (ca. 30 B.C.-A.D. 45) between Judaism and Hellenism during the very years of Christ's life on earth. It is from Philo's essentially non-historical view of allegory that the first three of the four kinds of allegory enumerated above developed in the Middle Ages.

Almost every Dante commentator since the fourteenth century has read the *Divine Comedy* as though its essential allegorical principle were that of Prudentius. This tradition of allegory is familiar to us today, because we in the English-speaking countries have been brought up on Spenser and Bunyan, as well as on the dream-vision poems of Chaucer. Thus we, like the literary critics of Dante's own time, often have only a certain kind of meaningful

---

medieval allegory, as is exemplified by the following comment, with its clear affinities to Isidore: "Allegory is simply the device of saying one thing to mean another, and its ulterior meaning may rest on things or on actions, or on both together" (*A Preface to Chaucer*, Princeton, 1962, p. 300).

[3] See E. R. Curtius, *European Literature and the Latin Middle Ages*, New York, 1963, pp. 203-207, for a brief discussion of "Homer and Allegory." Another effective brief treatment of the history of allegory from its ancient beginnings is J. Geffcken's article on "Allegorical Interpretation" in the *Encyclopedia of Religion and Ethics*, ed. J. Hastings, New York, 1913, pp. 327-331. See also the witty article, "Allegory," by Northrop Frye, in the *Encyclopedia of Poetry and Poetics*, ed. A. Preminger, Princeton, 1965, pp. 12-14.

fictiveness in mind when we say, see, or hear the word "allegory." For us, as for those, like Fulgentius, who saw in Virgil's epic only the external trappings of an inner experience, the struggle within an archetypal human soul as it grows from youth to maturity, allegorical poetry is concerned with the concrete primarily as the means of arriving at spiritual abstraction. This tradition of allegory is, in religious terms, the spirit of gnosticism, in which the objects of perception have value only as they lead us toward the ineffable, toward salvation through wisdom— as they are clues to the spiritualized, non-tangible, abstract essence of the universe. According to this theory, objects, whether theological or poetical, are the inadequate signs of ideas. Though it sounds much the same, this line of argument is precisely opposite to the Christian argument, which was first advanced in ways that were to become largely influential in the Gospels and in the works of Paul and of Augustine, and which can be grasped under the single text, Incarnation. The gnostic imagination, on the other hand, is predicated on the notion that allegory begins with an idea which is treated as object only to accommodate a weaker human understanding—the sort of humanizing of conceptual truth that is found in Platonic myth, every element of which is "worked out" by the author to correspond with the conceptual framework which necessitates his bitter instruction. There is no actual cave within which men sit in chains, deprived of the light of the sun; there is the allegorical reduction of a conceptual statement, something like: "Men, lacking the intellectual perfection it might be hoped they would possess, are unable to understand the relationship between the shadowy, imperfect presences of the actual world and the clarity of the real." This kind of allegory precludes, or at least supersedes, experience.

Perhaps no specifically Christian poetry—of which the

early medieval world can offer few major examples—can offer a more typical, charming, and effective example of a nearly pure allegorical imagination than that often referred to (and less often read) work of Prudentius, *Psychomachia*. We should be grateful to Prudentius for many reasons, one of which is that in his title he enunciated the approach of every allegorist who was to follow his technique. The title means "The War in the Mind" or "The Struggle for/in the Soul." Works like the *Roman de la rose*, Chaucer's dream-vision poems, Spenser's epic, and Bunyan's dream-journey—all these owe something to Prudentius (the very name works as a personification of the attributes a Christian poet should possess). In all such works the reader is made to understand that *this* is not actually happening; it serves only to represent *that*. The dream is public and the dreamer is the author, or the dreamer in the fiction, or you the reader. And all such allegories, no matter how densely and beautifully detailed they may be, begin and end with the understanding that they are not at first remove to be confused with actuality; that they are the record of the struggle within one idealized soul which stands for all Christian souls; that the trappings of external reality stand only and surely for the sacramental spiritual truths in which we must all be instructed. We can see the continuance of this medieval and later literary tradition in some contemporary literature, particularly in Dostoievski and in Kafka.[4]

[4] The scene in *Crime and Punishment* in which Raskolnikov's tentative confession to Sonia is overheard by the eavesdropping Svidrigailov through a closed door lends itself especially well to a recognition of the traces of this kind of allegory. If Raskolnikov and Svidrigailov represent, in some respects at least, opposing yet correlate consciousness of the same event, we perceive that a coagulate consciousness, a blend of Dostoievski, Raskolnikov, Svidrigailov, and the reader—or a postulated mind developed from all of these—is pictured as being comprised of two warring elements.

6

Although it might be difficult to prove that Prudentius' work had a direct influence on so much of later literature (it would seem, however, that no monastery library in the Middle Ages was without its copy),[5] it is easy to understand the contribution that his work made to Christian literature. Since the Christian life was to be understood as having one of its climactic moments in conversion, Prudentius had perfected a literary treatment that allowed such a momentous event (which is, after all, internal) to be displayed externally. In contrast, we might consider the climactic moment of Augustine's *Confessions* (VIII, xii). It takes less than a page to describe that moment of conversion in the garden. To be sure, this is one of the great moments of Western literature (we shall see that it had a literary as well as a spiritual effect upon Dante): the voice from outside the garden wall cries "Take and read"; Augustine, playing the Christian equivalent of the *sortes Virgilianaes*, opens to Romans 13:13; and finally he is a Christian. Augustine's life is told as history. A poet attempting to deal with a similar matter, the turning of the soul from sin toward redemption, would have been tempted by the literary in addition to the doctrinal. That temptation, in the case of Prudentius, is the probable cause of the invention or reinvigoration of allegory as a means of describing graphically what occurs within the soul: our mind is a battlefield.

[5] For the popularity of Prudentius, see M. Lavarenne's Introduction to his edition of *Psychomachia*, Paris, 1933, pp. 22-28, where he points out (p. 27) that more than 310 Prudentius manuscripts have survived to our own day. H. R. Jauss, "Form und Auffassung der Allegorie in der Tradition der *Psychomachia*," in *Medium Aevum Vivum: Festschrift für Walther Bulst*, ed. H. R. Jauss and D. Schaller, Heidelberg, 1960, pp. 179-206, speaks to the unique importance of the contribution of Prudentius (p. 186): "Prudentius hat in seiner *Psychomachia* zwar zum ersten Mal ein Werk geschaffen, in dem alle Figuren in Gestalt von allegorischen Personifikationen auftreten."

7

Prudentius' peculiar contribution was to make the war in the mind or soul a fit subject for poetry. A formal contribution, it in turn relies on a technique which is at least as old as fifth-century Athens and which is variously known as personification, philological, or (appropriately enough) Greek allegory. This technique applies principally to the mode of signifying rather than the method of presenting, and since it is the best known and best understood allegorical technique, should offer little problem in itself. In this study difficulties arise when the role of personification allegory in the *Divine Comedy* is considered. At the outset I wish to say merely that, although Dante's poem makes a certain use of this kind of allegory, the technique is basically inimical to his way of writing in the *Divine Comedy*.

In one tradition of Homeric criticism, which began in the fifth century before Christ, personification allegory came into existence first as an interpretive and critical device (Athena urging Achilles to sheathe his sword in *Iliad* I was seen by some commentators as the personification of the Wisdom of Achilles temporarily easing his anger—an example of the common role of psychomachia and personification in a literature which precedes Prudentius by a thousand years). The device became an important part of "creative" allegoresis in the myths of Plato.[6] In these myths we see clearly both the great benefits and the great drawbacks of philological allegory. The technique enables a teller to make his point clearly and attractively. At the same time (and in accord with Plato's negative notions of the possibilities of mimesis), it is immediately obvious that an allegorist should not surrender to his subject, should not be caught and drawn by something

[6] See J. A. Stewart, *The Myths of Plato*, London, 1905.

in the world that offers him the occasion for mimesis, as were Homer and the tragedians. Rather, he must at all times reduce his subject matter to its intellectual framework. These myths are allegorical representations of the abstract truth that a well-trained mind can grasp and present in simple, though often moving, terms. Now, as then, those who work from idea to representation necessarily deal with a more limited form of expression. In order to create, an allegorist must have thought through what he is going to create. What he imitates has no primary life of its own. It is this approach to art which is thoroughly attacked in the aesthetic principles of Aristotle. The *Poetics* call for an art which, like a living animal, is organic, an art based on imitation rather than on abstract formulation. The Platonic "muse" is the organization of actuality once one has grasped the principles which lie behind it; the Aristotelian "muse" is actuality itself. The first is deductive, the second inductive. Significantly enough, Aristotle does not discuss allegory. He is on the side of the poet, the man who encounters experience as it is, who gives it a form and even possibly a formulation, but who refuses to start from the formulation. R. P. Blackmur's often quoted "Poetry is life at the remove of form and meaning"[7] seems to me to be a thoroughly Aristotelian statement. The Platonist, when he condescends to art, would turn this around: "Art is meaning made decorational in ways that may or may not reflect actual life." The Platonist is not basically interested in the literary question of form because he respects only the philosophical distinctions about form. Thus literary form, for him, is extrinsic. It will be, of necessity, the allegorical form, in which imitation is primarily adjunct to philology rather than to experience.

[7] From the first page of his essay "A Critic's Job of Work."

The rules of any art are both doctrinal and technical. By technical I do not mean to indicate the small rules, but only the major distinctions concerning the methods by which the artist imitates—technical in the way that all sciences of observed behavior must insist on the laws of their techniques of observation. The pole of Platonism is aestheticism—the Pseudo-Longinus' contribution which points to the mystery of beauty itself. Most people would agree that the two essential ingredients of great art are significance and beauty; but theories which seek to institute the rules of either must perforce leave the work of art, and the world which somehow caused it, in order to insist on an ideal significance or an ideal of beauty toward which the given work of art aspires. Both are extrinsic to the first principles of *imitatio*, though indeed many things which do not imitate are beautiful and significant ("Beauty is truth, truth beauty" is an example which, although it may be neither beautiful nor true, or either one and not the other, happily coincides with the poles of this discussion). Aristotle was the first non-allegorical critic, the first who gave to the poet his right to imitate first and think later, though the thought must guarantee the imitation. He makes us ask the question, "Is Oedipus a true imitation of a man?" Sophocles imitated significantly and beautifully, to be sure. But the significance and beauty of his work depend upon the excellence of his imitation, which is not so for the Platonist. At least Plato, unlike his fellows in Homeric criticism, realized that the epics were imitative and not allegorical. He simply does not approve of imitations of imitations. Art is to be taken for walks on the philosopher's leash; it can make no claims of its own because it has no ideal—which is to say real—existence.

The Homeric problem became the Virgilian problem as well. This is partly because Virgil imitated Homer's imitation, and partly because he was a Roman and thus almost necessarily held history as his muse. The problem arose mainly because Christian Virgilians tended to be gnostics who could only imagine a value in the swirl of life and words of the *Aeneid* if Aeneas could be less than himself and more than a Roman. Their vulgar allegorizations of the *Aeneid* are monuments to Christian gnosticism.

Augustine's reaction to Virgil, like Plato's to Homer, is a fascinating study in the ways in which brilliant men cannot be duped, despite their inclinations.[8] In the *Confessions* Augustine condemns the *Aeneid*.[9] Yet it is important that he does not try to save his Virgil, whom he much admired, by allegorizing him. He, like Plato, objects that the poet tells us lies, and he recognizes that the lies ask to be dealt with as though they were truth, that the literal meaning of the poem demands to be faced—and rejected here, but not always—as history. The literary critics of his day who seek for hidden allegories seem to anger him more.[10] And, despite his protestations against

[8] See Karl Hermann Schelkle, *Virgil in der Deutung Augustins*, Stuttgart-Berlin, 1939, for a record of Augustine's great admiration of Virgil (Schelkle counts some 140 quotations) despite his averred disapproval. Nancy Lenkeith, in *Dante and the Legend of Rome*, London, 1952, p. 33, reminds those who take Augustine's attack on Virgil in the *Confessions* uncritically that at Cassiciacum, while he was nearing his conversion, Augustine read and discussed Virgil every day with his younger friends. It is at least amusing to remember that Augustine's first "triumph" as a young scholar came when he won a contest at school by doing the best prose rendering of *Aen.* I, 37-49 (*Confs.* I, xvii).

[9] Especially in Book I, xiii, where he chides himself for his youthful enthusiasm for the tale of Dido and Aeneas.

[10] Such, at any rate, is the implication of his description of the schools of rhetoric, *loc.cit.*, where "vela pendent liminibus," thus indicating that the mysteries of literature are taught within. *Velum* is the word which lies at the heart of the matter for the processes of personification allegory, in which the literal meaning is but a "veil" for the spiritual truth hidden behind the fictive words. (It has a more

Virgil, it is to the poet of Rome that he turns over and over again in *The City of God*. Indeed, one even has the nagging sense that the *Confessions* themselves take their literary form from the *Aeneid*—the Mediterranean wanderings of Augustine to find the "true city."[11] If the *Confessions* were a novel, we would have to concede that it would best be described as a realistic novel, not as an allegory; and so it would find a parallel to itself in the journey of Aeneas, which Augustine, unlike his more "sophisticated" fellow readers, did not see as allegorical.

The wanderings of his fellow readers are generally similar, having this in common: they "de-historicize" the *Aeneid*. Under their eyes the surface of the poem becomes the pretext for psychomachian, philosophical misunderstandings. "Medieval Virgil" means the disappearance of the actual Virgil and of the actualized Aeneas. The poem becomes a parable of the growth of the Christian soul. While many have pointed out that Virgil may be understood as a pre-Christian at least in some major respects, in recent times none has been foolish enough to contend that Virgil's method corresponds to the allegorical method superimposed upon him. His meaning may be close to, or assimilable into, a Christian structure of belief. His method, like Homer's, is "historical." Aeneas is an actual man. His story is history, not a public dream.

---

complicated significance when applied to the Bible.) The thresholds of the literary schools thus offer a picture of the practices taught by the *literati*, which lead to error.

[11] A few of the common and central elements include a journey from the city of destruction (Carthage) to Rome (Augustine will fare better at Milan, however); passionate women who lead the hero astray, while the good woman (Lavinia, Monica) leads to victory and truth; nocturnal flight from Africa: where Aeneas left Dido stealthily behind in Carthage to suicide, Augustine similarly steals away from Monica, who responds with a better faith.

This, at least, is what is to be understood at the poem's first remove.

So far my comments have been exclusively directed to the kind of allegory which was used in common by a handful of Christian poets and critics in the Middle Ages, one which had its roots in the critical processes of Platonism. Although it accounts for a major part of the allegorical concerns of the first thousand years of the history of literature in the West, we had better turn to an idea of allegory that is less firmly related to the conceptual similarities we can easily perceive between the first two kinds. This is allegory as defined by the rhetoricians and grammarians—allegory that can primarily be described, if not defined, by the single phrase of Isidore of Seville, who calls it *alieniloquium*,[12] or "otherspeech." In doing so, Isidore has in mind Cicero's kind of concern with the decorative possibilities of language in the mouth of the orator, and hence in the productions of the writer. In this respect allegory is treated as belonging to the art of rhetoric, the work being used to refer simply to seven (for Isidore—more or less than seven for others) figures of speech, or tropes.[13] This concern had come through Cicero to such

[12] *Etymologiae*, I, xxxvii, 22 (Migne, *P.L.*, LXXXII, col. 115).

[13] The chapter (xxxvii) in which Isidore discusses *allegoria* is indeed called "De tropis." James E. Shaw, in his important essay, *The Lady "Philosophy" in the Convivio*, Cambridge, Mass., 1938, p. 11, speaks generally to this point: "The secular view of allegory—the poet's view—is of course much broader than that of the theologians. Allegory was vaguely defined by the old Latin grammarians and rhetoricians as any kind of language that has a double meaning, an obvious and an implied meaning. It was listed as one of the tropes that belong to the 'ornatus difficilis,' but it is indistinguishable from metaphorical language in general, even though the name 'metaphora' is given to another particular trope which is described as the transference of a word suitable to one kind of creature to another. Cicero had said that a chain of metaphors is called 'allegory' by the Greeks, but that generically they are still metaphors (*Ad M. Brutum Orator*, xxvii, 94)."

writers as Quintilian. "Otherspeech" is, theoretically at least, unrelated to theories of allegory as a form or as a central technique of signifying; it is, rather, related to "allegorical" modes of embellishment. It is fitting to make a distinction between Greek, philological, or personification allegory, which necessarily implies a theory of signification, and rhetorical allegory, which implies only the grammarian's or rhetorician's interest in the way language may be made to function. The two may often come together; yet, in theory they are clearly separable, not only one from another but, more importantly for the purpose of this study, from the fourfold exegesis.

The argument concerning allegory in the *Divine Comedy* has a long history. Almost all of the earliest commentators chose to treat the allegory as though it were simply personification allegory. Nevertheless, most of these writers, including Dante's son Pietro, began their commentaries with gestures toward the precepts contained in the Letter to Can Grande. Essentially, however, the importance of Dante's borrowing of the technique of fourfold exegesis was lost to the critics until the twentieth century. The whole problem is densely complex when it is considered in a historical perspective. It is enough to say here that two predispositions—one toward personification allegory and one toward the belief that secular use of Christian exegesis was both impossible and would have been blasphemous—these two, in various permutations, lie at the root of six centuries of unenlightened criticism of the essential processes of Dante's poem.

CHAPTER I

THE ALLEGORY OF THE
COMMEDIA

Although the allegory of the theologians lies at the heart of Dante's poem, giving it form and meaning, we do not —nor did Dante—need to be theologians in order to understand the process. We require only a single paragraph from St. Thomas, one which lists the four senses of Scripture as literal/historical, allegorical, moral, and anagogical. The complex history of these four senses has recently been set forth in great detail by Father Henri de Lubac.[1] We may merely note here that Augustine came close to stating the four senses as Aquinas eventually would, with the exception that he omits moral and anagogical meanings of a passage in Scripture as numbering among the four.[2] It is perhaps in Cassian (ca. 360–ca.

[1] *Exégèse médiévale, les quatre sens de l'Écriture*, 4 vols., Paris, 1959-1964. This work has become the indispensable work in its field. Still extremely useful are the following: Beryl Smalley, *The Study of the Bible in the Middle Ages*, Oxford, 1952. The first chapter, "The Fathers," pp. 1-36, contains probably the best brief summary and review of the development of medieval exegesis which I have seen. C. Spicq, *Esquisse d'une histoire de l'exégèse latine au moyen âge*, Paris, 1944. Before the advent of Lubac's work, this was probably the most important and useful volume on the subject. The work concludes with a highly instructive "Table des commentaires bibliques," pp. 395-401, which presents in brief compass a record of what Biblical passages were dealt with by which commentators and where. Also to be recommended though perhaps not so highly, but especially to those who desire a fairly straightforward approach to the subject in English, is Robert M. Grant, *A Short History of the Interpretation of the Bible*, rev. ed., New York, 1963.

[2] In *De Genesi ad litteram (imperfectus liber)*, ca. A.D. 395, II, 5. The four senses of the Bible are given as *historia, allegoria, analogia, aetiologia*. The first of these corresponds to the *historicus vel litteralis*

435) that the later nomenclature of fourfold allegory first became established, if only tentatively so; but its roots issue from Origen (ca. 185–ca. 254) and develop in the text of Aquinas for the men of Dante's time. As Father de Lubac puts it, ". . . saint Thomas ne fait que reproduire un schème courant de son époque, fondé, suivant le principe

---

of Aquinas. Since the burden of the rest of Augustine's discussion is to affirm the historicity of Gen. 1:1, his understandings of the other three senses are not particularly clear in this treatment. In his words, they are as follows: "Allegoria, cum figurate dicta intelliguntur. Analogia, cum Veteris et Novi Testamentorum congruentia demonstrantur. Aetiologia, cum dictorum factorumque causae redduntur" (*P.L.* xxxiv, col. 222). However, another treatment of the four senses Augustine finds in Scripture is relatively clear in itself, and is further clarified by Aquinas. This occurs in *De Utilitate Credendi* iii, 5, where Augustine expounds the senses in a different order: "Secundum *historiam* ergo traditur, cum docetur quid scriptum, aut quid gestum sit. . . . Secundum *aetiologiam*, cum ostenditur quid qua de causa vel factum vel dictum sit. Secundum *analogiam*, cum demonstratur non sibi adversari duo Testamenta. . . . Secundum *allegoriam*, cum docetur *non ad litteram* esse accipienda quaedam quae scripta sunt, *sed figurate* intelligenda" (italics mine—*P.L.* xLii, cols. 68-69). This treatment reveals that Augustine's fourfold is actually twofold, since his "aetiological" and "analogical" senses are extensions of the historical. Aquinas, in his statement of the fourfold method (*S.T.*, i, i, 10), takes up the objection that Augustine's nomenclature in *De Util. Cred.* differs from his own: "These three—history, etiology, analogy—are grouped under the literal sense. For it is called history, as Augustine expounds, whenever anything is simply related; it is called etiology when its cause is assigned, as when Our Lord gave the reason why Moses allowed the putting away of wives—namely, because of the hardness of men's hearts (Matt. 19:8); it is called analogy whenever the truth of one text of Scripture is shown not to contradict the truth of another. Of these four, allegory alone stands for the three spiritual senses" (tr. in ed. of A. C. Pegis). In *De Util. Cred.* iii, 8, Augustine explains what he means by *figurate*: *allegoria* shows us that Jonah is the promise of Jesus (Matt. 12:39-40), the Exodus of the "futurae christianae plebis" (1 Cor. 10:1-11), Abraham's two sons allegories of the two Testaments themselves (Gal. 4:22-26). The three Scriptural texts used by Augustine to define *allegoria* give ample proof of the essential concord between him and Aquinas concerning the distinction between parable—"allegory" which is merely verbal—and a specifically

déjà mis en oeuvre par Origène, sur le texte même de la Bible."[3]

One of the difficulties facing an apologist for Dante's use of fourfold allegory's techniques is that today the tradition seems forgotten lore to anyone but a student of the development of the Christian exegesis.[4] And thus the arguments of Charles Singleton may seem arcane only because contemporary literary men look at Dante through the conventions of allegory peculiar to the Renaissance and later times. That is the simplest form of the problem against which we need only establish one fact: Dante's knowledge of the tradition as it was expressed in Aquinas. Therefore, we need not concern ourselves here with the history of the tradition; instead, we may refer to the large efforts of Father de Lubac and of others.

A second and larger problem is posed by what might be called the religious objection, a position which has many

---

figural allegory which is based upon events, while the first element in Augustine's own phrase, "non in verbis . . . sed in facto" (*De Trinitate*, xv, ix, 15) will be appropriated to describe what Augustine here has kept distinct from *allegoria* and *figura*, that is, metaphoric speech, which for him and for Aquinas is true only *in verbis*.

[3] *Exégèse médiévale*, vol. IV, p. 295.

[4] While most of the students of exegetical techniques in the *Divine Comedy* are literary scholars who have turned their attentions to theology, two important contributions have been made by scholars with primarily theological backgrounds or interests. One is by Johan Chydenius, *The Typological Problem in Dante*, in *Societas Scientiarum Fennica: Commentationes Humanarum Litterarum*, xxv, Helsingfors, 1958, 1-159. A more recent and probably more important work is that of A. C. Charity, *Events and Their Afterlife: The Dialectics of Christian Typology in the Bible and Dante*, Cambridge, 1966. The latter work devotes some ninety pages to the great influence of typology in the *Commedia*. In addition to its critical usefulness, it is also of bibliographical help to the literary critic of the poem, for, although its listing of critical works about allegory in the *Commedia* is not particularly thorough, its record of recent work in the problems of Biblical exegesis is extremely valuable.

followers, all of whom take their clue from Aquinas himself, who said, "The author of Holy Scripture is God, in
whose power it is to signify His meaning, not by words
only (as man also can do) but by things themselves."[5]
This is essentially the position of Bruno Nardi, who carefully examines the background of the argument in what
is the most clearly enunciated of a large number of arguments in this vein, and then abruptly decides that no
secular writer *can* write fourfold allegory.[6] This position
does not consider the possibility that Dante might have
attempted things not yet attempted, things technically
impossible or doctrinally incorrect, or that he might have
written, as Singleton has explained, in imitation of God's
way of writing.[7] The most amusing although infuriating
characteristic of this approach to the problem is that it is
always couched in hypothetical terms. That is, the question
is not phrased, "Did Dante borrow the techniques of fourfold exegesis?" but "Could Dante have borrowed the

[5] *S. T.*, I, i, 10. The wording would seem to reflect Augustine, *e.g.*,
De Trinitate, xv, ix, 15 (see note 2 above). The implication is that
although God may sometimes write like man, man can never write like
God. See also *Quodlibet*, vii, a. 16, for an even stronger statement:
"Unde in nulla scientia, humana industria inventa, proprie loquendo,
potest inveniri, nisi litteralis sensus . . . fictiones poeticae non sunt ad
aliud ordinatae nisi ad significandum; unde talis significatio non
supergreditur modum litteralis sensus."

[6] Nardi, referring to *Quodlibet*, vii, a. 16, puts his argument in the
following terms in his note to the *Convivio*, "I sensi delle scritture"
(in his book *Nel mondo di Dante*, Rome, 1944, pp. 55-61): "Piuttosto
resta da vedere se alla *Commedia* poteva applicarsi la teoria teologica
dei quattro sensi. Intanto è notevole che, secondo il parere di S.
Tommaso, a nessuna scrittura umana può attribuirsi altro significato
che quello letterale, sia che le parole debbano prendersi in senso proprio,
sia che debbano prendersi in senso figurato o metaforico, com' è il
caso nelle favole dei poeti" (p. 59).

[7] *Dante Studies 1: Commedia, Elements of Structure*, Cambridge,
Mass., 1965, p. 15.

techniques of fourfold exegesis?" It is a strange means of proceeding.

The third problem is the oldest. It can first be seen in the fourteenth-century commentaries on the *Commedia*. These often begin by citing Dante's famous Letter to Can Grande, and then go on to avoid completely any use thereof, preferring to read Dante as Fulgentius and Bernardus Silvestris read Virgil, that is, as personification allegory, in which Beatrice becomes Theology, Virgil becomes Reason, and so forth. These commentaries are significant documents, for through them we can see that the habit of theological allegory so deeply ingrained in Dante was almost immediately lost or denied in all but one of the commentaries on his poem written in the first seventy-five years after his death. The documents are, I believe, fascinating. My interest in them here will be confined mainly to an appendix to which, at this juncture, I refer those who are similarly fascinated.[8] For over six hundred years those commentators and critics of the *Divine Comedy* who have seen fit to deal with the allegorical problem at all have done so almost without exception through the philological approach, treating the *Divine Comedy* as one would with more justice treat *The Faerie Queene*. And those who have not been drawn to this approach have generally favored no method at all, objecting correctly that Beatrice and Virgil are primarily themselves, but for various reasons neglecting to think that the theological form of allegorical treatment is proper to the poem.

These three groups typify the three major forms of evasion or negation of Dante's allegorical principles. In the twentieth century two major Dante critics, one German and one American, have led the way to the discovery of

---

[8] See Appendix I: The Fourteenth-Century Commentators.

the allegorical method which lies behind the poem. Before putting this study into relationship with the work of Erich Auerbach and Charles Singleton, I think it would be useful to review, as briefly as possible, Dante's own statements about allegory, since Dante was not only the first but also the best critic of his own poem.

The first of these statements, as well as the later Letter to Can Grande, derives largely from Aquinas' definition of fourfold exegesis; it is best to begin with that:

"The author of Holy Scripture is God, in whose power it is to signify His meaning, not by words only (as man also can do) but by things themselves. So, whereas in every other science things are signified by words, this science has the property that the things signified by the words have themselves also a signification. Therefore that first signification whereby words signify things belongs to the first sense, the historical or literal. That signification whereby things signified by words have themselves also a signification is called the spiritual sense, which is based on the literal and presupposes it. For as the Apostle says (Heb. 10:1) the Old Law is a figure of the New Law and [Pseudo-] Dionysius says: 'The New Law itself is a figure of future glory.' Again, in the New Law, whatever our Head has done is a type of what we ought to do. Therefore, so far as the things of the Old Law signify the things of the New Law, there is the allegorical sense; so far as the things done in Christ, or so far as the things which signify Christ, are types of what we ought to do, there is the moral sense. But so far as they signify what relates to eternal glory, there is the anagogical sense."*

(S.T., 1, i, 10—tr. R. M. Grant)

* "Auctor sacrae Scripturae est Deus, in cuius potestate est ut non solum voces ad significandum accomodet (quod etiam homo facere potest) sed etiam res ipsas. Et ideo, cum in omnibus scientiis voces

The distinction with which Aquinas begins this celebrated passage, itself dependent, as Father de Lubac shows, on the formulations of earlier Fathers,[9] goes back at least as far as Augustine, who makes his classical distinction in *De Trinitate*, xv, ix, 15: "But when the Apostle speaks of allegory, he refers not to words, but to fact [non in verbis eam reperit, sed in facto]; as when he shows that the two sons of Abraham, one by a bondmaid, the other by a freewoman (these are not words but facts), are to be understood as the two Testaments."[10]

What both Augustine and Aquinas, as well as those who came between them, maintain is perhaps the most single significant distinction upon which Dante's own practice as a poet depends. The words of men are only vocables; the Word of God is a vocable but has the peculiarity of being also a thing, of having actual historical existence. This assertion resides with absolute perfection at the center of Christian theology, which is the Incarnation. Christ is no metaphor, although he is the

---

significent, hoc habet proprium ista scientia quod ipsae res significatae per voces etiam significant aliquid. Illa ergo prima significatio qua voces significant res pertinet ad primum sensum, qui est sensus historicus vel litteralis. Illa vero significatio qua res significatae per voces iterum res alias significant dicitur sensus spiritualis; qui super litteralem fundatur et eum supponit.

"Hic autem sensus spiritualis trifarium dividitur. Sicut enim dicit Apostolus *ad Hebr. Lex vetus figura est novae legis*, et ipsa nova lex, ut Dionysius dicit, est *figura futurae gloriae*. In nova etiam lege ea quae in capite sunt gesta sunt signa eorum quae nos agere debemus.

"Secundum ergo quod ea quae sunt veteris legis significant ea quae sunt novae legis est sensus allegoricus; secundum vero quod ea quae in Christo sunt facta vel in his quae Christum significant sunt signa eorum quae nos agere debemus est sensus moralis; prout vero significant ea quae sunt in aeterna gloria est sensus anagogicus."

[9] See note 3 above.

[10] Augustine refers to Paul's commentary (Gal. 4:22-26) on Gen. 16:15, 21:2, to which we shall return in the following chapter.

Word. Similarly, the words of God, as these are recorded in Scripture, have the unique quality of representing actuality; and it is here that the Hebrew sense of history, as represented by the Old Testament, enters Christianity. Scripture is the verbal record of living history, of the covenant between God and historical man. In the Bible, then, all that is recorded as fact is fact. Both Augustine and Aquinas, as well as others, had one difficulty to confront in order to make this distinction workable; for any one who reads Scripture notices that not all the words therein represent similarly. That is, some of the words of the Bible represent actual persons, places, events, and things, while others do not. Some of the words of God are merely words, like the vocables of mere human fabulists, and these are the words of parable. We are not concerned, for instance, with actual green bay trees, or with actual talents. This parabolic speech is employed exactly as philological allegory is employed, only to make a meaning clear, to tell a moral lesson. The objects it uses have the names and the semblances of actual objects, but they have no unique, historical being.[11] In other words, not all of Scripture (nor all of the *Divine Comedy*) is written in the historical mode; and only that part of Scripture which is in the historical mode may have four-fold meaning. A further distinction is also important: if parable is excluded from containing fourfold senses, so are certain non-further-signifying historical passages, those which merely buttress or adorn history that does have further significance.[12] The *locus classicus* for this doctrine, which should have served as a restraining influence on some

[11] See P. Synave, "La Doctrine de S. Thomas d'Aquin sur le sens littéral des Écritures," *Revue Biblique*, XXXV (1926), 40-65.
[12] See Robertson's fine discussion of this point in "Some Medieval Literary Terminology," *Studies in Philology*, XLVIII (1951), 687.

later exegetes whom it obviously failed to impress, is to be found in a justly celebrated passage of Augustine's *De Civitate Dei*:

"Nor are all the historical relations of these books mystical, but such as are not are added for the more illustration of such as are. It is the ploughshare only that turns up the earth, yet may not the plough lack the other instruments. The strings only do cause the sound in harps and other such instruments, yet must the harp have pins, and the others frets, to make up the music, and the organs have other devices linked to the keys, which the organist touches not, but only their keys, to make the sound proportionate and harmonious. Even so in those prophetic stories, some things are merely relations, yet are they adherent unto those that are significant, and in a manner linked to them."

(xvi, ii—tr. J. Healey)

I represent this additional distinction here because it is one which the Fathers made, and it is essential to their understanding of the limits of their own techniques. Thus we can see that Aquinas' opening distinction is not meant to cover all the words of Scripture, but only those which have what we could call historical meaning, and not all of these. The additional point is that no human author can write with other than parabolic words. If we accept, or if Dante accepted, Thomas' distinction, it is literally impossible that he wrote the *Divine Comedy* in fourfold allegory. In concert with Charles Singleton and with others who have followed him, let us be content to say that Dante wrote in imitation of God's way of writing. For, if Aquinas makes it explicitly impossible for a mere human to write in fourfold allegory, he in no way proscribes nor could he possibly prevent any human author from imitating the technique. The technique, after all, had enjoyed tremendous use as a critical device in the nine hundred years before Dante when it was applied, to be sure, only to Scripture, but with Dante it received its first and perhaps sole use as the central technique of signification in a fictional invention.

Although for most readers it will be tiresome, I hope those who have not dealt with these questions before will find useful a brief recapitulation of the four senses as they are defined by Aquinas. The literal or historical sense (as opposed to a literal sense which is merely *letters* which in turn form mere *words* that have only parabolic significance) tells us what happened. Now, literal senses in Scripture which have the characteristic of also being significantly historical (e.g., Jonah in the belly of the whale, or Moses leading the Israelites out of Egypt) have a further threefold signification. The second kind of meaning history has is spiritual, and the spiritual sense (which can only be found in words which make up history, and not in parable) itself is divided into three senses: allegorical, moral, and anagogical. The following chart makes the relationship visually immediate:

Fourfold allegory	LITERAL or HISTORICAL sense	
	ALLEGORICAL	three spiritual or allegorical senses
	MORAL or TROPOLOGICAL	
	ANAGOGICAL	

The second sense, the allegorical, is the most difficult for the neophyte to conceptualize, and also the most important for our purpose in reading the *Divine Comedy*. The literal sense, as the record of a fact or deed, takes on greater significance by being related to other facts or deeds within the historical procession that is Scripture; this would be a simple and non-theological way of describing the second sense. A simple and theological way would be

24

simply to say *typology*: Jonah's three days in the seacreature followed by his emergence are a *type* of the three days Jesus is to spend in the earth after the Crucifixion, which are to be followed by His Resurrection.[13] This is precisely the science which Aquinas points to in his use of the word *figura*, or in his brief sentence which defines the allegorical sense (the first spiritual sense): "Therefore, so far as the things of the Old Law signify the things of the New Law, there is the allegorical sense." Foreign as this way of thinking is to our time, it is simply enough understood. The *letters* of Scripture, when reporting events, have the peculiar quality of being able to signify words which simultaneously signify facts, which facts also simultaneously are figures, types, or shadows (*umbrae*) of other facts. Any significant event in Scripture will have a figural relationship to other events which either precede or follow it. Thus, the rib taken from Adam's side foreshadows for most exegetes the Church, which will be taken from the side of Christ, and which is the new Eve.

Migne, in his *Index figurarum* of the Old Testament, divides the *types* into five classifications: "figuras quae spectant ad Christum; quae ad Ecclesiam; quae ad apostolos et justos; quae ad Judaeos et Gentiles; quae ad haereticos et impios."[14] Through his summary of the uses of typology during one thousand years of exegesis, we can

[13] It is perhaps worth noting here that "significant," and thus frequently capitalized words, are, in the tradition of Christian exegesis, usually the names of events (e.g., the Annunciation, the Crucifixion), while in personification allegory they are almost without exception the names of moral abstractions.

[14] *P.L.*, vol. 219, *Indices*, vol. II, cols. 241-242. Index XLVIII (cols. 241-260) is concerned with the *figurae* of the O.T. as these are found in the corpus of the 217 volumes of the *P.L.*; Index XLIX, observing the same five classifications of figures, does the same for the commentaries on the N.T. (cols. 259-264). For what may be the first equivalence of the words "type" and "figure" Migne cites (cols. 241-242) the phrase "Typus seu figura" in Junilius Africanus, *P.L.*, LXVIII, col. 33.

see that the science was not restricted to finding prefigurations of Christ or of the Church (the essential respective positions of, to cite only two critics, A. C. Charity and D. W. Robertson, Jr.), though these were the most important uses; typology was used to find connections among all the major and many minor personages of the two Testaments. Thus Absalon is the type for Gregory the Great, Rabanus Maurus, Peter Damian, and others of those Jews who opposed David;[15] while Judas, for Hilary, looking backward, "novus est Absalon."[16] Consultation of Migne's valuable indices shows how widely spread and how versatile were the uses of typology.

This historical view of Scripture, which capitalizes so largely upon Hebrew history in order to build a Christian world order, easily lends itself to the moral purpose that the writings of any religion must contain. If the Fathers were in fairly constant agreement on various typological co-referents, their moral readings, their lucubrations on the third sense, varied more widely. Let us return to Jonah. The narrative of his miraculous experience is a figure, in the second, the allegorical sense, of the death and resurrection of Jesus. Morally, a greater freedom of interpretation necessarily accrues. "When things look blackest, never lose faith in the saving power of the Lord" would be an acceptable moral gloss on the passage. The powers of tropological invention tend to be limitless; nevertheless, the moral sense *is* limited by the relatively strict historical order from which it issues. We should not, for instance, argue that the Jonah story is a warning against deep-sea fishing, rather, that Jonah, as type of Christ, teaches us faith in Him.

The anagogical sense, Aquinas says, relates the literal

[15] Index XLVIII, col. 253.
[16] Index XLIX, col. 262.

event to eternal glory; to be simple, it relates history of this world to God's; or, it shows that things which have happened here point to the afterlife, which is eternal. The point of the anagoge is first to affirm that God's universal plan is operant, that this world is an *umbra futurorum*.[17] In our language we might want to call it the teleological sense, which assures us, by revealing a divine pattern in the affairs of men, that God is indeed in His Heaven, and that in Jonah He has pointed to His Eternality, which is our future, when those of us who are saved shall, like Jonah and because of Christ, be resurrected.

Thus, although the four senses of Scriptural exegesis serve different aims, the medieval system had an enormous attraction because in a single method it found a way of representing history, morality, and metaphysics simultaneously. It is not surprising that nine hundred years of effort went into the establishment and maintenance of this system of exegesis; and it is not difficult to see how radically different this kind of allegory is from that of its Greek predecessors, who handled the literal only as a pretext for *sententia*.

Before we come to Dante, perhaps it will be useful in our summary to make one further clarification of Aquinas' statement of fourfold allegory. Hardly a single treatment of medieval allegory likes to be without the following couplet, apparently a schoolmasterly mnemonic device popular with budding clericals who wanted naturally enough to sort out the four senses in their own minds:

> Littera gesta docet, quid credas allegoria,
> Moralis quid agas, quo tendas anagogia.

[17] See particularly the important study by Father Jean Daniélou, *Sacrementum Futuri: Études sur les origines de la typologie biblique,* Paris, 1950, *passim.*

[The literal teaches the deeds, the allegory what
    to believe,
The moral what to do, the anagoge whereto
    you should strive.][18]

Notice that the second sense, the allegorical, is not immediately clear. What to believe about *what*? The answer
is what to believe about, or how to read, the Old Testament's relation to the New. For the word *allegoria*, used
to represent the second sense of fourfold exegesis, is a
synonym for the words *figura* and *umbra*,[19] and thus the
medieval schoolboy was reminding himself that typology
was the means by which he must govern his reading of the
literal sense of the Old Testament.

A clarification is necessary concerning the word "allegory." Those who have thought about this problem before,
as well as those who may be dealing with it here for the
first time, have noticed the many discrete meanings we
have already found for this word merely within the
Christian exegetical tradition. We began by discussing
fourfold allegory, thus indicating the entire exegetical
technique. We have also referred, as Dante did, to the
three spiritual senses, which devolve from the literal
sense, as the three allegorical senses. And we must remember that the second sense is itself called the allegorical

---

[18] A twentieth-century schoolboy might rather put down:

Stephen Dedalus is my name,
Ireland is my nation.
Clongowes is my dwellingplace
And heaven my expectation.

The last line, at least, does resemble the anagoge. Lubac discusses
critically the traditional attribution of the distich to Nicholas of Lyra,
vol. I, p. 23.

[19] See Erich Auerbach's seminal essay, "Figura," tr. Ralph Manheim,
in *Scenes from the Drama of European Literature*, New York, 1959,
pp. 44-49.

sense, by which is indicated no more and no less than typology. It is a bit confusing, especially as the other kinds of allegory also involve different definitions of the word. We shall not review the others here, for we are about to come upon Dante's own distinction between the allegory of the theologians and the allegory of the poets in *Convivio* (II, i). This passage has been the cause of a great deal of confusion. The confusion, it seems to me, is to some extent justified in light of the confusions within the passage itself, and is aggravated by the lacuna in the original text, which has been filled in and then argued over by subsequent editors. Dante's statement in *Convivio* is perhaps of only peripheral interest here for the major reason that it describes his allegorical practice in *Convivio*, not in the *Commedia*. Yet, many of those who wish to argue against Dante's use of fourfold exegetical techniques in the *Divine Comedy* make their stand upon Dante's statement in *Convivio*. Even if the statement had never been contradicted by a later one, such as the one in the Letter to Can Grande, or more importantly, by practice in the *Divine Comedy* itself, this procedure would be dangerous. To argue that because Dante uses the allegory of the poets in *Convivio* he must also use it in the *Commedia* is so entirely without logic that I do not wish even to discuss the matter here. What can be immediately assented to is that Dante does use, when he writes allegorically in *Convivio*, the allegory of the poets. Because in the *Divine Comedy* he changes his mode of representation, the literal senses of the two works are not commensurate. The essential mode of *Convivio* is the veiled speech of philological allegory in which there is no literal sense *in facto* but only a tissue of fabrications of the sort indicated by Dante's own phrase *bella menzogna*, a tissue which must be puzzled over by the *dotti*, so that its meaning, which is all

that is really important about it, will become clear. This is
Dante's own position, and I find no more efficacious way to
deal with this celebrated passage than to offer a brief commentary of my own, some of which will repeat what has
already been said, and some of which will offer some
tentative new judgments.[20]

[20] The complete text, from the standard edition of G. Busnelli and
G. Vandelli, vol. I, Florence, 1934, pp. 96-103, follows here. For
their arguments concerning the lacuna and the way in which they
have restored the text, see Appendice I to *Convivio* II, "Sopra i quattro
sensi delle scritture," pp. 240-242:

"Dico che, sì come nel primo capitolo è narrato, questa sposizione conviene essere litterale e allegorica. E a ciò dare a intendere,
si vuol sapere che le scritture si possono intendere e deonsi esponere
massimamente per quattro sensi. L'uno si chiama litterale, [e questo è
quello che non si stende più oltre che la lettera de le parole fittizie, sì
come sono le favole de li poeti. L'altro si chiama allegorico,] e questo
è quello che si nasconde sotto 'l manto di queste favole, ed è una
veritade ascosa sotto bella menzogna: sì come quando dice Ovidio che
Orfeo facea con la cetera mansuete le fiere, e li arbori e le pietre a
sè muovere; che vuol dire che lo savio uomo con lo strumento de la
sua voce fa[r]ia mansuescere e umiliare li crudeli cuori, e fa[r]ia
muovere a la sua volontade coloro che non hanno vita di scienza e d'arte:
e coloro che non hanno vita ragionevole alcuna sono quasi come pietre.
E perchè questo nascondimento fosse trovato per li savi, nel penultimo
trattato si mosterrà. Veramente li teologi questo senso prendono altrimenti che li poeti; ma però che mia intenzione è qui lo modo de li poeti
seguitare, prendo lo senso allegorico secondo che per li poeti è usato.

"Lo terzo senso si chiama morale, e questo è quello che li lettori
deono intentamente andare appostando per le scritture, ad utilitade di
loro e di loro discenti: sì come appostare si può ne lo Evangelio,
quando Cristo salio lo monte per transfigurarsi, che de li dodici Apostoli
menò seco li tre; in che moralmente si può intendere che a le secretissime
cose noi dovemo avere poca compagnia.

"Lo quarto senso si chiama anagogico, cioè sovrasenso; e questo è
quando spiritualmente si spone una scrittura, la quale ancora [sia vera]
eziandio nel senso litterale, per le cose significate significa de le superne
cose de l'etternal gloria, sì come vedere si può in quello canto del
Profeta che dice che, ne l'uscita del popolo d' Israel d' Egitto, Giudea
è fatta santa e libera. Chè avvegna essere vero secondo la lettera sia
manifesto, non meno è vero quello che spiritualmente s'intende, cioè

"I say that, as is narrated in the first chapter, it conforms that this exposition be literal and allegorical." Dante, preparing to explicate the canzone "Voi che 'ntendendo il terzo ciel movete," the first canzone of *Convivio*, draws our attention to something he has said in the First Treatise

---

che ne l'uscita de l'anima dal peccato, essa sia fatta santa e libera in sua potestate. E in dimostrar questo, sempre lo litterale dee andare innanzi, sì come quello ne la cui sentenza li altri sono inchiusi, e sanza lo quale sarebbe impossibile ed inrazionale intendere a li altri, e massimamente a lo allegorico. È impossibile, però che in ciascuna cosa che ha dentro e di fuori, è impossibile venire al dentro se prima non si viene al di fuori: onde, con ciò sia cosa che ne le scritture [la litterale sentenza] sia sempre lo di fuori, impossibile è venire a l'altre, massimamente a l'allegorica, sanza prima venire a la litterale. Ancora, è impossibile però che in ciascuna cosa, naturale ed artificiale, è impossibile procedere a la forma, sanza prima essere disposto lo subietto sopra che la forma dee stare: sì come impossibile la forma de l'oro è venire, se la materia, cioè lo suo subietto, non è digesta e apparecchiata; e la forma de l'arca venire, se la materia, cioè lo legno, non è prima disposta e apparecchiata. Onde con ciò sia cosa che la litterale sentenza sempre sia subietto e materia de l'altre, massimamente de l'allegorica, impossibile è prima venire a la conoscenza de l'altre che a la sua. Ancora, è impossibile però che in ciascuna cosa, naturale ed artificiale, è impossibile procedere, se prima non è fatto lo fondamento, sì come ne la casa e sì come ne lo studiare: onde, con ciò sia cosa che 'l dimostrare sia edificazione di scienza, e la litterale dimostrazione sia fondamento de l'altre, massimamente de l'allegorica, impossibile è a l'altre venire prima che a quella.

"Ancora, posto che possibile fosse, sarebbe inrazionale, cioè fuori d'ordine, e però con molta fatica e con molto errore si procederebbe. Onde, sì come dice lo Filosofo nel primo de la Fisica, la natura vuole che ordinatamente si proceda ne la nostra conoscenza, cioè procedendo da quello che conoscemo meglio in quello che conoscemo non così bene: dico che la natura vuole, in quanto questa via di conoscere è in noi naturalmente innata. E però se li altri sensi dal litterale sono meno intesi—che sono, sì come manifestamente pare—, inrazionabile sarebbe procedere ad essi dimostrare, se prima lo litterale non fosse dimostrato. Io adunque, per queste ragioni, tuttavia sopra ciascuna canzone ragionerò prima la litterale sentenza, e appresso di quella ragionerò la sua allegoria, cioè la nascosa veritate; e talvolta de li altri sensi toccherò incidentemente, come a luogo e a tempo si converrà."

(1, i, 18), where he announced his intention as follows: "per allegorica esposizione quelle [canzoni] intendo mostrare, appresso la litterale istoria ragionata" ("I intend to explain these canzoni by allegorical exposition, after having explained the literal story"). If by "literal" and "allegorical" Dante means the same things in each passage, and there is no reason to believe that he does not, we may still have some difficulty in knowing exactly which kind of allegory he claims to be using. Later in the *Convivio* passage he announces that he intends to follow the allegory of the poets, in which the literal story is non-historical, a fable invented by the poet; and it is probable that he means to say that here in this passage, as well as in the First Treatise. And yet in the First Treatise he uses the phrase *la litterale istoria*, which seems to reflect Aquinas' *litteralis sive historicus*, the literal sense we find in the Bible. Nevertheless, Dante would not seem to want to imply the presence of that distinction. Whatever the case, his next sentence points clearly to Biblical allegory:

"And to make this understood, one should know that writings [*le scritture*] are to be understood and should be mainly expounded in four senses." A problem arises in the English translation of the word *scritture*, traditionally translated as "writings." In French, for instance, a translator says *écritures*, which means either "writings" or "Scripture," and at least may remind the reader of Holy Writ. Although it is not certain in *Convivio*, it is clear from Dante's later uses of the words *scrittura* and *scritture* (*scriptura* in Latin) in the *Commedia* and in the Letter to Can Grande that by them he means Holy Writ (in nine out of ten uses in the *Commedia*) or pagan writing on divine subjects which for him has similar authority.[21]

---

[21] In the *Commedia* Virgil refers to his own writing on the efficacy of prayer as *scrittura* (*Purg.* VI, 34). The Letter to Can Grande yields

However, in *Convivio* his practice is mixed, or his meanings sometimes uncertain. Nevertheless, the reference in the passage above would certainly seem to be a reference to fourfold Biblical exegesis. After ". . . in four senses," he continues: "One is called literal. . . ." And here, at this crucial point, occurs the famous lacuna. What is clear and I believe beyond argument, despite various opinions to the contrary, is that Dante begins to enumerate and define allegory in accord with the four senses of Biblical exegesis. What is not clear and in my opinion never shall be is whether he intended to make a clear distinction between Scriptural allegory and that of the poets, which he here invokes for his own canzoni. In my opinion he did not. Otherwise stated, I find that Dante has either deliberately or confusedly elided the necessary distinction. If such is the case, the restoration of Busnelli and Vandelli makes sense, for it also elides that distinction. These editors would have Dante continue: "and this is that sense which does not extend beyond the letter of the fictive words, as in the fables of the poets. The other [sense] is called allegorical. . . ." If that is indeed the way in which Dante did continue, we are forced to conclude that his critical theory of allegory, at the time of the writing of *Convivio*, was in some logical disorder, even if the practice of this sort of hybrid allegory is a common enough phenomenon. We need think only of Boccaccio's later set-

---

similar results: The focal paragraphs use the word to mean Scripture, and then paragraph 22 calls the writings of Lucan (concerning God) *scriptura paganorum*. It is interesting that one of the first, perhaps the first, modern criticisms of the poem to call for a fourfold reading of the *Commedia*, although it does so in a confused and confusing way, does in fact translate (or else makes use of a previous English translation) the word in this passage as "Scriptures." See S. Udny, "The Interpretation of Dante," *Living Age*, CCXXXVII (1903), 735-744 (p. 738).

ting forth of the four senses in *Genealogia deorum genti-lium* (1, 3), which takes the example of Perseus' killing of the Gorgon and elucidates the four senses as follows: "Now, this may be understood superficially in its literal or historical sense. In the moral sense it shows a wise man's triumph over vice and his attainment of virtue. Allegorically it figures [*designatur*] the pious man who scorns worldly delights and lifts his mind to heavenly things. It admits also an anagogical sense, since it symbolizes [*per fabulam posset figurari*] Christ's victory over the Prince of this World, and his Ascension" (tr. Osgood). Here a literal sense, which Boccaccio treats sensibly enough as a made-up myth, is found to have three further significances, which are given the names of the three spiritual senses from fourfold exegesis. It should be immediately obvious, however, that Boccaccio is here playing fast and loose with the rules of exegesis. First, he has inverted the usual order from allegorical, moral, anagogical to moral, allegorical, anagogical. This inversion tells us a great deal immediately. Let me give a simple example. If one attempts to tell the significance of Jonah's three days in the belly of Leviathan by first elucidating the "moral" sense, without having established the typological equivalence of Jonah and Jesus, he will, of necessity, play fast and loose, as does Boccaccio in the *Genealogia*, and as does Dante in the *Convivio*. The inversion of the order of the second and third senses is the sure sign of an exegete (of things sacred or profane) who has missed the point of the technique, which is to treat the literal historically, and thus first to find the historical connective that links literal and spiritual.

As for Boccaccio's actual analysis of the three spiritual senses, we find that the moral and allegorical are essentially the same, or if not that, at least essentially of the same order; that order is personification allegory. We note further that Boccaccio's anagoge is far more a forced typology than a true anagoge.

It is not my purpose to berate Boccaccio, for in literature the laws of theological explication de texte need not, and almost always do not, apply. I merely wish to take the example of Boccaccio to clarify the confusion of the allegory of the poets and the allegory of the theologians in Dante's text in *Convivio*. We may note in passing that Boccaccio is even more confused than Dante, even though it is more than likely that his own passage is borrowed from the one we are now examining.

Dante's missing definition of the second sense may then have been the one the editors have supplied, as Singleton maintains: "No one who knows the general argument of the whole work will, I think, make serious objection to the way the editors of the accepted critical text have filled the lacuna."[22] Nevertheless, it does seem to me worth the effort to keep the question open. For what Dante may have accomplished in the missing words of *Convivio* II, i, is a concise distinction between two kinds of allegorical sense. When we rejoin him, however, he is obviously discussing allegorical significance according to the poets: "One is called literal . . . and this is that sense which is hidden under the cloak of these fables; and it is a truth hidden beneath a beautiful lie: as when Ovid tells that Orpheus pacifies the wild beasts with his zither, and causes the trees and the stones to approach him; which means to say that the wise man with the instrument of his voice would make cruel hearts peaceful and humble, and would make

[22] *Dante Studies I*, p. 84. In addition to the present writer, G. R. Sarolli also has some reservations about the restoration of Busnelli and Vandelli in his recent and important study, "Prolegomena alla 'Commedia,'" *Convivium*, XXXIV (1966), 84.

move to his will those who live without science and art; and that those who have no life of reason are as stones." Clearly, as many have pointed out, this passage is in the tradition of secular allegory, in which the mere moral propensities of words, themselves *parole fittizie* making up a *bella menzogna*, lead the way to the hidden truth. This is not the process of Biblical exegesis, in which the Word of God, which exists as actual truth in itself in a literal sense that is also historical, and which in turn has further meanings, is the way to the revealed truth. Dante continues:

"And why this concealment was invented by the wise men will be divulged in the penultimate treatise." Although Dante did not finish *Convivio*, his thoughts on this matter are, I believe, almost the same as those which Boccaccio sets down, especially in his commentary on the first canto of the *Divine Comedy*.[23] These thoughts in turn represent the ancient tradition of the Greek allegorists, who claim that the poet must not make his meaning immediately clear, but must use allegory so that only the *dotti* will understand what would be misunderstood and thus misapplied by the ignorant.

"It is true that the theologians take this sense otherwise than do the poets; however, because it is here my intention to follow the method of the poets, I take the allegorical sense according as it is employed by the poets."

And so he does, in *Convivio*. What is noteworthy is that Dante omits, or the lacuna omits, the treatment of the second sense of theological allegory which we would expect from Dante in light of his claim for the applicability

---

[23] See Boccaccio's excursus on the word *poeta* (in Virgil's statement "Poeta fui"—*Inf.* I, 73), where he explains ". . . è l'uficio del poeta . . . nascondere la verità sotto favoloso e ornato parlare."

of the two other spiritual senses, the moral and the anagogical, his discussion of which immediately follows. For in the next paragraph, to summarize briefly its content, Dante goes on to discuss the third sense, the moral sense, for which readers must intently study *le scritture* (returning to the subject of fourfold exegesis Dante returns to this word, which replaces *favole*, the word he uses for the fictions of the poets). He concludes by returning to Scripture for the fact that only three of the twelve apostles were allowed to accompany Christ when He climbed the mount to transfigure Himself, and which supposedly teaches that in the most secret things we should have little company.

And in the following paragraph Dante goes on to discuss the fourth sense, which is called the anagogical, or *sovrasenso* (literally, supersense), in which "the things signified signify the supernal things of eternal glory."[24] Once again he uses the word *scrittura*, and, taking a Biblical example, is at pains to point out its literal truth, this time alluding to the Exodus, as he will again in the Letter to Can Grande and in *Purgatorio* II, 46. This long paragraph goes on to assert, in good Aquinian fashion, the importance of the literal, upon which all the other senses depend. He would seem to be, with little room for doubt, still referring to the theological allegory he has said he is not using. This is not altogether surprising. It would be thoroughly typical of him, as a man of his time, to adumbrate what is really of little use to his poem or the treatise upon it, simply because he knows about the

---

[24] There is close agreement here with Aquinas' definition of the anagogical sense (*S. T.*, I, i, 10—see above), as well as with his precedent phrasing—"things signified by words have also a signification." For the derivation of *anagogia* see Lubac, vol. II, pp. 622-624.

subject and feels it his pleasure and perhaps his duty to give us his knowledge.[25]

However, in the concluding paragraph of *Convivio* II, i, the fourth paragraph of the statement of Dante's allegorical principles, all that has been kept separate, or at least can be understood as being so, comes puzzlingly together: "For these reasons, therefore, I shall always first discourse upon the literal meaning of each canzone, and after that I shall discourse upon its allegory, that is, the hidden truth; and I shall sometimes incidentally touch upon the other senses, as the place and the time make appropriate."

How can Dante claim that a poem made up of *parole fittizie*, a poem which is a *bella menzogna*, a poem of which the literal sense is not historical, that such a poem has *four* senses, including two of the senses which are precisely reserved for Holy Scripture, as he himself has apparently reserved them in the previous commentary? I have a simple suggestion which may help to ease the problem. If, as I believe the several preceding pages demonstrate, Dante was capable of making, and did in fact make, some clear distinction between the two kinds of allegory—a distinction which has been often forgotten, lost, or misunderstood during the six centuries since he wrote—there is one reason why he might conclude his essay on allegory in the *Convivio* by eradicating, or at least weakening, his own distinction, bringing the two kinds of allegory together after having previously kept them apart, and it is this: although he admits that the poetry of *Convivio* is a *bella menzogna*, he also insists that it is of such high

[25] See the passage in the *Vita Nuova* (XL, 6-7) where, in explaining why the following sonnet makes use of the word "pilgrims," Dante rehearses the usual tripartite division of pilgrimages which observes the difference among those to the Holy Land, to Spain, and to Rome, all of which has essentially nothing to do either with the sonnet or with his commentary upon the sonnet.

purport that it can have the kind of significance usually found only in Scripture. And so, even though it is "against the rules" to do so, he tells us that he will occasionally apply the third and fourth (significantly enough, *not the second*) Biblical sense to his *parole fittizie*.[26] Under this scheme the poetry of *Convivio* is to be understood as being literally and allegorically fictive, but occasionally, in the moral and anagogical senses, theological. This makes the poetry of *Convivio* a hybrid.[27] Perhaps the difficulty of maintain-

[26] For Dante's actual application of the third and fourth senses to his *canzoni*, see Wicksteed's note to this passage in the Temple Classics *Convivio*, p. 67: "Instances in which the moral significance of texts is insisted upon may be found in II. 16:50-58, III. 1:45, IV. 17:106ff. We may perhaps regard such passages as the conclusion of IV. 22 as instances of the anagogical interpretation, which always refers in some direct way to things of heaven." Boccaccio, *Genealogia*, I, 3, concludes his statement on fourfold allegory, cited above, as follows: "But it is not my intention to unfold all these meanings for each myth when I find one quite enough." Osgood, his translator here (*Boccaccio on Poetry*, reprint of 2nd ed., Indianapolis, 1956, p. xviii) goes on to point out that Boccaccio only rarely departs from the "moral" or "allegorical" interpretation. In this, he is again like the Dante of *Convivio*. Still, Dante's discussion and handling of the spiritual senses, for all the confusion caused by joining two kinds of allegory, display a surer awareness of the tradition from which he claims he borrows than do those of Boccaccio.

[27] Dante's confusing mixture of the two kinds of allegory in *Convivio* is perhaps illuminated by going back over the four paragraphs he devotes to the subject sentence by sentence. I offer the following diagrammatic exposition in the interests of conserved space and time. (Roman numerals stand for the paragraphs, arabics for the sentences; P denotes the allegory of the poets, T that of the theologians.)

II. 1.	P (and/or T?)	exposition will be literal and allegorical
2.	T	four senses of Scripture
3.	T ...	one of these called literal (lacuna occurs here)
4.	....P	. . . Orpheus tale as truth hidden beneath beautiful lie
5.	P	why this kind of concealment invented
6.	P (*not* T)	here I follow mode of poets

ing the truth and the comeliness of such a creature led Dante to abandon it. That the *Convivio* is unfinished is perhaps the most important single fact about the work.

THE ARGUMENTS that surround Dante's Letter to Can Grande are not particularly germane to this discourse. About all those who claim that the Letter is not genuine, or that only its first four paragraphs are genuine, one thing is clear: Their desire to cast doubt upon the authority of the *Epistola* in all cases depends upon a desire to discredit the notion that Dante used the allegory of the theologians in creating the *Divine Comedy*.[28] However, it is astonish-

III. 1.	T	moral sense of Scripture: the Transfiguration
IV. 1.	T	anagogical sense of Scripture: Israel out of Egypt
2.	T	letter spiritually understood: departure from sin
3-4.	T	letter comes first, all others depend upon it
5-7.	T *or* P	anything, either natural (T) or man-made (P), only to be understood when we see how it is made
V. 1-2.	T *or* P	thus, since literal easier than allegorical, begin there
3.	P *and* T	first the literal, then the hidden truth (P); and then, on occasion, moral and anagogical (T).

[28] The modern quarrel probably begins significantly at the turn of the century. Francesco d'Ovidio, "L'epistola a Cangrande," in *Studii sulla Divina Commedia*, Palermo, 1901, pp. 448-485, argues against authenticity. He is answered by Edward Moore, *Studies in Dante*, III, Oxford, 1903, 284-374. More recently the debate has become warmer. Luigi Pietrobono, "L'Epistola a Can Grande," in *Nuovi saggi danteschi*, Torino, 1954, pp. 199-244, renews the argument, speaking for the negative. Francesco Mazzoni, "L'Epistola a Cangrande," *Rendiconti dell'Accademia Nazionale dei Lincei*, x, fasc. 3-4 (1955), 157-198, offers what is probably the closest to a definitive argument for authenticity. His argument is especially effective in that it is not committed to any theoretical result, but merely examines evidence within Dante's life, work, and times for constatation. He concludes (p. 197): "Scritta

ing that so much labor (which, according to most of the best scholarship on the question, has failed in its prime purpose) has gone into the destruction of the authenticity of this piece of literary criticism. Granting for the moment that it was not written by Dante, the Letter to Can Grande nevertheless tells us much about his poem.[29] Had

---

dunque a Verona, tra il 1315 e il dicembre del 1317 . . . è da Dante Alighieri. . . ." Bruno Nardi, presenting a summary of the critical debate in his *Il punto sull'Epistola a Cangrande*, Florence, 1960, attacks Mazzoni's arguments and his findings, while praising "il dotto latinista di Oxford" (p. 5), Colin Hardie, whose article, "The Epistle to Cangrande again," *DDJb*, XXXVIII (1960), 51-74, which takes up the negative side once more, appeared earlier in the same year. (Hardie's subsequent article, "Beatrice's Chariot in Dante's Earthly Paradise," *DDJb*, XXXIX [1961], 137-172, briefly returns to the problem.) It is worth noting that Hardie's argument does not take into account that of Mazzoni, either as it is advanced in the study just referred to, or in his other works (see Bibliography). The excesses of zeal which characterize the detractors of the Letter's genuineness are typified *à outrance* by the following hypothetical argument offered by Professor Hardie: "If there is anything in this argument, the *Epistle* was originally written by an unknown struggling *grammaticus* some years after Dante's death to an unknown signore of a city other than Verona. The discoverer of the *Epistle*, who jumped to the conclusion that Dante wrote it, may have found it without any superscription and perhaps at Verona, if, for instance, it was written in 1327 to the signore or some notable of Treviso just before its capture by Cangrande and carried off to Verona by Cangrande, who died before he could himself take notice of it" (pp. 55-56). All of which, being true, might only prove that there was an extremely bright young (or old) struggling *grammaticus* hanging around a city other than Verona in the early fourteenth century. For a reasonable attempt to understand the reasons for the opposition of the doubters of authenticity, see A. C. Charity, *Events and Their Afterlife*, pp. 199-207, where Bruno Nardi's long-held disbelief in genuineness is put in clear perspective. The most recent finding, another negative one, is that of Allan Gilbert, "Did Dante Dedicate the *Paradiso* to Can Grande della Scala?" *Italica*, XLIII (1966), 100-124.

[29] G. R. Sarolli, quoting from E. Gilson in the same vein, has recently also made this point in his "Prolegomena alla 'Commedia,'" *Convivium*, XXXIV (1966), 78.

the detractors tested their theories against the poem rather than against this external piece of evidence, they might have come to wiser decisions regarding the poem. They might even have come round to acceptance of the authenticity of the *Epistola*, which, almost all of Dante's first commentators, including his son Pietro, quote approvingly.[30] Thus, although I do not wish to become involved in the quarrel concerning the authorship of the *Epistola*, I do wish to refer to that text now, since it discusses more clearly than any other single document of Dante's time the allegorical conventions which inform the poem. In doing so it would be less than honest were I not to confess that the work seems to me to be in no way a forgery.

The dedication gives us the signature of the author, which contains the acerbic flavor of Dante and which is worth re-remembering for its own sake: "Dantes Alagherii florentinus natione non moribus" ("Dante Alighieri, a Florentine by birth, not by character").[31]

Paragraph 1: "Verum ne diuturna me nimis incertitudo suspenderet, velut Austri regina Ierusalem petiit, velut Pallas petiit Elicona, Veronam petii . . ." Dante, paying Can Grande della Scala an exaggerated compliment, uses a technique that has often been noticed throughout the *Divine Comedy*: the coupling of a Christian and a pagan source in order to clarify a contemporary event. As playful

[30] See Appendix I.

[31] Here and elsewhere (with the exception of *Convivio*—see note 20 above) I quote from *Le opere di Dante*, ed. M. Barbi, E. G. Parodi, F. Pellegrini, E. Pistelli, P. Rajna, E. Rostagno, G. Vandelli, 2nd ed., Società Dantesca Italiana, Florence, 1960. I hope that the following excerptions from the first six paragraphs of the Letter (XIII in modern editions, X in earlier) will serve to remind the reader of what precedes the more familiar contents of paragraphs 7 and 8. For purposes of convenience, and especially in order to avoid a certain coyness that otherwise results, I have taken the liberty of calling the author of the Letter "Dante," rather than "the author of the Letter to Can Grande."

as the compliment may be, I think it is worth noting that Dante here uses the technique of figuralism: Dante had heard so much of Can Grande's magnificence that he had to come to Verona to see for himself ("Lest immeasurable incertitude hold me in suspense any longer, just as the queen of the South sought Jerusalem, or as Pallas sought Helicon, sought I Verona"). The typology has to do with the place sought rather than the seeker: Verona is, playfully, the New Jerusalem, the New Helicon. I have paused over this passage because it is evidence that the writer is willing to borrow from Scriptural exegesis for a mundane purpose—an idea that has frequently been attacked by those who doubt that Dante would have thought of this kind of writing as being permissible or possible.[32]

Paragraph 4: Dante concludes the fourth paragraph, which is the limit of his dedicatory praise, with the announcement that he will now assume the office of the lecturer (*sub lectoris officio*) in offering an introduction to his own work.

Paragraph 5: The introduction begins by quoting Aristotle's *Metaphysics*: "sicut res se habet ad esse, sic se habet ad veritatem" ("as a thing relates to existence, so it relates to truth"). This quotation is put to the task of the further Aristotelian distinction between substance and accident, the

---

[32] Professor Gilbert (see note 28 above) objects that Dante would not have compared himself to a woman, especially not to the Queen of Sheba. The extravagance of the entire passage would allow for exactly such immoderate figural play. (G. Boffito, "L'Epistola di Dante Alighieri a Cangrande della Scala," *Memorie della R. Accademia delle Scienze di Torino*, s. 2a, LVIII [1907], 6, cites Filippo Scolari, writing in 1819, who makes precisely the same objection Gilbert has recently made.) Furthermore, Matt. 12:41-42 contains the following appropriate *figurae*: Just as the men of Nineveh took heed of the words of Jonas, and as "the queen of the south" (Vulgate, "regina austri"; Dante, "Austri regina") heeded the wisdom of Solomon, so now should the scribes and Pharisees care to hear the teachings of Jesus.

distinction which Dante employs to relate the *Paradiso* (the part of the poem dedicated to Can Grande and hence introduced here) to the whole, since the existence of this part depends upon the first two *cantiche*.

Paragraph 6: And thus the introduction of this part, *Paradiso*, is to be understood as the introduction to the whole. Dante continues: "Sex igitur sunt que in principio cuiusque doctrinalis operis inquirenda sunt, videlicet subiectum, agens, forma, finis, libri titulus, et genus phylosophie" ("There are six things, then, which must be investigated at the beginning of any instructional work; namely, subject, agent, form, end, the title of the book, as well as the branch of philosophy it concerns").[33] He goes on to say that it is clear that of these six there are three respects in which this part, *Paradiso*, differs from the whole: subject, form, and title; the other three are the same for the part as for the whole, and therefore he will begin with these three.

Paragraphs 7 and 8: These paragraphs constitute the part of the *Epistola* generally quoted in full, for it is here that Dante goes into the theory of allegory which is to be

---

[33] For the possible influence of the Latin commentary of Guizzardo on Mussato's *Ecerinis* upon the formulation of Dante's *sex inquirenda*, see Mazzoni, "L'Epistola a Cangrande," p. 191, and the Temple Classics *Latin Works of Dante*, p. 364. Nardi, in his "Osservazioni sul medievale 'accessus ad auctores' in rapporto all'*Epistola a Cangrande*," which is found in his *Saggi e note di critica dantesca*, Milano, 1966, pp. 268-305, after carefully reviewing the scholarship on the problem, demonstrates, against Mazzoni, that there are a number of sources which might have served Dante here, among them the rather obvious passage from the first page of Servius' commentary on the *Aeneid*: "In exponendis auctoribus haec consideranda sunt: poetae vita, titulus operis, qualitas carminis, scribentis intentio, numerus librorum, ordo librorum, explanatio." Curtius, *European Literature and the Latin Middle Ages*, pp. 221-222, points to the *Life of Virgil* of Donatus, as well as to several others not mentioned by Nardi. As it turns out, Dante's six terms, so puzzling to the modern reader, are entirely commonplace within their time.

understood as the handling of the work's subject—that is
made clear by the first sentence of paragraph 8 (paragraph
9 concerns the *forma*, paragraph 10 the *libri titulus*). I
give these two paragraphs in full:*

(7) "In evidence, then, of what should be said, let it be
known that the sense of this work is not simple; nay, it
may be said to be polysemous, which is to say, of a number
of senses; for the first sense is that which is understood by
the letter, another, that which is understood by those
things signified by the letter. And the first is called literal,
the second, to be sure, either allegorical, or moral, or
anagogical. This mode of treatment, that it may be better
revealed, may be considered in the following verse:
'When Israel went out of Egypt, the house of Jacob from

* "Ad evidentiam itaque dicendorum sciendum est quod istius operis
non est simplex sensus, ymo dici potest polisemos, hoc est plurium sen-
suum; nam primus sensus est qui habetur per litteram, alius est qui habetur per significata per litteram. Et primus dicitur litteralis, secundus vero
allegoricus sive moralis sive anagogicus. Qui modus tractandi, ut melius
pateat, potest considerari in hiis versibus: «In exitu Israel de Egipto,
domus Iacob de populo barbaro, facta est Iudea sanctificatio eius, Israel
potestas eius». Nam si ad litteram solam inspiciamus, significatur nobis
exitus filiorum Israel de Egipto, tempore Moysis; si ad allegoriam, nobis
significatur nostra redemptio facta per Christum; si ad moralem sensum,
significatur nobis conversio anime de luctu et miseria peccati ad statum
gratie; si ad anagogicum, significatur exitus anime sancte ab huius cor-
ruptionis servitute ad eterne glorie libertatem. Et quanquam isti sensus
mistici variis appellentur nominibus, generaliter omnes dici possunt allegorici, cum sint a litterali sive historiali diversi. Nam allegoria dicitur
ab 'alleon' grece, quod in latinum dicitur 'alienum,' sive 'diversum.'
"Hiis visis, manifestum est quod duplex oportet esse subiectum, circa
quod currant alterni sensus. Et ideo videndum est de subiecto huius operis,
prout ad litteram accipitur; deinde de subiecto, prout allegorice senten-
tiatur. Est ergo subiectum totius operis, litteraliter tantum accepti, status
animarum post mortem simpliciter sumptus; nam de illo et circa illum
totius operis versatur processus. Si vero accipiatur opus allegorice, subiectum est homo prout merendo et demerendo per arbitrii libertatem iustitie
premiandi et puniendi obnoxius est."

a people of strange speech, Judea became his sanctification, Israel his power.' For if we consider the letter alone, signified to us is the departure of the children of Israel out of Egypt, at the time of Moses; if the allegory, our redemption wrought by Christ; if the moral sense, the conversion of the soul from the grief and misery of sin to the state of grace; if the anagogical, the departure of the holy soul from the servitude of this corruption to the liberty of eternal glory. And although these mystic senses are called by many names, they may all in general be called allegorical, since they are different from the literal or historical. For *allegory* is meant by the Greek *alleon*, which is equivalent to the Latin *alienum* or *diversum*.

(8) "Once we grasp these facts, it is manifest that the subject, around which the senses run, one after the other, is of necessity twofold. And that such is the case concerning the subject of this work ought to be clear, as it is first to be understood literally, and then expounded allegorically. Thus the subject of the whole work, so far as it is to be understood in the literal sense, taken simply, is the state of the souls after death;[34] for the process of the entire work situates itself in this and around this. If, to be sure, the work is to be understood allegorically, the subject is man, as he is liable to rewarding or punishing

---

[34] Bruno Nardi, "I sensi delle scritture," in *Nel mondo di Dante*, Rome, 1944, p. 60, argues that this is indeed *not* the subject of the *Commedia*: "Veramente, a volere esser precisi, il 'subiectum totius operis litteraliter tantum accepti,' non è lo 'status animarum post mortem,' ma il viaggio di Dante Alighieri fiorentino attraverso i tre regni d'oltre-tomba, pei quali egli può conoscere quello che è lo 'status animarum post mortem.' " While it is surely just to insist that the actions of Dante's voyage are the subject of the poem, it is not equally true that what he sees during the voyage—precisely "the state of the souls after death"— is not. The twin subject of the poem includes what Dante does and what Dante sees, as I argue at the conclusion of the third chapter.

justice, according as he is worthy or unworthy in the exercise of the freedom of his will."

The first thing we should notice about these passages when we compare them, as we inevitably do, with the passage on allegory in the *Convivio*, is that this time Dante does not combine in any way at all the allegory of the poets and the allegory of the theologians. The *Divine Comedy*, the epistle informs us, is to be understood through the techniques of allegory which are specifically and only Christian, not, as was the *Convivio*, by means of the allegory of the poets. Here there is no reference to Orpheus,[35] only to Scripture.

For now, I should like to put aside the *Epistola* and other matters dependent upon it and call to the reader's attention that much of what has been presented up to now

---

[35] C. A. Robson's recent important essay, "Dante's Use in the *Divina Commedia* of the Medieval Allegories on Ovid," in *Centenary Essays on Dante*, Oxford, 1965, which I discuss in my fifth chapter, points out that the only Ovidian reference which his system of accounting for Dante's references to the *Metamorphoses* expects to find and does not is one to Orpheus. In answer to Professor Robson's frank quandary, I would suggest the following hypothesis: Orpheus is missing from the *Commedia* (he is seen in *Inf.* IV, but not dealt with at all) because Dante has used him as an example of the allegory of the poets in *Convivio* II, i. Thus he might have thought it would have been confusing to those who remember the earlier work to be confronted with Orpheus, now treated at length not as *bella menzogna*, but as "historical" personage. (That is, in this view Dante has corrected his earlier non-historical treatment, but only gently.) For this is the way Dante treats the characters of Classical literature, as I am concerned to show in the next and following chapters. This argument is bolstered, it seems to me, by two facts. First, we know, from his treatment of it in *Convivio*, that Dante knew the Orpheus matter and considered it germane. Second, Orpheus is a "natural" as a *figura* of Dante in *Inferno*, as the Ovidian counterpart of Aeneas, who also visited the underworld. The omission of Orpheus from complex consideration in the *Commedia* is at least superficially comparable to Milton's easing him out of *Paradise Lost*, although the reasons for the two disappearances are probably not entirely commensurate.

is far from new. To those for whom it is old stuff I must apologize for having to include it. And needless to say, I count upon the work of others, to whom I have referred, to buttress what I have summarized. I refer those readers who still have grave doubts about the large degree of acceptance enjoyed by medieval exegesis in Dante's time again to the keepers of theological history, especially to Henri de Lubac.[36] I refer those who find it unlikely that Dante either knew or used this medieval system of thought to those few contemporary critics who have seen the matter clearly and put it well, above all to Erich Auerbach and Charles Singleton. I believe it is incumbent upon me to delineate, at least briefly, the differences between my position and that of these two illustrious precursors.

In all his many works on Dante, most of which are to some degree involved with Dante's use of this method of exegesis, Erich Auerbach never addresses himself to the full theoretical scope of the question.[37] Rather, from the time of his important essay, "Figura," he concerns himself primarily with Dante's use of the central technique

[36] In the few passages that deal with Dante in *Exégèse médiévale* Father de Lubac's position gives strong support to my own. Speaking of the analysis of Psalm 114 (Vulgate 113) in the Letter to Can Grande he says (vol. IV, p. 323): "Il est commenté de façon plus complète et plus exacte, parce que Dante n'entremêle pas, comme dans son premier texte [*Conv.* II, i] l'allégorie biblique et celle de la poésie profane. Ici encore, néanmoins, c'est bien son oeuvre à lui qu'il entreprend d'expliquer, non la Bible, tout en cherchant à bénéficier d'un rapprochement si auguste. Rapprochement d'autant plus légitime à ses yeux que, comme il le dit dans cette même lettre à Can Grande, il a voulu, en écrivant sa Comédie, 'arracher les hommes à leur état de misère et les faire parvenir à l'état bienheureux.' "

[37] See my Bibliography for the most important works. A complete bibliography of the works of Erich Auerbach is available in the English edition of his *Literary Language and Its Public in Late Latin Antiquity and in the Middle Ages*, tr. Ralph Manheim, New York, 1965, pp. 395-405.

of fourfold exegesis, figuralism; but he does not take up, either theoretically or practically, Dante's awareness and use of the other spiritual senses or of the theory as a whole. I cite, for instance, his pages on the figural nature of Cato,[38] which I believe achieve only a minimal insight into the complexity of Dante's poetic behavior at this juncture of the poem.

As for Charles Singleton, it is my belief that, after Filippo Villani, he is the first to see the structure of the *Divine Comedy* as Dante saw it. By that I mean that he is the first modern critic who became conversant with the actual poetic of the poem, which is, in his own phrase, the imitation of God's way of writing.[39] And yet I do not find in his work what I expect to find: the proof of the allegorical theory in the pure evidence of the text itself. For instance, to my knowledge Singleton does not (nor does

[38] "Figura," pp. 64-68.

[39] D. W. Robertson, Jr., "Some Medieval Literary Terminology," *SP*, XLVIII (1951), writing, to be sure, before Singleton made his exposition of this approach as clear as he has since made it, fails to see the accuracy or usefulness of this insight, nor has he subsequently, as far as I know, changed his mind about Singleton's great contribution: ". . . Professor Singleton confuses this distinction [between the allegory of the theologians and that of the poets] with that between verbal allegory and the allegory of things. It seems obvious, moreover, that the *Divine Comedy* is a poem, not a history, and certainly not a new chapter in Scripture" (p. 683n). I do not wish to tax Professor Robertson's good humor and patience, especially since he is not a Dantist, yet his inability to see the distinctions which Singleton was the first to clarify, despite his own great accomplishment as a medievalist, helps to illustrate the great difficulty which confronts those who attempt such studies as these in the face of an audience which has already made up its mind. The *Commedia* is a poem, and not a history; but it is a poem unlike most other poems in that it takes itself as history, and even as that kind of history which would be found in "a new chapter in Scripture." Robertson's later major work, *A Preface to Chaucer*, Princeton, 1962 (which, while discussing Dante's relationship to medieval theories of allegory, hardly mentioning the name of Aquinas), does not display greater hospitality to Singleton's seminal ideas.

anyone else for that matter) discuss Dante's straightforward use of the very words of exegetical theory in his
poem. Preferring to show Dante's awareness of the fourfold in more general ways, he does not, with a few notable
exceptions,[40] show how radically and beautifully Dante
turns the techniques of theology to poetry.

And the last is the task of this study.

It is my contention then, that the seventh and eighth
paragraphs of the Letter to Can Grande, whoever wrote
it, contain in germ all that the critic needs to know of the
plan of the poem in order to elucidate its essential techniques. The poem has a literal sense which operates whenever the actual events and persons of the afterworld are
described immediately, *historically*, as it were. It has a
figural or allegorical sense as what we see there relates to
history here (to keep in mind Dante's continual distinction between the two realms). It has a moral sense as what
we see there tells us what we should do here. It has an
anagogical sense as what we see there informs us of God's
purpose for the future, or at least shows us that there is
such a purpose by letting us see that nothing is either unknown to God or beyond His power, that all is in accord
with His plan.

Let me at once confess that this is simplemindedness itself. Let me add, however, that this simple formulation has
not been made before, except in the Letter to Can
Grande.[41] No one else seems to observe how simply stated

[40] Principally in his essays " 'In exitu Israel de Aegypto,' " *Annual
Report of the Dante Society*, LXXVIII (1960), 1-24 (reprinted in John
Freccero, ed., *Dante: A Collection of Critical Essays*, Englewood Cliffs,
N.J., 1965, pp. 102-121); and "The Vistas in Retrospect," *MLN*, LXXXI
(1966), 55-80 (first printed in *Atti del Congresso Internazionale di Studi
Danteschi*, Florence, 1965, pp. 279-304).

[41] In an article which I had overlooked when writing these words,
Francesco Mazzoni says much the same thing ("Pietro Alighieri inter-

50

Dante's subject is. And thus, even those who are in essential agreement with the document somehow balk at the notion of taking it perfectly straightforwardly. Let me continue by repeating the above formulation, this time making use of a concrete example from the poem. Take Ciacco the glutton (*Inf.* VI), for instance. (Any other character will serve as well.) The literal sense shows us, as Dante says, the state of this man's soul after his death. The allegorical sense makes evident the connection between his present life in the Circle of Gluttony and its past causes in Florence. The moral sense warns us against this particular sin. The anagogical sense asserts God's divine plan, which includes punishment for sinners. It is, I'm afraid, as simple as that. And, insofar as Dante's simple theory is concerned, I could end this book here, for it would be a great bore to move through the poem making similar observations, the only point of which is to assert that there is a valid constructive approach to the poem which accords with the practice and theory of medieval exegesis. As the mathematicians say, this is a true but not an interesting result.

Dante's use of the exegetical technique has two major effects, once we do realize that this is his technique. The first of these is amply discussed by Erich Auerbach and may be subsumed under the phrase "figural realism," which sets Dante's work aside from that of his contempo-

---

prete di Dante," *Studi danteschi*, XL [1963], 290n.): "Ed è questa la distinzione fondamentale fra i due piani, letterale e allegorico, del poema, almeno secondo l'autore dell'*Epistola a Cangrande* e i commentatori che seppero seguirlo: la lettera, il viaggio nei regni dell'oltretomba; l'allegoria, il continuo ricondurre, nell'ambito dell'*exemplum* e della *figura*, le immagini tipologiche della poesia alla concreta realtà dell'esistente, cioè a dire all'uomo considerato come soggetto d'attività morale, che tende, mediante i propri atti, ai fini voluti dalla Provvidenza per l'umanità."

raries, and prepares the way for the resurgence of Aristotelian ideas of imitation which typify the great works of literature at the close of the sixteenth century and after. The Judaeo-Christian historical tradition, centered for Christians in the doctrine of Incarnation, which for so many centuries had been attacked by heretical Christians (who may generically be referred to as gnostics), met similar opposition from literary men; this gnostic impulse was reinvigorated by that part of the fourteenth century which turned away from the ideas of imitation and of "historicity" in art in favor of the treatment of this world, and the consequent representation of this world, as being merely a veil, a cloak, that concealed and revealed the way to the next. The Christian Incarnational art of Dante, while it agrees that this world is an *umbra* of the next, treats this world as substantial shadow, as being actually existent and hence the tangible counterpart of a heavenly paradigm. It is essentially a matter of emphasis. Incarnational art, like Aristotle's philosophy, takes its beginning here. The gnostic impulse likes neither fact nor flesh of this world, preferring the non-physical intimations of the next, the spiritual realm. In my opinion, the best brief discussion of this conflict, as it centers in Dante and simultaneously is applied to the history of Western literature, is to be found in Erich Auerbach's Introduction to his *Dante, Poet of the Secular World.*[42] In the *Commedia* this world is to be treated literarily as historical fact, while for the other school, the school that embraces gnostic Christian poetic allegory and gnostic Christian allegorical criticism, this world and the literary works that are concerned with this world have only the currency

[42] Tr. Ralph Manheim, Chicago, 1961 (first published as *Dante als Dichter der irdischen Welt*, 1929), pp. 1-23.

of parable, and literature, to be worthy of the name, must be *bella menzogna*.

It is through such polarities that we can understand the major importance for the history of literature in Dante's borrowing of the techniques of fourfold exegesis. The principle of imitation that devolves from these techniques also has roots in the mimetic principles of the New Testament, in such remarkably vivid descriptions of human action as that which shows us Jesus writing with his finger in the dust while the scribes and Pharisees call for the stoning of the adulterous woman (John 8:6-8), or which shows us Peter, after denying his Lord, moving to a brazier in the dawn because he is so cold (John 18:18). It was this kind of imitation—which appeals to, and even demands, our total human attention, not merely that of a facile allegorical temper—which seems to have affected the Christian and poetic mimetic faculty of Dante. Although he almost certainly did not know Aristotle's *Poetics*, we can imagine how well he would have understood Aristotle's analysis of mimesis. In his mimetic intention Dante is greatly different from the poets of the thirteen hundred years since Virgil, the poets of his own time, and the poets of the three hundred years following him, with the single exception of the author of that other fourteenth century "Divine Comedy," the *Canterbury Tales*. These are the only two major works until the sixteenth century which, like the Bible, treat the literal as historical, and thus must perfect the techniques of mimesis as well as those of doctrine. (It is important to note that in this period the only "major minor" work—or so its author considered it—to use this approach is the *Decameron*, and this work is in some ways modeled on the *Divine Comedy*, with its hundred "cantos" and its attention to the literal. The gulf between Dante and the first Dante

53

professor is, however, evident in that Boccaccio could not
see his way, sharing this blind spot with his master,
Petrarca, to imitate the actual world in a work of doctrinal importance.) The great paradox of the medieval
period is that the major writers who were concerned with
the world as history were theologians, while most of the
literary artists were concerned with a theory of literature
which denied the importance or usefulness of imitation
and thus of a literal-historical sense. From Prudentius on-
ward the major tradition of medieval poetry, encompass-
ing such works as the *Roman de la rose* (despite the magnificent mimetic proclivities of Jean de Meun), the *De
planctu naturae*, Guinizelli's canzoni, Dante's *Convivio*,
Petrarca's *Trionfi*, and Chaucer's dream-visions—a tradition that went through the Renaissance to Spenser and
Bunyan—was to accept the role of the poet as fabulist, to
accept the Lucretian notion that fictions are all to be
treated as made up, as the honey on the rim of the draught
of doctrine.[43] It is then perhaps not surprising to find even
major scholar-critics neglecting, or failing to understand,
the unique importance of the *Divine Comedy*,[44] for it is

[43] Edward A. Bloom, "The Allegorical Principle," *ELH*, XVIII
(1951): "At the root of the allegorical concept is the traditional notion
that it is an essentially didactic device whose responsibility it is to delight
while it teaches" (p. 164).

[44] Such is the case in C. S. Lewis' major study of medieval allegory,
The Allegory of Love, Oxford, 1936, where (p. 48n.) Lewis
glides by the question of fourfold allegory in the *Commedia* and
at the same time dismisses it as a further subject of inquiry from his
book: "The experienced reader may be surprised to find no mention here,
and little mention below, of Philo, Origen, and the multiple senses of
Scripture. It must be remembered, however, that I am concerned much
more to explain a taste than to record the steps by which it found its
gratification; and that my subject is secular and creative allegory, not
religious and exegetical allegory. If Dante is and if I am right in detect-
ing a *nisus* towards allegory in Paganism itself, it will follow that the
exegetical tradition is less important for the understanding of secular

not typical of its time, although it is the great work of
its time and among the greatest works of all time.

If we were to see only this one ramification of Dante's
use of fourfold exegesis, even if the actual demonstration
of the technique's presence in his work were as simply and
dully exposited as my brief examples above have been,
we would see a major fact about the importance of Dante's
poetic theory and practice.[45] The aim of this study is to

---

allegory than is sometimes supposed. Certainly it will be difficult to prove
that multiple senses played any part in the original invention of any
erotic allegory. Dante himself, while parading four senses (*Conv.* II, i,
and Ep. xiii), makes singularly little use of them to explain his own
work." The point is exactly to prove that the theory of the four senses
lies behind the *Commedia*'s intended form and meaning. Lewis is right
about almost all secular allegory. His attempt to dismiss the greatest
"secular allegory" of all from exegetical consideration is one of the few
badly thought-out moments in his imposing corpus of criticism. His last
sentence, which tries to defend, or at least buttress, his position by
making the absence of Dantesque fourfold explanation a significant detail is wrong on two counts. The Letter to Can Grande, which Lewis
certainly seems to accept as genuine, is in fact the only criticism of the
Commedia by Dante we have, and it proclaims (it does not merely
"parade") his use of fourfold allegory; this would hardly correspond to
"singularly little use." Second, the absence of claims outside the poem
for its fourfold technique, if the Letter did not exist, would not necessarily say anything against its importance within the work.

[45] Two graduate students who are working with me at present, Robin
McAllister and Peter Schäffer, have given me cause to believe that two
areas of study which I have neglected will shed considerable light on
Dante's theory and practice of a mimetic and typological poetry. Mr.
McAllister has succeeded in convincing me that I have been entirely
negligent of the influence of Nominalism on Dante, and Mr. Schäffer
that the typological conceptual framework in which Dante beholds
present history perhaps owes more to the *Concordia utriusque Testamenti*
of Joachim di Fiore than to anything else, in that it was Joachim who
insisted, against received authority, that the Old Testament types extended
past Christ's life on earth and the founding of the Church to present
history. Probably the greatest student of Joachim in our century is Herbert Grundmann. See his "Dante und Joachim von Fiore," *DDJb*, XIV
(1932), 210-256. This last-minute note is by way of a rather ungrace-
ful *mea culpa*.

illuminate the *Divine Comedy* in the light of Dante's allegorical technique, which is not the mere activity of seeing, implied in each "historical" moment of the work, a fourfold scheme of interpretation. Yet it is my claim that this approach gives us first a way of seeing, as the Letter to Can Grande states, Dante's structure of the subject of the entire work; and second, more than any other critical approach so far directed at the *Commedia*, it helps us to understand the meaning of particular moments in the text itself, and thus serves as a bridge to the sense we may gain of the entire poem.

THE ROOTS OF UNIVERSAL
HISTORY

While Dante may have thought of his poem as finding its structural principles in the imitation of God's way of writing, and thus as being interpretable in all four senses, it is probably fair to conclude that he himself only infrequently "put things in" or "left things out" because of their moral or anagogical meanings. For him, as for the Scriptural exegete, the most important spiritual sense to attend to is the allegorical. As Dante himself implies (*Convivio* II, i, 8-12), since all spiritual senses are based on the literal, it is also true that the literal moves first and most significantly to the allegorical, for it is this sense which gives the historical relationship that is necessary to make the other two spiritual meanings clear. At any rate, while this study claims that Dante did indeed construct his poem in accord with the techniques of fourfold exegesis, it also maintains that his use of the second sense shows us exactly how he did so. Thus my position here is almost the same as Erich Auerbach's, who investigates the poem from the point of view of its adaptive uses of typology, while I would go on to say that Dante intended that the reader should also grasp, or at least feel the presence of, the other senses as well. It is in his adaptation of the second sense of Scriptural exegesis that Dante's theory of imitation may be clearly seen, and this then is the main subject of the following investigation.

To remind the reader of the conventions of figuralism, as well as its major Christian beginning, let us turn to Luke's Gospel, 24:27: "And beginning at Moses and all the prophets, he expounded unto them in all the scriptures the things concerning himself." Thus, according to Luke the first act of Jesus after the Resurrection was to give to his followers a lesson in Christian figures by telling them how the Old Law foreshadowed the New.

It is in Galatians 4:22-26 that we find the first explicit Christian use of the word "allegory" to refer specifically to the science which has come to be recognized in the synonymous words *allegoria, umbra,* and *tipos*:

"For it is written [Gen. 16:15 and 21:2] that Abraham had two sons, the one by a bondmaid, the other by a free-woman.

"But he who was [born] of the bondwoman was born after the flesh; but he of the freewoman was by promise.

"Which things are an allegory [*per allegoriam dicta,* from the Greek *allegoroumena,* that is, things meant allegorically]: for these are the two covenants; the one from the mount Sinai, which gendereth to bondage, which is Agar.

"For this Agar is mount Sinai in Arabia, and answereth to Jerusalem which now is, and is in bondage with her children.

"But Jerusalem which is above is free, which is the mother of us all."

Philo Judaeus and Paul are often represented as the two most important men of their time who made the attempt to harmonize, even synthesize, what is characterized as the Greek sense of idealist philosophy and the Hebrew sense of history—in other words, the attempt to reconcile the realms of pure spirit with the realms of deed and fact, the *invisibilia* with the *visibilia.* Because Philo tended to make the substance of things seen of trivial importance,

it is Paul who became the first great Christian theolo
of the Incarnation.

If Paul's hostility to the Old Law is manifest in the
citation above, as well as throughout his writings, he is
the first Christian exegete to declare that the Old Law
is historically related to the New, and thus indispensable
both as the prefiguration of the coming of the New Law
in Christ, and as the historical record of man since his
birth in Adam—the universal history. We can see in
Paul's commentary on the two passages in Genesis the
essential line along which figuralism will develop over a
thousand years.

Let us return to the notion of *figura*. Two citations help
clarify its point. Johan Chydenius, in the *Typological
Problem in Dante*,[1] defines the second sense as distinct
from what he calls Greek allegory: "Greek allegory, in
which the immediate sense is seen as a mere fiction taking
the place of something else, is essentially distinct from
Christian typology, which always implies that the two
events, promise and fulfillment, have taken place in time
as real historical facts." Auerbach, in his famous essay,
"Figura,"[2] says this: "Figural interpretation establishes
a connection between two events or persons, the first of
which signifies not only itself but also the second, while
the second encompasses or fulfills the first." As we might
say it, "The function of the allegorical sense is to relate
two historical events or things or persons, each of which
has a discrete and particular historical reality in time, so
that the relationship between them may express spiritual
significance."[3]

[1] Helsingfors, 1958, p. 23.

[2] *Scenes from the Drama of European Literature*, p. 53.

[3] C. R. Post, *Mediaeval Spanish Allegory*, Cambridge, Mass., 1915,
pp. 4-5, makes the following more general observation: "Allegory starts

The only case that I know of a fully developed four-fold explication of the poem is Singleton's analysis of the arrival of the pilgrim ship in *Purgatorio* II. He makes use of the one text in the poem where a fourfold reading is most obviously called for in his study "In exitu Israel de Aegypto."[4] The newly arrived souls come singing a four-fold gloss on themselves when they sing this Psalm. The Letter to Can Grande, whoever wrote it, is of absolute use to us here. In the literal sense we see a ship of one thousand souls who have been saved—that is the state of their souls after death. They are allegorically (or figurally or typologically) related to the Jews Moses led out of

---

with an idea and creates an imaginary object as its exponent. If one starts with an actual object and from it receives the suggestion of an idea, one is a symbolist. The primary difference between symbolism and allegory is that the former sees 'sermons in stones'; the latter from phantom stones builds sermons." This distinction has had considerable usefulness in criticism of contemporary literature (see W. Y. Tindall, *The Literary Symbol*, Bloomington, Ind., 1955, *passim*). It would make of Dante a symbolist and not an allegorist, which is very close to Nardi's position, for instance, as well as to Singleton's nomenclature. Essentially, I believe, it is the correct position. That is, Dante is not an allegorist if by allegory we mean personification allegory. If the only distinction we keep is that between symbolist and allegorist, Dante is a symbolist. But that is not to make great enough distinction. Allegory, in the *Commedia*, devolves from fourfold allegoresis, which could well be characterized as symbolism made specific and historical. Nardi and the other critics who argue against the arid allegorizations of the *Commedia* make the mistake, it seems to me, of lumping fourfold allegory with personification allegory. Similarly, see A. Pagliaro, "Simbolo e allegoria nella Divina Commedia," *L'Alighieri*, IV, 2 (1963), 3-35, where the author distinguishes between Dante's two kinds of allegory, calling that which we find in the first two cantos "allegoria," and the essential technique of the rest of the poem "simbolo" (e.g., ". . . Virgilio simbolo della ragione sommessa alla fede e Beatrice simbolo della ragione illuminata dalla fede, cioè della sapienza teologica . . . ," p. 16). While Pagliaro's study begins by making the necessary distinction, it declines to a semantic confusion, for this kind of "symbol" is surely just personification allegory.

[4] See Ch. I, note 40.

bondage in Egypt, roughly two thousand years earlier—
as the *Epistola* implies, the second sense represents our
redemption wrought by Christ *as it was prefigured* in the
flight from Egypt. Morally, we see the results of "the
conversion of the soul from the grief and misery of sin
to the state of grace," and anagogically, again quoting,
"the departure of the holy soul from the servitude of this
corruption to the liberty of eternal glory." In light of the
seventh paragraph of the Letter to Can Grande, it is difficult to read this passage any other way.

Dante apparently desired—in turning from *Convivio*,
which he confesses is a *bella menzogna*, a beautiful lie,
and which makes use of the allegory of the poets as he calls
it—to create in the *Commedia* a new kind of fiction, based
essentially on the allegory of the theologians. It would
have been considerate of Dante to have taken up the
phrase *bella menzogna* in the Letter to Can Grande, to
have reworked it in accord with his poetic practice in the
Commedia. To do that for him, we might call the *Divine
Comedy* a *menzogna vera*, that is, a poem the literal sense
of which is treated as true and not imagined.[5] Singleton
has said this best: "The fiction of the *Divine Comedy* is
that it is not fiction."[6] This is more or less the major

[5] Compare Singleton's discussion of Plato's "true lie" in *Dante Studies
1*, p. 69.
[6] In "The Irreducible Dove," *Comparative Literature*, IX (1957),
129, replying to R. H. Greene, "Dante's 'Allegory of Poets' and the
Mediaeval Theory of Poetic Fiction," *Comparative Literature*, IX
(1957), 118-128, who argues: "But this is not the 'allegory of the
theologians' which Dante mentions in the *Convivio*. It is the 'allegory of
Christian poets,' making fictions which veil the truth according to the
ancient art of poets. . . ." (p. 128). This is essentially the same position
as that taken by C. S. Lewis (see Ch. I, note 44). The modern debate on
the secular or even ecclesiastical uses of fourfold interpretation has had
a large American following. It was perhaps initiated by the article of
Harry Caplan, "The Four Senses of Scriptural Interpretation and the

61

message of Ulrich Leo's work *Sehen und Wirklichkeit bei Dante*,[7] in which the late Professor Leo speaks of the radical importance of vision (forms of the verb "to see" are the most frequently used words in the poem, appearing over four hundred times, an average of more than four

Mediaeval Theory of Preaching," *Speculum*, IV (1929), 282-290. Among those who have been affected by what Caplan and those who followed his reopening of the old topic have had to say, there often remains a certain discomfort, especially about the conclusions drawn by Singleton. Three recent examples are M. W. Bloomfield, "Symbolism in Mediaeval Literature," *Modern Philology*, LVI (1958), 73-81, who demurs as follows (p. 79n.) : "I have never seen this fourfold meaning completely worked out in the case of any literary work, including Dante's." Bernard Stambler, *Dante's Other World*, New York, 1957, pp. 54-78, has a strangely inconclusive debate with himself and Singleton, and ends up with Dante writing a third kind of allegory in the *Commedia*—what kind it is hard to say, except that it would seem to have been described with some adequacy in Post's "symbolism" (note 3 above). Probably the most important recent study which has taken Singleton into account and yet remains, though not hostile, unconvinced, is Joseph Mazzeo's "Dante's Conception of Poetic Expression," *RR*, XLVII (1957), 241-258, printed as Chapter II of the author's *Structure and Thought in the Paradiso*, Ithaca, 1958, pp. 25-49. Mazzeo, perhaps because he is primarily interested in the Neoplatonic influences on Dante's thought, or perhaps because he is concerned with real distinctions rather than actual ones (*i.e.*, that only God can really write fourfold allegory, that Dante's version of it is to be understood as a metaphorical approximation of God's way of writing—which is one step back from Singleton's simple and brilliant solution of the problem, *imitation* of God's way of writing), ends up by saying (p. 37) : "Dante's conception of allegory, however, remains ambiguous. Nardi is undoubtedly right in maintaining that Dante did not understand the allegory of the theologians. It is true, at least, that he did not understand it as theologians wanted it understood." More recently, two other expositors of Dante's allegory have shared this tack, which falls between the deniers of the fourfold allegory and the supporters of Singleton. Each of them, like Mazzeo, creates an epicycle—or so it seems to me— by positing the roots of a theory which would honor the fourfold at one remove: Dante's literal sense is to be understood as a metaphoric approximation of the literal sense of Scripture. This position is accurate enough if we wish to uphold the Dantesque equivalent of the old

per canto) in the poem precisely because its fictional pretense is that it is real.[8] Is not this the burden of Dante's comments, in the Letter to Can Grande as well as in *Convivio*, on the major importance of the literal sense?

Dante bases his poem's structural techniques in the fourfold exegesis of the Bible for two main reasons: first, to make the poem capable of seeing God, which it does in *Paradiso* xxxiii, as well as the order of the whole universe as this is known to God alone; then, to make it a *real* poem, and not just the usual fiction of a poet. Thus Dante's

---

astronomy ("only God can write that way"); Singleton, as Copernicus, makes the epicycle superfluous. See Phillip W. Damon, "The Two Modes of Allegory in Dante's *Convivio*," *Philological Quarterly*, XL (1961), 144-149, reprinted in slightly different form as an appendix, "Dante's *Canzoni* and the 'Allegory of Poets,'" pp. 329-334, in the author's *Modes of Analogy in Ancient and Medieval Verse*, Berkeley and Los Angeles, 1961; and see the opening argument of G. R. Sarolli's "Prolegomena alla 'Commedia,'" *Convivium*, xxxiv (1966), 77f.

[7] Frankfurt am Main, 1957. Although Leo attacks the conventional allegorical interpretations of the *Commedia*, he, like Bruno Nardi, balks strongly when presented with a fourfold reading. See especially his attack on Singleton in his "Vorrede zu einer Lectura Dantis," *DDJb*, XXXVIII (1960), 18-50. He is tangibly in error when he claims that the Letter to Can Grande supports only a twofold, and not a fourfold, reading. The *Epistola*, as its own wording makes abundantly clear, is merely reflecting Aquinas' own distinction between the literal and the allegorical sense, when the allegorical sense includes all three spiritual senses. For Leo, as for others discussed in notes 3 and 6 above, Dante is a "symbolist," not a "theological poet."

[8] Bruno Nardi has said this with some power in his *Dante e la cultura medievale*, Bari, 1949, p. 397: "La differenza che v'è tra una finzione poetica, poema o romanzo che sia, e la visione dantesca, è questa, che chi narra le avventure d'Ulisse, d'Enea o di Renzo e Lucia, ha coscienza che quello che narra è finzione poetica, cioè 'bella menzogna'; Dante invece tratta gli oggetti della sua visione come realtà." This seems to me absolutely just for Dante. However, it would also seem to me to apply with equal force to Homer and to Virgil. Nardi's point would have been more just had he used works in the mold of the *Roman de la rose* as his examples of fiction which is *bella menzogna*.

allegory is vastly different from the personification allegories of Bunyan and Spenser, and even of his own *Convivio*; for the events in his allegory like the events in
Scripture, are to be understood as actually occurring in
history, except of course, as is also true in the Bible, when
we deal with parable, which the writer inserts in order to
make a moral meaning clear by words alone.[9]

To begin, I would like simply to demonstrate Dante's
own use of the terminology of the second sense. *Figura*
and *ombra* are the words which occur frequently in the
Commedia (*allegoria* and *tipos* do not occur in the *Comedy*) and could have the signification we seek.[10] The former word is used more than twenty times and the latter

[9] In the *Commedia* Dante draws our attention to two such "parabolic"
passages by warning the reader that he must "look under the veil."
This use of personification allegory is discussed in Chapter VI.

[10] Inattention to precisely such detail is the mark of almost all recent
argument concerning Dante's use of fourfold exegesis in the *Commedia*,
even in those studies which argue for its presence. Surely the text
of the poem was one of the first places to look. Further, four passages
in *De Monarchia* show us Dante using the terminology of the second
sense with precision and force. In III, iv, 2, he discusses the exegetical
meaning of the sun and the moon at the beginning of Genesis, which
have been understood allegorically (*allegorice*) to signify the two
regimens, the spiritual and the temporal. That he is thinking in relatively orthodox typological terms is made evident first by his following
reference to the famous passage in *The City of God* (XVI, ii—discussed
in Ch. I) which distinguishes between further-signifying and non-
further-signifying historical passages in the Bible by use of the analogy
of the ploughshare and the other parts of the plough, which are also
necessary (III, iv, 7). When Dante resumes his point (III, iv, 12), he
substitutes the synonym *typice* for the earlier *allegorice*. It is, or should
be, enlightening to see Dante using the adverb "allegorically" with
strict typological sense, and not with the connotation of Greek allegory
which is so often urged upon him. And further on in *Monarchia* III
(ix, 18) we find him returning to the exegetical vocabulary, explaining the typological significance of the conversation between Peter and
Jesus concerning the sword (Matt. 10:34: "I came not to send peace,
but a sword"), "si verba illa Christi et Petri typice sunt accipienda."
For *figura* see III, XVI, 7.

almost sixty in its singular form alone, according to the
Concordance. In most instances it is readily apparent that
Dante does not use these words to denote or connote figural
awareness; most of the time they have their usual meanings. Yet surely Dante knew what they meant with reference to Scriptural exegesis. I cite two passages alone, one
for each word. First, for *figura*, in *Paradiso* xxv Beatrice
is addressing St. James, who is about to give Dante his
oral examination on Hope:

> Inclita vita per cui la larghezza
> de la nostra basilica si scrisse,
> fa risonar la spene in questa altezza:
> tu sai, che tante fiate la figuri,
> quante Iesù ai tre fé più carezza.

> [Illustrious living soul, by whom largesse
> of this our court was chronicled,
> make hope resound unto this height;
> thou art able, who so often figured it
> when Jesus showed more favor to the three.]

(Par. xxv, 29-33)

James was the "chronicler" of the court of heaven (Jas.
1:17), and it was James, accompanied by Peter and John,
who was with Jesus at His Transfiguration (Matt. 17:2,
Mark 9:2). These Biblical references are made in the
passage. What is of greatest interest to us here is Dante's
use of the verb *figuri*, which appears to be the only form
of the word *figura*, denoting the exegetically precise term,
which Dante uses, for none of his uses of the noun *figura*
have sure exegetical denotation, although on occasion some
do seem to carry at least an overtone of Biblical exegesis.
It is perhaps surprising that no critic or commentator, at
least none consulted by me, has pointed out the exegetical

precision of Beatrice's description of James. This is all the more surprising since the event to which the passage most urgently refers is the Transfiguration, which I am sure most readers of this book have already realized was precisely the text upon which Dante elaborated the moral (third) sense of fourfold allegory in *Convivio* II, i, 5. Now, do we find a moral sense here as well? Dante uses this Bible story as the example of the moral sense in *Convivio* by saying that "in the most secret things we should have little company." A pretty undistinguished reading, we might think. The particular moral reading is of little interest, as is the particular anagogical reading. Both are more important as directions in which the reader is to be moved—morally toward goodness, anagogically toward the awareness of God's plan, insofar as this can be understood by humans. Yet I think Dante might insist, if we could ask him, that the passage is meant to reflect four senses, that it is written in imitation of God's way of writing; and I believe we can be fairly sure that this is so because of his use in the passage of that exegetically potent word *figuri.*

To go one step further, if we cast our eyes down the page a mere thirty-three lines to *Paradiso* xxv, 55-56, we find Beatrice speaking of Dante as one to whom "it was granted to come from Egypt to see Jerusalem before his time of war is done."[11] This glancing reference, now not only to the Letter to Can Grande's definition of fourfold allegory but to the passage in *Purgatorio* II which Singleton elucidates in the fourfold manner, further vivifies the

[11] In his article "The River of Death: *Inf.* II, 108," in *The World of Dante* (ed. S. B. Chandler and J. A. Molinaro, Toronto, 1966, p. 25), John Freccero demonstrates a similar figural understanding of these lines, but apparently without having taken notice of the preceding passage containing the verb *figuri.*

use of the Biblical method at this moment in Dante's poem. I do not believe I need belabor the point, although it is one Dante himself belabors, returning to the formulation in the most personal and powerful form he gives it in *Paradiso* xxxi, 39, when he describes his arrival in the Empyrean as that of one who has come "from Florence to a people just and sane," that is, from earthly bondage to the City of God. The figuralism is evident.

For the word *ombra*, which, as we shall see, has greater exegetical currency for Dante than does *figura*, I cite for now *Purgatorio* xxi, the moment of Statius' completed purgation:

> Ed ecco, sì come ne scrive Luca
> che Cristo apparve a' due ch'erano in via,
> già surto fuor de la sepulcral buca,
> ci apparve un'ombra. . . .

> [and lo, just as Luke writes
> that Christ appeared to two who were in the road,
> just now risen from the sepulchral cave,
> there appeared to us a shade. . . .]
>
> (*Purg.* xxi, 7-10)

Dante and Virgil have, in the preceding canto, felt the Mount of Purgatory quake with joy. Throughout the *Commedia* there have been reminiscences of the earthquake that occurred at the Crucifixion. This particular earthquake is the direct result of the Crucifixion, without which neither Statius nor anyone else might come to bliss. And so even before the canto begins the sense of redemption in Christ is stronger than it has yet been in the *Commedia*. "*Ed ecco*" is the very language of Luke (24:15) as he is about to describe the appearance of the resurrected Jesus to Cleopas and someone else not named on the road near Emmaus. The "shade" is Statius, and Statius is *umbra Christi* here, just now "resurrected" from sin, on his way to Paradise. In the lines that follow, the whole scene from Luke is likewise resurrected by Dante with loving care. He does not merely concern himself with the significance of the scene, but with many of its smallest details: the Resurrection; the surprise of the two travellers who, like Dante and Virgil, are in their third day, Dante and Virgil in Purgatory, Cleopas and his companion saddened at the memory of the Crucifixion; the stigmata paralleled in the *segni* which Statius bears; even Virgil's making the appropriate sign of Christian recognition to the "resurrected" one; Statius' first words ("Frati miei, Dio vi dea pace"—line 13) reflecting the very words of Christ, as recorded in Luke 24:36: "Pax vobis, ego sum, nolite timere."[12] Further, the Biblical and musical "setting" for Canto XXI, the "Gloria in excelsis Deo" of *Purgatorio* xx, 136, reminds the reader and the Pilgrim of the angels' song to the shepherds (Luke 2:9-14), culminating in these lines, which promises that the Saviour is this day born in the city of David. The song sung by Dante's angels in the preceding canto in praise of the Lord at the birth of the Christ is amplified by the opening lines of Canto XXI, which refer to the "natural thirst" (*sete natural*) of the Samaritan woman for the saving water of Jesus (John 4:4-15). Here Dante, possibly correcting his earlier version of *la naturale sete* (*Convivio* I, i, 9), which is *di sapere* (*Convivio* I, i, 1), perhaps a too general and gnostic formulation for the later Christianity of Dante, explicitly makes

[12] Note should be taken that what is one of the earliest examples of Christian figuralism, to which I have already alluded, occurs in this passage (Luke 24:27): "And beginning at Moses and all the prophets, he expounded unto them in all the scriptures the things concerning himself."

Jesus the object of his thirst. Thus, the apparition of the saved Statius is the surest evidence Dante has yet been granted of the actual Salvation found in Christ. Statius comes as the figural messenger of Christ.

It should not be surprising to see that Dante has carefully constructed many of the elements of his scene from appropriate scenes in Scripture. It is slightly surprising though to follow his logic to its culmination in the following canto, where we find Statius advising Virgil that it was the Fourth Eclogue, three lines of which he quotes, which made him a Christian (*Purgatorio* xxii, 70-73). For where the "literary" source for the words we heard in Canto xx was Luke's second chapter, the source for the words which round off our experience of the Rebirth of Statius in Canto xxii is the vatic Eclogue of Virgil. Each promises a Saviour, the first in the words most quoted, even to the present day, as the emblematic notation of the birth of Jesus; the second in the words which Dante and his time considered the most prophetic of any uttered by a pagan. The message of each is Christ. The two quotations stand as a frame to the central action of the Resurrection of Statius, *poeta* and *cristiano*, the pivotal action of *Purgatorio*.

That *ombra* has here not only its Virgilian meaning—a shade, one who lives in the afterworld—but its full Christian figural significance as well seems obvious. It is difficult to imagine the troubles that commentators of the personification allegory persuasion must undergo in face of the tangible "historicity" of Dante's literal sense, at least as it reveals itself in these and similar passages, for it is clear that here we are dealing with *allegoria in facto*, allegory of event, and not a *bella menzogna* which is a mere philological veil.

In citing these two passages, I have intended to show

69

that Dante both knew and used the precise exegetical terminology of the Fathers, and that he embodied it with considerable effect in his poem, which can, indeed which must, be understood as it relates to its primary structural device, the imitation of God's way of writing.

However, if we are to treat the letter of Dante's poem as though it is also historical, a difficulty confronts us when we start our reading of the poem at its beginning. The first two cantos of *Inferno* do not seem to ask for this sort of treatment. They seem to embody, rather, examples of Greek allegory in which personifications, or at least mere philological exponents of ideas, meet our attention. Boccaccio's commentary cites ten of these "allegories," some of which continue to puzzle modern critics.[13] The *selva oscura* would not seem to be an actual wood, nor the "straight way" any particular road. Here is what Singleton says of the setting of the first two cantos: "The stage is *there*; but where *there* is you may not say. The real sun, to be sure, shines down upon this place; and before we leave it, an historical person, Vergil, has stepped out upon it. . . . Neither may this dark wood nor the valley nor this hill be found on any map. Nor is any one of the three beasts who are met there such as would be hunted by any but a Hound (with a capital H) who is yet to come and who is, in fact, not a hound."[14] Although traces of the dominant allegorical mode of the poem are present, the dominant allegory of the first two cantos is a different one.[15] When we observe the very moment when the poem

[13] In his commentary explaining the "allegories" of the first canto of *Inferno*. These include Dante's "sonno," the "diritta via," the "selva," the "tre bestie."

[14] " 'Sulla fiumana ove 'l mar non ha vanto,' " *RR*, XXXIX (1948), 272.

[15] For an excellent discussion of the shadowy unreality of the first two cantos see John Freccero, "Dante's Firm Foot and the Journey

changes its fictive technique, that is, when we turn the
page to Canto III, we are witness to one of the great moments in the history of Western fiction.[16] For suddenly
we are asked not only to read what our author has written, but to see what he has seen. And what do we see?
We see something that seems like the least thing a poet
who has found the way of writing by seeing would ask
us to see with him: we see some letters on a page, which
are supposed to be the words Dante saw carved upon the
Gate of Hell. Why does he begin the visionary part of
his poem with words and not things? I think that here
Dante is playing a game with us, and it is a very high
game, one which tests our abilities to understand the importance of his fictional technique in the *Commedia*. We
remember, and certainly he remembers, the distinction
that Augustine, Aquinas, and many others made between
two kinds of words: those that are only words and those
that have the quality of also signifying things. What
Dante insists here at the outset is that the letters of which
his words are composed are not made up but are real,
that they have the tangible actuality of letters sculpted
in stone, and if we extend the argument only a little, that
they are the model for all the words which report what
he saw throughout the *Commedia*—for this is the mode of
vision essential to his poem. In most editions of the poem
these nine lines are printed in upper case. We do not have
an autograph manuscript of the *Divine Comedy*, and so

Without a Guide," *Harvard Theological Review*, LII (1959), 245-
282. Chapter VI of this study returns to the question of the allegory
involved there.

[16] Singleton, *Dante Studies 1*, p. 9: "In a sense it might be regretted
that somehow a curtain does not fall at the end of the Canto II *Inferno*
to mark off the first two cantos of the poem for the prologue which
they are."

71

we cannot know whether Dante wrote the lines in upper case. I would like to wager that he did.[17] But this is not important. What is important is that he is telling us that the literal sense of his poem is real, that his letters are the kind that signify words which in turn signify things, that this is not a poem made up of *parole fittizie* but of *parole vere*—or again, that the fiction of the *Commedia* is that it is *not* fiction. In the *Convivio* Dante admonished us about the prime importance of the literal sense; and here he asserts the nature of the literal sense of the *Commedia*: it is made up of "real" words, like these we see sculpted in stone at the outset. To my knowledge no one else has ever asked this kind of question of the opening lines of Canto III, and I think to do so yields a pleasing result, one which makes us consider, for instance, the difficulties of Virgil in guaranteeing the reality of his underworld—the Sybil, the golden bough, the mouth of Avernus; all this fanciful (though beautiful) trapping is done away with in a single stroke that takes us into the reality Dante claims for the fiction of the poem. For we should remember that the "author" of these sculpted words is God, that the first concretion imitated in Dante's journey to the afterworld is precisely "God's way of writing." The words over the gate and almost everything we shall see now for ninety-eight cantos are to be understood as having been made by Him, not by His poet. Thus, what is described as having been seen, like the events of Biblical narrative—not the parables, but the events—has a figural relationship to other past or present or future events, a moral sense, and an anagoge. We are able to test the theory immediately with the first damned souls we are made to see:

[17] For a second reason for drawing this conclusion, see Appendix II.

Poscia ch'io v'ebbi alcun riconosciuto,
vidi e conobbi l'ombra di colui
che fece per viltà il gran rifiuto.

[After I had recognized some among them,
I saw and knew the shade of him
who out of cowardice made the great refusal.]

(*Inf.* iii, 58-60)

While most of the commentators identify this *ombra* as that of Pope Celestine V, whose abdication in favor of Boniface VIII, so hated by Dante, would make him a likely candidate, some others suggest Esau, who sold his birthright for porridge, and still others, more persistently, Pontius Pilate. Since Dante's scorn is part of the *contrapasso* here—these men, the Neutrals, are not worthy of our attention—Virgil's words in line 51, advising Dante merely to look and pass on, make it clear that it is difficult to know whom Dante had in mind. A figural reading of the passage, one that does not rely upon, but may make some further use of, the word *ombra* (which means what it meant in Virgil—a shade—but which may also have the further Christian meaning *umbra futurorum*) may even help clear up this old commentator's tangle. And here we begin to see the extraordinary usefulness of figuralism. Assuming that the *ombra* is literally that of Celestine, we can tick off our simpleminded use of fourfold analysis: literally we see the damned soul of Celestine; figurally, the life of the caitiff prince of the Church which brought him to this pass; morally, how not to behave; anagogically, that God's Justice is always evident in the afterworld. However, the further uses of figural techniques are far more interesting. For in the refusal of

73

Celestine we may see the refusal of Pilate,[18] and perhaps even a reflection of that refusal of Esau. To be sure, none of this is certain. Nevertheless, I believe it is a more satisfying way of entertaining the possibilities than that of other commentators, all of whom must argue for one or for another identification. Seen with the eye of historical figuralism, each act in universal history has its past or future counterparts in other acts. It allows us a polysemous interpretation that is both multitudinous and precise.[19] Dante's use of this method, which can be more dramatically and certainly demonstrated in later passages, makes the likelihood of its applicability here greater than the context may seem to allow.

[18] See Yvonne Batard, *Dante, Minerve et Apollon*, Paris, 1952, Appendice III, "Le Grand Refus," for a recent argument that the *ombra* is that of Pilate. The most recent reinvestigation of the problem, containing essential bibliography in its notes, and reaffirming that the shade is that of Celestine is Nardi's "E rieccoci a 'colui che fece per viltà il gran rifiuto,'" in his *Saggi e note di critica dantesca*, Milano, 1966, pp. 321-331. For a theologian's discussion of a figural usage of the word *umbra*, see Jean Daniélou, "'Nous vivrons à son ombre.' (Lam., 4, 20)," the fifth chapter of his *Études d'exégèse judéo-chrétienne: Les Testimonia*, Paris, 1966, pp. 76-95. For a poet's discussion of the relationship between Dante's *ombra* and figuralism, see Allen Tate, "The Unliteral Imagination; Or, I, too, Dislike It," *Southern Review*, I (1965), 535-536.

[19] In a recent discussion, two of my students gave still another answer to the question raised by the *ombra* in Canto III. They saw, independently and with some urgency, Peter's triple denial of Jesus. They were at most, I believe, half-wrong. Figurally, one might argue, Peter's refusals are also present here, even though he who made them is in *Paradiso*. What is clearly at stake here is the denial of responsibility by one who holds divinely sanctioned office. For Dante, Celestine's abdication probably smacked of Pilate's, and perhaps even of Peter's momentary failures. Had Peter not come back to his Lord he might have become the first soul we see in Hell. There is no way of "proving" that Dante had Peter's denials in mind here. Nevertheless, I do not believe my students' replies would have surprised Dante in the least.

Before proceeding into the poem, we should certainly treat the roots of figuralism as they first enter the poem, blended with the other kind of allegory, in the first two cantos. In Canto IV we shall meet the poets of Antiquity, who greet Dante and include him among their number. In line 121 of that canto a strange thing happens, although perhaps we do not think it strange. So far every inhabitant of hell we have met, except Charon, who is something of an ornament, though he is treated as the actual guardian of Hell, is the shade of one who lived on this earth. Now suddenly we meet the shades of those who lived only in books, or so it would seem:

> I' vidi Elettra con molti compagni,
>> tra' quai conobbi Ettor ed Enea,
>> Cesare armato con li occhi grifagni.

> [I saw Electra with many companions,
>> among whom I recognized Hector and Aeneas,
>> Caesar armed, with his fierce eyes.]
>> (*Inf.* IV, 121-123)

For Dante the record of Troy is history; in his time he was not alone in so treating it. Thus Electra, here the mother of Dardanus, founder of Troy (*Aen.* VIII, 134f.), Hector, and Aeneas are for Dante as equally "historical" as Caesar. This much may introduce the problem of Dante's reading of Virgil, which is opened by the appearance of Virgil himself in Canto I.

All that must be understood is that for Dante the events recorded in the literature of pagan antiquity have, for purposes of his fiction, as much historical validity as do the events recorded in the Bible. The latter may be more "true" in his eyes, but the situations of Aeneas or Jason are as significant for Dante's theory of the "true lie" as

75

the situations of Moses or Rahab. I do not insist in our believing that Dante thought Jason stole away with Medea or that Theseus went down into that labyrinth or even that Aeneas went into Avernus; but I do think it helpful to recognize that he treats their stories in the *Divine Comedy* as though they had all actually happened, and that as real events they have significance for the real events of his poem.[20] Again Charles Singleton's phrase comes to mind: the fiction of the *Divine Comedy* is that it is not fiction. I believe Dante treats other poems, myths, and stories in the same way in the *Commedia*.[21]

Long study and great love have given Dante's readers a measure of understanding of the *Divine Comedy*'s relationship to the Christian and pagan works which precede it. And although the large indebtedness which the later poet confesses to Virgil ("il lungo studio e 'l grande amore/ che m'ha fatto cercar lo tuo volume"—*Inf.* I, 83-84), both in general and in particular, has been frequently discussed, readings of the *Commedia* are likely to continue to suggest yet undiscovered reciprocities between Virgil's epic and Dante's poem. Among recent studies, one of the most interesting is by Ulrich Leo, who argues that ". . . Dante, while writing the last chapters of the fourth book of the *Convivio* and of the fragment of the *De Vulgari eloquentia*, is evidently under the influence of having

[20] For a brief discussion, one with which I am in accord, of Dante's change of attitude toward the literal sense of pagan fiction, especially as it concerns his treatment of Virgil, see Charles Till Davis, *Dante and the Idea of Rome*, Oxford, 1957, pp. 122-123. In a similar vein, see E. K. Rand's remark (quoted by Lubac, vol. IV, p. 244): "I prefer the Virgil that Dante lets me see rather than the object revealed in the scholarly pages of Teuffel and Schanz. . . ."

[21] The following pages concerning Dante's use of Virgil have been somewhat revised from my first treatment of this subject, "Dante's use of *Aeneid* I in *Inferno* I and II," *Comparative Literature*, XX (1968), 142-156.

reread and understood more personally than before the *Aeneid* along with other Latin poetry."[22] Professor Leo, in discussing the development of Dante's poetry between *Convivio* and *Commedia*, finds that Dante's rereading of Virgil first becomes apparent in *Convivio* iv, xxv, at which point his quotations from the *Aeneid* and other classical texts become vivid and particular. In this context it is perhaps instructive to remember that *Inferno* i was undoubtedly composed with *Convivio* iv very much in mind; for in *Inferno* i we find translated from *Convivio* iv not only the "top of the arch of life," the thirty-fifth year which should mark a man's maturity, but also the concept that the young man who has entered the "wood of error" (*selva erronea*) of this life requires that the right path be pointed out to him by his elders (iv, xxiv). The mature guide in question, both within the drama of *Inferno* i and in Dante's own life as a poet, appears to have been Virgil. When Dante addresses Virgil's shade in *Inferno* i, 85, "Tu se' lo mio maestro e 'l mio autore," he may, Leo's research would indicate, be referring to his recent rereading of the master's poem in such a way as to make it seem almost

[22] "The Unfinished Convivio and Dante's Rereading of the Aeneid," *MedStud*, xiii (1951), 45; this article is reprinted in the author's later volume, *Sehen und Wirklichkeit bei Dante*. It supports with some detail the earlier contention of Karl Vossler, *Mediaeval Culture*, tr. Wm. C. Lawton, vol. ii, New York, 1929, p. 191: "At the point where his *De vulgari Eloquentia* breaks off, and his *Convivio* is laid aside, about 1305-1308, he had become by study, will, inclination, and taste a friend of the ancient classics." For a partial representation of the massive body of scholarship that surrounds Dante's relationship to pagan literature, consult the appropriate section of my Bibliography. The three works with which I find myself in closest agreement on this point are those by Auerbach, Davis, and Gmelin. Professor Davis' recent work is to my mind clearly the best in English on the problem, and is also valuable in that it contains an extensive bibliography. I have not yet been able to see the recent study of Domenico Consoli, *Significato del Virgilio dantesco*, Florence, 1967.

the proximate cause for the writing of the *Commedia*, and thus also offering an explanation for his abandonment of *Convivio*. Admittedly, such high claims, however attractive they may be, are not susceptible of proof. Whatever the conclusions we draw from it, Leo's article is further concrete evidence of Dante's close acquaintance with Virgil's work, further concrete demonstration that his readings of Virgil found their way with some immediacy into his own work.

Inferno I concerns the poet's, or any Christian's, confrontation of a crisis in his moral life. It would suggest that, at least in the struggle of this particular Christian, the *Aeneid* had been, or should have been of considerable aid. One sign of Dante's great respect for the author of the *Aeneid* is to be found in the very word he uses for Virgil's work: *volume*. This word is used six times again in the poem, always in *Paradiso* (II, 78; XII, 122; XV, 50; XIX, 113; XXVIII, 14; XXXIII, 86), and there to denote either the Bible or the Heavens: God's Book or His Creation, His Other Book. Thus the word inherits an exalted context when we rediscover it in *Paradiso*. The word *volume*, used for the *Aeneid* and for God's Book, is thrown into sharp relief by the other word for book that we find in *Inferno*: the *libro* which led Francesca and Paolo astray (V, 137). One of the words Dante uses for Virgil himself—*autore*—has a similarly honorific history in the poem. It is used once again in *Inferno* (IV, 113) to describe the inhabitants of the *nobile castello*, people of *grande autorità*, those pagans whose philosophy became the philosophy of Christendom, Virgil's fellow authors, as it were. The word then, like *volume*, reappears only in *Paradiso* (XXVI, 26, 40, and 47), where it is used to speak of God as the *verace autore*, of the *autorità* which descends from Heaven, and of the *autoritadi* concordant with human intellect. Virgil is no mere fabulist; he is an *autore*: his book is no mere fable; it is a *volume*.[23] Seen in this light the *Aeneid* becomes, in Dante's poem, the best book we have from Latin antiquity, the pagan counterpart to the Old Testament, the authoritative history of Troy on its way to becoming Christian, as the Old Testament is the history of the Hebrews on a parallel path. The *Aeneid* is the work of pre-Christian Latinity that Dante knew and loved the best, as Virgil himself tells us, when speaking as a character within Dante's poem he implies that Dante

[23] For discussions of the importance of these words see E. R. Curtius, "Das Buch als Symbol in der Divina Commedia," in *Festschrift zum sechzigsten Geburtstag von Paul Clemen*, Bonn, 1926, pp. 44-54: "Das Buch—in quo totum continetur—ist die Gottheit. Das Buch ist Symbol des höchsten Heiles und Wertes" (p. 53). Also see passages indexed under "Auctores" and "Book" in Curtius' *European Literature and the Latin Middle Ages*, tr. W. R. Trask, New York, 1953. For evidence that Dante consciously reflects a neat and established distinction between the words *volume* and *libro*, see Isidore of Seville, *Etymologiae*, VI, xiii, 2-3, where, to be sure, the distinction is primarily between methods and materials of manufacture. Nevertheless, Isidore's examples of *volumina* are the Hebrew "book of the law and books of the prophets," while his etymology of *liber* depends from Virgil's Tenth Eclogue, line 67, "alta liber aut in ulmo." Thus, by implication, a volume is holy, a book is not. For Dante some of Isidore's *libri* seem to have become *volumina*. This way of distinguishing between the credentials of various writings comes to Dante through Uguccione da Pisa, as we learn from *Convivio* IV, vi, 5: "L'altro principio, onde 'autore' discende, sí come testimonia Uguiccione nel principio de le sue Derivazioni, è uno vocabulo greco che dice 'autentin,' che tanto vale in latino quanto 'degno di fede e d'obedienza.' E così 'autore,' quinci derivato, si prende per ogni persona degna d'essere creduta e obedita. E da questo viene questo vocabulo del quale al presente si tratta, cioè 'autoritade': per che si può vedere che 'autoritade' vale tanto quanto 'atto degno di fede e d'obedienza.' " In addition to keeping clear distinctions in his use of the words *volume* and *autore* in the *Commedia*, Dante also treats the word *scrittura* similarly, using it nine times to refer to the Bible and once (*Purg.* VI, 34) to Virgil's writing. See note 21, Chapter I. It is pleasing to see that Dante uses each of these three significant words denoting books or writing or writers once in the poem to refer to Virgil's writing.

79

knows the *Aeneid* by heart: "l'alta mia tragedìa . . ./ ben lo sai tu che la sai tutta quanta" (*Inf.* xx, 113-114).

We have for some time understood that the opening scenes of the *Commedia* reflect the events of Exodus.[24] Might we add to Singleton's well-documented discussion of the figural pivotalness of Exodus at the poem's beginning the figural presence of Genesis as well? If Dante the Pilgrim, as he undertakes his pilgrimage, is figurally related to the experience of the Hebrew people—Adam's progeny on the way toward Israel and redemption—is he not also, if we attend to the place he is trying to leave, figurally related to Adam's Fall from Eden's forest and his progeny's subsequent experience of the Flood? Before Exodus is present in the poem, in a few large strokes which are neither inappropriate nor particularly surprising, we are presented with the figures of the first two great events of Genesis which concern our race. We can sense them in the dark wood that Dante metaphorically relates to dangerous waters, thus suggesting that the Fall and the Flood are the historical analogues to the Pilgrim's dire situation, which is, after all, causally related to Adam's sin. It would be unlike Dante not to begin at the Beginning. His journey to God begins in memory of the beginning of the race's journey—Adam cast forth from the Earthly Paradise, his offspring shortly after to be confronted by a flood—and all of this is present in and behind the first thirty lines of the poem.[25]

[24] See Singleton, " 'In exitu Israel de Aegypto.' "

[25] Although Charles Singleton, in a letter to this writer, expresses his doubts about this theory, I find another contemporary critic of Dante who, though not developing the parallel, would seem to support it; Aldo S. Bernardo, in "The Three Beasts and Perspective in the *Divine Comedy*," *PMLA*, LXXVIII (1963), 16, makes this brief statement: "In the first verse we have 'life,' in the seventh 'death.' The opening moments of Genesis immediately come to mind." More convincing on

If it is true that at the inception of the *Commedia* Dante draws our attention to Adam, is it not also possible that he would expect us to think of a parallel figure in pagan Latinity? What is perhaps classifiable as the first overt use of typological comparison in the poem, "Io non Enea, io non Paolo sono" (*Inf.* ii, 32), moved us backward in time for two noteworthy predecessors of Dante, each of whose particular experience of the afterworld is a prefiguration of the divinely ordained journey to a vision about to begin in the poem. In this exact comparison Dante suggests major relationships that the temporarily unwilling hero of the poem only negatively acknowledges: as one who will take a journey to a vision in the afterworld, he shall in fact be a new Aeneas, another Paul.[26] Is it not

this point is one of Dante's earliest interpreters. Filippo Villani's *Comento al primo canto dell'Inferno* (ca. 1400), ed. G. Cugnoni, Città di Castello, 1896, p. 99, explicating *Inf.* I, 11, the phrase *pieno di sonno*, has this to say: "Homini quippe dictum est: Sapiens eris, si te ipsum cognoueris. Ignorauit semitipsum Adam, quando, ratione in ipso penitus dormiente (quod colligitur per uerbum *pieno*), sensualitati factus est obediens." Filippo's commentary finds several other reminiscences of Adam in Canto I, mostly on the figural principle that Dante in his sinfulness is implicitly the new Adam. I shall return to the much-neglected work of Villani in my final chapter, where I shall examine again the figural relationships within Dante's first canto.

[26] For discussions in a similar vein, although neither employs the precise conceptual framework of Biblical exegesis or the actual text of the *Aeneid*, see Vincenzina Inguagiato, "Come Dante col Poema rinnovelli l'azione d'Enea e di s. Paolo," *Giornale dantesco*, XVIII (1910), 193-199; and Luigi Valli, *L'allegoria di Dante secondo Giovanni Pascoli*, Bologna, 1922, pp. 149-161. For a sense of the literal significance of the *Aeneid* which may well correspond to Dante's own sense of the meaning of Virgil's poem, see D. L. M. Drew, *The Allegory of the Aeneid*, Oxford, 1927. Drew argues that the essential allegory of the *Aeneid* is allegory of event and not the internalized moral allegory of the medieval commentators: "It is one of his methods to blend together events and scenes of different dates . . . , historical facts, which, if separated in their actual occurrence by time, are still the steps of one progression" (p. 4). Thus, he argues, Augustus and Aeneas are given

also probable that, as one who has lost the true way and in
his immediate surroundings is bewildered, fearful, and
lost, he is like Adam and Aeneas? To develop the Adamic
correspondence further seems unnecessary here. The parallel

parallel actions to perform, Aeneas being, and here I adapt his argument to my own, a "figure" of whom Augustus is the "fulfillment."
Drew's essentially "historical" reading of the poem would, I believe,
be similar to the approach natural to Dante, far more accessible to his
way of thinking than the internalized moral allegory of the medieval
Virgilians. It is this sense of the poem, and of Dante's understanding
of Virgil, which illuminates Helen Flanders Dunbar's appreciation of
the relationship between the two works in her important study, *Symbolism in Medieval Thought and Its Culmination in the Divine Comedy*,
New Haven, 1929, p. 311n.: "Dante makes his very life follow that of
Aeneas. For example, each shows temperance, in leaving Dido and the
Siren, respectively." That sort of intelligence for the figural presences
of Aeneas in Dante has not ever received surer treatment than in the
doctoral dissertation of Sister Marie Catherine Pohndorf, "Conceptual
Imagery Related to the Journey Theme in Dante's *Commedia*," University of Denver, 1965, esp. pp. 41-45. Sister Marie Catherine is to my
knowledge the first critic of Dante ever to combine into a single large
pattern the effects of Dante's allegorical techniques, derived from
Biblical exegesis, and his reading of Virgil. Since I came upon her work
only after completing the body of my own, the debt of gratitude I owe
her is not one of scholarly instruction, but of critical fellowship. If
she will forgive my presumption in saying so, the approaches of our
two works have more in common with each other than they do with any
other approach to the *Commedia*. Her dissertation is available, I should
add, through University Microfilms. A most recent study, which also
speaks to the Virgilian background, as well as to the allegorical techniques of the *Commedia* is Eberhard Müller-Bochat, "Der allegorische
Äneas und die Auslegung des Danteschen Jenseits im 14. Jahrhundert,"
DDJb, XLIV-XLV (1966-1967), 59-81. The author's comment on
Dante's relationship to Aeneas and Paul is as follows: "Äneas und Paulus
sind die Träger dieser Erfahrung. Mit ihnen beiden hat Dante sich
verglichen; an beiden hat er sich gemessen, wenn auch mit einem
demutsvollen Unterton der Selbstbeschränkung: *Io non Enea, io non
Paolo sono*. Das demütige Pathos dieser Stelle beruht nicht zuletzt auf
dem Kontrast zu Vergil. Der von der Sibylle den *descensus* fordernde
Äneas beruft sich auf Vorgänger, denen er sich ebenbürtig weiss:
Orpheus, Pollux, Theseus, Hercules (*Aen.* VI, 119-123)"—p. 59 and n.

follows from Singleton's work in such a way as to be merely
a footnote; it involves two large imagistic relationships—
dark wood and dangerous waters—developed in the first
thirty lines of the poem; and its general justness has been
frequently touched on in one form or another, if not in a
specifically figural analysis of the poem. The Virgilian
parallel, though perhaps not grasped as immediately as
the Adamic correspondence, is neither outrageous nor unlikely: as Dante discovers himself off the true way *nel
mezzo del cammin di nostra vita*, so Aeneas *in medias res*
discovered that he had been blown off course by the storm
which initiates the present action of the poem concerning
his voyage. Other details which reinforce and extend this
parallelism cluster around the first and central one and will
be taken up immediately.

The parallels between *Inferno* i and ii and *Aeneid* i
offer convincing proof that Dante consciously reflected
Virgil's first book in the beginning of his book. I must
admit at the outset my surprise that something so relatively
simple and natural should have gone unnoticed for more
than six hundred years. As a reason for this lack of perception I might suggest that Dante's way of writing, if not
easily grasped, has been clear enough, but our way of
reading the *Commedia* has been at fault, at least in two
major respects: first, hardly any attempt has been made to
deal with the poem in terms of the techniques of Biblical
exegesis; and second, only a few students of Virgil's influence on Dante after Pietro and Benvenuto da Imola, almost all of whom have written in the past seventy years,
have dealt with the actual text of Virgil's poem as it came
into Dante's poem.

Perhaps the common cause for both of these critical
failures is the preconception of most commentators that the

Commedia is to be dealt with primarily as internal action, not as significant outward event. Interestingly enough, this was the fate of Virgil's poem in Dante's own time. Only fairly recently has our civilization begun to read Virgil's poem as we are now beginning to read Dante's. To put this briefly, we might now say that for Dante Virgil's book had more in common with the Bible than with Prudentius' *Psychomachia* or Bernardus Silvestris' commentary on the *Aeneid*, and that the literal sense of the *Aeneid* was to be conceived as historical and actual (and thus meaningful in higher respects) rather than merely as a poet's deceit having meaning mainly in the moral lesson a reader might draw from the obviously fictitious and discardable *fabula*.

As we move through five passages and/or moments of the first two cantos, each of which contains several verbal or situational reflections of the *Aeneid*, it becomes difficult to disregard Dante's plan. One general comment is necessary here: in no way do I intend that his citation of Virgilian analogue be construed as displacing or replacing other previously understood analogues. Clearly, many of Dante's passages reflect several sources. This argument only maintains that among these sources Dante is consciously reflecting *Aeneid* I in his own first cantos, and goes on to assert that his reasons for doing so are structurally meaningful.

(1) The first reflection of the *Aeneid* is primarily situational. When Dante has left the dark wood, progressing toward the mountain, his experience of fear in the forest is summarized and translated by images of water. He is as one who, having pulled himself ashore after swimming through perilous waters, pants while he gazes back on the place of his near-destruction:

84

E come quei che con lena affannata
uscito fuor del pelago a la riva,
si volge a l'acqua perigliosa e guata,
così l'animo mio, ch'ancor fuggiva,
si volse a rietro a rimirar lo passo
che non lasciò già mai persona viva.

[And as one who, with panting effort
having come from the sea to the shore,
turns to the dangerous waters and gazes,
so my mind, that still was fleeing,
turned back to take in the pass
which never yet let slip a living man.]

(*Inf.* 1, 22-27)

After the Trojans survive the storm at sea in *Aeneid* 1,
they steer for the coast of what turns out to be Libya,
where they fling themselves, exhausted, on the shore—
"artus in litore ponunt"—(*Aen.* 1, 173). Then Aeneas
scales the cliff which stood above them,[27] seeking a prospect
of the sea, from which he has just escaped, for a possible
glimpse of other Trojan survivors—"et omnem/ prospec-
tum late pelago petit" (180-181). The sea (Dante and
Virgil share the word *pelago*), the exhausted survivors, the
shore with a cliff above it, the proximity of death by
drowning; all these are common to both scenes. And each

---

[27] Of the similar features of the two landscapes, we may note that
Virgil has two peaks ("geminique minantur/ in caelum scopuli"—1,
162-163) where Dante has one. And Virgil's forest, though dark
("tum silvis scaena coruscis/ desuper, horrentique atrum nemus imminet
umbra"—164-165), are above Aeneas, not around him. The place,
however, toward which Aeneas looks and Dante is forced down by his
terror at the beasts, is in both poems characterized by silence: "là dove
'l sol tace" (60) and Virgil's "sub vertice late/ aequora tuta silent"
(163-164).

85

hero, having arrived in a strange and frightening new landscape, begins by climbing upward in order to discover a way out of his present condition. Where the action of *Aeneid* i is the action of literal event, the corresponding moment in Dante's poem is given metaphorically, or, more precisely, in the first simile of the poem. The context of the first seven *terzine* has been exclusively Christian, with the exception of the epic reference contained in the words *nel mezzo* which we have already noted. In this first simile Dante broadens the reference of the beginning of the poem, first by the human immediacy of the exhaustion of the barely surviving swimmer, and then by his first suggestion, tacit though it is, of the correspondence between the two pilgrims, a correspondence that will be quickly developed and made more obvious as Virgil himself enters Dante's poem.

(2) Having started to climb the mountain, Dante comes upon the three beasts. Having scaled the cliff, Aeneas also sees three beasts—"tris litore cervos/ prospicit errantis" (184-185)—wandering on the shore. Here the situations have opposite meanings: Dante's animals will hardly serve to feed an army, as will the stags Aeneas subsequently kills and brings back to his hungry Trojan comrades, for these are like Spenserian beasts, inedible though morally significant. Yet the triad of animals common to both narratives is surely striking, and perhaps suggests that Dante was pleased to reflect his Virgil even at the cost of context, although it is possible to argue that Virgil's participle *errantis* had a moral force to suit Dante's purpose.[28] When

[28] In this connection it is interesting that Isidore of Seville's definition of allegory (for him merely one of the tropes) gives as its first example of *alieniloquium* (*Etymologiae* i, xxxvii, 22) precisely these lines of *Aeneid* i. Isidore claims that the three stags are allegorical representations of either the three leaders of the Punic Wars or of the

86

we examine the beasts more closely, however, we find out that Dante did appropriate the name (by false etymology) and aspect of his *lonza* from Virgil's lynx in a slightly later passage of *Aeneid* I,[29] a fact which tends to buttress the notion that the poet would have enjoyed this small though relatively interesting coincidence. The often cited passage in Jeremiah (5:6) is surely the likely source for this tri-form embodiment of sin. Yet, that Aeneas also confronts three beasts as he begins his journey must have pleased Dante greatly.

(3) The next event in Dante's poem after the Pilgrim flees from the beasts is the coming of Virgil. Dante, having passed a piteous night, his heart filled with fear—". . . la paura . . ./ che nel lago del cor m'era durata/ la notte . . ." (19-21)—sets out up the mountain, as Aeneas sets out after an equally disturbed night—"Aeneas per noctem plurima volvens" (305)—which began as he brought food for his comrades, pretending to be hopeful when the heart in him was not—"premit altum corde dolorem" (209). The language and feeling of the descriptions of the heroes' nocturnal desolation are at least similar. And each hero starts out at dawn: "principio del mattino" (*Inf.* I, 37) and "ut primum lux alma data est" (306). Dante's encounter with

---

three Wars themselves. His interpretation obviously had no effect on Dante; yet the fact that an allegorical significance is attached to the lines might have encouraged Dante to make his own gloss—in this case one involving philological, and not theological, allegory.

[29] Moore, *Studies in Dante*, I, pp. 180-181, follows Pietro di Dante and Benvenuto da Imola when he points out the Virgilian echo in the "lonza . . ./ che di pel maculato era coverta" (I, 32-33) of *Aen.* I, 323, "maculosae tegmine lyncis." Tommaseo (see note 30 below) also makes this citation. Here again, although a Virgilian source seems certain, context does not fit, for the lynx of the *Aeneid* is merely a part of the imaginary garments of the imaginary sister Venus asks Aeneas about in order to disguise her own identity.

the three beasts occurs now, during his first morning, while Aeneas' adventure with the stags takes place the night before he sets out to explore Libya. These are the approximately similar settings for the major encounters about to occur in each poem. Each hero stands in need of divine assistance, and each receives assurance from someone sent on a mission by higher authority: Venus appears to her son; Virgil appears to Dante. That Dante thinks of the Virgilian passage here is established by one of his most obvious quotations of Virgil, although only one commentator of the many I have consulted notes the correspondence.[30]

> Quando vidi costui nel gran diserto,
> "Miserere di me," gridai a lui,
> "*qual che tu sii*, od ombra *od omo certo*!"
> > (*Inf.* 1, 64-66: italics mine)

[. . . o quam te memorem, virgo? namque haud tibi vultus
mortalis, nec vox hominem sonat; o, *dea certe*
(an Phoebi soror? an Nympharum sanguinis una?),
sis felix nostrumque leves, *quaecumque*, laborem . . .]
> > (*Aen.* 1, 327-330: italics mine)

The very locution of Dante's address to Virgil, the first spoken words in the *Commedia*, is a quotation of his master and author, picking up both the *quaecumque*, "who ever you are," in his *qual che tu sii*, as well as the *o, dea certe* in *od omo certo*. Here the situations are perfectly parallel: both heroes seek aid from a being whose nature or whose order of being is not certain, while both have

---

[30] In his commentary, *La Commedia di Dante Allighieri, col comento*, Venice, 1837, which contains more citation of Virgil than any other commentary that has come to my attention, N. Tommaseo points out (p. 13) the parallels between these four lines of Virgil and Dante's two-line response.

been sent someone by divine power to aid them. And the situational parallel is sealed by the precise verbal under-lining of the two Virgilian quotations in a single line of Dante's first speech as a character in the poem; the speech is, appropriately enough, addressed to Virgil, who appears just now for the first time as a character in the poem. What-ever Virgil's moral meaning in the *Commedia*, he is al-ways first the actual Mantuan, whose *Aeneid* Dante knows by heart, for it is the most real thing Dante knows about Virgil. The quotation here is Dante's acknowledgment of the long debt of gratitude and the strong desire to honor, both of which are accomplished through the courtesy of quotation.

(4) In *Aeneid* I Aeneas describes himself to his mother in words that may have recalled to Dante his pilgrim's situation: "Sum pius Aeneas . . . (378), fama super aethera notus . . . (379), Italiam quaero patriam . . . (380), ipse ignotus, egens, Libyae deserta peragro . . ." (384). Dante is also known above, seeks in his poem and in his life the Italian homeland, and is currently in poor estate, making his way over a "piaggia diserta" (*Inf.* I, 29).[31] Shortly afterwards, Virgil tells of Beatrice's coming to Limbo to intervene on Dante's behalf, just as the *Aeneid* narrates the intervention of Venus on behalf of her son on Olympus. Virgil's speech begins with the prophecy of the Veltro (100-111). In the *Aeneid*, Venus is reassured of her son's eventual safety by Jupiter's prophecy (257-296), which begins by promising success for Aeneas in words that are literally more applicable to the Pilgrim: "sublimemque

[31] I am indebted to A. B. Giamatti for first calling to my attention the possibility of a connection between the desert landscapes of Aeneas' Libya and *Inf.* I. For a discussion of *desertum* as a technical term in Richard of St. Victor, see G. H. Williams, *Wilderness and Paradise in Christian Thought*, New York, 1962, p. 5of.

feres ad sidera caeli/ magnanimum Aenean" ("thou shalt bear the lofty and great-souled Aeneas to starry heaven"— 259-260). Then Jupiter goes on to foretell the coming of a great temporal leader, Augustus Caesar, who will close the doors of war and shackle Furor forever. In Virgil's prophecy in the *Commedia* the beast over whom the Veltro will triumph is characterized by her loathsome hunger, "che mai non empie la bramosa voglia,/ e dopo il pasto ha più fame che pria" (98-99); in the *Aeneid* Furor is characterized by bloody jaws, "ore cruento" (296). Perhaps the form of the Virgilian prophecy is responsible for Dante's somewhat confusing telescoping of the three beasts into a single *bestia*, symbol of all sin, or of all civil disobedience, or of both.[32] More than the striking resemblance between the disruptive appetitive natures of these two personified enemies of peace and order, we find in the entire shapes of the two prophecies extraordinary similarity of form, intensity, and context. If this does not solve the vexing question of the identity of the Veltro and of the DXV, it does suggest that if Dante had the *Aeneid* in mind he was thinking of a temporal leader, one on the order of the great Augustus. And a temporal leader of that order may surely in turn prefigure, in his ability to bring justice to human affairs, the Second Coming of

[32] The vexed question about the meanings of the three beasts, the history of which is as long as Dante criticism, has no place in this discussion. Two recent important contributions are: Bruno Nardi, "Il preludio alla Divina Commedia," *L'Alighieri*, IV, 1 (1963), 3-17, which finds, *inter alia*, that the she-wolf represents, when taken abstractly, Avarice, and, when understood historically, indicates Boniface (p. 13). Aldo S. Bernardo's article, "The Three Beasts and Perspective in the *Divine Comedy*," *PMLA*, LXXVIII (1963), 14-24, argues convincingly, it seems to me, for the generic identification of each of the beasts with one of the three great areas of sin punished in *Inferno*, the leopard with Fraud, the lion with Violence, and the she-wolf with Incontinence.

Christ and the ultimate Kingdom on earth. The analogous passage in the *Aeneid* gives Virgil's prophecy a larger and surer dimension in the poem by revealing Dante's probable source and thus his preoccupation. Surely, for Dante, this passage in the *Aeneid* must have been the locus classicus for any prophetic revelation of a coming temporal leader. And since the prophecy comes from the very mouth of Virgil, it is at least likely that Dante would have modeled his own version of Virgilian prophetic utterance on the most noteworthy exemplum in the original.[33]

(5) Virgil fills the central section of Dante's second canto with his description of Beatrice's compassionate visit to his station in Limbo. He describes her tears: "li occhi lucenti lacrimando" (*Inf.* II, 116). Venus, as she appeals to Jupiter for the safety of her son, also weeps from compassion: "et lacrimis oculos suffusa nitentis" (228). The tearful pleas of the two ladies are similarly answered in their respective heavens. Jupiter sends Mercury to Libya to make the usually haughty Carthaginians receive Aeneas with kindness so that he may escape the desert and begin his journey to Italy. In the *Commedia* Mary sends Lucy to Beatrice, who in turn comes to Virgil and then appears to Dante in a desert place and leads the new Aeneas on his journey. The similarly shining tears of mercy have similar results; the *misericordia* of each lady initiates the divine action by which the human action of each poem may commence. One may certainly argue that there are any number of classical ladies whose tears bring benevolence. It is probably fair to respond that if Dante had any of these other tears in mind, they in turn would remind him of

---

[33] That Dante was thoroughly familiar with this passage is demonstrated by his Italian translation in *Convivio* IV, iv, 11, of two of its lines (*Aen.* I, 278-279): "his ego nec metas rerum nec tempora pono:/ imperium sine fine dedi." See also *Epistola* VII, iii, 13.

Virgil's *lacrimae*. And it is perhaps justifiable to conclude in light of the evidence that, at this point in the poem if Dante has any Virgilian tears in mind, they are most likely to be these in *Aeneid* I. For certainly the resulting parallelism between Beatrice and the pagan goddess of love who lends her name to a sphere of the heaven where Beatrice is in glory would not have seemed amiss to the author of the *Divine Comedy*. And once again it is in Virgil's own voice that we hear these words which appropriately echo the similar words and actions from the corresponding episode in his *Aeneid*. Dante, like Goethe, is too great a poet not to imitate a great predecessor.

THUS A great deal of the action of *Aeneid* I, lines 157-386, is recapitulated in the action of *Inferno* I and II.[34] In some cases it is difficult to be certain of the degree of ex-

---

[34] The notion that, if Dante reflected the counterpart moment of the *Aeneid* at the beginning of *Inferno*, he might do a similar turn at the opening of *Purgatorio*, was difficult to part with. Book VII, the landing in Italy, seemed the natural place to look. However, supporting evidence is meager. Moore, without advocating a schematic reason for the parallel he finds, and following both Pietro di Dante and Benvenuto da Imola, shows the sure connection between the concluding lines of *Purg.* I and those of *Aen.* VI which describe the preparations for Aeneas' descent to Avernus: "In connexion with the above passage we may compare the 'aurea bractea' with which Aeneas was armed by the direction of the Sybil in Aeneid, vi. 140 . . . with the Christian equivalent of the reed with which Dante was girt . . . by the advice of Cato, Purg. i. 94. Also the spontaneous renewal of the plant, Purg. i. 134-6, is borrowed from Aeneid, vi. 143, 'Primo avulso non deficit alter Aureus.' Nor must we omit the bathing of Dante's face with the dew, Purg. i. 95-6, 121 seqq., and the corresponding act on the part of Aeneas, Aeneid, vi. 635,6"—*Studies in Dante*, I, p. 170. If Dante has taken his *giunco* from Virgil's golden bough, the borrowing suggests that Dante is self-consciously marking a parallel between Virgil's "invention" of the underworld and his own "invention" of the geography of Purgatory, which he considers himself to be the first poet to see. Thus the figural connectives in this passage join not only the Pilgrim and Aeneas, but also the Poet and Virgil.

plicitness Dante intends in his echoes of Virgil. The weight of the evidence is probably sufficient to rule out mere chance or unconscious imitation as explanations for the parallelism in the passages we have examined. Dante's own words on the subject, "Long study and great love have made me search your volume" (*Inf.* 1, 83-84), seem explicit enough. Perhaps we should not be surprised to find that Dante weaves into the fabric of his poem the actual words and events of its greatest pagan predecessor as well as the situation of Adam at the beginning of God's Book; for we have always found throughout the poem, side by side, characters from both worlds in a continuous historical procession which not unnaturally begins with the inceptions of the two great histories: that of the earthly Rome beside that of the Rome of which Christ is Roman.

How much of Dante's conception of Virgil was shaped by his time is difficult to ascertain. It is certain that Dante was aware of the several allegorical treatments of the *Aeneid* that so influenced many medieval and renaissance writers. While Comparetti and some later commentators and critics unwisely neglect the "medieval Virgil,"[35] seems

[35] In this connection it is perhaps worth noting that Fulgentius' *Expositio Vergilianae continentiae* declares that the shipwreck in *Aeneid* I denotes the birth of man, and that, accordingly, the rest of the poem shows the development of the human soul to maturity (see note 56 below). Charles Till Davis points out (pp. 122-130) that where Dante seems to have relied on Fulgentius and other medieval Virgilians to some degree in the *Convivio*, the Virgil of the *Commedia* comes straight from the source, in this position agreeing with Domenico Comparetti's judgment in *Vergil in the Middle Ages*, tr. E. F. M. Benecke, reprint of 2nd ed., Hamden, Conn., 1966, esp. pp. 195-231. Nevertheless, in Dante's handling of the parallels between his Pilgrim and Adam, the first man, there is a possible overtone of the non-historical view of the *Aeneid* of Fulgentius and others. The entire question of Dante's reliance upon the medieval Virgilians has not received widespread attention to date. However, two noteworthy articles appeared in 1932. H. T. Silverstein, in "Dante and Vergil the Mystic," *Harvard Studies and Notes in*

overemphasis equally unwise. To see in Dante's reading of
Virgil a culturally impossible act, to chain Dante to an
essentially secondhand understanding of a poem he quotes
over and over again, is surely even less defensible than to
turn him into a poet of the Renaissance. Fortunately, we
do not have to make this arbitrary and rather useless choice
between Dantes. As the greatest medieval poet, he gave,
as has so often been said, one thousand years of human
history their fullest single expression. Why are we surprised that a man of his obviously supreme gifts possessed
the ability to be totally of his own time and simultaneously
to outstrip it? Many aspects of the *Commedia* suggest to
us the work of writers centuries after Dante. To name but
two, we might consider his "self-conscious" use of himself

Philology and Literature, XIV (1932), 51-82, discusses "the nature of
the indebtedness to the *Aeneid* as it was transformed by both the
allegorical commentaries and the mythographers" (p. 53), giving
eight examples from the *Commedia* (none from Cantos I or II). R.
Palgen, in "Die Virgilsage in der Göttlichen Komödie," *DDJb*, XIV
(1932), 1-26, claims that ". . . Dantes Vergil der Vergil des Mittelalters
ist und nicht eine schemenhafte Konstruktion Dantes nach der Lektüre
der Aeneis . . ." (p. 21), a conclusion he offers again in "La Légende
virgilienne dans la *Divine Comédie*," *Romania*, LXXIII (1952), 332-390,
and in the chapter "Dantes Vergil-Gestalt" of his *Werden und Wesen
der Komödie Dantes*, Graz, 1955. Although I dispute strongly the conclusions Palgen draws from his research, I would certainly admit that
there is some reflection of the medieval Virgil in the *Commedia*. The
entire problem is a matter of degree. Those who approach Dante's treatment of the classical authors as reflecting primarily the medieval commentators in the *Commedia* are dedicated to a scholarly principle which
seems attractive, but which turns out to be simply incorrect in its
central preoccupation, one which fails to explain the acutely literal translations or references to the *Aeneid* and to other classical works that
are so frequently and vibrantly evident throughout the *Commedia*.
Müller-Bochat (see note 26 above), p. 66, points to three passages in
Pietro's commentary which would seem to have been influenced by
Bernardus' commentary on the *Aeneid*. But he does not go on to argue
that the sins of the son had been first visited on the father.

as narrator of the *Commedia*,[36]—"Everyman" with a particular history—and his use of classical letters in a Christian work. If we cannot observe either of these phenomena without thinking of the Renaissance, we must not forget that they are also a natural outgrowth of Dante's thoroughly medieval preoccupations and practices. Karl Vossler has spoken to this point with some force:

"For if we observe how in Italy and in the more naive Northern Europe the classical world was justified by pious, unwary monks, laymen, and heretics, how they made Virgil a prophet or a magician, Ovid a teacher or morals, Hades a Hell, Olympus a Paradise, Orpheus or Apollo a Redeemer, Horatian love-songs chants of the Church; how they prayed at Ovid's grave, as though at a sacred spot, and half-piously, half-inadvertently, regarded Cato, Seneca, Pliny, Statius, and Trajan as Christians, how they were edified by the humanity and greatness of these figures and their works without questioning their historical environment, how they took delight in what they had in common with them and ignored what was alien—when we weigh all this, we understand that there existed in the Middle Ages a spontaneous, blindly loving humanism. . . ."[37]

[36] See R. M. Durling, *The Figure of the Poet in the Renaissance Epic*, Cambridge, Mass., 1965, *passim*.

[37] *Medieval Culture*, II, 132. For a similar statement see Bruno Nardi, "Tre momenti dell'incontro di Dante con Virgilio," in his *Saggi e note di critica dantesca*, Milano, 1966, pp. 220-237 (first published in *L'Alighieri*, VI, 2 [1965], 42-53): "Molto s'è parlato e dissertato, in questi ultimi anni, dopo la celebre opera del Burckhardt, intorno all'umanesimo del Rinascimento e al preumanesimo medievale, non che sul loro contributo al rinnovamento filologico, scientifico, filosofico e perfino politico e civile, e molte cose sono state dette giustamente a precisare meglio concetti unilaterali o confusi, e molti miei cari amici hanno recato in queste discussioni il frutto prezioso di sagaci e pazienti ricerche delle quali mi guarderei bene di negare l'importanza; eppure io sono ancora del parere che nessuno abbia assimilato

Dante's Virgil is first and foremost the Virgil of the *Aeneid* and not the Virgil of the commentators. We rarely find in Dante the phraseology that we find in these commentators—the phraseology we find continued in such writers as Boccaccio, who treats Dante in the spirit of medieval Virgilianism, claiming that in Dante's poem Virgil represents "la ragione delle terrene cose" ("reason in earthly affairs"),[38] and who insists that his task as commentator on Dante's poem is, in a similar vein, "to explain the difficult text, the multitudinous tales, and the sublimity of the senses which are hidden beneath the veil of our Dante's *Commedia*" (". . . spiegare l'artificioso testo, la moltitudine delle storie e la sublimità de' sensi, nascosi sotto il poetico velo della *Commedia* del nostro Dante. . . .")[39] There is, moreover, the problem of ascertaining *which* medieval Virgilians served as guides to Dante. A cursory review points to a number of important possible sources which might be summarized as follows:

1. The pagan grammarians who accept the *Aeneid* as a great poem without tampering with it. The major example here is the commentary of Servius (ca. 375), which reflects the lost work of the earlier grammarian, Donatus (ca. 350). Servius, as distinguished from the later pagan and Christian commentators, essentially avoids allegorical explanations. One must read some 122 pages of his com-

---

mai tanto dell'umanesimo classico quanto Dante" (p. 235). Perhaps the best brief and general treatment of this problem as it concerns especially the fourteenth century in Italy is B. L. Ullman's study, "Renaissance—the Word and the Underlying Concept," *Studies in Philology*, XLIX (1952), 105-118, which cites from a number of contemporary documents in order to establish the picture of a time already taken up with a sense of its own novelty in being curious about the antique.

[38] In the *proemio* of his *Comento*.   [39] *Ibid.*

mentary, including the first 222 lines of *Aeneid* i, to get even a faint whiff of the allegorist's midnight oil. From lines 223-224, ". . . cum Iuppiter aethere summo/ despiciens . . . ," Servius adduces the fact that Jupiter shares his high place with Venus "because some happiness may issue from the company of a woman" ("quod per mulierem aliqua felicitas possit evenire").[40] The bulk of his work accords with the brief and cogent description of it given by Émile Thomas: "Expliquer Virgile par Virgile a été la pratique constante de Servius."[41] We must turn to other sources to find an allegorized *Aeneid* which might accord with the allegorizations of Virgil urged upon Dante by some scholars.

[40] *Servianorum in Vergilii carmina commentariorum*, editionis Harvardianae, ed. E. K. Rand *et al.*, Lancaster, Pa., 1946, p. 122. This magnificent Servius-by-committee helps a modern reader see what Servius himself actually was concerned with in Virgil's poem. The medieval Servii are less likely to conform to the original. For discussions of this problem, see, among others, J. J. H. Savage, "The Manuscripts of the Commentary of Servius Danielis on Virgil," *Harvard Studies in Classical Philology*, XLIII (1932), 77-121; J. J. H. Savage, "The Manuscripts of Servius' Commentary on Virgil," *HSCP*, XLV (1934), 157-204; E. K. Rand, "Une nouvelle édition de Servius," *Académie des Inscriptions & Belles-Lettres, Comptes rendus des séances de l'année 1938*, pp. 311-324.

[41] *Essai sur Servius et son commentaire sur Virgile*, Paris, 1880, p. 234. Elsewhere Thomas concludes: "Cependant on doit croire qu'il avait, même en ces matières, plus de sens que ses contemporains quand on le voit se dégager d'un défaut alors général, je veux dire des *explications allégoriques*" (p. 243). His description of the practices of such ancient grammarians as Quintillian, which he sees paralleled by the practice of Servius, is worth noting. "Les devoirs du grammarien ancien peuvent se résumer ainsi. Il donnait d'abord une interprétation *littérale* du texte où, considérant les mots séparément, il déterminait leur sens dans le passage commenté, leurs autres significations, leur âge, suivant qu'ils étaient créés par l'auteur ou empruntés par lui à un écrivain ancien, enfin leur emploi au propre et au figuré. Il passait ensuite à l'interprétation *littéraire*, où, rattachant les expressions et les développements au plan de l'ouvrage, il recherchait les intentions de

2. Macrobius (ca. 400), who was also a grammarian, and a Neo-platonist as well. Thus, in the *Saturnalia*, although it is not a commentary on the *Aeneid*, we find: a near apotheosis of Virgil;[42] Virgil a sage (". . . Maro omnium disciplinarum peritus"—1, xvi, 12); and, the *Aeneid* a sacred poem (". . . sacri poematis"—1, xxiv, 13).[43] The sense of Virgil that emerges and projects itself into the later Christian view contains the germ of the future theories of a "secret doctrine."

3. The early Christians who rejected all pagan *fabula* as being unfit for the edification of a Christian. Here there are many practitioners, all with one position in common: an official refusal to deal with Virgil or other pagans as bearers of the truth. Thus they refuse to allegorize Virgil. But if we look at two leading exponents of this central position, we find a surprising adherence to the text of the *Aeneid*. Prudentius' *Psychomachia* (ca. 400), while never naming Virgil, is at great pains to imitate the master, especially in his bloody battle scenes. If we take the trouble to count Lavarenne's citations of the *Aeneid* in his edition of the text,[44] we find eighty-five taken from all parts of the poem, plus six from the *Georgics*, and one from the *Eclogues*—a total of ninety-two quotations of Virgil in a

---

l'auteur et tâchait de faire comprendre la composition du poème, la correspondance de ses parties, le choix des descriptions et le caractère des différents personnages." See Comparetti, *Vergil in the Middle Ages*, pp. 59-60 for similar appreciations.

[42] F. Eyssenhardt, ed., *Conviviorum primi diei Saturnaliorum*, Lipsiae, 1893, v, ii, 1: "bene opifici deo a rure Mantuano poetam conparas." The work, the full title of which may remind the reader of the title of the *Convivio*, is in dialogue form, which accounts for the second person singular of the verb.

[43] See Curtius, *EL&LMA*, pp. 443-445, for a brief discussion of these matters.

[44] Paris, 1933.

poem of 915 lines. And Lavarenne cites only the surest resonances. If Prudentius' religion kept him from owning Virgil, his poetry did not.

Similarly, Augustine only a few years later officially disowns Virgil in the *Confessions*;[45] yet, while refusing to allegorize the *Aeneid* he continually cites it. Book XVIII of *De Civitate Dei*, throughout its historical account of the founding of Rome (Chapters xv-xxi), treats the *Aeneid* as historical record. A particularly pleasing example is the first sentence of Chapter xix: "Troy being now taken and razed, Aeneas with ten ships filled with the remains of Troy came into Italy, Latinus being king there, Mnestheus at Athens, Polyphides in Sicyon, Tautanes in Assyria, and Abdon judging Israel."[46] This kind of universal history defies Augustine's earlier attacks on Virgil; its acceptance of the literal sense of the *Aeneid*, though not supposedly typical of the Middle Ages, may well be more typical than is admitted by those who argue for the extensive influence of the allegorized *Aeneid*.

4. The later Christians who, paralleling the grammatical and rhetorical interests of pagans like Donatus and Servius, may attack the *Aeneid* because they find it literally untrue but applaud it because it is good. This paradoxical position is found in many places; Jerome and Augustine variously embrace it, each of them authorizing the Christian teacher to study the Classics in order to improve his necessarily useful rhetoric. Some two hundred years after these Christians' attempts at a very partial compromise, Isidore of Seville seems less upset about Virgil's paganism, citing him

---

[45] See Foreword, notes 8 and 9.

[46] Healey's translation. In a copy of the Everyman's Library text once owned by my friend Jeffrey Hart I find, in his handwriting, the correct marginal notation, "Takes Virgil literally."

as rhetorician endlessly, and on occasion, but only on occasion, stooping to allegory.[47]

5. The Christian allegorists. First among them, if only chronologically, is Fulgentius, whose *Liber de expositione Virgilianae continentiae*[48] (ca. 525) is the first explicit allegorical explanation of the *Aeneid*. Its second title, *De allegoria librorum Virgili ad Chalcidium grammaticum*, points to its affinities with early Christian neo-platonism. Like Chalcidius' commentary on the *Timaeus*, Fulgentius's brief explication of the *Aeneid* is interested only in drawing "orthodox" significance from the wealth of the poem. Fulgentius was an African, which fact may or may not help to explain his bombast and self-congratulation. His exposition of Virgil begins by heralding itself as the first to come to grips with the true and heretofore hidden meaning of the poem, which is to record the history of the human soul from birth to maturity. It is a thoroughly undistinguished performance and only barely an amusing one. Where Servius often demonstrates a keen and straightforward appreciation of Virgil's purpose (as when he says, ". . . intentio Vergilii haec est: Homerum imitari et Augustum laudare . . ."),[49] Fulgentius loves to fly from such mundane observations. Thus the shipwreck in Book 1 is the dangerous birth of the soul,[50] and the mist falls over Aeneas and his companions because the first thing a baby sees is his mother, while yet failing to understand her worth to him.[51] The second and third books contain many

[47] See above, note 28.

[48] Included in A. van Staveeren, ed., *Auctores mythographi latini*, Amstelaed, 1742, pp. 737-766.

[49] Rand, p. 4.   [50] van Staveeren, p. 748.

[51] *Ibid.*, p. 749. See Comparetti, p. 112, for suitable indignation: "But the process of Fulgentius is so violent and incoherent, it disregards every law of common sense in such a patent and well-nigh brutal

fables. Why? Because these two books concern childhood, and children love stories (". . . puerilis consueta est avocari garrulitas").[52] We move with Fulgentius through three stages of human life, from *natura*, through *doctrina*, and finally to *felicitas*.[53] We reach the second stage in Book VI when we come "ad templum Apollini, id est ad doctrinam studii,"[54] where we find the golden bough, which is to be understood as *scientia*.[55]

As discouraging as Fulgentius' efforts at criticism may seem to us today, he did find his followers, even unto Dante. As a contemporary critic points out,[56] when Dante discusses the first age of man in *Convivio* IV, xxiv, 9, he would seem to be echoing Fulgentius: "E lasciando lo figurato che di questo diverso processo de l'etadi tiene Virgilio ne lo Eneida . . ." ("And to pass over the figurative expression Virgil uses for the various progress of our ages in the *Aeneid* . . ."). Here Fulgentius' sentence, "Ergo sub figuralitate historiae plenum hominis monstravimus statum ut sit prima natura: secunda doctrina: tertia

---

manner, that it is hard to conceive how any sane man can seriously have undertaken such a work, and harder still to believe that other sane men should have accepted it as an object for serious consideration."

[52] *Ibid.*, p. 751.   [53] *Ibid.*, p. 747.   [54] *Ibid.*, p. 753.
[55] *Ibid.*, p. 754.
[56] See A. Pagliaro, "Simbolo e allegoria nella Divina Commedia," *L'Alighieri*, IV, 2 (1963), 3. It is interesting to speculate that this reference to Fulgentius occurs in the chapter of *Convivio* which immediately precedes the chapter in which Ulrich Leo finds evidence that Dante has come from a fresh re-reading of Virgil (see notes 22 and 35 above). If Leo is right, we arrive at a pleasing pattern: When Dante recaptures his Virgil, he discards his Fulgentius. I realize that this neat schematization must be treated skeptically, especially in light of *Conv.* IV, xxviii, 13, where Marcia, Cato's wife, is seen to signify "la nobile anima." In *Purg.* I, 78-90, she will be treated historically, as here she is allegorized in Fulgentian fashion.

felicitas,"[57] is Dante's probable source. Nevertheless, further influence of Fulgentius on Dante's later writing has not been demonstrated.

A more interesting Virgilian is Bernardus Silvestris (ca. 1150), whose commentary[58] indicates his similar interest in finding in the *Aeneid* the progress of the human soul from birth to maturity. Bernardus deals only with the first six books. In his neo-platonist vein the longest and richest commentary on Book VI, where the golden bough, not unlike the one of Fulgentius' version, is *philosophia*.[59] The commentary on Book I sets forth some general introductory statements about the poem, including the following clear announcement of the kind of allegory Bernardus practices: "Integumentum vero est genus demonstrationis sub fabulosa narratione veritatis involvens intellectum, unde et involucrum dicitur" ("This kind of showing forth is truly a covering that conceals, wrapping up the sense beneath a fabulous telling of the truth, whence it is called an envelope").[60] The first book concerns, as in Fulgentius, *infantia*; the second, *pueritia* (Bernardus spends only 22 lines on Book II); the third, *adolescentia*; the fourth, *natura iuventutis*; the fifth, *natura virilis aetatis*; the sixth, the maturity accomplished in the deep truths of philosophy.

This way of reading Virgil, whether found in Fulgentius or Bernardus, treats, as Bernardus clearly states in his discussions of *integumentum* and *involucrum*, the literal sense of the *Aeneid* as discardable *fabula*. Whatever Dante's knowledge of moralized Virgil—and he undoubtedly was aware of the tradition—it is clear that in the *Commedia*,

[57] van Staveeren, p. 747.

[58] G. Riedel, ed., *Commentum Bernardi Silvestri super sex libros Eneidos Virgilii*, Gryphiswaldae, 1924.

[59] Riedel, p. 58.   [60] *Ibid.*, p. 3.

even though there may be traces of this way of reading Virgil, his essential method is to treat the literal sense as historical. Thus, of all the medieval Virgils, the one we find in Augustine's writings when he deals with Virgil as historian is the one that has most in common with the Virgil of the *Commedia*. To be sure, elements of the allegorizing interpretations of other medieval Virgilians appear in Dante's work. Yet the major impulse behind Dante's sense of Virgil springs from his reading Virgil as Virgil "read" himself; treating the literal sense as historical, as the record of actual events; treating the story of the *Aeneid* as history, a history parallel to that recorded in Scripture, the two strains making up for him the major components of his universal history.[61]

[61] One of the important medieval documents with which Dante was surely familiar and which gives at some length a synoptic history of the matter of the Hebrews and that of Troy is Isidore of Seville's table of the six ages of man (*Etymologiae* v, xxxix). Étienne Gilson argues strongly for Dante's direct reading of Virgil: "Dante connaissait sans doute Servius, qui était le Scartazzini de son temps, mais on notera que la simple lecture de Virgile lui en apprenait là-dessus autant que le commentaire . . ." (see his articles, "Trois études dantesques pour le VIIe centenaire de la naissance de Dante," *Archives d'Histoire Doctrinale et Littéraire du Moyen Age*, XL (1965), 71-126 (p. 100). Two important earlier assertions that Dante thought of the *Aeneid* not only as being similar to Scripture in its historical narrative but as having similar authority are found in Nunzio Vaccaluzzo, "Le fonti del Catone dantesco," *Giornale storico della letteratura italiana*, XL (1902), 140-150: "L'Eneide era il vangelo pagano di Dante e la sua parola aveva per lui quasi l'autorità della Scrittura" (p. 142); and E. G. Gardner, *Virgil in Italian Poetry*, London, 1931, p. 16: "[Petrarch] can still read moral allegories into the *Aeneid*, which Dante attempted in the *Convivio*, but nowhere in the *Commedia*. . . ." For a modern historian's discussion of the "historicity" of the *Commedia*, see Peter G. Bietenholtz, "Clio and Thalia: The Place of History in Dante's *Comedy*," *Canadian Journal of History*, I, 2 (1966), 1-25.

CHAPTER III

THE FIGURAL DENSITY
OF FRANCESCA, ULYSSES,
AND CATO

The *Commedia* is to be treated as universal history,[1] beginning in the Beginning, concluding with the Alpha and Omega, the vision of the Godhead:

> Et quia, invento principio seu primo, videlicet Deo, nichil est quod ulterius queratur, cum sit Alfa et O, idest principium et finis, ut visio Johannis designat, in ipso Deo terminatur tractatus, qui est benedictus in secula seculorum.

> [And because, once the origin and beginning has been found, that is, God, there is no reason to seek further, since He is Alpha and Omega, that is, the beginning and the end, as John's vision designates, the treatise ends in God Himself, who is blessed throughout the ages.]

(Epistola XIII, 33)

We will now be concerned with the middle.

Until now we have been investigating two aspects of Dante's figuralism: the relatively simple and intuitable fourfold reference of the being and actions of each individual soul we see in the afterworld, and the more complex relationship between Dante's experience of the afterworld and universal history. We shall have little more to

---

[1] See Helen Flanders Dunbar's treatment of the *Inferno* as reflecting the stages of the life of Christ and of the six ages of man, *Symbolism in Medieval Thought*, pp. 284-310, for an earlier approach to this subject.

say about the former. The latter, which we have only begun to investigate, will now be studied in conjunction with
a third aspect which is possibly the most interesting of all.
So far we have been discussing the figural relationships
that connect the poem to Dante's view of history: Celestine
to Pilate and others, Dante to Adam and to Aeneas and to
Paul. But once it begins to unfold before our eyes, the
poem itself becomes a point of reference, so that Dante can
now use his figural techniques to refer simultaneously to
event in history and to previous event within the poem.
This process has its final sophistication in what I am
tempted to call "verbal figuralism," the technique of repeating a word used earlier in the poem in such a way
as to "fulfill" its meaning. In my earlier treatments of
three of the words which refer to the Bible and to the
Aeneid—*volume, autore, scritture*—I have alluded to this
process. Some further discoveries await us along these
lines. The theory which makes such poetic behavior possible is a fairly simple one, and if Dante never stated it,
we can easily state it for him. If the poem mirrors universal history, that is, if it behaves like the literal sense of
the Bible, then, as it develops it takes on the propensities
of universal history by which its inner verbal consistencies
are also ordered by a sense of "historical" progression. The
two books outside itself with which the poem has most in
common, if we pay attention to Dante's borrowings and if
we exclude Aristotle, are, naturally enough, the Bible and
the *Aeneid*.[2] Dante's quotations of his own poem are at
least as numerous. As examples of Dante's complex use of
figuralism we shall examine three of the most famous
passages in the work, those concerning Francesca, Ulysses,
and Cato.

[2] Moore, *Studies in Dante*, I, counts some 255 specific references in
the *Commedia* to the Bible, some 130 to the *Aeneid*.

Canto v tempts some to read no further. Francesca's power to seduce is so great and so beautiful that she has come, for many readers, especially nineteenth-century readers, to embody the greatest moment in the *Divine Comedy*. The canto is divided into four parts. The first (lines 1-24) shows us the judge of the damned Minos, that parody of judgment (he "judges" with his tail, not his head) to whom the sinners eagerly confess their besetting sin—the one act that might have saved them for God's Grace had they been similarly eager on earth.

The second movement (lines 25-51) shows us the spirit of the place, the swirling and conflicting winds of passion in which we see an implied hierarchy of birds, starlings and cranes, which will be completed later in the doves to which Paolo and Francesca are compared.

The third introduces the element which will be of most interest to our purpose, an only slightly surprising element: books. Virgil tells us who the "cranes" are, that is, he points out the great stars of love. Dante and Virgil see among them Semiramis, Dido, Cleopatra, Achilles, Paris, Tristan, the beginning of the list which Dante says numbered more than a thousand. Here are his concluding words:

"Vedi Parìs, Tristano"; e più di mille
    ombre mostrommi, e nominommi, a dito
    ch'amor *di nostra vita* dipartille.
Poscia ch'io ebbi il mio dottore udito
    nomar le donne antiche e' cavalieri,
    pietà mi giunse, e fui quasi *smarrito*. (italics mine)

["See Paris, Tristan"; and more than a thousand
    shades did he point out with his finger, naming
    those whom love parted from this life.

After I heard my teacher
  name the ladies and the courtly lords of old,
  pity overcame me, and I was as one who had
    lost the way.]

(Inf. v, 67-72)

The knights and ladies of old, the matter of Hebrew and
Trojan and Roman antiquity coupled with the matter of
France, all the great sad tales of love, overpower the emo-
tions of Dante, who had in his earlier poems sung of
earthly love. The effect of the scene upon the Pilgrim is
to remind him (tacitly) and us of his condition at the
beginning of the poem, when he had lost, on the road of
our life ("di nostra vita"), the true way ("ché la diritta
via era *smarrita*"),[3] suggesting that, as the action on the
Terrace of Lust and the meeting with Beatrice in the Earthly Paradise will later also suggest, Dante's own life was
nearly lost to God through lust. Lust and literature are
the two elements which are put into focus by this section of
the canto, and we are prepared for the encounter between
the once lustful poet, Dante Alighieri, and that lustful
lady, who had also read the matter of French romance,
Francesca.

If I may be permitted a digression, I should merely
like to point out that this great canto, which dwells in the
memory of almost every literate Western man, is remembered for this scene of seemingly epic proportion. And yet
the part that we remember is less than half the canto,
occupying a mere seventy lines after the seventy-two of
introduction. Dante's gift of poetic compression has never
been equalled.

[3] The echo here of the first canto's "smarrita" has been noted recently by O. Lagercrantz, *From Hell to Paradise*, tr. Alan Blair, New
York, 1966, p. 1; and by A. C. Charity, *Events and Their Afterlife*,
p. 215.

Having drawn our attention, if we are careful readers, to his own sinful condition at the commencement of the poem, Dante now lets us see Francesca. The fourth part of the canto is itself divided into five movements: Dante wants to find out about these two lovers who stand out among the great lovers of history; he calls them and they come. Francesca has her first speech. Dante is moved and wants to know the details of their love affair. Francesca has her second speech. While Paolo weeps, Dante faints, falling like a dead body.

The action which is being imitated here is the mutual action of passivity to love and passivity to literature. It only seems to be a curious combination. In the first of Francesca's two speeches, the three invocations of Amor that begin three *terzine* remind us of the code of the *fideli d'amore*[4] (one of them is a near quotation of Guinizelli's great canzone in Dante's own earlier love poetry).[5] But the full impact of the combined focus is better seen in her concluding speech:

E quella a me: "Nessun maggior *dolore*		(1)
che *ricordarsi* del tempo felice		(2)
ne la *miseria*; e ciò sa 'l tuo dottore.		(3)
Ma s'a conoscer la prima radice		(4)
del nostro amor tu hai cotanto affetto,		(4)
dirò come colui che piange e dice.		(5)
a b c b		

---

[4] Robertson, *A Preface to Chaucer*, p. 85n., points out that Pietro employs the definition of love found in Andreas Capellanus in order to define the lust of Paolo and Francesca.

[5] "Amore e 'l cor gentil sono una cosa" (*V.N.*, xx), which would also seem to echo the famous canzone, "Al cor gentil ripara sempre Amore."

Noi leggiavamo un giorno per diletto
  di Lancialotto come amor lo strinse:
  soli eravamo e sanza alcun sospetto.
Per più fiate li occhi ci sospinse
  quella lettura, e scolorocci il viso;
  ma solo un punto fu quel che ci vinse.
Quando leggemmo il disïato riso
  esser baciato da cotanto amante,
  questi, che mai da me non fia diviso,
la bocca mi baciò tutto tremante.
  Galeotto fu il libro e chi lo scrisse:
  quel giorno più non vi leggemmo avante."
                              (italics mine)

[And she to me: "There is no greater pain
  than to recall the happy time
  in misery; and this thy teacher knows.
But if to know the first root
  of our love thou hast so great desire,
  I shall tell as one who weeps and speaks.
One day for pleasure we were reading
  of Lancelot—how love constrained him;
  we were alone and had no caution.
Many times our eyes were impelled to meet
  by that reading, which drew the color from our faces;
  but one passage alone it was that overcame us:
When we read that the longed-for smile
  was kissed by so great a lover,
  he, who from me never shall be parted,
Kissed my mouth all trembling.
  A Galeotto was the book and he that wrote it:
  that day we read in it no further."]
                              (*Inf.* v, 121-138)

109

Although the passage deserves better than to be used to prove a point, I am afraid that bookishness constrains me. There are many books, at least four, directly referred to in the passage, which begins, unsurprisingly enough, with reference to Virgil's book as Francesca's pointed "and this thy teacher knows" makes clear.[6] And naturally enough the reference is to a conversation between Aeneas and Dido, the archetypal star-crossed lovers, one of whom was destroyed by lust, as Virgil has just now shown us. When Dido asks Aeneas to retell the Troy story his answer is:

"infandum, regina, iubes renovare *dolorem*, (1)
Troianas ut opes et lamentabile regnum
eruerint Danai, quaeque ipse *miserrima* vidi (3)
et quorum pars magna fui. *quis* talia *fando* (5)b
Myrmidonum Dolopumque aut duri miles Vlixi
temperet a lacrimis? et iam nox umida caelo (5)c
praecipitat suadentque cadentia sidera somnos.
sed si tantus amor casus cognoscere nostros (4)
et breviter Troiae supremum audire laborem,
quamquam animus *meminisse* horret luctuque (2)
    refugit
incipiam." (5)a

(italics mine)

["You command me, O queen, to renew my
    unspeakable grief, to tell
How the Greeks cast forth the Trojan might

---

[6] As many commentators have pointed out, Dante would also seem to have in mind a similar passage in Boethius' *De Consolatione Philosophiae* (II, 4): "In omni adversitate fortunae infelicissimum est genus infortunii fuisse felicem." Enzo Esposito, "Dante traduttore di Virgilio," *L'Italia che scrive*, XLVIII (1965), 335-336, has written on the resonance of *Aen.* II, 3, in *Inf.* XXXIII, 4-6, as well as in this passage.

And the sorrowful royal authority, to tell of the
    most wretched events
I witnessed and of those of which I was myself
    a great part. Who of
The Myrmidons, or of the Dolopes, or what
    soldier of stern Ulysses
Could refrain from tears in relating such things?
    And now moist night
Hastens from the sky, and the setting stars advise
    sleep.
But if you have so much desire to know of our
    ruin
And briefly to hear the last struggle of Troy,
Although my mind dreads to remember and
    draws back from grief,
I shall begin."]

(*Aen.* ii, 3-13)

Virgil's eleven lines come out as six in Dante. Their
appositeness has to some degree been noticed. I should
merely like to celebrate it. As Aeneas, questioned by Dido,
has lost the realm of Troy to the Greeks, so Francesca,
questioned by Dante, has lost the realm of God's kingdom
to her lust. The verbal reminiscences are so striking that
it would be futile to deny Dante's reading of the *Aeneid*
here. Rather than elaborating, I have italicized the words
common to both passages in order to point out the corre-
spondences.

And so Francesca's second speech finds its first literary
source in the *Aeneid*; its second literary source is further
north and of later date. The particular Old French version of the Lancelot romance which Dante knew has been
brought to light by Paget Toynbee.[7] The story does not

---

[7] See his "Dante and the Lancelot Romance" (first published in the
Fifth Annual Report of the Dante Society of America, 1886), in *Dante*

require retelling here, for it is both familiar and clear enough in Dante's treatment. And now we notice that the entire second speech, with the exception of the last line, has come from other books, their language and their situations adapted to Dante's purpose, which is to reveal the misuse of literature that promotes the sin of lust in Francesca. Francesca herself says that, when she and Paolo read of that kiss in an orchard, she read for pleasure, and not—the medieval reader surely went on to consider—for instruction.

"That day we read in it no further." If the rest of the speech reflects earlier literature, what about this concluding line? T. K. Swing has found, I believe, the "source" of Dante's line in the *Confessions*, viii, xii, at the very moment of Augustine's conversion.[8] Augustine has heard a voice, beyond the wall of the garden where he sits, advising him, or so it seems, to "take and read." He picks up his St. Paul and, playing the Christian version of the *sortes Virgilianaes*, reads Romans 13:13 and the following verse, which counsel strongly against the lusts of the flesh.

Studies and Researches, London, 1902, pp. 1-37. See also the recent study by Anna Hatcher and Mark Musa, "The Kiss: *Inferno* v and the Old French Prose *Lancelot*," *Comparative Literature*, xx (1968), 97-109.

[8] *The Fragile Leaves of the Sybil*, Westminster, Md., 1962, p. 299. Renato Poggioli's recent celebrated study, "Tragedy or Romance? A Reading of the Paolo and Francesca Episode in Dante's *Inferno*," *PMLA* (1957), 313-358, which is a graceful and cogent examination of the verbal, literary, and psychological components of the episode in the mode of a modern De Sanctis, has failed to see Augustine here, and neglects to discuss the earlier Virgilian parallel. One of its major points is based upon this line: Poggioli maintains that the words "quel giorno" imply that on subsequent days Paolo and Francesca returned to their dalliance in romance. This interpretation, which gives the scene the ominous resonance of continuance, and by which I own myself convinced, does extremely well by the first two words of the line, but misses the important reference that resonates in its conclusion.

It is enough. Augustine gives over his chambering and wantonness, of the flesh and of the spirit, and becomes a Christian in heart and deed, never to waver again. For a Christian reader this is rather an important moment, surely one that Dante knew and respected. After reading these verses, Augustine stops reading because he does not need to read any more. He says: "Nec ultra volui legere." ("And I did not wish to read any further.") Surely these words lie behind Dante's "quel giorno più non vi leggemmo avante." Francesca has undergone an experience precisely opposite to that of Augustine—and that is exactly her problem. For in this passage, united in its bookishness, one Book stands out implicitly from all others, the one that has the power to lead to Grace, the Bible. The Bible performed the ultimate instruction of Augustine; the Lancelot story, by giving delight rather than instruction, helped to perform the ultimate destruction of Francesca, who read about the wrong garden and who loved the wrong Paul.

Dante's own bookishness shows through this passage in a wonderfully clear light. Most readers do not even notice the other works, so intent are they on the drama which Francesca relates. They are not supposed to notice, for Dante has used the other works without any desire to show off erudition. It seems to have taken six hundred years for the Augustinian parallels, like the Virgilian parallels in the opening cantos, to be observed. Dante uses the past without display partly because of the spiritual necessities of his message, partly because of his own theory of history as it applies to what we might think of as his theory of literature, and partly because of his easy familiarity with the Classics. The enormous amount of earlier and imposing events that he evokes in these eighteen lines is testament enough to the utility, grace, and success of the method. In and behind Francesca we *see*—and this is the important thing, the form of reference is not arid and scholarly—we see Aeneas in conversation with Dido, his heart heavy with defeat, "come colui che piange e dice"; the night air preparing us for the love story which will end in Dido's self-destruction, as Francesca's love brought on her self-destruction. We see the embrace of Lancelot and Guinevere and know the dire results that will flow therefrom. We see Augustine reading Romans and know that this action led to Grace, insofar as the evidence of Grace can be known on this earth. Even if we do not see these things, Dante did, and I believe that he expected some of us who read his poem to see them also. Figural analysis does not, it seems to me, deaden the poem; it helps to open up its inner life.

THE CANTO of Ulysses has much in common with that of Francesca; it even happens to contain the same number of lines (142). And like that earlier canto, it begins relatively slowly and quietly (as does the Farinata canto), preparing us for the enormous experience we are about to witness. As in the Francesca canto over one-half of the canto is preparation; indeed, the epic, uninterrupted speech of Ulysses only begins at line 90, and is thus limited to a mere fifty-three lines.

The Ulysses-motif is one of the strongest and most deeply felt in the *Commedia*. In *Inferno* it establishes the voyage theme which will be the dominant motif for the poem itself as it rises toward its conclusion. The Ulysses-motif also, I believe, points us back not only to the inception of the poem, but to the experiences that Dante invokes at the commencement of his work and that refer to the types of his own experience as these have been recorded in previous literature. For this study I am primar-

ily interested in the conclusion of Ulysses' speech; and
in order to reach it, I should like to notice three passages
on the way.

The Ulysses canto begins by concluding the previous
canto with the bitterly ironic address to Florence, whose
fame is spread abroad in Hell.[9] As Dante and Virgil
descend, the Poet interrupts the action to make the following comment:

> Allor mi dolsi, e ora mi ridoglio
>> quando drizzo la mente a ciò ch'io vidi,
>> e più lo 'ngegno affreno ch'i' non soglio,
> perché non corra che virtù nol guidi;
>> sì che, se stella bona o miglior cosa
>> m'ha dato 'l ben, ch'io stessi nol m'invidi.

[I felt grief then, and feel grief now again
> when I turn my mind to what I saw,
> and more than I am wont I rein my talent in
lest it run where virtue guide it not,
> so that, if kindly star or better thing
> has granted me its boon, I need not hold it
> against myself.]

(Inf. XXVI, 19-24)

It is clear that Dante thinks of Ulysses as one who
allowed his considerable powers to run where virtue
guided not. He himself, as a man and as a poet, will be
charged with the same kind of venturesomeness by Beatrice, probably with specific reference to *Convivio*, although

---

[9] The invective against the city refers to the five Florentines Dante
has just seen among the thieves in Canto XXV. Although we tend to
think of the "borders" of the one hundred cantos as being firm and
strictly ordered, in actuality they frequently show a freedom, even a
playfulness, that would seem better suited to Cervantes. (See Raymond
S. Willis, Jr., *The Phantom Chapters of the Quijote*, New York, 1953.)

this point is much debated. At any rate, it is a sort of "There but for the Grace of God go I" passage, and serves to introduce the similarity between Dante's past and Ulysses' great adventure which the later passages will clarify by developing.[10]

Next, the Poet keeps us distant from the great Ulysses by making him and his fellows resemble the fireflies of early evening, seen from above by a resting peasant. But it is the second simile, immediately following this one— again comparing the souls of the false counsellors to other lights, this time in a context that does not diminish their size but emphasizes the untrustworthiness that has brought them to this pass—which we should consider:

[10] The very day I took this work to press I received, upon return- ing home, my copy of *Dante Studies* in the mail. It contains the ex- cellent study of Ulysses by David Thompson, "Dante's Ulysses and the Allegorical Journey," *Dante Studies*, LXXXV (1967), 33-70. Since then I have been able to correspond with Professor Thompson at some length, both in debate and in agreement about many of the matters treated in this book. My own sketchy treatment of Ulysses, although in no way indebted to his, has much in common with his approach. There are areas of disagreement between us, especially concerning Dante's use of Bernardus Silvestris. Nevertheless, I have read no other treatment of perhaps the most treated canto of the *Commedia* which is as illuminating as his; while I do not wish to give a protracted representation of his argument here, I hope that my strong endorse- ment of his essay will not keep those who disagree strongly with me from giving it the full attention it deserves. Since this protruding and tardy footnote is the only place in my work where his name appears, I should also mention that his study, "Figure and Allegory in the *Commedia*," which I have read in typescript, is scheduled to appear in a forthcoming volume of *Cornell Dante Studies*. It is also only just that I record a general sense of disagreement with this study, at least in the form in which I read it. I do so with no sense of ingratitude, for I expect that David Thompson will show similar disagreement with my own work, either privately or publicly. I look forward to read- ing anything he has to say, for we share similar interests in the *Com- media*.

E qual colui che si vengiò con li orsi
   vide 'l carro d'Elia al dipartire,
      quando i cavalli al cielo erti levorsi,
che nol potea sì con li occhi seguire
   ch'el vedesse altro che la fiamma sola,
      sì come nuvoletta, in su salire. . . .

[And as he who was avenged by the bears
   saw Elijah's chariot at its departure,
      when the horses rose, erect, toward heaven—
since he could not follow with his eyes
   so as to see anything but the flame alone,
      like a little cloud, going on up. . . .]

(*Inf.* xxvi, 34-39)

So, the simile concludes, only the flames of the sinners, as they move along their ditch in Malebolge, are visible to Dante. Dante brings in the Elijah-Elisha story (II Kings 2:11-12; 23-24) to set up a negative typology for Ulysses: as Dante himself is like Elisha, who was also the bearer of the true record of an ascent to God because he was singled out for this privileged vision, so Ulysses, the great voyager, is *not* like Elijah (whom Dante shall himself ultimately resemble), for his awesome voyage was precisely the inversion of the divine voyage, taking him and his men to perdition. That is what Dante the Poet knows about the various relationships intended in the simile. Dante the Pilgrim would seem to be a good deal less sure, for despite the fact that as a poet he now reins in his poetical power in order to be morally inoffensive, as the voyager who is there, he is filled only with pity and admiration. Indeed, so great is his excitement at the prospect he sees before him, which has been introduced with the two similes concerning flame, that he almost falls down among the sinners, so eagerly does he lean forward (43-

45). The poet does not use such details lightly. Surely we are to associate Dante's near fall ("la caduta") with the sin he has previously committed, and with the sin of Ulysses, whose false counsel is that venturesome experience is all.[11]

These three passages associate Dante with Ulysses. We shall see what further use the poet makes of the association at the conclusion of Ulysses' speech, which starts as the horn of the flame speaks,[12] beginning, like Dante's own poem, *in medias res*, and then bringing together the Ulysses matter from classical literature.[13] Ulysses pridefully points out (line 93) that he had himself been detained by Circe on an island not far from the one that Aeneas would only later name Gaeta, after his nurse (*Aen.* VII, 1f.). He describes the beginning of the voyage with a display of his artful rhetoric, quoting one of his own speeches

[11] R. P. Blackmur once in conversation suggested a line from Confucius as the epigraph for the relationship between Ulysses and his men revealed by Canto XXVI: "Greatness is a national calamity."

[12] André Pézard, *Dante sous la pluie de feu*, Paris, 1950, p. 283f, points out the importance for all sins in *Inferno* punished by fire of the tongues of fire which descend upon the Apostles (Acts 2:1-11), speaking in tongues. Thus the speaking tongues of flame of *Inferno* XXVI are a parody of the Pentecostal fire, as is pointed out by Terence P. Logan, "The Characterization of Ulysses in Homer, Virgil and Dante: A Study in Sources and Analogues," *Eighty-Second Annual Report of the Dante Society* (1964), p. 42.

[13] Gmelin's *Kommentar*, vol. I, Stuttgart, 1954, pp. 388-390, points out the many sources, including Horace, *Epist.* I, ii, 17-22; Cicero, *De Finibus* v, xviii, 49; Ovid, *Meta.* XIV, 435f. See also Phillip W. Damon, "Dante's Ulysses and the Mythic Tradition," in *Medieval Secular Literature: Four Essays*, ed. Wm. Matthews, Berkeley and Los Angeles, 1965, pp. 24-45; and the recent major study by Giorgio Padoan, "Ulisse 'fandi fictor' e le vie della Sapienza," *Studi danteschi*, XXXVII (1960), 21-61. For a summary of recent discussions and a suggestive "medieval" reading of the episode, see August Rüegg, "Zum Danteschen Ulisse Problem," *DDJb*, XLIII (1965), 172-198.

to his tiring shipmates,[14] which convinced them to plunge
into the journey:

"Li miei compagni fec'io sì aguti,
    con questa orazion picciola, al cammino,
    che a pena poscia li avrei ritenuti;
e volta nostra poppa nel mattino,
    di remi facemmo ali al folle volo,
    sempre acquistando dal lato mancino.
Tutte le stelle già de l'altro polo
    vedea la notte, e 'l nostro tanto basso,
    che non surgea fuor del marin suolo.
Cinque volte racceso e tante casso
    lo lume era di sotto de la luna,
    poi che 'ntrati eravam ne l'alto passo,
quando n'apparve una montagna, bruna
    per la distanza, e parvemi alta tanto
    quanto veduta non avea alcuna.
Noi ci allegrammo, e tosto tornò in pianto;
    ché de la nova terra un turbo nacque,
    e percosse del legno il primo canto.
Tre volte il fé girar con tutte l'acque;
    a la quarta levar la poppa in suso
    e la prora ire in giù, com'altrui piacque,
infin che 'l mar fu sopra noi richiuso."

[14] The speech is modeled on Aeneas' speech to his companions in
Aen. I, 197-207, as is pointed out by Gmelin, *Kommentar*, I, p. 392,
possibly following C. H. Grandgent, *La Divina Commedia di Dante
Alighieri*, Boston, 1933, p. 236, who makes the same ascription. After
only thirty-five years Grandgent's commentary receives much less attention than it should command. It has been "replaced," in bookstores
at least, by English translations or by Italian editions of greater textual
accuracy. His commentaries and notes, however, remain, in the opinion
of this writer, the very best in this language, and often superior to
those in other tongues.

["My companions I made so eager
  for the journey with this brief speech
  that I then could have hardly held them back;
turning our stern to the morning,
  we made oars wings for the foolish flight,
  always gaining to the left.
Night already showed all the stars
  of the other pole—ours was so low
  that it did not rise from the sea surface.
Five times rekindled and as many times
  was quenched the light beneath the moon
  since we had entered on the deep passage,
when a mountain came into our view, dark
  with distance, and to me it seemed
  I had never seen one so high.
We rejoiced, but soon we turned to weeping;
  for from the new land arose a whirlwind
  which struck a blow to the bow of the ship.
Three times it drove her 'round together with
      the waters;
  the fourth it made the poop go up
  and made the prow go down, as Another willed,
until the sea was closed again above us."]

$$(Inf. \text{ xxvi, } 121\text{-}136)$$

The words that tie Ulysses' experience to Dante's in the first canto of the poem are perhaps not altogether striking at first: *cammino, passo, acque.* Ulysses' "road" is not a true way, but a false one; he has entered a "passo che non lasciò già mai persona viva" (*Inf.* 1, 27) while Dante escapes, in *Inferno* 1, from his *passo*, the "acqua perigliosa" (24) that will drown Ulysses and his men. And both scenes occur under the shadow of the purgatorial mount.[15] Still, I would not argue urgently for the identification except that a later passage in *Purgatorio* will, I believe, also make the connection. The concluding four lines of the speech and of this canto also make the connection by returning to the matter of the shipwrecked Trojans of *Aeneid* 1, the matter that was parallel to Dante's condition in *Inferno* 1. For the ship that whirls around three times and then sinks has a noble antecedent, as Moore has pointed out.

> . . . ast illam ter fluctus ibidem
> torquet agens circum et rapidus vorat aequore vertex.

> [. . . but a wave whirls the ship, driving it
> three times around in the same place, and then a
> sudden eddy swallows it up in the sea.]
> (*Aen.* 1, 116-117)

The ship in point is that (in *Aeneid* 1) which carried the Lycians and the faithful Orontes and which goes down within sight of the land that would have saved its sailors, as does Ulysses' ship. Ulysses had begun his speech with a vaunt over Aeneas. But his ship is like the Trojan ship that failed, not like Aeneas' ship. It is a ship of the damned. Aeneas, in his piety, is the hero; Ulysses, in his heroicness, is the failure. The quotation of Virgil here is a fine touch, for there speaking with Ulysses he stands—the creator of the epic tradition against which, in Dante's eyes, Ulysses aspired. With them is the Tuscan who has inherited both epic traditions, who, as a character in his own poem, has survived that metaphoric storm at sea (in the "lake" of

---

[15] Although there has been some debate on the identification of the *colle* of *Inf.* 1, 13 (subsequently referred to as the *dilettoso monte*—1, 77) as the Mount of Purgatory, it is difficult to understand why. Gmelin, *Komm.* 1, p. 29, says it is "nur eine traumhafte, visionäre Vorschau des Läuterungsberges."

his own heart) in Canto I, and who is the inheritor of the tradition of Aeneas despite his temporary identification with Ulysses.

If the use of the *Aeneid* and Dante's own words point us back, the Ulysses episode also points us forward. A single word of it, one of the best examples of "verbal figuralism" I have found in the poem, will suffice for now, although the dream of the Siren in *Purgatorio* XIX will also serve the purpose shortly. The word appears twice in the passage. It is *poppa*, the poop of a ship. Ulysses' poop, where he as captain stands, is an inverse poop.[16] It has turned its back to the morning. When the word reappears in the poem, it will be in conjunction with the voyage to the mountain which Ulysses failed to reach, a voyage which is the answer to Ulysses' voyage: "Da poppa stava il celestial nocchiero"—"on the poop stood the heavenly pilot" (*Purg.* II, 43). The ship of the thousand souls is the fulfillment of the voyage of which, within the poem, Ulysses' voyage was the *figura*, and here the very words tell us exactly that. Nor does this "verbal figuralism" cease here. Proceeding perhaps into the realm of excess, Dante's first description of Beatrice upon her entrance into the poem is the following simile:

> Quasi ammiraglio che in poppa ed in prora
> viene a veder la gente che ministra
> per li altri legni, e a ben far l'incuora. . . .

> [As an admiral who to the poop and to the bow
> comes to see the men who sail
> the other ships, and heartens them to do well. . . .]
> (*Purg.* XXX, 58-60)

---

[16] A point made by Professor Fredi Chiappelli, addressing a recent Colloquium of the Department of Romance Languages of Princeton University, 27 February 1967.

so Beatrice first appears to Dante, whose poem has by now become a ship (*Purg.* 1, 2, and elsewhere). Historically, the images make an imposing string: the ill-fated ships in *Aeneid* 1, which are answered by the shipwrecked but safe Aeneas; the damned voyage of Ulysses; the voyage that is Dante's poem; the pilgrim ship that arrives safely at the shores of Purgatory, an angel on its poop; and now, also on a poop, Admiral Beatrice, who is Supreme Commander of the fleet of which Dante's bark is one. It may smack of the exertions of Crashaw, this last; its "historical" footing in the poem helps it work.

CATO's LIFE would seem to have qualified him for occupancy in every area of Inferno. If we think of him as a virtuous pagan, we should expect to find him in Limbo. If we are disturbed about his having given his wife to another man, we should look for him among the Panderers. More logically, since he was a suicide, we should expect to see him in the form of a bleeding tree in Canto XIII. Worst of all, since he opposed Caesar, we should feel that Dante missed by a single canto, that he should have put Cato in *Inferno* XXXIV, which we have just finished reading and where we have seen the dire punishment inflicted upon Brutus and Cassius, who also opposed Caesar.

Grace, however, is always a surprise.

The stoic rigidity of Cato certainly reminds us of Hell. In a way he is a fitting bridge between the two *cantiche*, because he has endured sin, and yet is miraculously saved. The mark of his worldly error is still to be seen in his office, for he must work as God's customs officer and may not yet complete his purgation and ascend to heaven.

Whatever rationale we may find for his salvation by Dante, we must remember that Dante expected us to be amazed, a fact sometimes forgotten by those who are

puzzled by Cato's location.[17] After the opening invocation and the following evocation of dawn at the antipodes,
the place Ulysses saw in harsher circumstance and darker
light, Dante holds back joy for a moment to show us Cato:

> vidi presso di me un veglio solo,
>> degno di tanta reverenza in vista,
>> che più non dee a padre alcun figliuolo.
> Lunga la barba e di pel bianco mista
>> portava, ai suoi capelli simigliante,
>> de' quai cadeva al petto doppia lista.
> Li raggi de le quattro luci sante
>> fregiavan sì la sua faccia di lume,
>> ch'i' 'l vedea come 'l sol fosse davante.

[I saw near me a solitary old man,
>> worthy of such reverence in his appearance
>> that no son owes more to a father.
A long beard with white hair mixed in
>> he wore, which blended with the locks
>> that fell upon his breast in double strand.
The rays of the four holy lights
>> so adorned his face with light
>> that I saw him as though the sun were before him.]

(Purg. I, 31-39)

The first figural presence that emanates from Cato is
that of Moses. This shade—the benign but stern lawgiver of Purgatory (his function parallels that of Charon

[17] A fairly early study which did much to show that Cato was less
of a surprise as the guardian of Purgatory to the medieval than he
has been to the modern reader is Nunzio Vaccaluzzo, "Le fonti del
Catone dantesco," *Giornale storico della letteratura italiana*, XL (1902),
140-150. This short piece speaks to the many and various classical
texts which permeated the medieval sense of Cato. A good summary
of recent criticism concerning Cato's presence in the poem is available
in Silvio Pasquazi, "Catone," *Cultura e Scuola*, IV (1965), 528-539.

in Hell), who stands outside the Promised Land but may not enter (at least until the Day of Judgment), and who stands beneath a mountain,[18] his face ablaze with light, as Moses stood at the foot of his mount, his face so bright he had subsequently to veil it from the sight of men (Exodus 34:29f)—this shade must first be conceived as figured in Moses. What of a second detail, the beard and/ or hair that falls in double strand upon his breast?[19] If that detail also yielded the medieval iconography of Moses the identification would be even more certain, and one of my students, Mr. William Johnson, did indeed show ample evidence of this in a paper he wrote for me. In Christian art the tradition of the horned Moses, from Jerome's mistranslation in the Vulgate, apparently gave rise to the iconographical forked beard of Moses, which seems merely a form of aesthetic balance: horns and forked beard making counterpart shapes. At any rate, a fountain, a cathedral, and an illustrated Bible Dante might have been acquainted with, all show Moses with a forked beard.[20]

Naturally Moses is present here, for this is the place which is to be figurally understood as the place where the Exodus of each Christian soul is accomplished. Surely

[18] See also *Purg.* IV, 67-70, where Mt. Sion is the antipode of Mount Purgatory.

[19] For the color and general appearance of Cato's beard, see Lucan, *Pharsalia* II, 372f, as is pointed out by Gmelin, *Komm.* II, p. 35; see also G. Barone, "I capelli e la barba nella *Divina Commedia*," *Giornale dantesco*, XIV (1906), 262-277.

[20] Wm. Johnson, "The Figure of Moses in the *Divina Commedia*," May 1967, points to the Fonte di Piazza in Perugia of Niccolo Pisano; to the exterior of the Cathedral of Siena, where stand Moses and the dean of the cathedral sculpted by Niccolo's son, Giovanni Pisano; and to an illustration of the so-called *Corbolinus Bible*, a Florentine Bible dated 1140, showing Moses with his beard divided in two. For more professional treatment of the *barbe bifide* of Moses, see Louis Réau, *Iconographie de l'art chrétien*, vol. II, Paris, esp. pp. 177-178.

Moses is figurally present in the next canto when the souls
of the angel ship sing "In exitu Israel de Aegypto."[21]
And, taking our clue from that typology, we realize that
if Moses is figurally present here, Christ must be also,
for Christ, whose face was once similarly shining, during
the Transfiguration (Matt. 17:2), is figured by Moses,
leading us out of bondage to salvation.

A passage some thirty lines further along makes the
second identification evident. Virgil describes the worthi-
ness of Dante to Cato:

> "Or ti piaccia gradir la sua venuta:
> libertà va cercando, ch'è sì cara,
> come sa chi per lei vita rifiuta.
> Tu 'l sai, che non ti fu per lei amara
> in Utica la morte, ove lasciasti
> la vesta ch'al gran dì sarà sì chiara."

["Then let it please you to look with favor upon his
    coming:
he goes seeking liberty, which is so dear,
as he knows who for it gives up life.
Thou knowest this, since death for it was not
    bitter in Utica, where thou didst leave
the vestment which on the great day shall be so
    bright."]

(*Purg.* 1, 70-75)

For any Christian the phrase, "he who for liberty gives
up life," can point only to Christ's sacrifice. This is the
true *gran rifiuto*, and it was prefigured in a sort of pre-
imitation of Christ by the suicide of Cato, which is why
Dante can say in *Convivio*, "E quale uomo terreno più

---

[21] See again Professor Singleton's article, " 'In exitu Israel de
Aegypto.' "

degno fu di significare Iddio, che Catone? Certo nullo."
("And what earthly man was more worthy of signifying
God than Cato. Surely no one.")[22] The topic of the first
canto of *Purgatorio* is rebirth. Dante has issued forth from
the womb of Hell to be reborn in salvation. The negative
presence of Christ in *Inferno* xxxiv—Satan's three heads,
perverse figures of the three crosses at the Crucifixion,
among a number of other details—has been well noted.[23]
And in the following canto Dante again makes us feel the
presence of Christ, this time, as is only appropriate, reborn. We see Him in the dawn itself, which is understood
as His attribute. The components of Dante's dawn are
"oriental zaffiro" (line 13), "oriente" (line 20), and the
"bel pianeta" (line 19) which is the Sun rising.[24] He is
also present, iconographically, in the constellation Pisces
(line 21) (in which Venus, the morning star, is visible)
since the Fish is His sign. And the canto ends with the
sure symbol of the Resurrection, "l'umile pianta, cotal si
rinacque/ subitamente là onde l'avelse" (lines 135-136),
the rush which girds Dante and which, though plucked,
renews itself in the same place where it was plucked.[25]

Cato's suicide then, as distinct from the suicidal sin
which leads to *Inferno* xiii, is to be thought of, despite
the fact that it apparently broke moral and Roman law, as

[22] IV, xxviii, 15. Other laudatory references to Cato occur in *Convivio*
(IV, v, 16; IV, xxvii, 4), *Monarchia* (II, v, 15-17), and *Inf.* XIV, 15.
One particularly Christlike utterance of Cato in the *Pharsalia* which
may have caught Dante's eye is (II, 312): "Hic redimat sanguis
populos" ("Let my blood ransom the people").

[23] Singleton, *Dante Studies 1*, pp. 33-38; Freccero, "The Sign of
Satan," *MLN*, LXXX (1965), 11-26.

[24] For Christ as Sun God see Dunbar, *Symbolism in Medieval
Thought*, passim.

[25] See Chapter II, note 34, for Moore's identification of the *giunco*
with Virgil's golden bough. Dante's magic wand, though modeled
on Virgil's, is Christological.

prefiguration of Christ's "suicide," as Charles Till Davis almost realizes: "The contradiction is impossible to account for, unless we assume that Cato is to be considered as transcending his historical context, as *the type of the man* who masters his own passions and lives justly. . . ." (italics mine).[26] Not quite. The historical Cato's motives are understood by Dante as implying the kind of devotion to liberty that is the mark of Christ, Who sought and found true liberty for all men. And so, for Dante, Cato becomes *figura Christi*.[27] Dante may well think of him as his "father" (line 33).

Thus, Cato is figured in Moses, is a figure of Christ, and of Dante. These four liberty-seekers are brought tightly together by the action of the canto. That is enough, except that we are still without the detail which reinforces the Cato-Dante parallel with one of Dante's many reflections of his reading in the *Aeneid*. Almost all commentators and critics who pay any heed to Dante's Classical reading cite this detail, and yet none, apparently, has seen the submerged play on words that it contains. The reflection alluded to here is a noteworthy moment in the text of the *Aeneid*, the description of the shield of Aeneas, on which is depicted (*Aen.* VIII, 670) the judge of those who kept the laws and who have died well for Rome: "secretosque pios, his dantem iura Catonem"—"Cato giving them the laws." In view of Virgil's authority in Dante's eyes, that reference would probably be quite enough to make Cato the "lawgiver" of *Purgatorio*. And yet there is that one further touch in Virgil which must have made Dante start

---

[26] *Dante and the Idea of Rome*, p. 116.

[27] This point is twice made by Erich Auerbach: "Figura," pp. 65-67; "Typological Symbolism in Medieval Literature," *Yale French Studies*, no. 9 (1952), pp. 3-10.

and smile: the line contains his own name.[28] (Even the Latin declension works for the pun: Cato's name, in Italian, is *Catone*, the ablative of the Latin; the ablative of *dans, dantis*, is, of course, *dante*.)

So much for a sketchy discussion of the figural relationships which lie outside the poem in *Purgatorio* I. What of those that come from within? Canto I, it seems to me, looks back primarily to four places in *Inferno*: Cantos I, XIII, XXVI, and XXXIV. Charles Singleton has dealt at length with the first cantos,[29] and I have above alluded briefly to the Ulysses theme and to the presence of Christ in the last canto of *Inferno*. Let us think back to Canto XIII for a moment, and especially to three actions and two words. In lines 31-32 Dante breaks off a twig from the ruined tree that is the soul of Pier della Vigna (the business, as Dante out-Virgils Virgil, is of course borrowed, as are Pier's first words, from *Aeneid* III, 22f). Dante here, in *Purgatorio* I, plucks a plant that immediately grows back, as Pier's cannot. Essentially the same action or state is later referred to when the nameless Florentine suicide,

[28] Discussing the Prophet Nathan's presence in Paradiso, Professor Sarolli has pointed out Dante's possible reaction to finding a pun on his own name in "Dante 'scriba Dei,'" *Convivium*, XXXI (1963), 414-422. In his discussion "Equazione tipologica Natàn-Dante" he points to Isidore of Seville's derivation of Nathan's name (*Etymologiae* VII, viii, 7), "Nathan, *dedit*, sive *dantis*." For an early interpreter's insistence on a similar etymological derivation of Dante's own name, see Boccaccio, *Vita di Dante*, Chapter II. A modern interpreter, also interested in such lore, is Walter Arensberg. His book, *The Cryptography of Dante*, New York, 1921, argues, *passim*, for the presence of frequent secret anagrams in the *Commedia*. He is not, I believe, convincing.

[29] Once more see "'In exitu Israel de Aegypto.'" For another approach to the connectives between these two cantos see Harri Meier, "Zu Inferno I und Purgatorio I," *Romanische Forschungen*, LIV (1940), 284-289.

who has become a bush, asks Dante and Virgil to amass beneath him the scattered leaves that are all he has left of his human semblance. The leaves have been broken off and cannot grow again, like the branch of Pier that Dante has broken. In both moments the *giunco* of *Purgatorio* I is prefigured. Because these men committed suicide from despair, they are punished eternally in this way. The *giunco* is the answer to them, the foliage that can be re-born, as they might have been reborn in Christ had they sought him. And the further punishment that awaits these particular sinners, the suicides, upon the Day of Judgment is that they will get their bodies back, only to have them hang upon the trees that they had become. Surely they can be seen here as being forced to enact eternally a cruel and perverse imitation of the form of Christ's sacrifice or more properly, of Judas' suicide, itself a perverse prefig-uration of the Crucifixion. That Dante had the canto of the suicides very much in mind when he composed *Purgatorio* I is further evidenced by his use of two words in the two cantos. *Purgatorio* I contains the first of several uses of *libertà* or the adjectives and adverbs formed from it which are to be found in *Purgatorio* and *Paradiso*. In fact, there is only one previous occurrence in *Inferno*, and that is in Canto XIII. Pier has asked that Dante reestablish the memory of him in the world above when he returns. Virgil responds (line 85) by telling him to tell his story to Dante, so that Dante will be able to do freely (*libera-mente*) what Pier has requested. Perhaps the cruel point of Virgil's words is that Pier has no liberty at all—he gave that up when he took his own life—while the living Christian he addresses still possesses his freedom. At any rate, I find it arresting that the word, introduced here among the suicides, will not be used again until it is used to refer to Cato (and indirectly to Jesus and Dante), who is also a suicide, in *Purgatorio* I. The second bit of "verbal figuralism" is even clearer. At the very beginning of Canto XIII Dante describes the boughs of the horrible trees as being "non rami schietti"—branches that are not smooth, but knotted and gnarled (line 5). He uses the adjective *schietto*, smooth, only once more in the poem: *Purgatorio* I, 95. There it describes the *giunco*, which is smooth, and most importantly, the very opposite in its function and its meaning to its Hellish counterparts. The "unsmooth branch" is the "type" of Judas; the "smooth rush" is the "type" of Christ.

I will not speak further of this way of looking at the verbal connectives of the *Commedia*. Although Dante did not invent the technique—it is at least as old as Homer— I think it is useful to consider it in light of his allegorical practice. It is not surprising that the very words in the poem should have the same kind of figural relationship as have events.[30]

Bringing fourfold exegesis, historical figuralism, and "verbal figuralism" into critical play in Dante's poem reveals the relationship between subject matter and structure in the *Commedia*. One dimension of the subject matter is past, another present and future. For instance, when we look at Francesca or Ulysses or any other inhabitant of the afterworld, we see first his present state *in morte* and, almost simultaneously, that this state is the fulfillment of his life on earth. Dante's figural sense

---

[30] In a sense, Dante's technique of repeating words in such a way as to make all previous uses of the words more certain and meaningful is a universal literary technique, one about which twentieth-century criticism has been most perceptive. Nevertheless, I would argue for the particularity of a figure-fulfillment relationship in his work, claiming that "verbal figuralism" is not an empty critical phrase, but corresponds to Dante's way of thinking about the words he uses, words pregnant with, in A. C. Charity's phrase, "events and their afterlife."

might seem different from Aquinas' in that it moves from *now* to *then*, while the exegetes, when exemplifying the second sense, usually move from *then* (Moses) to *now* (Christ). In other words, in Dante's poem the traditional order is apparently reversed in that we see the fulfillment and then look for the *figura*. As A. C. Charity (one of the few writers who has troubled to discuss the point)[31] indicates, this reversal is orthodox and is also the natural result of Dante's subject matter which is, as Dante tells us in the Letter to Can Grande, the state of the souls after death. If we were shown Francesca *in vita* and then made to envision her destination in the afterworld, the usual exegetical order would be maintained. We do, however, through what we see *now* in light of the past gain the moral and anagogical senses and these move us into the future, first as they concern the choices we should make in our lives as a result of what we have been shown, second as they point to God's divine plan, which will be wholly apparent only at the end of time.

What I hope my discussions of the figural elements in Dante's treatment of three of his major characters has made tacitly clear is that Dante is a great deal freer in his adaptation of the Biblical technique than St. Thomas would have warranted.[32] Aquinas, or any other clerical

[31] He discusses "post-figuration" in *Events and Their Afterlife*, p. 204. And see the similar discussions by Rosemond Tuve, *Allegorical Imagery*, Princeton, 1966, pp. 47 and 403.

[32] Gerhard von Rad, "Typological Interpretation of the Old Testament," tr. John Bright, in *Essays on Old Testament Hermeneutics*, ed. Claus Westermann, Richmond, Va., 1963, pp. 17-39, finds that typology is easily and naturally adapted to the uses of the poet. Although his comments make no particular reference to Dante, I believe they may be of interest here: "It might be well to make it clear at the outset that what we are accustomed to understand under the heading of typology is, in a broad sense, by no means a specifically theological concern or, indeed, a peculiarity of ancient Oriental thought.

writer, is obviously concerned with nothing but the two Testaments. Indeed, a major portion of traditional exegesis is concerned only with figures of Christ in the Old Testament, as is only natural. For Dante, however, the technique has only a normal extension into all literature, his own poem included.[33] And thus he is free to think of Francesca *in vita* as the figure of Francesca *in morte*; and of Dido and Guinevere as figures of Francesca's lustful life; and of Augustine's reading of Paul as the negative and corrective figure of her reading. Thus one kind of figural density accumulates around that subject which is the state of the soul after death.

Nevertheless, despite the fact that Dante claims only this one subject matter, there is clearly another, as Professor Nardi says.[34] The Letter to Can Grande is right as far as it goes, but there is another subject matter and it involves what Dante the Pilgrim does in the poem, while

---

Rather, typological thinking is an elementary function of all human thought and interpretation. . . . And, above all, without this interpretive, analogical sort of thinking there would be no poetry. The poet goes ceaselessly to and fro; he sees the often insignificant, obvious things and recognizes in them ultimate value. In the movements of the elements, the passing of the years and the days, in the most elementary relationships of man with man, in simple mechanical performances—in everything regularity reveals itself, in which the smallest as well as the greatest things participate" (p. 17).

[33] Both Helen Flanders Dunbar and A. C. Charity have argued well for the single configuration of Dante as type of Christ. Their approaches do not go deep or wide enough, however, and so fail to illuminate enough of the poem's structure or meaning.

[34] ". . . il viaggio di Dante Alighieri fiorentino attraverso i tre regni d'oltretomba. . . ." See Ch. I, note 34. See also Filippo Villani's keen appreciation of the twin subjects in Appendix I. A recent brief and clear statement of what the author calls the poem's "double focus" is T. M. Greene's "Dramas of Selfhood in the *Comedy*," in T. G. Bergin, ed., *From Time to Eternity*, New Haven, 1967, esp. pp. 117-118.

the state of the souls after death involves what he sees. Thus we have a dual and related system of subjects and the Poet must imitate two sets of actions, those of the lively dead souls alongside those of the developing Pilgrim. It is not difficult to find an exact counterpart in other literature. One example will suffice, though many come to mind: the "subject" of the play-within-the-play in *Hamlet* is what Claudius sees *and* what he does when he sees it.

The system of meaning which unites these two subjects, as I have attempted to demonstrate, especially in my treatment of Cato, is figuralism. Cato has four senses of "meaning," and has also figural extensions which amplify these. Dante, interacting with Cato, has also four senses of meaning: literally, he begins the ascent of the mountain which leads to Grace; figurally, his actions in the afterworld point toward the ascent he will make if he does not fail when he returns to the earth after his death (here the figure-fulfillment relationship accedes to the normal order); morally, his ascent teaches us how to be good Christians, a purpose similar to that of Augustine's *Confessions*, for instance; anagogically, God's Grace and His plan are demonstrated in choosing Dante to go for all of us. In addition, and of more interest and significance, Dante the Pilgrim's actions at various points of the journey have further figural extensions: when he comes to Cato he is figurally related to Ulysses (who failed to come this far), to Cato himself (who likewise sought liberty), and most importantly, to Christ (Who descended into Hell and ascended on the third day, and to Whom the Pilgrim is figurally related in many other ways).

The two subjects are drawn together and made mutually relevant through the figural relationships with which they intertwine. For instance, Cato figured in Moses figuring Christ; Dante figured in Ulysses by contrast, figured in

Christ, and also figured by Cato. The result is that all the figures come together; and the result of this, as I have said so many times, is that the literal sense of the *Divine Comedy* is joined to universal history.

CHAPTER IV

THE WOMEN OF *PURGATORIO*:
DREAMS,
VOYAGES, PROPHECIES

Purgatorio xix presents the second of Dante's three programmatic dreams on the mountain. It is a passage which
looks back to the first cantos of *Inferno*; to the central
cantos of *Purgatorio* (the center of the poem as a whole),
which discourse on love; to its immediate context which is
the discussion and presentation of "Sloth," or better,
accidia,[1] the action of the soul which gives physical surrounding and moral necessity to this dream; and to the
context of the first Purgatorial dream. If we look forward,
we see that the passage also creates a context for the third
Purgatorial dream, for Matelda's role in the poem, and for
the coming of Beatrice. One basic figural pattern for all
this is, I believe, the voyage and that voyager of *Inferno*
xxvi, Ulysses.[2] Thus one of the common elements is a man
on a ship and the woman who attracts him to her island.
The moral choice that is revealed can be expressed in terms
of which woman, and therefore which island, one sails for.
For the poem as a whole, then, the focus of these thirty-

[1] For a detailed discussion see Siegfried Wenzel, " 'Acedia' 700-1200,"
Traditio, xxii (1966), 73-102.

[2] It is curious that Dante first refers to the greater truth contained
in morning dreams—which is only naturally pointed to in *Purg.* ix,
16-18, as preparation for the dream which is about to occur as well
as for the two that will come later in *Purgatorio*—in the canto of
Ulysses (*Inf.* xxvi, 7). It would seem that the proximity of Ulysses,
for Dante, in some way suggests dreaming. For a summarizing discussion of Dante's use of the morning dream, and of the appearance
of the *topos* in other literature, see Charles Speroni, "Dante's Prophetic
Morning-Dreams," *Studies in Philology*, xlv (1948), 50-59.

six lines is intense. Before proceeding we had better look
at the passage:

mi venne in sogno una femmina balba,
   ne li occhi guercia, e sovra i piè distorta,
   con le man monche, e di colore scialba.
Io la mirava; e come il sol conforta
   le fredde membra che la notte aggrava,
   così lo sguardo mio le facea scorta
la lingua, e poscia tutta la drizzava
   in poco d'ora, e lo smarrito volto,
   com'amor vuol, così le colorava.
Poi ch'ell'avea il parlar così disciolto,
   cominciava a cantar sì che con pena
   da lei avrei mio intento rivolto.
"Io son" cantava, "io son dolce serena,
   che i marinari in mezzo mar dismago;
   tanto son di piacere a sentir piena!
Io volsi Ulisse del suo cammin vago
   al canto mio; e qual meco si ausa,
   rado sen parte; sì tutto l'appago!"
Ancor non era sua bocca richiusa,
   quand'una donna apparve santa e presta
   lunghesso me per far colei confusa.
"O Virgilio, o Virgilio, chi è questa?"
   fieramente diceva; ed el venia
   con gli occhi fitti pur in quella onesta.
L'altra prendea, e dinanzi l'apria
   fendendo i drappi, e mostravami il ventre:
   quel mi svegliò col puzzo che n'uscia.
Io mossi gli occhi, e 'l buon maestro "Almen tre
   voci t'ho messe!" dicea. "Surgi e vieni:
   troviam l'aperta per la qual tu entre."

[there came to me in dream a stammering woman,
   squint-eyed and crooked on her feet,
   with clumsy-fingered hands, sallow of complexion.
I gazed on her; and as the sun invigorates
   cold limbs made heavy by the night,
   thus did my look make nimble
her tongue, then made her wholly erect
   in a moment, and then to her bewildered countenance,
   as love requires, so it gave color.
As soon as her power of speech was thus set free
   she began to sing in such a way that with difficulty
   I might have turned my purpose back from her.
"I am," she sang, "I am the sweet Siren,
   who leads mariners astray in mid-sea,
   such pleasure do I give when I am heard!
I turned Ulysses from his wandering way
   to my song; and he who becomes used to me
   rarely departs, so thoroughly do I satisfy him!"
Her mouth had not yet closed again
   when a lady appeared, holy and alert,
   alongside of me, to put that other to confusion.
"O Virgil, O Virgil, who is she?"
   she said sternly. And he came
   with his eyes fixed upon that honorable one.
The other one he seized, and opened her up in front,
   rending her garments, and showed me her belly;
   that awakened me with the stench which came
     from there.
I moved my eyes, and my good teacher said,
   "At least three
   calls have I sent thee! Arise and come:
   let us find the opening by which thou mayst enter."]

(*Purg.* xix, 7-36)

The poetic source of this dream lies in the preceding canto. To my knowledge this fact has not been pointed out, at least not with the verbal detail which makes some of the Siren's meaning plain. The first half of Canto xviii (seventy-five lines) is devoted to Virgil's exposition of love. This exposition in turn hinges upon Virgil's forty-nine lines of discourse (which conclude Canto xvii) upon the negative side of love, which is reflected by the Seven Sins. And this discourse, in turn, springs from Marco Lombardo's disquisition upon free will, our better nature (*miglior natura*), and the necessary guides which should supervene in human affairs to direct human conduct (*Purg.* xvi, 79-129). Each of these three cantos contains a major doctrinal exposition; these occur in logical order, moving from the condition of the soul at birth, through its turning to sin, and finally to Virgil's assertion that the faculty of the free will is to control the natural instinct to love. Numerically and doctrinally these three cantos are at the center of *Purgatorio* and of the entire *Commedia*.[3]

Dante, in his imperfection, having heard the doctrine of love expounded by Marco and by Virgil, now enters the Terrace of Sloth, where, schematically enough, he becomes somnolent (*Purg.* xviii, 87). The sight of the hurrying spirits who had once been, as Virgil says (107-108), negligent, dawdling, and lukewarm, temporarily awakens Dante to alert observation of their reformation, exemplified in the courteous words of the Abbot of San Zeno, uttered on the run. Then, however, at the conclusion of the canto Dante again falls into a state of rambling ("vaneggiai"—line 143) and finally goes off to sleep ("e 'l pensamento in sogno trasmutai"—line 144) as he had done

<hr />

[3] See Singleton, "The Poet's Number at the Center," *MLN*, lxxx (1965), 1-10. And see, in rebuttal, R. J. Pegis, "Numerology and Probability in Dante," *MedStud*, xxix (1967), 370-373.

previously in line 87 ("stava com'om che sonnolento vana"). Exactly what *accidia* meant to Dante is not altogether certain. Surely here it is the sin of slothfulness, expressed through images of laziness, sleepiness and wandering of the mind, perhaps refracting the sleepiness of Adam which characterized the Pilgrim as he was about to have his first dream in *Purgatorio* IX, 10—perhaps in some indirect way as well, the errant Ulysses. The result of his own *accidia*, within the context of his own life, is probably to be understood as his dreaming of false philosophy, as the passive mental state which allows false gods to lead one astray; for the spiritual action which the Pilgrim now enacts before us is, as the poet now tells us in the vivid and concluding phrase of Canto XVIII, to turn thought into dream. What this means explicitly is simple: Dante has heard the wise and true words of Virgil, but he translates these into a dream that initiates itself as the record of the spiritually passive man who is easily caught in the snare of falsehood. As his first dream took place, literally and figuratively, in Pride, so this dream takes place in Sloth, and the final one will take place in Lust. The Siren comes, not only from Dante's reading in the Ulysses literature, but from the text of Virgil's discourse on love. In other words, Dante's dream is triggered by the very words of Virgil on the subject of misdirected love, or rather, by his own summary of the words of Virgil, which even gives the detail a final touch of verisimilitude: Dante's dream is induced by his own words:

> ché s'amore è di fuori a noi offerto,
> e l'anima non va con altro *piede*,
> se *dritta* o *torta* va, non è suo merto.
> (italics mine)

[for if love is offered us from without,
   and if our soul goes on no other foot,
   it is not to her merit that she go crooked or straight.]

(*Purg.* xviii, 43-45)

As the woman[4] appears in Dante's dream, she comes on
crooked feet; so the soul of the lover goes on crooked feet
when it loves the wrong object. Her crookedness mirrors
her ability to lead men astray. This becomes clear enough
with her reference to Ulysses. Had she been drawn by
Spenser, her name would have been Errour (*F.Q.* i, i,
13f). The power she has to lead men astray depends upon
her being taken for the one who leads to the truth; in
Dante's structure, it depends upon her being mistaken for
the true Beatrice. She is the false Beatrice, whom Dante
makes erect ("drizzava") despite the reality of her crookedness. Those three words of Canto xviii, *piede*, *dritta*,
torta, give a conceptual basis for the figuration of the Siren
in the dream.[5]

The story which the dream recounts is simple enough: a
man is drawn to an ugly woman to whom he mistakenly
grants the power of a beauty which leads him on. She sings
of her power, citing her abilities to mislead Ulysses.[6] Suddenly another woman appears and prevails upon Virgil to
reveal the actual condition of the Siren, which he does. We
are back in *Inferno*, ii, 49f: Virgil tells Dante how Beatrice
came down to Limbo and directed him to lead the Pilgrim

[4] Gmelin is among the recent commentators to call the reader's
attention to the distinction Dante draws between *femmina* and *donna*.

[5] This was recently pointed out by my student Roger Nierenberg in
a paper he submitted to me which discussed the verbal interrelationships
among *Inf.* i, *Inf.* ii, *Purg.* xviii, and *Purg.* xix. I believe that Mr.
Nierenberg is the first reader of the poem to mark the significance of
these three words for the dream that follows in the next canto.

[6] For Dante's confusion or deliberate telescoping of the Sirens and
Circe, see Moore, *Studies in Dante*, i, pp. 264-266.

through Hell. She describes her lover as one who is attacked by death on the waters. Virgil's description of her
coming gives Dante heart to begin his trek through Hell.
These broad outlines are recapitulated in the dream: a
sailor (namely Ulysses) is led astray in mid sea (the one
who misleads him portrayed as a woman) and Beatrice appears to ask Virgil to put her sailor back on the right path,
which he does in the dream by showing Dante the naked
truth about the Siren as he has done earlier in the poem
by showing him all of Inferno. One of the things that
attracts us about this dream is its similarity to actual
dreams.[7] With the possible exception of the Siren herself,
who at first seems little more than personified Error, the
dream has its sources in actual experiences in the dreamer's
past life within the poem that contains him, and eventually
in the life that was the pretext for the poem. That the Siren
is a reflection of a real woman is nevertheless a possibility;
but for this I should like to delay until we have examined
more of *Purgatorio*. What clinches the relevance of *Inferno*
II at this point in the poem are the similes concerning the
effects of love that we find in both passages:

> Quali i fioretti, dal notturno gelo
>   chinati e chiusi, poi che 'l sol li 'mbianca
>   si drizzan tutti aperti in loro stelo,
> tal mi fec'io di mia virtute stanca,
>   e tanto buono ardire al cor mi corse,
>   ch'i' cominciai come persona franca. . . .

> [As little flowers, closed and bent down
>   by nocturnal cold, when the sun whitens them
>   grow erect and open on their stems,

---

[7] For a "modern" reading of the dreams of *Purgatorio* see Francis
Fergusson, *Dante's Drama of the Mind*, Princeton, 1953, esp. Chapter IV.

so became I, with my flagging powers;
    and so much good ardor flowed to my heart
    that I began as one freed from toil. . . .]
                    (*Inf.* ii, 127-132)

Virgil's words about Beatrice have a warming effect
upon the fearful Dante. In the simile which begins in the
fourth line of the dream, Dante's gaze is like the sun
which warms the limbs (not flowers, to be sure) made
heavy by night in that it gives the *femmina balba* the
power of speech, color in her cheeks, and most importantly
for our purpose, in that it makes her erect. The similar
rhythms and meanings of the two similes are probably
enough, but the repetition of the verb *drizzare* is further
proof that Dante was thinking back to the earlier passage.
The love which Dante lavishes upon the Siren is a perverse
imitation of the love that Beatrice has lavished upon him.
In addition, the use of the word *smarrito*, in line 12, picks
up Beatrice's own words (*Inf.* ii, 64) when she tells Virgil
that she fears Dante is already so far off the path (*smarrito*
—and see *Inf.* i, 3, "ché la diritta via era smarrita") that
she has come too late to aid him. Here the poet displaces
his own quality, that of being lost to the true way, making
it a part of the capacity of the Siren: it is she who has led
Ulysses and Dante astray.

If the dream moves us back to its proximate cause in the
words of the previous canto, and if it moves us further
back for its ultimate cause in what Beatrice tells Virgil in
Canto ii, it also prepares the way for much that is to come,
especially having to do with Beatrice, who enters the poem
offstage, as it were, confronting Virgil some time before
Dante arrives in the poem in Canto i, and who now enters
the poem in dream,[8] shortly to come in actuality in *Purga-*

---

[8] Other identifications of the *donna* seem far from the point. Scartazzini's commentary, for instance, says she is a "simbolo della ragione

torio xxx. Before moving forward, I should like to review the relationship of this dream to the first one, which occurs in *Purgatorio* ix, and then to see the rhetoric which the three dreams establish before the vision of Beatrice takes place.

---

naturale che mostra all'uomo la fallacia dei falsi beni e la mendacità delle loro lusinghe." In so far as Dante treats her as a personification, this analysis works. Once again it is probably more reasonable to look upon the literal as historical, or at least upon the literal sense of the dream as reflecting the "historical" Beatrice. This is Gmelin's procedure, *Komm.* II, p. 304: "Dante hat sie absichtlich nicht mit Namen genannt, aber ihre Rolle gleicht am meisten derjenigen Beatrices selbst," an estimation in which Singleton concurs (" 'In exitu Israel de Aegypto' "). The Siren's first words are, significantly, a parodistic preview of Beatrice's self-nomination in *Purg.* xxx, 73, "Ben son, ben son Beatrice." The Siren has opened her discourse with the words "Io son . . . , io son dolce serena." There is probably a resonance here of Dante's understanding of the meaning of God's Hebrew name, which he and his period took to be "I am that I am." It would seem likely that Dante's parallel use of the formulaic repetition of the *son* mirrors his sense of God's self-nomination. Isidore of Seville, *Ety.* VII, i, discusses the ten Hebrew names for God. The ninth one is most interesting (VII, i, 16): "Nonum *Tetragrammaton*, hoc est, *quatuor litterarum*, quod proprie apud Hebraeos in Deo ponitur, יהוה id est, duabus יהיה *ia, ia*, quae duplicata ineffabile illud et gloriosum nomen Dei efficiunt; dicitur autem ineffabilis, non quia dici non potest, sed quia finiri sensu et intellectu humano nullatenus potest, et ideo quia de eo nihil digne dici potest, ineffabilis est." While Dante's understanding of the *meaning* of God's name depends from Exod. 3:14, "Ego sum, qui sum" (Isidore's sixth name of God—and see Augustine, *De Civitate Dei*, VIII, xi), he also may have been aware of this other tradition which also involves a formulaic repetition, and which has the further advantage of being closer to the Italian "io, io," which might have been, in Dante's eyes, a kind of reflection of the *tetragrammaton*. This might help explain why Adam tells him (*Par.* XXVI, 134) that *I* was the first name of God, and not *EL* (which Dante thought it was in *De vulgari* I, iv, 4). Whether or not this is so, the parallel between the Siren and Beatrice would seem to be nothing else but clear, though the precision of the verbal parallel has gone, I believe, unnoticed until now. For a brief discussion of Jerome's influence on Dante's rejection of *EL* for *I*, see Phillip Damon, "Adam on the Primal Language," *Italica*, XXXVIII (1961), 60-62.

The three dreams of *Purgatorio* parallel in some respect the three visions of Beatrice, which Dante recounts in *Vita Nuova*, at least in that they are numerically relatable to Dante's age in each of the three visions: nine, eighteen, and twenty-seven are the numbers of the cantos which contain the dreams—or they are if we count the fact that Dante *says* that he dreamed in the concluding line of Canto XVIII ("e 'l pensamento in sogno trasmutai"—"and I turned thought into dream"). Insofar as Dante has deliberately invoked those earlier and truer visions, they would seem to be of structural use mainly by playing against the dreams, thus preparing him and us for the new vision of Beatrice. The patterns of allusion in the three dreams which Dante uses to this end are extraordinarily rich, even for him. The first dream (*Purg.* IX, 13-42) takes place while Dante is being carried up toward the gate of Purgatory proper by Lucia, and is prepared for with the phrase, "quand'io, che meco avea di quel d'Adamo,/vinto dal sonno" ("When I, who had with me something of Adam, overcome by sleep"—lines 10-11), a phrase which makes a figural pattern between Adam's sleep on the grass of Eden, which ends in God's making of Eve from his rib (Gen. 2:21-22), and Dante's sleep in the grass of the Valley of the Princes, which will be the occasion for the coming of Lucia, who shall take him up toward Beatrice. More than that, once the dream itself is introduced, Dante moves back in literary time for three classical rapes:

> Ne l'ora che comincia i tristi lai
> la rondinella presso a la mattina,
> forse a memoria de' suo' primi guai. . . .

> [At the hour near morning when the swallow
> begins her sad lays,
> perhaps in memory of her first woes. . . .]

(Purg. IX, 13-15)

ed esser mi parea là dove fuoro
    abbandonati i suoi da Ganimede,
    quando fu ratto al sommo consistoro. . . .

[and it seemed to me that I was there where
    his own people were abandoned by Ganymede,
    when he was snatched up to the highest consistory. . . .]

(Purg. IX, 22-24)

Non altrimenti Achille si riscosse,
    li occhi svegliati rivolgendo in giro
    e non sappiendo là dove si fosse,
quando la madre da Chirone a Schiro
    trafuggò lui dormendo in le sue braccia,
    là onde poi li Greci il dipartiro. . . .

[Not otherwise did Achilles startle up,
    directing his awakened eyes in a circle
    but not knowing where he was,
when his mother from Chiron to Scyros
    carried him off secretly, sleeping in her arms,
    thence where then the Greeks took him off. . . .]

(Purg. IX, 34-39)

The three rapes are temporally arranged one at the beginning, one during, and one at the conclusion of the dream. The second one, concerning the rape of Ganymede by Jove in the form of an eagle, or by the eagle of Jove, is the substance of the dream itself. Since the dream occurs in the canto before the arrival of Dante and Virgil on the Terrace of Pride, it is particularly fitting because it is the dream of a mortal who is singled out from his fellows and carried up to heaven to be among the immortals, an event which certainly has its forward resonances for the journey Dante will soon himself undertake in *Paradiso.* But the important thing is that in the dream the prefiguration of his ascent to the fiery sphere is painful and awakens him, and thus, from the opening comparison, makes the version of the rape resemble that of Philomela, and that of Achilles. The three classical allusions, all of which directly apply to the uneasy internal state of the Pilgrim, can be expressed figurally as follows: as Philomela was raped by the husband of Procne; as Ganymede was raped by Zeus; and as Achilles was carried off by his mother, apparently to safety but actually to his death; so Dante was *not* to be raped, but borne safely by Lucia toward his vision of God. For the other three there was no efficient grace.[9] The pagan tales, which Dante amalgamates from Virgil, Ovid, and Statius,[10] are played against the Christian *figura* of the eagle as the bird of God's empire.[11] There are many Biblical passages wherein the eagle is a symbol of God's Grace. Gmelin's *Kommentar* cites Deuteronomy 32:11.[12] Some might prefer the Words of the Lord to Moses in Exodus 19:4: "Ye have seen what I did unto the Egyptians, and how I bare you on eagles' wings, and brought you unto myself." In the Vulgate the noteworthy words run, "quomodo portaverim vos super alas aquilarum, et assumserim mihi." Another apposite Scriptural passage is to

[9] Whoever or whatever Lucia is, she would seem to act in this capacity in *Inf.* II and here.

[10] Gmelin, *Komm.* II, pp. 162-163.

[11] Erich Auerbach, "Figurative Texts Illuminating Certain Passages of Dante's *Commedia*," *Speculum*, XXI (1946), 474f.

[12] *Komm.* II, p. 163. "Sicut aquila provocans ad volandum pullos suos, et super eos volitans, expandit alas suas, et assumpsit eum, atque portavit in humeris suis." ("As an eagle stirreth up her nest, fluttereth over her young, spreadeth abroad her wings, taketh them, beareth them on her wings.") The next verse continues, "So the Lord alone did lead him, and there was no strange god with him." The passage refers to Jacob in the desert, a fact which makes it a highly likely candidate; as we shall see, Jacob's experience is later in the poem used as a figure of Dante's own. Singleton, " 'In exitu Israel de Aegypto,' " prefers the eagle of Exodus, while also citing this one.

be found in Isaiah 40:31: "But they that wait upon the Lord shall renew their strength; they shall mount up with wings as eagles. . . ." The Vulgate runs, "assument pennas sicut aquilae."[13] The Pilgrim has difficulty understanding the exalted mission expressed in the dream until Virgil explains to him that Lucia has borne him up, that his dream should be interpreted in favorable ways.

What I find particularly arresting here is the rhythm of three plus one (like the repeated rhythm of the nine plus one making ten in the *Iliad*) which Dante brings back to his poem here.[14] That is, we have three versions, in and around the dream, of destructive rapes, which turn out to be negative versions of the actual and positive event. In all three negative versions Dante is implicitly to be identified with the young, attractive object of lust (in itself a disguised, prideful assertion of his desirability, the sort

[13] The Apocryphal Gospel of Nicodemus, describing the Harrowing of Hell, also contains an eagle that Dante might have known and surely would have liked (xx, 3). At stake is a conversation between Satan and Inferus (Hell) concerning the advent of Jesus to their realm after the Crucifixion. Inferus asks, "Who is this Jesus?" Satan informs him that it is indeed the one who drew Lazarus up from death. Inferus then remembers his terror on that occasion, hoping that this time Jesus will be kept far hence. He continues, "Nec ipsum Lazarum tenere potuimus, sed excutiens se ut aquila per omnem agilitatem et celeritatem salivit exiens a nobis" (text from J. C. Thilo, *Codex Apocryphus Novi Testamenti*, Leipzig, 1832, p. 711): "And we could not keep this Lazarus, who, shaking himself like an eagle, shot forth with all agility and speed, and left our kingdom." Dante being carried up by an eagle which is *figura Christi* and Lazarus called from death to life, going up like an eagle—the resemblance is one that Dante may or may not have had in mind.

[14] We have seen it once already in the sinking ship of Ulysses (*Inf.* xxvi, 139) which is driven thrice around before it plummets to the bottom. T. K. Swing, in *The Fragile Leaves of the Sybil*, pp. 143-146, discussing what he calls "cumulative representation," has pointed out that the four areas of Cocytus are actually a "three plus one." Three subsumed in one creates a rhythm, I need hardly point out, pleasing to a Christian poet.

148

of thing that is put in the mouth of Brunetto Latini in *Inferno* xv) who is destroyed, or at least removed from human companionship, by the appetite he causes in others in the first two cases, and by the unwitting complicity of his mother in the third case, where Dante is implicitly an enemy of Troy as well as one who is to be destroyed by being carried off. This rhythm will confront us again at an important juncture. First let us briefly consider the third dream.

The sleep that Dante has in Canto xxvii is singularly untroubled, for he has just passed through the fire which turns lust to love, the fire which signifies the end of purgation. The dream he has here is relatively brief and simple, full of the kind of lovingness that Freud has shown us our dreams actually rarely contain. The dream begins with Dante's formulaic details—an astronomical reference to the hour of the morning at which the dream occurs, followed by those focal words which remind us that this is dream, thus uncertain, and in need of close reading: "mi parea veder" (ix, 19), "mi venne in sogno una femmina balba" (xix, 7), "in sogno mi parea/donna vedere andar" (xxvii, 97-98). The astronomical references are in each case telling: Canto ix begins with a reference to Tithonus and Aurora, the former coming from the bed of his lover, thus setting the sensual tone for the dream that is to follow, while the formulaic time detail that immediately precedes the dream concerns the hour of the morning which the swallow chooses to begin its sad singing, thus introducing the notion of rape which the following classical references will develop shortly; the second dream and Canto xix begin with the reference to the coldness of Saturn and the Moon, combined with the natural coldness of the Earth before dawn, which establishes the slothfully contemplative mood for the dream of a false contemplation,

that of the cold woman who is revived by Dante's gaze as
cold limbs are warmed by the sun; and the third dream is
initiated by the happier astronomical reference to Cytherea
(XXVII, 95), Venus as the morning star. This takes us back
to the same planet as it appeared to Dante and Virgil upon
their arrival at the purgatorial mount in Canto I, lines 19-21,
where, on Easter Sunday morning, Venus is redolent not
only of Beatrice, but of Christ, since she is in conjunction with
Pisces the appropriate sign of Jesus.[15] Here, however, it is
not the planet "reborn," which Dante describes, but the
planet shining for the first time, as at the Creation. The
planet is appropriate not only as the forerunner of the
dream of innocent love, but as the indication of the figural
event corresponding to the place and action with which the
Pilgrim is now involved: the arrival in Eden. Here is the
dream:

> giovane e bella in sogno mi parea
>   donna vedere andar per una landa
>   cogliendo fiori; e cantando dicea:
> "Sappia qualunque il mio nome dimanda
>   ch'i' mi son Lia, e vo movendo intorno
>   le belle mani a farmi una ghirlanda.
> Per piacermi a lo specchio, qui m'adorno;
>   ma mia suora Rachel mai non si smaga
>   dal suo miraglio, e siede tutto giorno.
> Ell'è de' suoi belli occhi veder vaga,
>   com'io de l'adornarmi con le mani;
>   lei lo vedere, e me l'ovrare appaga."

[15] Dunbar, *Symbolism in Medieval Thought*, pp. 140-141, 303,
308n., 435, although not discussing the Christological significance of
the constellation, does point out the importance of the ancient Christian symbol for Dante.

[young and beautiful—in dream I seemed
  to see a lady going through a meadow
  gathering flowers; and singing she said:
"Know, whoever asks my name,
  that I am Leah, and I go plying
  my fair hands to make me a garland.
To please me at the glass here I deck me;
  but my sister Rachel never departs
  from her mirror, sitting there all day.
She is pleased to see her own fair eyes,
  as I to deck me with my hands;
  she by sight and I by work am satisfied."]

                  (*Purg.* XXVII, 97-108)

Dante says that sleep which contains dream often has the news before it happens ("il sonno che sovente,/ anzi che 'l fatto sia, sa le novelle"—lines 92-93). Although almost certainly not intended as such, the statement could be taken as a playful definition of figuralism; the dream that Dante has is certainly the figure—it "has the news"—of what is immediately to come, his meeting with Matelda. As Leah, the type of the active life, precedes Rachel, the type of the contemplative life, in the dream, so does the active Matelda precede the contemplative Beatrice. The figural patterns that emerge from this dream are richer and more pleasing than this simple equation, however. As T. K. Swing points out[16] (and to my knowledge he is only the second reader of Dante to point this out)[17] the figural proportion, Leah:Rachel as Matelda:Beatrice is deepened by the additional proportion, Jacob:Dante. As Jacob toiled

[16] *The Fragile Leaves of the Sybil*, p. 95. And see note 12 above.
[17] Giovanni Pascoli, *La mirabile visione*, 3rd. ed., Bologna, 1923, p. 462: "Il nuovo Enea è anche un Giacobbe novello." Swing's sense of the passage is more precisely articulated.

for seven years in order to gain the hand of Rachel, only to be given that of Leah (Gen. 29:10f), so Dante has toiled up seven terraces of purgation with the promise of Beatrice, only to find Matelda. To be sure, he has not to toil up seven more terraces to gain Beatrice, but he will have to undergo a final trial before she will smile upon him.

Who Matelda is, or is modeled on, is still an unsolved mystery of Dante scholarship. Of all the statements of possible solutions, I prefer Grandgent's.[18] The three Matil-

[18] Rejecting the conjectures of many earlier commentators, Grandgent argues as follows (p. 582): "Matilda's fresh girlishness would seem to preclude the possibility of identification with a grave ruler like the Countess Matilde of Tuscany; her amorousness, her active rather than contemplative existence should exclude the suggestion of a nun—such, for instance, as that German St. Mechteldis of Hackeborn who, towards the end of the 13th century, had a vision (*Liber specialis gratiae*) of seven terraces of purification in the vicinity of a beautiful garden." He goes on to postulate that Dante's method of symbolism, proceeding from the actual to the general, makes the most likely conjecture one that would see behind and in Matelda the traces of an actual Florentine girl, a friend of Beatrice, suggesting as a possibility the girl whose untimely death is mourned in *Vita Nuova* VIII. Whether or not Dante is referring to a girl he has already celebrated in his earlier poetry seems to me less important than the notion that she is in his mind a Florentine coeval of Beatrice, one whose relationship to his *donna* is in proportion to that of Leah to Rachel, of John the Baptist to Jesus. A. B. Giamatti, *The Earthly Paradise and the Renaissance Epic*, Princeton, 1966, p. 107n., follows Grandgent. Why Matelda bears that name is still, if the various medieval Matildas are rejected, a vexing question. I recently came across an article which confirms the desperate acrosticism which led me, a few years ago, to the conjecture that Dante spells the name with an *e* rather than an *i* so that it will spell *ad laetam* ("toward joy") backwards, or nearly so. This observation, in which I put little stock, had already been made, as I recently discovered, by Jacques Gould, "Une nommée Matelda . . . ," *Revue des études italiennes*, n.s., I (1954), 20-60. A brief and helpful bibliography of the Matelda problem is available in Gmelin, *Komm.* II, p. 442. For a differing view, in which Matelda is linked to Astraea (Dante refers to Astraea in *Mon.* I, xi, 1, as well as in *Ep.* VII, i, 6) see Singleton, *Dante Studies* 2, pp. 184-201. See also Renato Poggioli,

das of medieval repute do seem severe as models for Matelda. Who or whatever she represents, it is better, perhaps, to admire what she is: a woman before death and all our woe came into the world, the unfallen Eve.[19] Surely that is the figural extension of this young girl, so alone and so happy in her solitude; "eine *figura* der Eva vor dem Sündenfall," as Gmelin says.[20] I believe his approach is buttressed by the sort of verbal detail which helps make a case good. When Leah, who is figurally related to Matelda as well as to Eve, defines herself in the last line of the dream, she uses a verb we do not find elsewhere in the *Commedia*: *ovrare*. Why was man put into the Garden of Eden? Even Voltaire[21] remembered the Vulgate: "Tulit ergo Dominus Deus hominem, et posuit eum in paradiso voluptatis, ut operaretur, et custodiret illum" ("And the

---

"Dante *Poco Tempo Silvano*: Or a 'Pastoral Oasis' in the *Commedia*," *80th Annual Report of the Dante Society* (1962), pp. 1-20, which takes issue with Singleton's findings.

[19] It is worth noting that the last word of the Siren's song in the second dream (*Purg.* XIX, 24) and the last word of Leah's speech in the third (*Purg.* XXVII, 108) are the same: *satisfy*. The Siren says, "He who becomes used to me seldom departs, so thoroughly do I satisfy (*appago*) him." Her kind of satisfaction is countered radically by Leah's; she is satisfied by working ("e me l'ovrare appaga") with her hands, as Eve should have been satisfied. In the poem Matelda is figured in Leah, and thus partakes of Leah's active form of satisfaction. In this way she is the figural answer to the Siren and to fallen Eve, and is redolent of Eve before the Fall. "Thus Matelda figures the condition of man as it was, and was to have been, in Eden"—Singleton, *Dante Studies* 2, p. 211.

[20] *Komm.* II, p. 440. Giamatti, *The Earthly Paradise and the Renaissance Epic*, p. 110, also sees the unfallen Eve in Matelda: "She is an Eve who will not fall."

[21] In the last chapter (XXX) of that work which is so thoroughly concerned with the earthly paradise, *Candide*. Why was man put into the Garden of Eden? Pangloss quotes God's word: "ut operaretur eum." As usual, Voltaire misquotes from memory.

Lord God took the man, and put him into the garden of Eden to dress it and keep it"—Gen. 2:15).

One of the greatest advantages to a poet in borrowing from God's way of writing is that he is able at one moment to recreate many moments, not as mere verbal reminiscences but as concrete situational parallels which the reader, if he is adept, will be able to see simultaneously. In Matelda Dante is able to recapture the innocent experience of Eden. It is no wonder that at the conclusion of Canto XXVIII Virgil, Statius, and Dante all smile at the prospect of that place where "fu innocente l'umana radice" (line 142), as they gaze upon the place and the first woman, "la divina foresta" (XXVIII, 2) with its "bella donna" (XXVIII, 43).

When Dante, new as Adam, first sees Matelda, who is nameless until she is about to leave the poem (*Purg.* XXXIII, 119) so that we will not think of who she is but what she means, the poem comes back to the three plus one rhythm we remarked in the first dream, where we found three pagan references, notable for their threatening quality, answered by the Christian benevolence of Lucia's actual intervention on Dante's behalf. This time Dante is confused about who the lady really is. He wants to hear what she is singing. (The Siren sang; Leah sang.) As he asks her to approach, he tells her that she reminds him of Proserpina, "when her mother lost her, and she the spring" (*Purg.* XXVIII, 50-51). That was the time, if we remember our Ovid, when Pluto interrupted the flower-gathering of Proserpina and her mother by carrying off the daughter, from whose lap fell flowers. Once again Dante adverts to a classical rape. And then Matelda reminds Dante of Venus when, wounded by Cupid, she fell in love with Adonis (64-66). Again it is a matter of the threat of sensuality which causes disorder and death. Finally, Lethe, which lies between Dante and Matelda, seems to him as hateful as the water was to Leander for keeping him distant from Hero (73-75). All of the Ovidian reminiscence has the same theme; the destructiveness of sensual passion. Somewhere, behind the Ovidian, lies the Biblical. For, if this is the Garden before the Fall,[22] it must remind us of the Fall which is to come.[23] The action of the three Classical stories is joined at a point where the doomed lovers awaken to love, are alive but about to die, for here they are parallel to the moment before the Fall.

Now the "four":

"Voi siete nuovi, e forse perch'io rido"
    cominciò ella "in questo luogo eletto
    a l'umana natura per suo nido,
maravigliando tienvi alcun sospetto;
    ma luce rende il salmo *Delectasti*,
    che puote disnebbiar vostro intelletto."

["You are new, and perhaps because I smile,"
    she began, "in this place set aside
    to human nature for its nest,
some doubt keeps you wondering;
    but the psalm *Delectasti* sheds light
    that may uncloud your understanding."]
                    (*Purg.* XXVIII, 76-81)

As though reading Dante's mind, Matelda explains to the three poets that although the place where they are is Eden, it is Eden before the Fall, and more than that, it is an Eden which shall never suffer the Fall again, for it is the Earthly Paradise regained which is in question here. Thus she may smile, for where Dante's past experience

---

[22] Ovid's description of the place from which Proserpina "falls" is Edenic to a Christian poet: "perpetuum ver est" (*Meta.* V, 391).

[23] This is precisely the topic of a part of Matelda's ensuing speech to Dante (lines 91-96).

makes him (and us) think of the events that sent man forth from Eden—expressed in terms of the sensual destruction of Adam and Eve that has remained a commonplace throughout Christian history even though the Bible does not condemn them for their libido, making that a function of their prideful disobedience instead—her innocent knowledge goes beyond tragedy to a sort of Christian romance: here the human root was innocent, and (the thought is unexpressed but necessarily implied) here it becomes innocent again:

> "Qui fu innocente l'umana radice;
>   qui primavera sempre[24] ed ogni frutto;
>   nettare è questo di che ciascun dice."

> ["Here the human root was innocent;
>   here it is always spring, here is every fruit;
>   this is the nectar of which each one tells."]
>   (*Purg.* XXVIII, 142-144)

This is the corollary which Matelda promised Dante, Virgil, and Statius as a grace. She has first told them that the weather here is the weather of heaven and not that of earth, and now she tells them that the Golden Age, of which the Classical poets tell, was like this place—with one significant exception: those places were *then*, but this place is *now* and forever (as her use of the present tense in line 144 makes clear). Parnassus is gone; Eden lives. It is perhaps our very historical imaginations which prevent us from seeing the full import of Matelda's message. That is, we do not think of this place as the actual Eden, for we think of the actual Eden as being *then*, and as suffering its Fall and desertion. But this is not a shadow of Eden;

---

[24] Dante's "primavera sempre" is probably a translation of Ovid's "perpetuum ver est." See note 22 above.

this is the actual place. Adam and Eve cannot be here because they are in the Empyrean; but they are represented here by Dante and Matelda, who shall not fall. And this, I believe, is exactly what Matelda tells us by her reference to the Psalm. The verse she quotes is Psalm 92:4[25] in the Vulgate: "Quia delectasti me, Domine, in factura tua, et in operibus manuum tuarum exultabo." ("For thou, Lord, hast made me glad through thy work: I will triumph in the works of thy hands.") And this verse is probably enough to understand Eden reasserted by the Psalmist, and now regained in Christ, where once it was lost in the work of the hands of Adam and Eve. Without consulting the commentaries Dante knew, one can readily guess what he would have seen figurally present in the penultimate verses of the Psalm:

12 The righteous shall flourish like the palm tree: he shall grow like a cedar in Lebanon.
13 Those that be planted in the house of the Lord shall flourish in the courts of our God.
14 They shall still bring forth fruit in old age; they shall be fat and flourishing.

The work of Christ's hands was to make Eden come green again, and now we meet Matelda, a new Leah, the unfallen Eve, doing the works of her Lord, keeping the Garden as once it was kept and should always have been kept, as it is by Leah in the dream, *ovranda*.

Thus Matelda's playful coyness about her smile is useful in reminding us that when we see Eden we, like Dante, expect a fall to follow. This then is the "four," the Christian truth which answers the fears expressed through the

[25] 91:5 in the English Bible. Singleton, *Dante Studies* 2, p. 206, cites Abelard's gloss on this verse of the Psalm (*P.L.* CLXXVIII, col. 762) as also pointing in the direction of Eden.

pagan references. And now the reader is prepared for the full implementation of that rhythm. For just as the first of the dreams, and then the first of the occurrences in Eden, is experienced through three negative associations followed by clarifying actuality, so the three dreams themselves create a rhythm, if not of the false at least of the less true, which is answered not by a dream but by the true vision of Beatrice. Canto xxx initiates the action of what is in a sense a "fourth dream," or at least what is rhythmically present as the inheritor to those three dreams involving ladies.[26] And what follows, as many commentators have noticed, is clearly related to Dante's final vision of Beatrice in the *Vita Nuova*, the vision that he tells us, at the conclusion of that work, he has had but is not yet capable of expressing.[27] The rhythm of the *Vita Nuova*, to which I alluded at the beginning of this discussion, will perhaps not seem unrelated now to the rhythm of the three plus one of the Purgatorial dreams, which are capped by the coming of Beatrice. As the earlier work took its roots in three visions of Beatrice that are somehow less real than the ultimate vision that cannot be described, the *Purgatorio* contains the record of three dreams that are somehow less real than the presence of Beatrice that Dante does now finally describe.

[26] That Dante thought of the vision atop the mountain as a "fourth dream" is attested by the fact that the Pilgrim falls asleep (*Purg.* xxxii, 64-72) after the appearance of the Griffin. As before he has fallen asleep and had dreams, now he has had or been vouchsafed a vision and then falls asleep. The reversed order sets the "fourth dream" above the first three, for, although it is itself a veiled vision in that what he sees is a symbolic version of the Christ, it has nevertheless greater reality than what he has previously seen in dream; he sees the real Beatrice, although she is still veiled.

[27] In the last section (xlii) of the *Vita Nuova* Dante says he had "una mirabile visione" of Beatrice. Many commentators, rightly, I believe, point to this passage as the germ of the *Commedia*.

No ONE has contributed more to our contemporary understanding of Beatrice than Professor Singleton.[28] Although
those who still see her as Theology may continue to ad-
vocate the application of personification allegory to her
poetic being, they will no longer find a ready audience.
Another school, represented by most contemporary *dantisti*,[29] see her as "historical" but as "meaning herself,"
and feel uncomfortable with what to them seems the false
"theologizing" of Singleton. However, we should now
understand that Beatrice is literally herself and yet achieves
her full meaning in the poem only when we understand
that, at least in various significant moments,[30] she is without
doubt also *figura Christi*. I shall not elaborate here, for
Professor Singleton's work makes that unnecessary.

Beatrice, entering the poem as a figure of Christ, soon
after becomes, as we noticed earlier, Dante's "admiral."[31]
She thus inherits the voyage theme begun in *Inferno* I,
reinvigorated by Ulysses in Canto XXVI, made sacrosanct
in the pilgrim ship of *Purgatorio* II, and tacitly understood
in each of the three dreams of *Purgatorio* in which Dante
is travelling with or toward a woman (Lucia, Siren, Leah).
In *Purgatorio* XXXI Dante makes his confession to Bea-

[28] Especially in *An Essay on the Vita Nuova*, Cambridge, Mass.,
1949; and in *Dante Studies 2: Journey to Beatrice*, Cambridge, Mass.,
1958. Perhaps the greatest twentieth-century lover of Beatrice is Charles
Williams, whose work, *The Figure of Beatrice*, New York, 1961, makes
up in warmth for what it neglects to see in Dante's structure.

[29] Those critics who, rejecting centuries of arid allegorizing, also
reject the notion that Dante's "symbolism" has any interesting connection with fourfold allegory, have been discussed in Chapter II, notes 3,
6, and 7. They include such writers as Barbi, Nardi, and Hardie.

[30] For instance, and it is only one instance, it is difficult to avoid
the Christological bearing of Dante's final salute to Beatrice, "che
soffristi per la mia salute/ in inferno lasciar le tue vestige" (*Par.* XXXI,
80-81).

[31] The *ammiraglio* of *Purg.* XXX, 58.

trice. It causes him grief (the "other sword" of *Purgatorio*
xxx, 57, that Beatrice has promised will follow his grief
at the loss of Virgil). When she asks why his progress
stopped at her death, Dante is so stricken he is barely able
to answer. He refers to "present things with their false
pleasure" (*Purg.* xxxi, 34). Beatrice makes his sin more
explicit:

"Tuttavia, perché mo vergogna porte
    del tuo errore, e perché altra volta,
    udendo le serene, sie più forte,
pon giù il seme del piangere ed ascolta:
    sì udirai come in contraria parte
    mover dovieti mia carne sepolta.
Mai non t'appresentò natura o arte
    piacer, quanto le belle membra in ch'io
    rinchiusa fui, e sono in terra sparte;
e se 'l sommo piacer sì ti fallio
    per la mia morte, qual cosa mortale
    dovea poi trarre te nel suo disio?
Ben ti dovevi, per lo primo strale
    de le cose fallaci, levar suso
    di retro a me che non era più tale.
Non ti dovea gravar le penne in giuso,
    ad aspettar più colpi, o pargoletta
    o altra vanità con sì breve uso.
Novo augelletto due o tre aspetta;
    ma dinanzi da li occhi di pennuti
    rete si spiega indarno o si saetta."
Quali i fanciulli, vergognando, muti
    con li occhi a terra stannosi, ascoltando
    e sé riconoscendo e ripentuti,
tal mi stav'io; ed ella disse: "Quando
    per udir se' dolente, alza la barba,
    e prenderai più doglia riguardando."

["Nevertheless, so that thou now bear shame
   for thy wandering, and so that another time,
   hearing the Sirens, thou shalt be stronger,
put off the sowing of tears and take heed:
   so shalt thou hear how in another direction
   my buried flesh should have moved thee.
Never did nature or art bring thee
   so much pleasure as the lovely limbs wherein I was
   closed up that now are dispersed in the dust;
and if the highest pleasure so failed thee
   by my death, what mortal thing
   should then have drawn thee to desire it?
Surely thou shouldst, at the first shaft
   of false things, have risen up
   after me who was so no longer.
Thou shouldst not have let thy wings be weighed down
   to await more shots, either a young girl
   or other vanity of such short duration.
The young bird waits for two or three;
   but in the sight of full-fledged birds
   in vain is the net spread or the arrow shot."
As little boys, feeling shame, not speaking,
   stand, eyes to the ground, listening,
   conscience-stricken and repentant,
so stood I; and she said, "Since
   hearing brings thee grief, lift up thy beard
   and thou shalt have more grief by looking."]
                                 (*Purg.* XXXI, 43-69)

However, if Beatrice makes Dante's sin more explicit,
she has not made it more clear. In precisely what activity
did Dante's fault lie? He says (*Purg.* XXXI, 34) only that
it was "present things." Beatrice refers to a "mortal thing"
(line 53) as well as to "false things" (line 56). The mix-

ture of singular and plurals, combined with the abstract manner of reference, has given the commentators a heavy chore. The debate on this passage has continued since Pietro di Dante claimed in his commentary on the *pargoletta* that she is not to be understood as an actual woman, but as the allegorical representation of some reprehensible intellectual pursuit. Without reviewing the vast subsequent scholarship on the issue, we may take it that the question has three major resolutions: 1) the *pargoletta* does represent an actual love of Dante's; 2) she is not an actual woman, but false Philosophy; 3) she is both of these.

The following[32] seem to me the major questions which the passage, itself restating Beatrice's first expression of Dante's wandering in *Purgatorio* xxx,[33] calls to our attention: 1) What was Dante's "wandering" toward what "Sirens"? 2) Who or what was the "mortal thing" that drew Dante to desire it? 3) Is this "mortal thing" the same as the plural "false things" that appeared after Beatrice's death? 4) Who or what are the *pargoletta* and the *altra vanità*?

If we could answer these four questions with any certainty, we would be in a position to "solve" the difficulties of this passage once and for all. Unfortunately, such certainty does not seem possible to me. Nevertheless, I do propose the following hypotheses:

First, the Sirens have two major references with which to be reconciled. The first is from the dream of the Siren in *Purgatorio* xix, where she is that woman who has the power to lead Ulysses and other mariners from the true way. As such, she represents or shares the qualities that

[32] The discussion which follows is heavily indebted to that of Grandgent, pp. 612-614.

[33] *Purg.* xxx, 124-132. She says that Dante turned his steps from her to follow a way not true, false visions of the good ("imagini di ben seguendo false").

characterize all seductive and dangerous women, and she is figurally related to Circe and Eve. She is the woman who leads to death, and as Dante makes clear in the dream, she actually has only the power lent to her by men; in herself she is powerless, crippled, and ugly. Here the poem itself is a source of light. But there is a difficulty. Beatrice does not refer to the Siren, but to the Siren*s*. Who are they? Grandgent and others rightly (I believe) send us to Boethius, *Consolatio Philosophiae*, I, i, when Philosophy tells the author, whom she finds in the presence of the Muses of Poetry, whom she calls *Sirenes*, that he must be frequented instead by the Muses of Philosophy. Grandgent argues that Dante uses this passage from Boethius literally, that he accepts, in other words, the classical chestnut that poets are liars and only philosophers are to be trusted. My solution is that Dante, for whom the passage was indeed a potent one, for obvious reasons wants nothing to do with the distinction between philosopher and poet; he is interested only in the distinction between true muse and false muse that couples with the distinction he makes throughout his poem between mere writer and *autore*, mere book and *volume*, mere words and *scrittura*. Thus, in answer to the first question, Beatrice's indictment is of false thinking, and while it tacitly may include a reference to sexual aberration, its primary thrust is against aberrations of thought.

This could hardly be the case, however, for the second question because the phrase *cosa mortale* can hardly be applied directly to anything but a mortal woman, especially since Beatrice draws contrasting attention to her own *belle membra*. To which particular mortal woman Beatrice alludes is perhaps not at all important. But we do know that Dante loved others, according to his own words in *Vita Nuova, Convivio* as well as in the *Rime*. The lady in question would seem most likely to be the *donna pietosa* who comforts him after Beatrice's death in the latter parts of the *Vita Nuova*, and who becomes, in *Convivio* ii, ii, *la donna gentile* who is also the Lady Philosophy.[34] While in the *Vita Nuova* she is almost certainly to be understood as an actual woman, it is the burden of *Convivio* to assure the reader that she is to be understood as an allegorical personification of Philosophy.[35] One way to reconcile the apparent contradiction in the first two versions of Beatrice's charge against Dante is to find that they correspond to Dante's own versions of the woman, the first to *Convivio*, written in fairly frank imitation and admiration of the personification allegory of Boethius and the second to *Vita Nuova*, where the woman is a woman.

The third question is thus answerable with an affirmative. The "mortal thing" is indeed describable by the plural "false things"—as are the Sirens. In other words, I find that Beatrice, having enunciated the double charge against Dante singly, now, coming back to his offense for the third time, treats the two together: it was a false thing to love that girl; it was a false thing to love Philosophy more than me. One of the reasons I believe there has been so much difficulty with this passage is that hardly anyone can bring himself to think that philosophy can be bad in Dante's eyes; but, it is the Lady Philosophy whom Beatrice condemns now, not philosophy. There is no con-

[34] For what remains, in my opinion, although I am not in full agreement, still the most penetrating analysis of the sometimes puzzling relationship between the *donna gentile* of the *Vita Nuova* and the Lady of the *Convivio* see James E. Shaw's acutely reasoned answer to Barbi's argument in the introduction to Busnelli and Vandelli's edition of the *Convivio*: *The Lady "Philosophy" in the Convivio*, Cambridge, Mass., 1938.

[35] See especially *Conv.* II, XII, 5-6.

tradiction. The Lady Philosophy does not represent philosophy; she is a false muse—or a Siren.

In Beatrice's fourth statement of the charges against
Dante she puts the case in terms of a *pargoletta* or "other
vanity of such short duration." Is her "or" used here as
the connective between equivalents, or is it to be understood as the connective between two separate elements? In
other words, is the *pargoletta* the same as the "other vanity"? It is probably impossible to be at all sure here, but
I would opt for a double reference: the first to Dante's
infidelity to Beatrice with an actual *pargoletta*; the second
to his flirtation with the Lady Philosophy, who is to be
understood as the wrong kind of thought: the sins of the
flesh and the sins of the spirit.[36]

The necessity for locating his fault in two such distinct
categories is, I believe, the result of his two differing treatments of the fault. That is, in *Vita Nuova* he treats the
pargoletta as an actual woman, while in *Convivio* he treats

---

[36] In his important study, "Dante's Prologue Scene," *Dante Studies*,
LXXXIV (1966), John Freccero points (p. 2) to the Augustinian
provenance of Dante's hitherto puzzling line, "Che di necessità qui si
registra," explaining why he has written his own name into the text
of the *Commedia* (*Purg.* XXX, 63). Freccero shows that Dante's own
passage in *Conv.* I, ii, 12, which tells, citing the example of the *Confessions*, that one may speak of oneself when the practice serves a
doctrinal purpose, resolves the puzzle completely. I shall have occasion,
in Chapter Six, to recur to Freccero's excellent piece. For now, in this
context, I should like to point out that its central insight, which involves the explicit model Dante found in *The Confessions*, should
probably be carried further than Freccero allows it to proceed: Dante
shares with Augustine the same besetting sins as he sets out on his
journey toward redemption, namely, lust and Neo-platonism. Coming
before Beatrice he is forced to review them more vividly and generically
than he has before, and they become focussed in the two-pronged pang
for the lady of the flesh and the lady of the mind, each of which is
answered by Beatrice.

her as an allegorical one, and now he must be contrite, confess, and give satisfaction for both forms of wandering. The one form occurred in his outward life, the other in his thought; at least this is what his writings have left on record. Thus I would find the rejection of the Sirens, "false things," and the "other vanity" to be in essence the rejection of his theories of poetry and truth as these are put forth in *Convivio*. We do not know why or when Dante gave over the plan of completing that work. One imagines his turning aside from it suddenly in order to begin the *Commedia*. As *Convivio*'s essential fictive technique is the allegory of the poets, so *Commedia*'s is the allegory of the theologians. In other words, Dante, in his own mind, has turned aside from one literary convention to embrace another truer one. This may even suggest that *Convivio* becomes the locus which is represented by the dark wood and lost way of *Inferno* I, which employs the shadowy personification allegory of the previous work in order to establish the point of departure for the new true poetry that is fully initiated when the poem turns to actualistic mimesis in Canto III, for which we are prepared by the coming of the shade of the actual Virgil and the imitation of his actual poem in Canto I.

Yet the rejection of errors of theory is balanced by the rejection of the *pargoletta*. The word has an interesting history in Dante's work. Some of the commentators cite its appearances in the various of the *Rime*.[37] In the *Rime* the word is always used for someone other than Beatrice, a second lady who draws Dante to herself. However, it is also interesting to notice an earlier passage in the *Purga-*

[37] Most recently Gmelin, *Komm.* II, p. 492: the "Pietra" canzone (no. 100), line 72; the first line of the *ballata* (no. 87) "I' mi son pargoletta bella e nova"; the second line of the sonnet (no. 89) "Chi guarderà già mai sanza paura/ ne li occhi d'esta bella pargoletta."

torio (Canto XVI) which makes use of a coinage based on this word. The passage might properly have come first in these deliberations which have begun with the dream of the Siren, for it occurs in the center of the *Purgatorio* and contains the first statement offered by the poem of the meaning of love. This statement, the reader will recall, is followed by Virgil's two subsequent "treatises" on love in XVII and XVIII, and thus is in a very real sense the springboard to the dream which, as we have seen, takes its immediate root in Dante's response to the conclusion of the three-part discourse on love. Marco Lombardo has told Dante that man, who is free, is also subject to a "greater power and a better nature" (*miglior natura*—lines 79-80). In his discourse on the twin themes of human responsibility and human frailty which necessitate strong and just earthly leaders of the race, led by a king who can discern at least the tower of the true city (lines 95-96), Marco paints a picture of the human soul at its birth when it is necessarily and forgivably concupiscent (for a parallel passage concerning the development of the soul from its original "innocent" concupiscence see *Convivio* IV, xii, 15-18):

> Esce di mano a lui che la vagheggia
>   prima che sia, a guisa di fanciulla
>   che piangendo e ridendo *pargoleggia*,
> l'anima semplicetta che sa nulla,
>   salvo che, mossa da lieto fattore,
>   volontier torna a ciò che la trastulla.
> Di picciol bene in pria sente sapore;
>   quivi s'inganna, e dietro ad esso corre,
>   se guida o fren non torce suo amore.
>   (italics mine)

[From the hand of Him who regards it with delight
  before it exists, there issues, in the manner of a
    little girl
who, crying and laughing, babbles like a baby,
the simple soul that knows nothing,
  but, moved by a joyful Maker,
  gladly turns to what beguiles it.
First it tastes the flavor of a trifling good;
  there it becomes deceived, and runs after,
  if no guide or curb untwists its love.]
                    (*Purg.* XVI, 85-93)

Marco Lombardo's description of the new-born soul
gives the sharpest of points to the conclusion of Beatrice's
charge to Dante (*Purg.* XXXI, 68), which is to lift up his
beard. What the remark implies, in light of Marco's
speech, is that Dante's behavior is appropriate in a child
but not in a man. His passive action in being drawn to
the Sirens is put sharply into focus by the poet's return
to the concepts and language of Marco's discourse. Beatrice
was, or should have been, the "guide or curb" of Dante's
love. Instead, he turned to a *pargoletta*. Beatrice's language parallels that of Paul (I Corinthians 13:11: "Cum
essem parvulus, loquebar ut parvulus, sapiebam ut parvulus, cogitabam ut parvulus. Quando autem factus sum
vir, evacuavi, quae erant parvuli." "When I was a child,
I spoke as a child, I understood as a child, I thought as
a child: but when I became a man, I put away childish
things"). The echoing of Paul's dictum in the word
pargoletta, as well as in the doctrinal whole of Beatrice's
admonition, is particularly to the point since all of Corinthians 13 is concerned with the supremacy of *caritas* and
includes in its penultimate verse (the one which happens to
follow the one cited above) Paul's promise that where

now we see as through a glass darkly, in eternity we shall see face to face. In the poem Dante is about to gaze on the mirroring eyes of Beatrice and see reflected there the dual-natured Griffin, emblem of Incarnate God.

If the simple soul "babbles like a baby" when it issues as a little girl from the hand of God, Dante's mature soul had no right to allow itself to be directed toward the *pargoletta*, and Dante should not have to be made to stand guilty before Beatrice like a *fanciullo*, for he has a beard. The two words, remembered here from their earlier context, give Dante's encounter with Beatrice a sharper focus within the dialectic on love. Furthermore, the "childishness topos" (which, whenever it is introduced into the poem, clearly distinguishes between normal "innocent" childishness and inappropriate guilty childishness)[38] not only draws together the opening discourse on love in Canto XVI with Dante's encounter with the accusing Beatrice in Canto XXXI, it also brings us back where we began, that is, with the dream of the Siren, who is *una femmina balba*, a stammering woman; it also directs us nearly to the top of Paradise, where Beatrice picks up that word, thus rounding off this strand of the dream matter and its ramifications in the *Purgatorio*. The word *balba*, which only appears once in the poem (*Purg.* XIX, 7), means "stammering" and is a form of the same verb as the participle *balbuziendo*, which Beatrice twice employs during her denunciation of cupidity in *Paradiso* XXVII, 121-148. That passage makes clear that, for Dante, *balba* connotes a particularly childish defect of speech. As Dante is about to enter the Primo Mobile he has his last view of Earth and sees there "il varco/ folle d'Ulisse" ("the

---

[38] Compare, *inter alia*, *Purg.* VII, 31; XV, 3; XVII, 34; XXIII, 111; XXVII, 45; and *Par.* XXII, 2; XXVII, 128; and most notably the *voci puerili* of the saved infants in *Par.* XXXII, 47.

mad track of Ulysses"—lines 83-84), that Ulysses who, after his appearance in *Inferno* xxvi, has been so present in or behind the actions of the poem in Cantos I, II, xix, and xxxi of *Purgatorio*.[39] Here we have come to the roots of time (118-119), as Beatrice tells us, where human adventure in time seems even more vain. Let us examine the passage:

> "Oh cupidigia che i mortali affonde
> sì sotto te, che nessuno ha podere
> di trarre li occhi fuor de le tue onde!
>
> Ben fiorisce ne li uomini il volere;
> ma la pioggia continua converte
> in bozzacchioni le susine vere.
>
> Fede ed innocenzia son reperte
> solo ne' parvoletti; poi ciascuna
> pria fugge che le guance sian coperte.
>
> Tale, balbuziendo ancor, digiuna,
> che poi divora, con la lingua sciolta,
> qualunque cibo per qualunque luna.
>
> E tal, balbuziendo, ama e ascolta
> la madre sua, che, con loquela intera,
> disia poi di vederla sepolta.
>
> Così si fa la pelle bianca nera
> nel primo aspetto de la bella figlia
> di quel ch'apporta mane e lascia sera.
>
> Tu, perché non ti facci maraviglia,
> pensa che 'n terra non è chi governi;
> onde sì svia l'umana famiglia.
>
> Ma prima che gennaio tutto si sverni
> per la centesma ch'è là giù negletta,
> raggeran sì questi cerchi superni,

---

[39] See Harvey D. Goldstein, "*Enea e Paolo*: A Reading of the 26th Canto of Dante's *Inferno*," *Symposium*, xix (1965), 316-327.

che la fortuna che tanto s'aspetta,
   le poppe volgerà u' son le prore,
   sì che la classe correrà diretta;
   e vero frutto verrà dopo 'l fiore."

["O greed, thou so sendest down mortals
   beneath thee that not one has power
   to draw forth his eyes from thy waves!
The will still flourishes in men;
   but the continual rain turns
   true plums into blasted fruit.
Faith and innocence are found
   in little children alone; then they both
   flee before the cheeks are covered.
One child, still stammering, keeps the fasts,
   who then, once his tongue is loosened, devours
   every kind of food no matter what the month.
Another, stammering, loves and obeys
   his mother, who, once his speech is whole,
   then longs to see her in her grave.
Thus becomes black the white skin
   of the first visage of the fair daughter
   of him who brings morning and leaves evening.
Lest thou marvel at this,
   reflect that on earth there is none to govern;
   which is why the human family strays.
But before January is thoroughly unwintered
   by the hundredth part that is forgot below,
   these celestial circles so shall spin
That the tempest, so long awaited,
   shall turn the poops where are the prows
   so that the fleet shall run on straight;
and true fruit shall come upon the flower."]
                    (*Par.* XXVII, 121-148)

The matter of dream, of woman, of voyage which we examined in *Purgatorio* has a heavenly issue and recapitulation here. A brief summary of what has developed in the canto before Beatrice's speech will perhaps be helpful.

In the first lines Dante hears all Paradise praise the Trinity. The joyous mood is broken by St. Peter's violent invective against those who have usurped his place (the words "il luogo mio" are repeated three times in his vehemence—lines 22-23), the failing clergy of the present time, who have made of Rome an intestine for blood and pus to flow to Hell (25-27). As Peter predicted, not only has his own color turned to red with rage, all of Paradise has similarly changed complexion, as has Beatrice. This must have been how heaven looked at the Crucifixion, Dante reflects (35). His description of the change in color is as follows:

> Di quel color che per lo sole avverso
> nube dipinge da sera e da mane,
> vid'io allora tutto il ciel cosperso.

> [With that color which the sun's opposition
> paints a cloud at evening or at morning
> saw I then all heaven empurpled.]
> (*Par.* xxvii, 28-30)

The words here are an evident borrowing from Ovid's description of Diana's blush (*Metamorphoses*, iii, 183-185)[40] when that virgin is spied in her nakedness by

---

[40] This has been pointed out by Moore, *Studies in Dante*, i, p. 227; and by Grandgent, p. 906. Ovid's lines run:

> Qui color infectis adversi solis ab ictu
> Nubibus esse solet aut purpurae aurorae,
> Is fuit in vultu visae sine veste Dianae.

Alessandro Ronconi, "Per Dante interprete dei poeti latini," *Studi danteschi*, xli (1964), 5-44, also notes the correspondence. His con-

Actaeon. Diana's blush should remind us how often the "blushing trope" is used in the first part of this canto: lines 13-15, concerning the planet Jupiter's hypothetical change from white to red; lines 19-20, Peter's "trans-coloration" from white to the red of indignant anger; line 34, Beatrice's "transmuted" semblance; line 54, Peter's reddening ("arrosso"). It is not surprising that Dante thinks of Ovid's use of the blush of innocence offended as a locus classicus for the sudden metamorphoses of Peter, of Beatrice, and of all heaven at the Crucifixion. (A sudden change in color is at the heart of a perplexing passage in the speech we have just now read and will soon consider.)

Peter resumes his denunciation of the existing Church, whose officers are wolves among their flocks. He sum-marizes (59-60): "O good beginning,/ to what vile end must thou fall?" He then concludes that Providence will not let things remain as they are. Dante looks up to follow the saint's path back to the Empyrean, and then follows Beatrice's bidding to look down for the last time at the Earth; there he can make out both ends of the Mediter-ranean: Cadiz, whence Ulysses sailed to his death; and the Phoenician shore, whence Zeus, in the form of a bull, carried Europa on his back out to sea and seduction (82-84)—another disastrous sea voyage.[41] Then, looking on Beatrice's smiling face, he rises with her into the *Primo Mobile* (97). The first thing Beatrice does upon arrival is to follow in the train of Peter's outburst against earthly

cluding general comment is especially worth quoting (p. 44): "In questo impasto stilistico, in questa trama di allusioni che si muovono nelle due direzioni classica e biblica, si riflette il grande incontro dell'-umanesimo e della religiosità di Dante: incontro di scienza umana e scienza divina."

[41] Also cited by Moore, I, p. 349, as of Ovidian provenance: *Meta.* II, 868-873. Again the subject of Dante's reference is the sexually assaulted virgin.

173

cupidity, initiating the speech which we have just read here.
And now she reverts to the subject of the language of childhood as a point of reference for her attack on human
degeneracy: only *parvoletti* are innocent and faithful. We
are returned to the language of Marco Lombardo in
Purgatorio xvi, where the simple soul that babbles in its
innocent pursuit of pleasure must eventually be controlled
by its own free will and by human leadership, and to the
language of *Purgatorio* xxxi, where Dante is charged by
Beatrice with having loved a *pargoletta* when he was a
grown man.

The next two *terzine*, with their stammering[42] children,
continue this logic. The message is simple enough: while
we are young, even though we cannot speak properly, our
natural impulses are easily governed by our mothers; once
we perfect our abilities, in this case of eating and of speaking, we use these powers only for *cupidigia*. As our will
puts forth flower but, because of the rain of cupidity, that
which should turn to fruit rots on the bough (124-126),
so the "innocent" child begins well enough, but also gives
way to cupidity and becomes corrupt. Dante continues
the logic with a fourth *terzina* in the same vein. This one
is something of an unsolved puzzle in the commentaries;
but some commentary is called for, although it is digressive. I repeat the Italian and offer three recent English
translations:

> Così si fa la pelle bianca nera
>   nel primo aspetto de la bella figlia
>   di quel ch'apporta mane e lascia sera.

[42] I have kept my translations of *balba* and *balbuziendo* the same
in order to underscore the close relationship between the two words.
Actually, the "lisping" of Wicksteed and of Sinclair seems to me more
appropriate.

[So blackeneth at the first aspect the white skin
   of his fair daughter who bringeth morn and
   leaveth evening.] (Wicksteed)
[So the white skin turns black at the first sight
   of the fair daughter of him that brings morning
   and leaves evening.] (Sinclair)
[Thus is blackened, in the sight of God, the
   white skin of human nature, the sun's fair child.]
   (Grandgent, an "interpretation" rather than a
   translation)

As is clear from these versions, the phrase that is most
unclear in Dante's text is *nel primo aspetto*. There are
three major possibilities. One is reflected by Sinclair's translation: the white skin turns black when it sees the fair
daughter, who is, for Sinclair and some others, Circe,
daughter of the sun. Grandgent, in accord with Scartazzini,
has the white skin turn to black in the sight of God, trans-
lating *nel primo aspetto* as "in the primal sight." The
Wicksteed translation is cautious, not taking a side and not
trying to make the meaning of the phrase clear: "at the first
aspect" means anything and nothing. The problem is complicated by Gmelin's recent reading "der Ausdruck *primo
aspetto* bedeutet dann das direkte Licht" ("The expression
means then, direct light"), as Gmelin argues that the
precedent phrase (*Par.* xviii, 18), *secondo aspetto* (Dante
sees the joy of Heaven reflected on Beatrice's face), shows
that Dante has kept in mind the medieval distinction between *lux prima* and *lux secunda*.[43] In English this would
work out to the following: "Thus is turned to black in
God's direct light the white skin of the fair daughter of
him who brings morning and leaves evening." Although

[43] His argument follows closely that of Bernardino Catelani, "La
figlia del sole nella *Divina Commedia*," *L'Alighieri*, i (1890), 139-
144.

that solution is at least reasonable, I am not convinced that it is likely. Instead, it would seem to me more probable that Dante here uses *aspetto* in the simple and clear way he uses it so frequently in the *Commedia*, to mean the look in someone's face (as Brunetto Latini has a *cotto aspetto*, or a baked look—*Inf.* xv, 26). Thus I have translated the phrase as I have above, "the white skin of the first visage," as it seems to me both Dante's usual sense of *aspetto* and the most direct literal sense within the passage are both served best in this manner. This reading is also supported by the rhythm of the entire canto, which moves from innocent youth to guilty maturation.

The literal sense of the passage is not its primary difficulty, however. Whose skin is Dante referring to? The commentators have found many possible sources. Gmelin[44] alludes to several earlier ascriptions: the Moon, the Earth, Aurora, Circe, and human nature itself. Scartazzini, retaining, it seems to me, more of the sense of the underlying theme of the canto, which is the degeneracy of the Church, claims it is the Church which is here understood as being originally innocent but now dark with its wrongdoing.

The problem is not easily solved. I should rather like to add to the confusion by suggesting that what Dante possibly has in mind is the darkening of the visage of Proserpina, who, raped by Pluto as a young girl, is returned to her mother, Ceres, for half the year. Here are Ovid's lines describing her appearance when she returns to her mother:

Vertitur extemplo facies et mentis et oris;
Nam modo quae poterat Diti quoque maesta videri,
Laeta deae frons est, ut sol, qui tectus aquosis
Nubibus ante fuit, victis e nubibus exit.

[44] *Komm.* III, 477.

[At once her aspect changes, within and without;
Where once even Pluto saw her brow full of sadness,
Now it is joyful, as the sun, hidden a moment before
Behind rain-clouds, comes out of them their conqueror.]
(*Meta.* v, 568-571)

Proserpina, as Dante might well have concluded from this passage for his own poetic purpose, was first white of brow and then dark. Proserpina is the daughter of Ceres and Jove. That Dante has thought of Jove as the sun-god is apparent in *Purgatorio* xxix, 120, where it is Jove who destroys the careening chariot of Phaethon and puts the sun back in its proper orbit. Thus Proserpina "fits" as the fair daughter of him who brings morning and leaves evening. In addition, we have seen Dante frequently use Jove as a circumlocution for the Christian God, especially in *Purgatorio* vi, 118, where "O sommo Giove" is his apostrophe of Christ. And, if Dante is referring to the Ovidian here, it is probable that he will be adjusting that tale to a Christian significance.

As we have seen before, Proserpina is a figure of Eve[45] for Dante. If he is thinking of her story now, it is more than likely that he will be also thinking of Eve's. As Proserpina, the daughter of Jove, has her youthful countenance changed from white to black, so Eve, the daughter of God, lost the innocence with which she was made— metaphorically turning from white to black.

There is another passage, this one from Scripture, which would seem to be even more apposite.[46] It is from the Canticum Canticorum, I:5-6:

[45] See my discussion of *Purg.* XXVII, 49-51, above, and 191n.
[46] For this ascription see Erich Auerbach, "Figurative Texts Illustrating Certain Passages of Dante's *Commedia*," *Speculum*, XXI (1946), 485-488. Also H. D. Austin, " 'Black But Comely' (*Par.* XXVII, 136-138)," *Philological Quarterly*, XV (1936), 352-357. For an interesting

Nigra sum, sed *formosa*, filiae Jerusalem, sicut tabernacula Cedar, sicut *pelles* Salamonis.

Nolite me considerare, quod fusca sim, quia *decoloravit me sol*: filii matris meae pugnaverunt contra me, posuerunt me custodem in vineis: vineam meam non custodivi.   (italics mine)

[I am black, but comely, O ye daughters of Jerusalem, as the tents of Kedar, as the curtains of Solomon.

Look not upon me, because I am black, because the sun hath looked upon me: my mother's children were angry with me; they made me the keeper of the vineyards; but mine own vineyard have I not kept.]

The *beautiful, black* daughter, *discolored by the sun* (the King James does not preserve the literal sense of Dante's Vulgata here)—and even the word for skin, *pelles*, although its literal meaning is not the same in Dante's passage (the same can be said for the correspondence between the Bible's *filiae* and Dante's *figlia*)—these elements the Biblical passage and Dante's *terzina* have in common. And perhaps for Dante, in the concluding utterance of the comely bride-to-be there is an Edenic reminiscence in the "vineam meam non custodivi," for, al-

argument, one whose steps are of more use than its surprising conclusion that the *bella figlia* is Lucifer, see J. E. Shaw, " 'And the Evening and the Morning Were One Day' (*Paradiso*, XXVII, 136-138)," *Modern Philology*, XVIII (1921), 569-590. C. Spicq, *Esquisse d'une histoire de l'exégèse latine au moyen âge*, Paris, 1944, pp. 395-401, presents a "Table des commentaires bibliques" which shows that medieval exegetes compiled more commentaries on the Psalms and the Song of Solomon than on any other books of the Bible. Moore cites Cantic. I, 5, for *Purg.* XI, 116-117, thus buttressing the notion that Dante had Solomon's Song close to mind while writing the *Commedia*, although one hardly needs to be told this.

though the sense of the Canticum must be turned totally around, that is a fairly precise recapitulation of Eve's failure in the garden, which she was to "operaretur, et custodiret" (Genesis 2:15) with Adam. In that case, Dante might have found, in either passage or in both, ancient configurations which fitted his meaning here. Both Proserpina and the comely maid of Solomon are easily relatable, figurally, to Eve. And Eve, as we know, is for the medieval poet or theologian the type of the Church. Through this process, which is speculation, and about which I feel a certain uncomfortable venturesomeness, I come eventually to Scartazzini's identification of the *bella figlia* with the Church.[47] Nevertheless, it does seem to me that Dante is here making a literary allusion, not a made-up allegory which is ascertainable *in verbis* alone, which is Scartazzini's process. The passage is hinged by *così* to the two preceding *terzine*, which are based on the sort of observation of children that marks the early books of Augustine's *Confessions*, seeing in the infant the beast which must be regulated. And if the passage is hinged to the poetry of observation, it would be customary of Dante to have "guaranteed" his observation with a literary allusion. Prosperina works well here because she, like the first child, eats her own perdition (in this she is again like Eve), for she, Ovid tells us, could have left Hades forever had she refrained from eating while she was there: that is the command of Jove. Unfortunately, she ate the seven pomegranate seeds.[48] It is

---

[47] The passage in *Par.* XXII, which also attacks the degeneracy of the Church, or, at least, of her officials, uses similar language: "bianco fatto bruno" (line 93). Austin (see note 46 above) also points this out.

[48] *Meta.* v, 536-538. Proserpina "decerpserat arbore pomum," which is as close to describing Eve's sin as we may expect Ovid to come. While the whole of Dante's passage and the whole of Ovid's story have many elements in common, there are also some which they do not. Perhaps the most arresting detail which would argue for an intentional cor-

a good story for a Christian poem, whether Dante meant us to consider it or not; again, I am not at all sure that he did.

The upshot of the preceding nine lines is Beatrice's reassertion of Marco's lament that there are no good governors on earth, and that is why faith and innocence are found in little children alone and why the human family goes off the path it should follow. And this rounding off of her argument is followed by a prophecy. As Dante carried us back to the language of the initiation of the discourse on love in *Purgatorio* XVI and to the language that continued Marco's *pargoleggia* in Beatrice's charge to Dante, we will not be surprised that for the language of the prophecy he returns to the voyage of Ulysses. Dante has already seen traces of the voyage: in this canto when he looked back to earth; during the arrival of the pilgrim ship with the celestial captain on its poop in *Purgatorio* II; within his dream of the Siren, who turned Ulysses in *Purgatorio* XIX; and when Beatrice appeared as admiral in *Purgatorio* XXX.

Strangely enough, the prophecy's opening time reference literally intends us to understand that it will not be long until "January is thoroughly unwintered." Dante is mocking the Julian calendar's making of the year a quarter of an hour too long (roughly one-hundredth of a day), the result of which would be that relatively soon January would begin in spring-like weather, because since the

---

respondence is the common reference to the breaking of fast-laws. The child who eats all manner of food no matter what the month in Dante's passage is perhaps his version of Proserpina, who is not allowed to return to the earth without ties to the underworld: "Non ita fata sinunt, quoniam jejunia virgo/ Solverat" (*Meta.* V, 533-534). Her breaking of the fast-laws (*jejunia*) is answered by the faithful and obedient child of Dante's line (130) who keeps the fasts (*digiuna*), while that same child will later break them.

calendar was instituted in 46 B.C., it had been eating up the year at the rate of roughly one hour each five years, or about eleven days between 46 B.C. and Dante's time. As Dante has just now arrived in that heaven where time has its roots (118), it is a fitting denunciation of man, who cannot even tell time correctly. The calendar is another sign of man's neglect of the things that come from God.

What the prophecy promises is the coming of "la fortuna che tanto s'aspetta." *Fortuna* would seem here to have its secondary meaning of a storm at sea.[49] Yet it seems likely that Dante intends the word both ways, making an elevated pun on it. As the spheres in the line before are thought of as turning to bring the prophecy about in God's own time, as it were, I think it fairly natural that Dante here considers them as the axle of fortune's wheel, an image he has frequently used (*Inf.* VII, 96; xv, 95; xxx, 13; *Par.* XVI, 84).[50] The spheres are the eternal turnings upon which human time turns, and Fortune's tempest awaits all those who have left God's way. Benvenuto da Imola's commentary says that the word signifies "adventus veltri, qui debet extirpare cupiditatem de mundo, qui multum expectatur et desideratur" ("the coming of the Veltro, who shall banish cupidity from the world, and who is much awaited and much desired"). Seeing in the Beatricean prophecy a rehearsal of Virgil's earlier promise of the Veltro (*Inf.* I) should probably be augmented by the recognition of

[49] According to D. Du Cange, *Glossarium mediae et infimae latinitatis*, Paris, 1846, its third meaning, for which he cites several thirteenth-century uses. The first two are "Bona" and "Thesaurus inventus," the third "Maris tempestas." For a discussion of Dante's polyseme sense of the word, see Giuseppe Berretta, " 'Fortuna' e responsabilità umana in Dante," *Filologia e Letteratura*, XII (1966), 243-252.

[50] Although he more often means the goddess by *fortuna*, Dante has also previously used the word to signify a storm at sea (*Purg.* XXXII, 116), as well as a more generalized disaster (*Par.* XVII, 26).

Beatrice's own prophecy of the DXV (*Purg.* xxxiii) behind this Paradisal one. Without becoming embroiled in the enormous body of scholarship that surrounds these two prophecies,[51] I would like to observe here that each, at its first remove, prophesies the coming of a great temporal leader. As I have noted earlier, the model for the Veltro of Virgil is Jupiter's prophecy of the coming of Augustus in *Aeneid* i.[52] Thus, although each prophecy is given in deliberately obscure language (a fact which too many of the commentators brush past), we can be fairly sure that Dante intends his reader to understand that someone will come to govern the earth as it ought to be governed, whether this be Henry VII of Luxembourg, or Can Grande della Scala, or simply *some*one, *some* new Augustus. For both passages it is hard to imagine a literal meaning other than this. However, and here again figuralism is of use to Dante and to his reader, the bifocal vision of Scripture could have taught Dante to see the great leaders of this world as figures of Christ. One need only think of the examples of Moses and David. And so, if the two great prophecies foretell the coming of a temporal leader, they both also foretell, easily and naturally, a second future event which will be the fulfillment of the *figura* which

[51] For a survey of recent criticism on the Veltro problem see Bruno Maier, "Le principali 'cruces' della 'Divina Commedia' nella critica contemporanea," *Cultura e Scuola*, IV (1965), 275-277. For the place of the Veltro among other "enigmas" of the *Commedia* see the most recent treatment of this aspect of the poem, Paul Renucci, "Dantismo esoterico nel secolo presente," *Atti del Congresso Internazionale di Studi Danteschi*, Florence, 1965, pp. 305-332. The most important recent attempts to identify the Veltro are: Vittorio Cian, *Oltre l'enigma dantesco del Veltro*, Torino, 1945; Leonardo Olschki, *Dante 'Poeta Veltro,'* Florence, 1953; Erich von Richthofen, *Veltro und Diana*, Tübingen, 1956; R. E. Kaske, "Dante's 'DXV' and 'Veltro,' " *Traditio*, XVII (1961), 185-254; G. R. Sarolli, "Dante 'scriba Dei,' " *Convivium*, XXXI (1963), 513-544.

[52] See Chapter II, note 33.

that temporal savior is; that is, each prophecy foretells the Second Coming of Christ, as Kaske and Sarolli so effectively demonstrate. The language of each passage bears out this second and simultaneous meaning. Here is Virgil's description of the Veltro:

> Questi non ciberà terra né peltro,
>   ma sapienza, amore e virtute,
>   e sua nazion sarà tra Feltro e Feltro.

[He shall not feed on land or wealth,
    but on wisdom, love and power;
    and his nation shall be between Feltro and Feltro.]
                                        (*Inf.* i, 103-105)

Without going into the various scholarly discussions of what or where Feltro is, I accept one of the most simple and accepted solutions,[53] namely that the places are Feltre in Venezia and Montefeltro in Romagna, and that the hoped for leader is thus, in this passage, Can Grande della Scala, whose *nazione* is Verona, which Dante sees as growing under his command to include in its sphere of control and guidance all of northern Italy. This cartographical method draws a line north-south between two Italian cities, and indicates a large area within Italy itself. But why didn't Dante say, then, between Feltre and Feltro? One might argue that he did but that his amanuensis botched it. I would prefer to argue that Dante wanted to repeat the name of one of the two towns, since, although to my knowledge no one has thought of it, the configuration yields simply and easily the promise of Christ to come again. We know that, as He judges from the Great White Throne, His *nazione* shall be the whole world, as His

---

[53] Although it is vigorously opposed in Sapegno's commentary, as well as in others.

birthplace (an alternate reading of *nazione* frequently advanced) was once this world. If one draws a great circle arc (Dante likes such geometric behavior, and resorts to it frequently himself—and, although we are sometimes surprised when we are reminded of the fact, he did know the world was a globe, despite Queen Isabella's later apocryphal ignorance) through the point on the globe that is Feltre (or Montefeltro, or *any* town) one ends up by girdling the world, that is, indicating all of it. And so, if the temporal leader is to be Can Grande (or anyone else), whose domain is expressed cartographically, so he in turn prefigures the Second Coming,[54] its boundaries similarly expressed. Thus, although the Veltro himself is first of all an opaque and almost all-purpose prophetic embodiment, if the language of the whole prophecy is suitably obscure, the kind of thought it expresses and relies on is readily understandable.

Similarly, Beatrice's prophecy, which balances Virgil's in perfect aesthetic harmony, occurring 102 lines from the end of *Purgatorio* as Virgil's Veltro appears 101 lines from the beginning of *Inferno*, balances it also with respect to content. Dante has seen the "anti-triumph" which represents the decline of the West, culminating in the flight of the Imperial-Divine eagle from the chariot and his replacement by the giant and the harlot, usually identified as Philip IV of France and the Papacy, which has become the

[54] The difficulty with most of the Veltro criticism is, it seems to me, its desire to find a single reference. The Hound is found to mean, variously, either a particular governor *or* Christ to come. Olschki (see note 51 above) argues even less convincingly for Dante as the Veltro. Dante is the poet *of* the Veltro, to be sure, but the Veltro is itself, a veiled reference to the Emperor, earthly, and then divine. Lubac, vol. IV, p. 257, cites Philargyrius glossing the *nova progenies* of the Fourth Eclogue: "Augustum dicit; aestimavit enim Virgilius quod de Augusto Praedixit Sibylla, cum de Christo omnia prophetavit."

Whore of Babylon in Dante's eyes. Here are Beatrice's words:

> . . . un cinquecento diece e cinque,
> messo di Dio, anciderà la fuia
> con quel gigante che con lei delinque.

> [. . . a five-hundred, ten and five,
> one sent from God, shall kill the thief
> with the giant who offends with her.]
>
> (*Purg.* XXXIII, 43-45)

This is the one, the heir of the eagle, who shall come to power soon. Grandgent's suggestions here are excellent, I believe.[55] As a number, 515 (almost certainly modeled on Revelation's number of the beast, 666, which spells out, for the commentators of that Book, DCLXVI, and thus DIC LUX, or thus, as Gmelin points out,[56] *dicit essem lucem*, for Satan claiming that he, Lucifer, is the light and not Christ) spells out, with a similar transposition of its Roman letter-numerals, DXV, thus DVX, thus DUX (V and U being interchangeable in Latin), or "leader." Whether the king is Henry VII or Can Grande or someone else is not of primary interest here. What is of interest is that at the first remove the prophecy is of a temporal leader. But, as Grandgent points out in his analysis of *Purgatorio* XXXIII (he does not note the pregnancy of that number as bearing Christological potency for Dante, who will look on the Incarnate Godhead in *Paradiso* XXXIII),

---

[55] Pp. 635-637. Kaske's argument for the *Vere dignum*, while extraordinarily well documented and on the whole convincing, contains, as does his entire solution of the problem, an unfortunate unilateralism. Assuming that Dante had the *Vere dignum* closely in mind, he nevertheless would have been totally unsusceptible to obvious suggestiveness had he himself not been also aware, and expected his reader to be aware, that a D and an X and a V, only slightly juggled, spell "dux." But see Kaske, *Traditio*, pp. 199-201.   [56] *Komm.* II, p. 523.

Christ is also present here. He cites the traditional Greek abbreviation of the Christ, the Chi and the Ro, which comes out in Latin looking like a P superimposed upon an X, and goes on to say that this sign was sometimes interpreted as "Deus Christus Venturus," "The Lord Christ to come." Charlemagne whose coronation took place on Christmas Day in the year 800, was the last true Emperor for Dante (see Canto VI *Paradiso*, where that is Justinian's opinion). Thus, adding 515 to 800 indicates a date on which Dante expects his man to be victorious: 1315, ten years after the Papacy moved to Avignon.[57] He was, perhaps, almost right, since Henry VII died in 1313 as he was about to lay siege to Florence. What we want—whether we propose a unilateral reading either for a temporal or a spiritual redeemer, or a bilateral one, such as the one I am tentatively proposing here—is a reason for the number as number. In other words, who or what is a 515? (Beatrice is a nine, after all.) And here, it seems to me, none but Grandgent, following Davidsohn, has given an even slightly plausible explanation, one that even the scholarship and ingenuity of men as schooled and ingenious as Kaske and Sarolli have not overtaken. I confess that I share with most *dantisti* the desire to "solve" the riddle. I have not solved it, despite many a long night when I felt close to it, delving in the Apocrypha, the Fathers, Biblical concordances; looking for numbers in Ovid, Statius, Lucan, and of course Virgil; letting Dante make a fool of me too. Nevertheless, I should like to put down here my two best conjectures. First, of all the documents which may serve to elucidate Beatrice's prophecy, I find none so enlightening as Dante's own Epistles, those three probably written dur-

[57] This is the opinion of R. Davidsohn, "Il cinquecento dieci e cinque del *Purgatorio*," *Bullettino della Società Dantesca Italiana*, IX (1903), 129-131.

ing 1310 and 1311 at the height of passionate hope for the deliverance of Florence and of all Italy by Henry VII (*Epistolae* v, vi, and vii). There we find Henry referred to as the second Moses (*Moysen alium*) leading his people from Egypt (v, i, 4); he is "divus et Augustus et Cesar" (v, ii, 5), thus holy and Roman; again he is Caesar (v, iii, 7) and Augustus (v, iii, 10), but now by "Augustus" Dante refers to Julius Caesar, for he refers to that "Augustus" who defeated Pompey at Pharsalia, and that was Julius; he shall be like an eagle swooping back down to find invading crows in its nest (v, iv, 11); in him the power both of Peter and of Caesar is joined ("biffurcatur Petri Cesarisque potestas"—v, v, 17); he is ordained by Jesus, we are exhorted to honor him by Peter and by Clement, Peter's successor (v, x, 28, 30). *Epistola* vi continues the same themes: the barricaded Florentines are warned that Henry is the triumphant and divine bearer of the Roman tradition and that it is as though Isaiah had foretold that he would come after Christ (vi, vi, 24)— perhaps no other passage in the *Epistolae* shows a joining of temporal and divine elements as forceful as this one. *Epistola* vii begs Henry to shorten the delay which has joined itself to his mission: Henry, crossing the Apennines, is successor of Caesar and of Augustus (vii, i, 5); he brings to mind the prophecy made in Virgil's Fourth Eclogue (vii, i, 6); his delay reminds us of the question of John the Baptist, "Art thou he who should come or do we look for another?" (vii, ii, 7); embracing his feet Dante said silently to himself, "Behold the Lamb of God! Behold him who hath taken away the sins of the world!" (vii, ii, 10); his coming is prophesied in Virgil's prophecy of Augustus (*Aeneid* i, 286f—Dante quotes two of its lines here—vii, iii, 13); John, his firstborn son, is "alter Ascanius" (and thus Henry is the second Aeneas by implication—vii, v, 18); Henry should remember Samuel's words to Saul, and not be infirm of purpose as was Saul (Dante will return to I Samuel shortly when he urges the new David to slay the new Goliath, but here he cites only the negative part of the story—vii, v, 19); Henry, the new David (the second stem of Jesse—"proles altera Isai") is urged to kill Goliath and thus deliver Israel, in the Babylonian captivity and longing for sacrosanct Jerusalem (vii, viii, 29-30).

This brief recitation of the figural analogues to Henry we find in the *Epistolae* gives an immediate sense of how thoroughly Dante intermingled the temporal and divine elements of his messianic urge for a new emperor. In light of the above demonstration from Dante's own most prophetic writing outside the *Commedia*, I find it impossible to consider it likely that the prophecy in *Purgatorio* xxxiii is only of the Second Coming of Christ. To go on to say that the temporal ruler Beatrice promises is in turn a promise of the Second Coming seems to me, on the other hand, altogether in keeping with what we have been able to learn about Dante's own expectations as well as his inclinations. What we still lack, however, for this temporal leader is a number, precisely, a 515. If Dante was thinking of Henry when he wrote *Purgatorio* xxxiii, either before or after the year 1313 and Henry's death, Davidsohn's suggestion is attractive: 1315 is possibly the year of the awaited coronation, and that would be 515 years after the coronation of Charlemagne. However, few authorities would accept the necessary complications that would force us to grant that *Purgatorio* xxxiii was written before 1313, or even 1315 (which date itself would still leave those who support Davidsohn's theory in the difficult position of having to argue that Dante retained the mystical importance of the date even after he no longer held any genuine hopes for the recovery of Italia in that year). It would be pleasing to find, in a source Dante undoubtedly knew, a 515 which is not relative to such dubious criteria.

"Julius Caesar, an. v. Hic primus monarchiam tenuit. VM. CLV." That is the inscription to be found in Isidore of Seville's universal history of the world (*Etymologiae* v, xxxix, 25). It is the concluding entry for the Fifth Age. Translated it means that in the year 5,155, numbering from the Creation, Julius Caesar was five years old, and that "he was the first to hold the monarchy." Did Dante possibly have this fact and those numbers in mind when he wrote the enigmatic prophecy? I should like to think so, but cannot urge upon the reader any sense of proof. I invite him to take the single mathematical step with me that makes this solution attractive: if Caesar was five years old in the year 5,155, then he was born in the year 5,150. And *that* number is a 515, just as, for Dante, the number 90 is also a "nine." If then, when Dante thought of the new ruler to come, whether he thought of him as Henry as a hoped for but as yet unknown ruler, or as any particular ruler (Henry's son John?), he thought of him as the new Julius, we would not, or should not, be surprised.

At any rate, as Charlemagne was the last true Emperor, figuring the next true Emperor in the line of the great Augustus, in which Julius, "primus monarchiam tenuit," so all the great earthly emperors foreshadow the true Empire on Earth at the Second Coming. Beatrice's words, like Virgil's, have the power to reveal while concealing. The DXV is also the Christ who shall slay all sin forever. Beatrice reminds us of Eve and of Adam in line 57 when she says of the tree which we have just seen robbed of its foliage, that it has been robbed once before. Surely she alludes to Eve's, and then Adam's, eating of the apple. Thus Eve and Adam stand behind the thievish woman and

189

the giant as historical figures of this pageant, which has hidden current history under its veil (Philip and the Avignonian captivity of Holy Church, turned harlot), and now reveals its root in the primal disobedience, the fruit of which Christ shall put away forever at the Last Judgment.

Beatrice's prophecy in *Paradiso* XXVII has its beginning in the earlier prophecies of the *Commedia*. And if Benvenuto da Imola sees the trace of the Veltro here, I will not argue. The *fortuna* is thus a storm at sea for those who live in the rain of *cupidigia*, it is the rightful wheeling of the wheel of Fortune, and it shall be a piece of good fortune, a windfall,[58] to the race when justice comes again, as that shall be the day on which the rest of the Paradisal flower is petaled, that day on which Christ sends all who rest on earth and are worthy to their eternal reward. Beatrice's last words, "and true fruit shall come upon the flower," would seem to move us anagogically upward toward Paradise as well as morally forward below. But what is of greatest interest to me here is the implicit reference to Ulysses, who becomes again the type of errant man. For it was his *poppa* that was faced the wrong way, turned to the morning (*Inf.* XXVI, 124) where his *prora* should have been, and that was then lifted up, inverted, as his ship sank (line 140). It is Beatrice who is the true admiral in *Purgatorio* XXX, 58, who is "in poppa ed in prora"[59] taking care of her fleet, as the temporal leader-Christ is the true admiral who shall turn our fleet around and make it run

[58] See the second meaning of *fortuna* given in Du Cange (see note 49 above), which is "Thesaurus inventus."

[59] Isidore, discussing the parts of ships, begins with *puppis* and *prora* (*Ety.* XIX, ii, 1); "*Puppis* posterior pars navis est, quasi *post*. *Prora* anterior, quasi *priora*. . . ." This derivation of the two words, although thoroughly commonplace, may have offered Dante some reinforcement for his morally significant naval architecture.

diretta after it has so long been off the way ("onde si svia l'umana famiglia").[60] Again this reminds us of the dream of the Siren's use of that word, which in turn reflected the opening moment of the poem where Dante, going as one fulfillment of all earlier divagational journeys, had lost *la diritta via*. In the poem these journeys have been expressed primarily in terms of the errant Dante and the wandering Ulysses.

This concludes the examination of the extraordinary use of figural techniques that intertwine through the discussions of love, the dreams, and the encounters with Matelda and Beatrice in the *Purgatorio*, and it prepares the way for a related subject, the figural relationships of the voyager Dante in *Paradiso*.

[60] This final reference to *Par.* xxvii offers an opportunity to point to another source, direct or indirect, that may stand behind Dante's *bella figlia*. The first two lines of Prudentius' poeticized "history of the Bible," his *Dittochaeon*, describe Eve as white, becoming black because of the deceitful venom of the serpent: "Eva columba fuit tunc candida; nigra deinde/ facta per anguinum malesuada fraude venenum."

CHAPTER V

DANTE'S VOYAGE: HISTORY
AS "SHADOWY PREFACES"

As Beatrice explains in Canto IV: Paradise, that is, the actual place where God is, is the Empyrean. Thus the rest of *Paradiso*, that is, the poem, is not Paradise, but an accommodative metaphor (*Par.* IV, 28-63),[1] actually a series of nine metaphors, in which the truth of Heaven is gradually made clear by the kind of analogy that Grace alone affords, as spirits who actually dwell in the Empyrean with God descend from their seats in the celestial stadium-rose to make the hierarchical structure and meaning of God's truth known to man.

Thus, true Paradise has two introductions: the first as we enter the poem, when Dante is the poet who has already had his vision and asks God, his Muse, to help him tell it; and then again, in Canto XXX, as he is about to enter the Empyrean. Since, in the temporal succession of the journey, the latter occurs first, I should like to begin with it. The canto opens with reference to the waning of the last hour before daybreak. As Aurora advances, the lights of the stars disappear one by one. Just so, within the poem, the rest of the universe, the material spheres, are now dimmed by the pure intellectual light of the Empyrean. Dante's preparation for another event is also evident in his nine

[1] This discussion includes Dante's example of accommodation: the condescension of Scripture to human intelligence when it attributes feet and hands to God (lines 43-45). So here in Paradise God allows his souls to appear to Dante in the appropriate spheres, while actually they are in the Empyrean. For an excellent discussion of *Paradiso*'s movement toward abstraction, and then toward concretion, see Fredi Chiappelli, "La struttura figurativa del *Paradiso*," *DDJb*, XLIII (1965), 25-41.

opening lines, for they conclude by saying that in the reddening brought by Aurora, handmaid of the sun, the last to disappear is the most beautiful star (line 9). Surely this is the morning star, Venus, the last star that we can see at dawn. And just as God's greater light makes all the lovely lesser lights disappear, even to the most beautiful, so the anticipation of Dante's direct vision of that light prepares us for the disappearance of Beatrice. In each case the loss is not an unhappy one. And in Canto XXXI Dante will not grieve at the loss as he grieved in *Purgatorio* xxx when he found his Virgil gone. But now, before she goes, he will see her more brilliant than ever before, so brilliant indeed that all that has been said of her before, gathered in one praise, would be insufficient to praise her now (19-21), and so brilliant that no other poet, comic or tragic, was ever so baffled about how to express a point in his theme (22-24). In the following lines Dante bids his formal farewell to Beatrice as the subject for his poetry (28-33), and she, as his guide, bids her farewell to Dante (38-45), promising him that he is about to see the angels and the saints, the latter as though in the flesh, as they shall appear at the Last Judgment. This promise perhaps reminds the reader that Dante will shortly gaze upon the very miracle of Incarnation, and at any rate certainly prepares us and him to experience a greater and higher reality than ever before experienced in the poem. Now suddenly an effulgence like lightning takes Dante's normal sight away, to prepare, Beatrice tells him (53-54), his eyes to behold the Empyrean. As many commentators point out, the word the poet uses to describe the action of this vivid light is a notable one: *circunfulse* (49).

Factum est autem, eunte me, et appropinquante
Damasco media die, subito de coelo *circumfulsit*
me lux copiosa.   (italics mine)

CHAPTER V

[And it came to pass, that, as I made my
journey, and was come nigh unto Damascus about
noon, suddenly there shone from heaven a great
light round about me.]   (Acts 22:6)

It was, Dante tells us with the single verbal echo, like
the light that shone upon Saul on the road to Damascus,
the light that enclosed the voice of Jesus. Dante is, figurally
speaking (we shall return to the theme shortly), Saul,
becoming a second Paul. What Dante sees next is technically the last accommodative metaphor of the poem. Unlike
the objects of sight in Cantos i-xxix, what he now sees is
actually as it is; it is his sight that is incapable of seeing
with the certainty it shall soon achieve. And so he sees as
he can understand, not as what he sees actually is. First we
examine what he sees, and then what Beatrice tells him
about his vision.

> E vidi lume in forma di rivera
>   fluvido di fulgore, intra due rive
>   dipinte di mirabil primavera.
> Di tal fiumana uscian faville vive,
>   e d'ogni parte si mettean ne' fiori,
>   quasi rubin che oro circunscrive.
> Poi, come inebriate da li odori,
>   riprofondavan sé nel miro gurge;
>   e s'una intrava, un'altra n'uscia fori.

[And I saw light in form of a river
    of flowing effulgence between two banks
    painted with wonderful spring.
From this flood came forth living sparks,
    and everywhere they nestled in the flowers,
    like rubies set in gold.

Then, as though intoxicated with the odors,
   they plunged deep again in the marvellous torrent;
   and, as one went in, another came out.]

(Par. xxx, 61-69)

". . . il fiume e li topazii
ch'entrano ed escono e il rider de l'erbe
   son di lor vero umbriferi prefazii.
Non che da sé sian queste cose acerbe;
   me è difetto da la parte tua,
   che non hai viste ancor tanto superbe."

[". . . the river and the topazes
that go in and come out, as well as the smiling foliage,
are shadowy prefaces of their own reality.
Not that they are unripe in themselves;
   rather, the defect is in thee,
   whose eyes are not yet similarly exalted."]

(Par. xxx, 76-81)

Since this is the last moment in the poem when the
Pilgrim sees with earthly vision, it should not be a surprise
that he sees the realm of God, the Empyrean, as though it
were the Earthly Paradise, which is a prefiguration of the
Empyrean. The word *giardino* is used four times in the
poem,[2] beginning in *Paradiso* XXIII. In XXVI, 110, Adam
refers to the Earthly Paradise. The three other times (*Par.*
XXIII, 71; XXXI, 97; XXXII, 39) the word is used, once by
Beatrice and twice by Bernard, to designate the celestial
rose of the Empyrean. But this garden, though understandable to some degree by the analogue of Eden, is of a
different order. Thus, before Dante is able to see the

---

[2] Johan Chydenius, *The Typological Problem in Dante*, p. 109,
makes this observation.

Empyrean as it is, he sees it as it is not; that is, he sees it as though it were merely Eden.[3] And so, just as Dante had to be rebaptised in Lethe and Eunoe, now he must have his eyes "baptised" in the river of light, at Beatrice's direction.[4] At some distance this is an amusing action to behold (lines 85-89), for Dante bathes his eyes in an accommodative metaphor, in something that is other than it seems to be. It is perhaps instructive to recall that in the Canto I of *Inferno* the Pilgrim nearly drowns in a metaphor—the lake of his heart from which he scrambles to shore (lines 20-24). Nevertheless, we should take the moment seriously, for it marks the completion of the spiritual development of the Pilgrim, which has been one of the two prime subjects of the poem for ninety-seven cantos.[5]

Dante is seeing the celestial rose through a glass darkly. In a moment, in a very few lines in fact, he shall see face to face. To express the relationship between the two visions Dante resorts to the language of biblical exegesis, as is totally natural to him. The phrase *umbriferi prefazii* makes his vision *now* the prefiguration of his vision *then*; to put it another way, the river of light[6] is the *umbra* of which the rose is the fulfillment. That Dante uses a Latinate word here, as Gmelin points out, is probably significant. We have previously observed that he does use the Italian *ombra*, in some cases, with exegetical precision, or at least the overtone of exegetical precision. But Gmelin's

[3] The language is strikingly similar to the description of Eden in *Purg.* XXVIII, 25f.

[4] A student of mine, Herbert Marks, has suggested in a paper that this "third baptism" may reflect a Church tradition which requires triple immersion in cases of adult baptism.

[5] The other being, as the Letter to Can Grande states, "the state of the souls after death." See Chapter I, note 34, and Chapter III, note 34.

[6] For a discussion of a probable source for the "river" see Edw. C. Witke, "The River of Light in the *Anticlaudianus* and the *Divina Commedia*," *Classical Review*, XI (1959), 144-156.

comment on the phrase, while it does point to what he calls its "diverse nuances of meaning" ("verschiedenen Bedeutungsnüancen"—*Komm.* III, p. 520), fails to see what is, for the purposes of this study, the most cogent nuance of all. The Latin *umbra* has its Virgilian meaning of shade, its Ovidian and Virgilian resonance of those shady pastoral places, and its refraction of its exegetical use by the various Fathers of the Church and the later commentators known to Dante. Since we are about to leave the mortal realms of God's universe to experience the truth *sub specie aeternitatis*, to leap into the anagoge, as it were, it is fitting that Dante should have given the moment a structure in terms of the notion of *figura* and fulfilment. Strictly speaking, this should be the last use of figuralism in the work, since we are about to leave the realm of figures, the mortal realm, to gaze upon pure fulfilment. As we shall see shortly however, such is not the case.[7]

[7] The notion that various parts of the *Commedia* are primarily devoted to a single sense of the four senses of exegetical practice has been advanced by Francis Fergusson, *Dante's Drama of the Mind*, pp. 180-182 (and repeated in his later study, *Dante*, pp. 94-95). Though sharing many of his contentions about Dante's use of the fourfold, I differ sharply here. His scheme makes *Inferno* literal, the first twenty-seven cantos of *Purgatorio* moral, the Earthly Paradise figural (allegorical), and *Paradiso* anagogical. This would be roughly akin to reading the Bible under the following rubric: Old Testament history literal, its prophetic books, Psalms, and Solomon moral, Gospels and Acts figural (allegorical), Revelation anagogical. There is a certain critical insight thus attained, it seems to me, into both works. However, we must realize that neither Augustine, Aquinas, nor Dante ever went on record as thinking of the Bible in this light. What is most wrong with this way of adapting fourteenth century practice to twentieth century purposes is that it erases the great advantage the medieval mind built into the system, that of having four senses simultaneously. Furthermore, the theory is easily defeated by Dante's poem itself, which is everywhere (with the exceptions spoken to in my sixth chapter) literal/historical; which uses figural techniques in each *cantica*, including the last canto of *Paradiso*, which should be completely anagogical according

What Dante sees after his eyes are made perfect is the rose with its population of the souls of the blessed. He compares the moment to that of the unmasking (at a ball?), when those who are hidden behind masks suddenly make themselves clearly visible (lines 91-96). What he sees is, more importantly, expressed geometrically in the phrase which makes the linear river become round rose (89-90), thus projecting a sense of history become eternity. The implications of this will become clear in the last three cantos. For now Dante has finished his preparation for that vision, which concludes with the penultimate invocation of the *Divine Comedy*: "O splendor of God, by which I saw/ the high triumph of the true kingdom,/ give me the power to tell how I beheld it!" (lines 97-99).

As I suggested at the opening of the chapter, there are actually two introductions to the Empyrean, the one we have just examined in Canto xxx, as well as the one that is to be found in Canto i. That canto must also serve primarily as introduction to the entire *cantica*, to be sure. And yet its first line, "La gloria di colui che tutto move," is the basis for the last line in the poem, "l'amor che move il sole e l'altre stelle." This circling movement turns precisely about God, the triune point from which all radiates, and somehow, as the *cantica* begins, we are still at that point. That is, the first thirty-six lines of *Paradiso* i "take place" after the action of the entire *Commedia* is finished, that is, after Dante has returned to earth to write the poem. To make this more clear, let us answer the following question: why does *Paradiso* not begin with the sphere of the Moon, which is the next body up from Earth? The an-

---

to the scheme; which gives moral instruction *passim*; and which denotes its anagogical propensity from the moment we find God's name on Hell Gate.

swer, I believe, is that in ascending from the Earthly
Paradise there is only one destination, and that is to be
with God Himself. To make the ascent to the Moon
Dante's first goal would be to turn the poem into a sort
of pre–seventeenth-century adventure-voyage poem, while
its actual import is nothing less than Revelation. The second question that devolves from this is harder to answer,
although it has seemed not to bother the commentators at
all: where is Dante before he lands in the Moon (*Par.* II,
25)? One answer is, with Beatrice. But where is she? With
God. Somehow, Dante's doctrine and logic would seem to
suggest that *Paradiso* opens its action (after the invocation
concludes the "front matter," line 36) in a place which is
not a place, but a state of spirit. And that place, although
Dante's imperfect intellect (if *Inferno* is the record of the
correction of his will; if *Purgatorio* is the record of the
perfection of his will; then *Paradiso* would seem to be the
record of the correction and, finally, perfection of his
intellect)[8] cannot grasp the fact, is in God's heaven, that

[8] If there is anything to this schematization, it may be advanced in
the following precise way: *Inferno* is entirely devoted to the correction
of the will; *Purgatorio* I-XXVII, the last line of which has Virgil
awarding Dante crown and mitre over himself, records the perfection
of the will through the purgatorial experience of the sins experienced
first in Hell; *Purgatorio* XXVIII shows us a Dante who, though morally
fit, is of weak understanding (he immediately fails to understand
Matelda in her true light, finding only that she is like pagan ladies of
love), the correction of which moves to progressively higher spheres,
until he reaches the river of light in *Paradiso* XXX; going beyond that
barrier, his intellect is perfected in the last three cantos. Two pleasing
formulations additionally accrue to the scheme. First, the three guides
of the *Commedia* have clearly delineated tasks: Virgil, correction and
perfection of Dante's will; Beatrice, correction of his intellect (no
wonder so many readers find her unpleasant); Bernard, perfection of
his intellect. Second, the place where each of the two changes of guide
occur is a new place, first the literal Earthly Paradise (*Purg.* XXVIII)
and then the river of light, itself a shadow of the Earthly Paradise.

is, the Empyrean. Perhaps this explains the frequent references in Canto 1 to the Empyrean (lines 4, 23, 93, 106-
108, 122), which is the goal of the ascent, and the absence
of references to the intervening spheres. And yet it is impossible for Dante and Beatrice to be in the Empyrean for
the simple reason that they are going to go there. We
do know that Dante's trip through Paradise takes no time
as it is experienced, although it takes twenty-four hours if
we measure his absence from Earth, and if he can perceive
the effect of time on the Earth from his vantage point in
the heavens, which he does, as is shown by his differing observations of the Earth's surface in Cantos xxii and xxvii.
Thus we are faced with the paradox that, as *Paradiso* opens,
Dante would seem to be with God, and yet cannot be in
the Empyrean. Perhaps it is not worth worrying about.
What does emerge from the paradox is one important fact:
the nine spheres that precede Empyrean offer Dante a
course in spiritual astronomy. In the nine spheres the order
of the Empyrean as well as the order of the Spheres will
appear to him. He will see unity in diversity, and then
diversity in unity. The souls who "appear" to him do so
only as "accommodations" to his mortal intelligence, while
they are actually elsewhere. So Piccarda and Cacciaguida

Further, we remember that Virgil appears to Dante in the ruined version
of Eden which is the *selva oscura of Inferno* 1. Two other general
schemes of this kind, each different from the other and both different
from mine, have recently appeared. Francis X. Newman, "St. Augustine's
Three Visions and the Structure of the Commedia," *MLN*, LXXXII
(1967), 56-78, working from *De Genesi ad litteram* XII, points to a
tripartite structural deployment of the *Commedia* according as it moves
from corporeal to spiritual to intellectual—Augustine's distinctions—
vision. Giorgio Petrocchi, "Dante and Thirteenth-Century Asceticism,"
in T. G. Bergin, ed., *From Time to Eternity*, New Haven, 1967, pp.
46-47, refers to Aquinas' distinctions concerning the three phases of
ascetic perfection (*S.T.* II-II, q. 24, art. 9): those of the *principianti,
progredienti,* and *perfecti.*

and all the other spirits send Dante a message of themselves which appears to him in a sphere where the message will be most appropriate. This, reflecting the notion of accommodative metaphor which allowed God, for greater human understanding, to write of Himself in the Bible as though he had human attributes, allows Dante to reject his *Timaeus* and keep it too.

And so the *cantica* begins with, in a sense at least, greater "reality" than we shall have again until Canto xxx. And the first action of the *cantica* is perhaps the most important one of all: Dante must become transhumanate.

The *cantica* begins with Dante writing it, his experiences completed. He is concerned, like Homer, only with the power of memory (line 9). He invokes Apollo for that power (13f), asking that "l'ombra del beato regno/ segnata nel mio capo io manifesti" ("I may show forth the shadow of the blessed kingdom/ which is insigned within my head"—23-24). (It is probably worth noting that in Italian the verb *segnare* often means "to mark with the sign of the Cross.") Again we have an interesting use of the word *ombra*. Here, if we take it exegetically, and I believe we may,[9] it makes Dante's experience of Empyrean and of the rest of *Paradiso* the figure of which the poem is the fulfilment. Once again, it would seem to me, Dante has borrowed from the exegetical tradition to plead the cause

[9] My reading here would seem possibly to be in accord with Sapegno's commentary, III, p. 6: "Ma qui è veramente un'*ombra* tenue e sbiadita della visione reale." Sapegno goes on to cite a similar usage in *Paradiso* XIII, 19: "l'ombra de la vera." Of this later passage Auerbach ("Figura," p. 63) says: "Here his poetry is characterized as an *umbra* of truth, engraved in his mind, and his theory of inspiration is sometimes expressed in statements that may be explained along the same lines. But these are only suggestions; an investigation purporting to explain the relation between Neoplatonic and figural elements in medieval aesthetics would require broader foundations."

that his words are not *parole fittizie*, but the kind of words that have the power to denote events themselves significant of other events. Thus, since the experiences were so great that they shook his memory, the remembrance of them is shadowy; but as they were also true, they are *ombre*, and that kind of shadow is real. The parallel between *umbriferi prefazii* and *l'ombra del beato regno*, each phase occurring in a passage which points to the experience of the Empyrean, even sets up a time scheme between the beginning and end of *Paradiso*: as Dante's imperfect vision of the celestial rose was an *ombra* of the truth he was about to see, so that truth is an *ombra* of what he is about to tell.

Canto I *Paradiso*, within fifty-seven lines (13-69), contains possibly the most dense Ovidian atmosphere and actual quotation of the *Metamorphoses* in the entire *Commedia*. C. A. Robson, in a recent study of the use Dante made of the medieval allegories on Ovid,[10] attempts to show that Dante made systematic reference to forty-seven of the myths recorded in the *Integumenta* of John of Garland (c.1234) and in the prose allegories of his predecessor, Arnulf of Orléans, claiming that Dante's actual imitation of Ovid is limited to less than a dozen passages, out of a total of some seventy which reflect the work of Ovid.[11] At

---

[10] "Dante's Use in the *Divina Commedia* of the Medieval Allegories on Ovid," in *Centenary Essays on Dante*, Oxford, 1965, pp. 1-38. For an earlier and more general study of the problem see L. K. Born, "Ovid and Allegory," *Speculum*, IX (1934), 362-379.

[11] As do Dante's Virgilian borrowings, his Ovidian reminiscences raise the question of his debt to the medieval commentators. An acquaintance with these documents was almost surely his as a young man. However, those who see his debt to them as being major and lasting simply overestimate, in my opinion, the force of these curiously mindless documents on the mind of a poet who had read widely and deeply in the very works these commentaries treat in so cavalier a way. A few hours with Fulgentius, Bernardus Silvestris, or, for that matter, John of Garland, should be enough to convince an impartial reader that the

the outset let us note again that the subject matter of *Paradiso* I is transhumanization: how a mortal becomes capable of moving up to another order of being. In Dante's case, this involves explaining, or actually not explaining, how Dante Alighieri could so change his human nature that he was able to see God's Kingdom. Thus there is no work in the Classical canon, with the exception of the Myth of Er in Plato's *Republic* (which Dante knew, not through Cicero's redaction of it in *De Republica*, but through Macrobius' version of the *Somnium Scipionis*),[12] which is as worthy a predecessor as the *Metamorphoses*, which give

---

Divine Comedy, though perhaps reflecting a formulation here and a phrasing there, was markedly uninfluenced by their relatively crass attempts at literary criticism. The fact that Dante, who refers with exhaustive plenitude to almost every literary man we could expect him to have known throughout the entire corpus of his work, and the fact that Dante not once refers to any one of these candidates often urged as influences upon him, provide, I submit, information enough to cast deep doubt upon such urging. It is the worst face of the history of ideas that shows itself in the notion that the literature of a given period is primarily the reflection of the minor literati of that period, that each medieval poem is the product of the same composite mind— that of the learned pedagogue Mr. Medieval. Professor Palgen's numerous works on this subject (see Chapter II, note 35) would almost have us believe that instead of encountering Ovid, Horace, Lucan, and his guide, Virgil, Dante should have been greeted in *Inferno* IV by Fulgentius and the other Virgilians, as well as by the author of the *Ovide moralisé*. The firmness of Palgen's conviction that Dante had his Classics through the mediating screen of lesser men is recently revealed again in his article, "Le teofanie nella 'Commedia,'" *Convivium*, XXXIV (1966), 115-139, where he argues (p. 136) for a commentator's influence on Dante's Glaucus because he finds the word *deifiez* in the *Ovide moralisé*. Are we to believe that Dante required the commentator's authority to understand that Glaucus was turned into a sea-god? It is as absurd to believe that Haydn will only be known to future generations as the man who wrote the music for "Deutschland über alles."

[12] See Curtius, *European Literature and the Latin Middle Ages*, p. 360, for a discussion of Dante's use of the *Somnium* in *Paradiso* XV, 25.

the histories of humans who are, to use Dante's word, transhumanated, and, in Ovid's term, metamorphosed. Thus the Ovidian book of changes is of particularly acute resonance for Dante here, where he must set down his own astonishing change, first prepared for in Lethe and Eunoe, and now effected by the gaze of Beatrice (line 67). Here Dante employs three Ovidian myths: Apollo and Daphne (13-15, 32-33), Apollo and Marsyas (19-21), and Glaucus (67-69).

> O buono Apollo, a l'ultimo lavoro
>   fammi del tuo valor sì fatto vaso,
>   come dimandi a dar l'amato alloro. . . .
> Sì rade volte, padre, se ne coglie
>   per triunfare o cesare o poeta,
>   colpa e vergogna de l'umane voglie,
> che parturir letizia in su la lieta
>   delfica deità dovria la fronda
>   peneia, quando alcun di sé asseta.

[O good Apollo, for the final labor
  make me such a vessel of thy worth
  as, for the gift of thy loved laurel,[18] thou requireth. . . .
So few times, father, are they [the laurel leaves] gathered
  to celebrate the triumph of Caesar or of poet—
  fault and shame of human wills—
that the Peneian bough, when it makes anyone athirst
  for itself, must give birth to joy
  in the joyous Delphic deity.]

(Par. I, 13-15, 28-33)

The Ovidian resonance of the passage is undoubted, even though, for instance, as Gmelin points out,[14] the phrase "a

---

[18] In lines 25-27 Dante will announce that he will come to Apollo's chosen tree in hopes of being crowned with laurel.

[14] *Komm.* III, p. 27.

l'ultimo lavoro" is likely to have been suggested by Virgil's invocation at the beginning of his final Eclogue, "Extremum hunc, Arethusa, mihi concede labore . . ." (*Ecl.* x, 1), while the plea to Apollo for the granting of his leaves is likely a reflection of Statius' *Achilleis*, with its opening invocation of Apollo, "Da fontes mihi, Phoebe, novos ac fronde secunda/ Necte comas . . ." (*Ach.* i, 9f). Nevertheless, the tale of Daphne's transformation is the tale which stands behind Dante's construction of Apollo as God the Father, the best of all possible Muses, by whom he asks to be made a vessel like Paul (see *Inferno* ii, 28, where Paul is "lo Vas d'elezione").[15] Was Dante influenced by John of Garland here, as Professor Robson proclaims? "Perhaps, however, the most revealing of Dante's debts to the forgotten John of Garland is to be found in the latter's allegorization of Apollo's pursuit of Daphne as the scholar's pursuit of fame:

> Mentibus hec arbor sapientum virgo virescit
> Que quamvis fugiat victa labore viret:
> Est virgo Phebi sapientia facta corona
> Laurus, quam cupida mente requirit homo."[16]

Robson claims that there is little doubt that Dante had these lines in mind when he wrote lines 13-15 of his invocation. Let us see.

In the passage which immediately precedes lines 28-33, Dante tells Apollo that he will come "al tuo diletto legno." In Ovid, when Apollo finally catches up with the fleeing girl, she turns into a tree, and Apollo kisses what is now

[15] And see the discussion of Apollo as Christian muse in P. Renucci, *Dante disciple et juge du monde gréco-latin*, vol. ii, Paris, 1954, pp. 204-206.

[16] Robson, p. 16.

tree: "Oscula dat ligno" (1, 356).[17] I find it easy to believe that Dante was pleased by this climactic moment in the myth—a god covering a tree with kisses is pretty good Ovid—and kept it in his own quieter form: "thy beloved tree." The phrase *amato alloro* (line 15) would also seem to echo the kiss—and certainly not the commentary. To be sure, it is not unlikely that Dante remembered his schoolboy's Ovid, for the distichs are built for memory, with their internal repetitions of similar sounds (for instance, this one on Mirra: "Rem miram mirare novam Mirram per amorem/ In mirram verti quam dat amarus amor"),[18] their easy explanations, their brevity. Yet when the words of John of Garland and Dante are in common with their source, as they frequently are, it is at least probable that Dante has the original Ovid in mind. For the Apollo-Daphne story, the key passage from Ovid follows; as we shall see, it illuminates the entire passage in Dante, giving a context to what has not been seen before in Ovid's light, once again supporting the notion that Dante was bookish in the way that Montaigne was bookish, that he was a great scholar for whom literature was a form of life and not merely a pretext for simple-minded interpretation.

Where John of Garland may share with Dante the words for "tree" (*arbor* in the *integumentum*—Ovid has *ligno*, Dante *legno*), *corona* (in Dante, *coronarmi* in line 26), *labore* (in this case I would argue for sheer coincidence with Dante's *ultimo lavoro*, since the context is different and the source more likely in Virgil), and most

[17] The edition of the *Metamorphoses* I quote from here and elsewhere is that of R. Merckel (Leipzig, 1851 and 1875) as edited by J. Chamonard, 2 vols., Paris, 1953.

[18] John of Garland, *Integumenta Ovidii*, a cura di Fausto Ghisalberti, Messina, 1933, p. 68 (lines 413-414). The passage offers, by the way, an extraordinary example of metacism. See Villani's quotation of Gregory on this subject, Appendix I.

convincingly, *requirit* (for the *dimandi* of Dante—but here
in John of Garland it is man who *requirit*, not Apollo),
the text of Ovid's poem, and not the *integumentum*, contains the seminal words and concepts which shaped Dante's
few lines.

> ... Mihi *Delphica* tellus ...
>   ... servit.
> Juppiter est genitor. *Per me quod eritque fuitque*
> *Estque, patet*; per me concordant carmina nervis ...
>   ... *opiferque per orbem*
> *Dicor* ...   (italics mine)

> [... To me the Delphic land ...
>   ... is in service.
> Jupiter is my father. Through me what shall be, was,
> And is revealed; through me songs harmonize
>   with the strings of the lyre ...
>   ... and "aid-bringer" throughout the world
> Am I called ...]
>   (*Meta.* I, 515-522)

If the only word the two passages have in common is
Delphic, it is probably of more use and greater interest
to wonder at Dante's reading of this passage in terms of
the justification it conceivably granted him within Ovid's
own text for his use (which is not by any means foreign
to his poem) of pagan deity as suitable expression for
Christian God. It seems to me that a Christian poet, and
especially Dante, would have little difficulty in seeing in
the passage an unconscious understanding, even a predic-
tion, of Christ. If Jove is God the Father, as he is called
several times in the *Divine Comedy*, Apollo is His Son.
The following lines are almost too Christological to be believed, while those concerning Apollo's lordship over

minstrelsy are appropriate enough for musaic appropriation by Dante. And the concluding epithet is easily con-
verted to *salvator mundi*. Although I am not certain that
Dante had all or any of these things in mind when he
wrote his invocation to Apollo, I would not be surprised
if he had. And that *Delphica/delfica* conjunction, if assur-
ing evidence, is not definitive proof, since Dante could have
known of Apollo's Delphic origin through any number
of sources. However, I think the passage is at least interesting enough to present as a possible source for Dante's
formulations of his muse. A second passage is a great deal
more convincing as the source for his very words.

The passage immediately follows the woody kiss, as
Apollo addresses his tree:

> Cui deus: "At quoniam conjunx mea non potes esse,
> Arbor eris certe" dixit "mea. Semper habebunt
> Te coma, te citharae, te nostrae, *laure*, pharetrae.
> Tu ducibus Latiis aderis, cum *laeta triumphum*
> Vox canet et visent longas Capitolia pompas.
> Postibus Augustis eadem fidissima custos
> Ante fores stabis, mediamque tuebere quercum.
> Utque meum intonsis caput est juvenale capillis,
> Tu quoque perpetuos semper gere *frondis* honores."
>
> (italics mine)

> [To whom the god: "Since thou canst not be my wife,
> At least thou shalt be my tree," he said. "Always shall
> My hair, my lute, my quiver keep thee, laurel tree.
> Thou among the Latin chiefs shall be when joyful
> Voices sing of triumph, when the Capitol shall see
> endless processions.
> In the doorway of Augustus, most faithful guardian,

Thou shalt stand before the gate, safeguard of
the oak between.[19]
And as my head is youthful, hair unshorn,
Thou shalt also bear the perpetual honor of thy
leaves."]

(Meta. i, 557-565)

This passage, I believe, is the locus for a good deal of
Dante's briefer passage, especially as the words *laeta*,
triumphum, and *frondis* would seem to be directly proc-
essed from Ovid. What makes this seem more probable
than anything else is the one line of Dante's invocation
that has had no attention in light of a possible Ovidian
source—"per triunfare o cesare o poeta." For this line,
or so it seems to me, is keenly reflective of the Roman
pomp which Ovid treats here. For him it might well
serve as a point of departure for his *Paradiso*, "that Rome
of which Christ is Roman"—a point of departure that
causes sadness when he reflects how little has occurred
since the time of Augustus in politics and in poetry that
has justified the use of the laurel crown. And, since Dante
goes as the poet of God and the poet of Empire, the
passage in Ovid[20] certainly would have seemed to him
just and sane for his own point of departure. "The scholar's
pursuit of fame"—Robson's words—is not enough, it
seems to me.

[19] "Those in triumph wore the laurel crown. Before the house of
Augustus, on the Palatine, rose two laurel trees, framing the doorway,
above which was fastened the civic crown of oak bestowed upon that
prince." Chamonard's note, vol. I, p. 380.

[20] For the line "triumph of Caesar or of poet" Gmelin, *Komm.*
III, p. 29, cites the *Achilleis* of Statius, I, 15f.: "Cui geminae florent
vatumque ducumque/ Certatim laurus. . . ." It is certainly an apt
citation, one first made by Moore, but not one which removes the
concurrent appositeness of Ovid's passage.

Indeed, if an argumentative digression may be allowed me, when we pay close attention to Robson's "proof texts" with an impartial mind, it sometimes becomes entirely doubtful that he has proven even the slightest reliance on John of Garland, Arnulf of Orléans, or Giovanni del Virgilio.[21] Questioning Moore's assertion (in *Studies in*

[21] This question, closely related to the problem of Dante's reliance on the medieval Virgilians, has been examined less. Palgen (see note 11 above) is the most consistent and energetic proponent of the most absolute position favoring the influence of the commentators over that of the original. Perhaps Comparetti is the best example to cite at the other extreme. Certainly, faced with a choice of extremes, I choose the latter. As opposed to Robson, who at least cites commentators whom Dante was likely to have known, Palgen points to the *Ovide moralisé* as the specific moralized Ovid which influenced Dante, and that is a dubious position. C. de Boer, in the introduction to his edition of the work, which appeared in installments between the years 1915 and 1938 in *Verhandelingen der Koninklijke Akademie van Wetenschappen te Amsterdam*, XV, XXI, XXX, XXXVII, XLIII, gives the probable dates of its appearance as sometime between 1316 and 1328 (XV, p. 11). That is a bit late for Dante. A similar difficulty exists in the case of Giovanni del Virgilio's commentary. If Dante was to use any commentary, he would have most likely used his friendly rival's. But did he know it? F. Ghisalberti, "Giovanni del Virgilio espositore delle 'Metamorfosi,'" *Giornale dantesco*, XXXIV (1933), p. 5, points out that del Virgilio was at Bologna lecturing on Virgil, Statius, Lucan, and Ovid in 1322-1323, after Dante's death. He supposes that the allegories on Ovid were given in some form or other as part of these lectures, but confesses that it is impossible to know whether they were written down before or after that time. Thus Giovanni del Virgilio is another highly dubious source. (See P. H. Wicksteed and E. G. Gardner, *Dante and Giovanni del Virgilio*, Westminster, 1902, Appendix I, "Del Virgilio on Ovid's *Metamorphoses*," pp. 314-321, for a brief discussion of the nature of the work.) Ghisalberti's discussion includes full bibliography through 1933. See also his "'L'Ovidius Moralizatus' di Pierre Bersuire," *Studi romanzi*, XXIII (1933), 5-32, for discussion of another later commentary on Ovid, one that de Boer (p. 21) cites for its several resemblances to the French *Ovide moralisé*. John of Garland and Arnulf of Orléans were chronologically in a position to influence Dante; that is beyond doubt. See Ghisalberti's discussion of the latter in his "Arnolfo d'Orléans: un cultore di Ovidio nel secolo XII," *Memorie del Reale*

Dante, First Series) that there are about seventy passages in the *Commedia* directly modeled on Ovid, Robson concludes that less than twelve of these actually are. And then, examining a dozen passages which he claims could only have been formulated in light of the commentaries, he leaves us with the impression that the forty remaining passages are similarly commentator-inspired. But when we examine his passages, we do not find the convincing proof Robson claims. For instance, discussing Dante's treatment of Hecuba (*Inf.* xxx, 13-21), Robson cites for Dante's "forsennata latrò sì come cane;/ tanto il dolor le fé la mente torta" ("gone mad, barked like a dog,/ so much grief having made her mind go wrong") Arnulf's "pre nimio dolore insanuit . . . sicut faciunt canes" ("she went mad because of grief beyond measure . . . [barking] as do dogs"). This appears to be an apt citation. As Robson points out, Ovid says she "barked," not that she "barked like a dog"; that is, in Ovid she had become a dog, while in Dante and in Arnulf she is still a woman, barking like a dog. However, when we look over the passage in Ovid (*Meta.* xiii, 404-575), we find we are told that Hecuba lost her human form for dog form at the outset (line

---

Istituto Lombardo, Cl. lett., xxiv (1932), 157-230. Ghisalberti had earlier argued for points of contact between Dante and the commentaries on Ovid: "L'enigma delle Naiadi," *Studi danteschi*, xvi (1932), 105-125; "La quadriga del sole nel 'Convivio,' " *Studi danteschi*, xviii (1934), 69-77. Recently he claims to have found the thirteenth-century codex (Biblioteca Ambrosiana) used by Dante to make the two readings discussed by Ghisalberti in the *Studi danteschi* articles (above), and suggesting, tentatively, nine other treatments of Ovid in this codex which might have influenced Dante. This most recent finding, "Il commentario medioevale all'*Ovidius maior* consultato da Dante," *Rendiconti dell'-Istituto Lombardo, Accademia di scienze e lettere*, C (1966), 267-275, is mainly important, or so it would seem to me, for giving us a text that we may now study in the fairly sure knowledge that it corresponds more or less to the text Dante used—if he indeed did so.

405), but that at the climax of the story (line 569), when, having tried to speak, she barks ("Latravit, conata loqui"), she is at the moment of her transformation, still in human form, but inhuman because of her action in tearing out Polymestor's eyes (lines 560-564). The bark is the first dog-like action performed by that distraught old lady; that is the dramatic point of Ovid's story, and it gives the story its immediate pathos. She is indeed still a woman, her voice become a dog's in her last human moment, as her metamorphosis is about to take place. Thus, we have no authorization to accept Robson's conclusion on the basis of his evidence alone. Further, Dante's entire Hecuba passage is rich in details condensed directly from Ovid. Another writer on this subject claims as many as fifteen direct points of contact between *Metamorphoses* XIII, 404-575, and *Inferno* XXX, 13-27.[22] One must admit that Arnulf's recapitulation is like Dante's. There is one very good reason for the similarity: each of them is describing the same original. That, it seems to me, is as good an explanation as Robson's.

Since it is not useful to generalize in such matters, I shall offer a few more examples of ways in which Robson's "proofs" are at best assertions. To do the complete job would require far too many pages, however, and a few examples must suffice. For *Inferno* XXX, 4, "Atamante divenne tanto insano" ("Athamas became so insane"), he cites Arnulf, "Ino et Athamas maritus eius de sanis facti sunt insani." Robson admits that Dante takes his following lines (7-9) straight from Ovid, but insists that Dante relies on the commentator for this simple recapitulation

---

[22] G. Brugnoli, "Dante *Inf.* 30, 13 sgg.," *L'Alighieri*, VII, 1 (1966), 98-99. A. Ronconi, on the other hand, sees Seneca's behind Dante's Hecuba (less convincingly, in my opinion), in "Per Dante interprete dei poeti latini," *Studi danteschi*, XLI (1964), 13.

of the facts of the story. If Robson will admit that lines
513-514 of *Metamorphoses* IV form the action Dante
describes, what about lines 512 and 515, which tell us that
Athamas was "furibundus" and "amens"? Did Dante need
the commentator's word *insani* for his own *insano*, or did
he use *insano* because that's what *furibundus* and *amens*
mean, and because *insano* rhymes with *tebano* and *mano*
(lines 2 and 6)? In this same passage Robson argues for
Giovanni del Virgilio at line 12: "E quella s'annegó con
l'altro carco" ("and she [Ino] drowned herself with the
other burden"): "Ino dum esset ebria necuit se cum alio."
Here I think Professor Robson is thoroughly wrong. The
Latin verb *neco* may mean "drown" (cf. Pliny), but the
Oxford Latin Dictionary cites this meaning as late and
rare. *Neco* usually signifies a less specific kind of killing,
usually accomplished with a weapon of some sort. But that
is of little consequence. Look at Ovid (IV, 528-530): "Ino
. . . Seque . . . Mittit onusque suum . . . unda"; surely, as
the translation *carco* for *onus* makes clear, that is Dante's
source. Is it true that the *glossae* "played a more decisive
part in the shaping of the mythological foundation of the
Commedia than the text of Ovid himself" (Robson, p. 9)?
Even if we were to grant his premise—and I am far from
being convinced we should—we gain very little from it,
since the moralizations of Ovid are rarely evident even in
Robson's own citations, which give us claims mainly for
verbal reminiscence of plot summary. If the commentaries
had any effect on Dante at all, that effect would seem to
have been marginal and nominal. And sometimes, as in
my last example, Robson is thoroughly unconvincing even
when arguing for this minimal influence. For *Purgatorio*
XII, 37-48, Niobe and Arachne, Robson cites the verse
commentary which names Arachne, then Niobe, and he

says: "Dante has inverted the order of the two fables . . ." (p. 11). No he hasn't. Ovid presents them in the same order as Dante (VI, 5-145 and 146-312). Further, Robson points to Arnulf for Niobe's "VII filios and VII filias." Where, we may ask, did Arnulf learn about the seven sons and seven daughters of Niobe? From Ovid, where Dante also did (*Meta.* VI, 146-312, mentions the seven sons twice and the seven daughters once).

In sum, although I have questions about all of Robson's "proof texts," I shall forbear going on in this manner. I have taken this much time and space for refutation because his essay is an important and provocative one, and likely to have a large effect, especially on those who do not take the time to study the pertinent documents. Again, I am not claiming that Dante did not know these *integumenta*. He knew them the way some of us "know" the Latin trots, "College Outline Series," and other unspeakables of our youth. What I am claiming is that he simply didn't use them. I break my promised silence for one last look at John of Garland, Professor Robson, Ovid, and Dante. For *Purgatorio* XXV, 22-23, "come Meleagro/ si consumò al consumar d'un stizzo" ("how Meleager was consumed in the consuming of a firebrand"), Robson cites John of Garland's "Fax est fatalis Meleagri perdere fortis." Ovid himself is far more to the verbal point, once again. Dante's *stizzo* is Ovid's *stipes* (VIII, 514), and his "consumed in the consuming" is Ovid's "ad ignibus arsit" (also line 514) or perhaps his "flamma . . . Uritur" (515-516). If Dante's repetitive verbal play seems to parallel that found in John of Garland, it probably reflects the similar playfulness of Ovid. And his word for "firebrand" is precisely the Italian cognate of the Latin *stipes*.

To return to the question of Dante's understanding and

use of Ovid, let us examine his curious presentation of Marsyas in this same passage in *Paradiso* i. Here the figural relationship seems clear: Apollo was challenged to a flute contest by the satyr Marsyas, who was defeated by the god (in Ovid's version), and was flayed alive by the angry god for his presumption. Dante puts in his plea for inspiration from God, not claiming that his own poetic abilities are sufficient, as Marsyas thought his musical ones were. As Marsyas and the daughters of Pierus, referred to by Dante in a precisely parallel passage in *Purgatorio* i, 7-12 (as several have noticed), thought they possessed in their own right the ability to outstrip Apollo and the Muses, respectively, so does Dante, seeking proper aid and inspiration, call upon Apollo here and the Muses there to aid his powers. The punishment of each offending party is levied by the gods for artistic presumption, and in each case Dante refers to them in order to establish the difference between their goals and his. Here is Dante's passage:

> Entra nel petto mio, e spira tue
> sì come quando Marsia traesti
> de la vagina de le membra sue.

> [Enter my breast, and inspire there
> as when thou drewest Marsyas
> from out the sheathe of his limbs.]

> (*Par.* i, 19-21)

The brief Ovidian narrative contains some of these elements. As he is flayed, Marsyas cries:

> "Quid me mihi detrahis?" inquit
> "A! piget. A! non est" clamabat "tibia tanti!"
> Clamanti cutis est summos direpta per artus,
> Nec quicquam nisi vulnus erat.

["Why dost thou draw me from
   myself?" he said.
"O! it hurts. O! fluting is not," he cried, "worth
   this!"
While he cried out the skin was stripped from all
   his limbs,
And he was nothing but a wound.]
                              (*Meta.* vi, 385-388)

As Gmelin says (*Komm.* iii, p. 28), there seems to be
a verbal reminiscence of Ovid's *detrahis* in Dante's *traesti*.
What is more, though less certain, Dante's *membra* may
be a translation of Ovid's *artus*, as each word does mean
the same thing, and there is no word that is cognate with
artus in Italian. Professor Robson admits, in answer to
his own question concerning Dante's intention here, "Did
he accept the allegorists' interpretation of it as the triumph
of wisdom over folly?": "Dante's practice elsewhere suggests that the flaying was meant to be fully realized, like
the transformation of Glaucus and the staining of the
mulberry, as a genuinely awesome *event* containing in itself some further significance" (pp. 24-25). That significance, we may merely note, goes further than negative
typology. For, where Marsyas was destroyed by being
drawn from his limbs, Dante prays to be drawn forth in
a better way from his. The paradoxical positive way in
which we may understand the story is made clear shortly
when it is adumbrated by a similar leaving behind of
humanity in the tale of Glaucus.

Dante, gazing on Beatrice gazing on the Sun, suddenly
sees as though "day were added to day" (61). The first
two metamorphoses of Ovid that Dante has referred to
in this canto are more concerned with the power or re-
actions of the gods than with the experiences of the meta-

morphoses. Now, as Dante suddenly becomes transhumanate, his experience is understood as it was foreshadowed
by that of Glaucus:

> Nel suo aspetto tal dentro mi fei,
>> qual si fé Glauco nel gustar de l'erba
>> che 'l fé consorto in mar de li altri Dei.
> Trasumanar significar per verba
>> non si poria; però l'essemplo basti
>> a cui esperienza grazia serba.

> [Gazing on her I became such within
>> as was Glaucus when he tasted of the grass
>> which made him a sea-fellow of the other gods.
> Signified by words transhumanation
>> may not be; therefore, let the example suffice
>> him for whom grace keeps it in store.]

(Par. I, 67-72)

Dante's two lines about Glaucus have ramifications
within his poem which are indebted to the incident in
Ovid. Here is that passage, or a substantial portion of it.
Glaucus, having appeared to Scylla in his new form, explains how he got that way. A fisherman, already dedicated to deep water ("altis/Deditus aequoribus"—lines
921-922 of Book XIII), sitting one day by a green meadow
whose grass had never been grazed upon by any herbivo-
rous beast (924-927), Glaucus pulls in a catch of fish and
places them in rows upon that grass. Suddenly (936) the
fish come to life, and while he, amazed, looks on, they
move through the meadow as they are able to move
through water, and thus manage their escape back into
the sea (927-939). Glaucus tastes the grass himself out
of curiosity ("Quae tamen has . . . vires habet herba?"—
942), and finds himself possessed by the urge to change

his nature (945-946).[23] Bidding farewell to the land, he dives into the water (948). His speech continues:

"Di maris exceptum socio dignantur honore,
Utque mihi quaecumque feram mortalia demant,
Oceanum Tethynque rogant. Ego lustror ab illis,
Et purgante nefas noviens mihi carmine dicto
Pectora fluminibus jubeor supponere centum.
Nec mora, diversis lapsi de partibus amnes
Totaque vertuntur supra caput aequora nostrum.
Hactenus acta tibi possum memoranda referre:
Hactenus haec memini. Nec mens mea cetera sensit.
Quae postquam rediit, alium me corpore toto
Ac fueram nuper, neque eumdem mente recepi."

["The gods of the sea, welcoming me with honor,
          condescend to make me their fellow;
To rid me of all I might bear of mortal things
They appeal to Oceanus and Tethys. Purified by these,
And after the incantation which, said nine times,
          purified my impieties,
I am ordered to immerse myself in one hundred
          flowing streams.
In no time, coming from all directions, torrents flow,
All those waters rolling over my head.
I cannot tell you more of these memorable events:
Only so much have I remembered; my mind forgets
          the rest.
When my senses came back to me I recovered another
          me in body
Than what I was before, and a mind not the same."]

(*Meta.* xiii, 949-959)

[23] Sapegno's commentary on *Par.* i, 67, "Nel suo aspetto tal dentro mi fei," points out that Dante almost certainly had these two lines in mind: Cum subito trepidare praecordia sensi, Alteriusque rapi naturae pectus amore.

The miraculous transformation of Glaucus into a god of the sea takes its verbal form, to be sure, from Ovid, especially the phrase "Di maris exceptum socio" in line 949. What is of perhaps greater interest, at least to this reader of the two poems, is the Christian potential in the image of the fish which Glaucus caught and which came back to life (936-939). As Dante has used the constellation of Pisces in the train of Venus to open *Purgatorio* (I, 21), thus implanting the Christological symbol at the root of that cantica, might he not have gotten at least amused satisfaction from the configuration he found in the Glaucus story, which he sets as the analogue to the first and central action of *Paradiso* I?[24] The fish which can swim on land, the man who can swim like a fish, this dual and reciprocal change of nature would most likely have struck Dante for its figural aptness here, in the poem which is going to see Christ, the "fish" Who came back to life. Gmelin's comment on Glaucus is worth repeating: "Der Vergleich ist wieder ein Beispiel für Dantes christliche Sicht des antiken Mythus, die in der vorchristlichen Ära das Wirken Gottes in den antiken Gestalten präfiguriert sah."[25] I take this to mean that the change in Glaucus' nature is a prefiguration of the change in human nature wrought by Jesus. I wonder whether Professor Gmelin would have objected to carrying Dante's figuralism to the revivified fish as well.

The inability to remember all the details of his watery adventure of which Glaucus tells seems very close to the

[24] Virgil, asking Statius about the latter's conversion, refers to Christ as "pescator" (*Purg.* XXII, 61-63); Dante shares the Christian's traditional belief that the sign of the fish is that of Jesus. See Chapter IV, note 15.

[25] *Komm.* III, p. 35: "The comparison is yet another example of Dante's Christian view of ancient myth, which saw God's processes prefigured in the pre-Christian era's ancient configurations."

inexpressibility Dante insists on also: "Trasumanar significar per verba/ non si poria." Again, all I can claim is that Dante would have been pleased by the passage in Ovid, that it would have made him feel more pleasure, doctrinal and poetical, in his reference. And, although this is something of a question, he might have expected some of his readers to know the passage well enough to share the pleasure with him. I shall want to return to the undersea experience of Glaucus at the conclusion of this chapter. Now it is time to turn to the pivotal figural presence of *Paradiso*, the voyager who replaces Ulysses as the archetypal *homo viator* for Dante: Jason.

Some years ago I considered writing an article on these two sailors, in part because I liked the title I envisioned: "The Purgatorial Ulysses and the Celestial Jason." We have seen how great a part of Dante's imagination of the voyage on the mountain takes root in the doomed voyage of Ulysses he describes in *Inferno* xxvi. Now that vast exploit is referred to by only a few words in *Paradiso*, words we have already noticed: "il varco/ folle d'Ulisse" (*Par.* xxvii, 82-83). Canto ii introduces the Argonaut who, because his goal is the Grail, becomes the most perfect imperfect expression of Dante's own journey; where Ulysses, for all his grandeur, could only stand figurally behind a voyager whose goal was less certain.

Dante begins *Paradiso* ii by reminding us, his readers, how far we have come. For where his poem was, metaphorically, in *Purgatorio* i, 2, merely "la navicella del mio ingegno," "the small ship of my wit," it has now become a great ship in whose wake we toss as in a *piccioletta barca* (as we shall be again described in *Paradiso* xxiii, 67, when the poem prepares to take the great leap to the vision of Mary, Christ, and Gabriel, the first taste of true Paradise), attempting to follow the man who in the preceding canto has been the first vernacular poet to call himself *poeta* (I, 29). And only some of us are even qualified to follow:

L'acqua ch'io prendo già mai non si corse . . .
Voi altri pochi che drizzaste il collo
    per tempo al pan de li angeli, del quale
    vivesi qui ma non sen vien satollo,
metter potete ben per l'alto sale
    vostro navigio, servando mio solco
    dinanzi a l'acqua che ritorna equale.
Que' gloriosi che passaro a Colco
    non s'ammiraron come voi farete,
    quando Iason vider fatto bifolco.

[The water that I take was never sailed before . . .
You other few who stretched up your necks
    early for the angels' bread, which
    gives earthly nourishment but not satiety,
to the deep salt may well commit
    your vessel, keeping to my furrow
    in the water before it falls back level.
Those glorious ones who sailed to Colchis
    did not gaze in wonderment, as shall you,
    when they saw Jason turned ploughman.]
                     (*Par.* II, 7, 10-18)

The Ovidian reminiscence here has been largely noted (*Meta.* VII, 100-120). It concerns the voyage of the Argo with the descendants of Minyas from Iolcos to Colchis in search of the Golden Fleece. The exploits of Jason, undertaken with the aid of Medea, result in their returning home with what they sought (VII, 155-158). Dante refers obliquely to Jason's turning of the terrible bulls to meek plow animals through his judicious use of Medea's *can-*

221

tatas herbas, or "enchanted herbs" (VII, 98). In Ovid, the natives of Colchis are the ones who are amazed at Jason's feat: "Mirantur Colchi" (120). Dante has taken the license of the poet to make the Argonauts the wondering ones, as he wants the parallel to the amazement of us, *his* "shipmates."[26]

No commentator that I have consulted, however, has looked back to the conclusion of Book VI of the *Metamorphoses* to observe the Argo setting sail from Iolcos and found in that moment a phrase that most likely caught Dante's eye in the concluding line of that Book: "Per mare non notum prima petiere carina" ("The first keel to cleave an unknown sea"—VI, 721). It is difficult to believe, in consideration of his large acquaintance with Ovid, that the Roman poet's treatment of the first ship on an untravelled sea would have escaped Dante. "The water that I take was never sailed before," and Dante continues by giving us the story of Jason, the man who seeks and finds the Golden Fleece. It would be natural for him to begin the action of *Paradiso* with the preparation for Jason's voyage in mind. It is the figure of the voyage of Dante who is, in *Paradiso*, another Jason, another Paul, as in *Inferno* he was the new Aeneas and the new Paul, despite his earliest doubts and disclaimers (*Inf.* II, 32) in what I have previously alleged is the first overt typological comparison in the poem. Yet seeking the bread of angels does not prevent Dante from thinking of himself as the new Aeneas. At least twice in *Paradiso* he does so: Canto XV, 25-27, when he is welcomed by his ancestor Cacciaguida as Aeneas was welcomed by the shade of Anchises (*Aen.* VI, 684-686); and Canto XXXIII, 64-66, when, at the last moment before the final enlightenment, he is like Aeneas

[26] See Gmelin, *Komm.* III, p. 51.

about to consult the Sybil, the poet's phrasing here echoing Virgil's passage in *Aeneid* III, 448-452.

Jason, as seeker of the Golden Fleece, not as seducer of Hypsipyle and Medea (for which sin Dante recognizes Jason by his kingly aspect—*Inf.* XVIII, 85—amongst the Panders and Seducers in the first bolgia of Malebolge) is naturally a viable prefiguration of Dante's search for the Grail of his time. When Dante announces his longing to receive the laurel for the "sacred poem to which both heaven and earth have set hand" (*Par.* XXV, 1-2), and hopes that old cruelties shall be overcome so that he may receive it in Florence, "the lovely sheepfold where as a lamb I slept" (XXV, 5), the image of the lamb moves him naturally to the following lines:

> con altra voce omai, con altro vello
> ritornerò poeta; ed in sul fonte
> del mio battesmo prenderò 'l cappello.

> [with other voice now, with another fleece
> shall I return a poet; and at the font
> of my baptism shall I put on the wreath.]

(*Par.* XXV, 7-9)

Dante longs to be welcomed home in the Roman triumph he envisioned in *Paradiso* I ("the triumph of Caesar or of poet" of line 29), but now, as a Christian and a Florentine, he thinks of himself as a lamb, a good Christian metaphor surely, since he has elsewhere (*Inf.* XIX, 132, and especially *Purg.* XXVII, 77, 86) found an analogue for himself in the animal kingdom as a goat.[27] The lamb has

---

[27] Professor Sarolli points to the Christological implications of this analogue, yet somehow loses track of the major importance of the Jasonic motif in this passage, even though he does take Jason into some cognizance. See his study, "Dante's Katabasis and Mission," in *The World of Dante*, ed. S. B. Chandler and J. A. Molinaro, Toronto,

grown up, in the image, and so now is covered with the mature coat which replaces lamb's wool. The image makes simple literal sense, and also, obviously (I assume that the point is obvious, although, Scartazzini, Moore, Grandgent, Wicksteed, Sapegno, and Gmelin do not observe it) refers to the voyage of Jason. The line means not only that Dante, the lamb, will have another pelt, but that Dante, the poet, shall return from heaven with a new Fleece, not the Golden Fleece of Jason, but the true *vello*, granted by the Grace of God. Ovid uses the same word that Dante does, *vellus*, and he uses it at the beginning and end of the journey of the Argo to Colchis. It is unlikely that Dante did not have it in mind here. The pivotal position of Jason at the beginning and the end of Dante's heavenly voyage would also assure the reference here.

The last human reference in the *Commedia* is to Jason. It occurs as Dante accedes to the ultimate and highest vision, his vision of the Incarnate Godhead. That probably seems blasphemous to some. For what Dante brings off is the figural appropriateness of Jason's voyage for the Fleece to his own voyage to God. It is the moment in the poem where all things converge:

> Oh abbondante grazia ond'io presunsi
> ficcar lo viso per la luce etterna,
> tanto che la veduta vi consunsi!
> Nel suo profondo vidi che s'interna,
> legato con amore in un volume,
> ciò che per l'universo si squaderna;
> sustanze e accidenti e lor costume,
> quasi conflati insieme, per tal modo
> che ciò ch'i' dico è un semplice lume.

1966, pp. 97-107. Sister Marie Catherine Pohndorf's dissertation (see note 26, Ch. II) does see the importance of Jason's fleece here, p. 189.

La forma universal di questo nodo
    credo ch'i' vidi, perché più di largo,
    dicendo questo, mi sento ch'i' godo.
Un punto solo m'è maggior letargo
    che venticinque secoli a la 'mpresa,
    che fé Nettuno ammirar l'ombra d'Argo.
Così la mente mia, tutta sospesa,
    mirava fissa, immobile e attenta,
    e sempre di mirar faciesi accesa.

[O abounding grace, wherein I dared
    to fix my gaze on the eternal light,
    so long it therein was consumed!
In its depth I saw that it held in itself,
    bound by love in a single volume,
    that which is scattered in leaves through the
        universe:
substances and accidents and their relations,
    as though combined in such a way
    that what I tell of is a single light.
I believe I saw the universal form
    of this knot, for, telling of it,
    I feel my joy go past expanse.
A single moment causes me deeper oblivion
    than do twenty-five centuries upon the enterprise
    which made Neptune gaze in wonder at the
        shadow of the Argo.
So all my mind, suspended, was gazing,
    fixed, unmoving, and intent,
    and ever enkindled by its gazing.]
                      (*Par.* xxxiii, 82-99)

Of this moment T. S. Eliot has said, "I do not know
anywhere in poetry more authentic sign of greatness than
the power of association which could in the last line, when

the poet is speaking of the Divine vision, yet introduce the Argo passing over the head of wondering Neptune. . . . It is the real right thing, the power of establishing relations between beauty of the most diverse sorts; it is the utmost power of the poet."[28]

Dante's power of establishing relationships between histories of the most diverse sorts is what has been of primary interest to this study. And here, at the conclusion of the poem, we find Dante's figural technique itself raised to a level it could not have reached before—a level at which, as I have suggested, all the parts become the whole, all the pages become the book. And it is the many single leaves finally understood as unitary book that is the metaphor Dante uses to express his vision of the Godhead. This comparison implies a further fact about his poem: all the pages come together on this page. The mystic poet tries, in fact, to write only this page, the vision without its precedent experience, the knowledge without its precedent attempts and failures. Dante is not that kind of mystic poet. Rather, as his language itself implies, he is an Aristotelian as well as a Platonic poet, who proceeds up the ladder of sense dicta to the form of forms. And, as the presence of the Argo guarantees, he is greatly a literary poet, one who finds in literature of the most diverse kinds the guarantee of his particular knowledge and emotion. And he is a poet for whom all of human history, the universal history which is contained in the universal form, comprises the record of the substantial shadows of ultimate truth.

I confess that coming upon this moment in the poem for the hundreth time I am carried away by a *letargo*, which according to Curtius means "ecstasy" in Alanus ab

[28] "Dante," in *Selected Essays*, London, 1932, p. 268.

Insulis[29] and perhaps retains an overtone of that meaning here, and which makes discourse difficult. For those who also see and feel this passage so as to make adumbration unnecessary, I apologize for going on at all.

The poem and the universe are now *volumi*. Although the poem will go on to express the vision in terms of three circles in one, containing all color and smiling on it/themselves, a figuration which concludes with the climactic detail that this complex unity is painted with our effigy and thus is the approximate picture of the Incarnation (line 131), the journey has finished. We may say this because Dante has come out of it. In the midst of his description of the Godhead he has become the Poet, has finished being the Pilgrim: "For, telling of it, I feel my joy go past expanse. A single moment causes me deeper oblivion than do twenty-five centuries upon the enterprise which made Neptune gaze in wonder at the shadow of the Argo." It is a remarkable and beautiful trick, resembling the disappearance of Beatrice into her actual self, her task accomplished, in her last silent smile in *Paradiso* xxx, 26. Dante is back on earth writing the poem. The Pilgrim he was has become the history of the Poet he is. As Montaigne would put it, his book and himself have become consubstantial.

To Dante, as we have already seen in our examination of Ovid's concluding line to the Sixth Book of the *Metamorphoses*, the Argo was the first ship to cross the unknown waters from Iolcus to Colchis. E. R. Curtius has traced the development of the topos of the first ship from its origins in Pindar, through Apollonius Rhodos (by way of Euripedes, Ennius, and Cicero), to Valerius Flaccus, and finally up to Statius and the *Roman de la rose*, thence to

[29] E. R. Curtius, "Das Schiff der Argonauten," in *Kritische Essays zur europäischen Literatur*, Bern, 1950, p. 423.

Il Fiore, and, possibly, through various of these sources, to Dante, although he favors *Metamorphoses* VII, 120, as Dante's primary source.[30] We have already observed the cogency Dante found in this line, which contains the words "Mirantur Colchi," transformed by Dante to the form we discovered in *Paradiso* I, when we, his "shipmates," will be similarly amazed as were the Argonauts when they saw Jason's miraculous plowing. I would like to suggest another proximate cause, however. For here Dante employs a different image, invoking the surprise of the god of the sea at the first ship to sail over him. The passage I find resonating here is one I left dangling some pages ago, in which Glaucus becomes a god of the sea. At the moment during which Glaucus becomes divinized, after the nine incantations, in the one hundred flowing streams, he also is unable to express what he saw; his mind also boggles. The cleansing of Glaucus (Ovid's word is, after all, *purgante*); the nine (Beatrice's number and that of the spheres Dante has passed through before his vision); the one hundred (God's and the poem's number); the being immersed deep under water and seeing

---

[30] *Ibid.*, p. 421. Even though Jason is in Hell (*Inf.* XVIII, 86), he, his ship, and the wondering Neptune lie in readiness for their climactic appearance in *Par.* XXXIII:

> Tra l'isola di Cipri e di Maiolica
> non vide mai sì gran fallo Nettuno,
> non da pirate, non da gente argolica.
>
> (*Inf.* XXVIII, 82-84)

Here Dante has Neptune gazing on the Greek host sailing to the investment of Troy, since his phrase "da gente argolica" comes from Virgil's "neque me *Argolica de gente* negabo" (italics mine—the citation also made by Gmelin, *Komm.* I, p. 419). The speaker here is Sinon, *Aen.* II, 78, confessing he is one of the Greeks who fought against Troy. Thus here the sea-god is conceived as the spectator of a criminal act that issues from Argos, the home of Sinon, while he will later be conceived as the amazed spectator of the voyage of a ship named Argo, sailing for a better cause on a better journey.

memorable things which the mind/memory (Ovid and Dante share the word *mente*) cannot hold; and the insistence on the transhumanation at the conclusion of Ovid's passage which Dante adverts to, paralleling the experience of St. Paul, in the Glaucus passage in Canto I—all of these elements are present in both places, and I think it is not too much to believe that Ovid's lines stand as a sort of locus classicus for all of Dante's images of the sea god's miraculous experience and vision which are central to *Paradiso*.

In other words, I am arguing for the Ovid passage as a source of Dante's Neptune, who, despite Curtius' excellent work, has so far not been identified with any particular literary source. Within the logic of Dante's use of figural techniques is the resultant telescoping of similar persons, actions, and events. Contained in the *ombra* of Celestine, I have argued, are the *ombre* of Pilate and others. The *ombra* of the Argo, I would similarly argue, even without benefit of Ovid, contains the shadows of other ships, other voyages; and just so does Glaucus come back into the poem as an *ombra* of Neptune, each of their visions prefiguring the vision of Dante.

The *terzina* is not, at first glance an easy one.[31]

> Un punto solo m'è maggior letargo
> che venticinque secoli a la 'mpresa,
> che fé Nettuno ammirar l'ombra d'Argo.

[31] My own translation of these lines is, admittedly, to a certain degree an interpretation, one that is fairly close to Grandgent's. See also the commentaries of Scartazzini, Sapegno, and Gmelin for good discussions and summaries of other discussions of the difficulties of these three lines. Also, for an adroit analysis of the key words of the passage, *letargo* and *punto*, see Peter Dronke, "Boethius, Alanus and Dante," *Romanische Forschungen*, LXXVIII (1966), 119-125; also Georg Rabuse, "Un punto solo m'è maggior letargo," *DDJb*, XLIII (1965), 138-152.

[A single moment causes me deeper oblivion
than do twenty-five centuries upon the enterprise
which made Neptune gaze in wonder at the
shadow of the Argo.]

Dante the Pilgrim has just seen the universal form. It is
so exalted a vision that he cannot remember it. Among
the many discussions of this difficult *terzina*, one word
has received little attention: what is an *impresa*? Literally, the word denotes an "enterprise." Previously in the
Commedia the word is used three times with two firmly
established meanings. In *Inferno* II, 41 and 47 (once again
we see how Dante goes back to his beginnings), the word
is used to mean the journey Dante must take with Virgil,
overcoming his cowardice. Then, in *Inferno* XXXII, 7,
Dante uses it in one of his several self-conscious interrup-
tions of narrative to tell his readers that describing the
bottom of the Universe is not an *impresa* to be taken as a
game, not for a tongue which still calls "mamma" and
"pappa." Here the enterprise is the poem he is writing.
Now, in the only other use of the word in his poem, *impresa* becomes a reflection both of the journey *and*, by
implication, the poem: the Pilgrim's voyage *and* the Poet's
vision. It does so in the following way: the enterprise represented by the Argo, the Jasonic motif, is what Dante
is seeing. But what he is doing is completing what he has
previously called his *impresa*, that is, his record of his
journey. Indeed, Dante, in this last figural moment in the
poem, has two figural identities: he is Jason *and* Neptune.[32]
The Pilgrim is Jason, on the way to getting the Fleece;

[32] In terms of the Classical matter Dante here evokes, he is figurally
related to the builder of the first ship ("primaeque ratis molitor Iason"—
Meta. VIII, 302) and to the beholder of that first ship's voyage ("Per
mare non notum prima petiere carina"—*Meta.* VI, 721), seen from
below as a keel cutting the water.

the Poet is Neptune, watching him do so. Now Neptune is not to be understood as God, but as a god of the sea; he is the figural extension of Glaucus, who, a sea god, saw marvellous things and couldn't remember them to tell about them, struck dumb with amazement at the new things.

If God is Alpha and Omega, the penultimate moment of the poem that sees God should contain Alpha and Omega.[33] Dante is about to describe the Godhead, who is that. Here he gives us a kind of Alpha and Omega of human history, not in terms of Adam and Judgment Day, but in terms of the first ship and the last one, the voyage of 1223 B.C.[34] and that of 1300 A.D. The voyage over waters never sailed successfully before is, I need not remind the reader, one of the dominant motifs of the *Commedia*. In *Inferno* I Dante gazes on waters that no one ever left alive (27). In *Inferno* XXVI Ulysses almost sails to the Mount of Purgatory, but sinks. In *Paradiso* I, 7, the poet tells us that these waters (Paradiso itself) were never sailed before. And now the first voyage (one wonders if Dante thought also of Noah's voyage here, as he more probably did in *Inferno* I) is remembered with the

---

[33] As the Letter to Can Grande tells us, in its concluding (thirty-third) paragraph. It is worth pausing to consider the fact that the *Epistola* and the *cantica* it describes are each divided into thirty-three elements, as Curtius, *EL&LMA*, p. 222, has already noted. Bruno Nardi, "Perché 'Alfa ed O' e non 'Alfa ed Omega,' " in his *Saggi e note di critica dantesca*, Milano, 1966, pp. 317-320, gives a strong argument for the former reading ("Alfa ed O") as against the latter for *Par.* XXVI, 17. Interestingly enough, Dante also has it "Alfa ed O" in *Epistola* XIII—a small detail which would certainly buttress Nardi's case for the orthography of the line in *Par.* XXVI, if he would only admit the genuineness of the *Epistola*. Or perhaps we should admit his argument on its own strength, and then suggest that *it* lends support to the argument for genuineness.

[34] Gmelin, *Komm.* III, p. 572, discusses Dante's chronology for the Argonauts, giving pertinent bibliography.

last one, which is his own to see God. The midpoint of the sector of the arc of this history, thirteen centuries from either terminus, is the Incarnation, the *terminus ad quem* and *a quo* for the poem and for all human life. The size of these three lines is enormous.

And, what is especially pleasant for me to conclude with, these lines also make their focus felt with that word which for the Biblical exegete is so cogent: *ombra*. Neptune saw the *ombra* of the Argo. That is, he saw not only the visible sign of great and awesome human endeavor in the form of a shadow on the waters above him, he saw *in it*, or at any rate we do, the *figura* of the voyages which were to follow, the most recent of which is the great poem. As Neptune's eyes moved from the shadow to the substance of the ship, so now Dante's eyes have moved from the shadows he first saw in the blessed kingdom, those *umbriferi prefazii*, to the triune *substantia* of all things.

CHAPTER VI

OTHER KINDS OF
ALLEGORY

Now, having finished my claim for the centrality of four-fold allegory to the *Commedia*, I should like briefly to observe the contraindications. To tell the whole story of the allegory of Dante's poem would take many more pages, for there are many kinds and degrees of allegory in the work. This diversity has been well discussed by a critic whose interest in the poem has always avoided partisanship to a single notion. I hope, despite the singlemindedness of what has gone before, to ally myself with those of even critical temperament who have unfailingly put the poem itself ahead of any theory of it. This approach typifies the work of men like Thomas Bergin, who has wisely interceded between unilateral arguments and the poem itself. As Bergin has said: "Instead of thinking simply of *the* allegory of the *Commedia*, we must, after the most cursory of glances at the work, conclude that it is a question of various allegories, sometimes sharply different in genesis and purpose, frequently interweaving, and not always easy to distinguish."[1] In other words, the poem is "polysemous" in many respects.

In my introductory remarks I pointed to four kinds of allegory that flourished before and during Dante's time. These were the two kinds of philological or personification allegory, the one descending from the Homeric tradition of critical literary study and the other probably traceable to the same source, including the use of personification allegory in Christian fictions like the *Psychomachia*. The

[1] *Dante*, Boston, 1965, pp. 250-251.

third kind was developed and given shape in the Middle Ages primarily by Isidore of Seville's *Etymologiae*, which synthesized Aristotle, Cicero, and Augustine, the three major writers on rhetoric of Antiquity and the early Christian era; this third kind of allegory is the domain of grammarians and rhetoricians, and may be referred to as "the allegory of the rhetoricians." If we may lump the first two, and I believe that literary history permits it, we may then, for purposes of clarification, speak of three kinds of allegory: the allegory of the poets, the allegory of the rhetoricians, and the allegory of the theologians. I need not remind the reader that the last category has been our exclusive interest in the foregoing discussion.

Dante's own literary career was long involved with the first of these, as his clear statement in *Convivio* ii, i (that he in that work is following the allegory of the poets and not that of the theologians) testifies. What of the second kind, the allegory of the rhetoricians? Here the issue is less clear, since Dante himself does not announce any intention in this direction. Nevertheless, I believe his behavior, both in the *Commedia* and elsewhere, reflects the tradition of allegory as it was formulated by Isidore and others. Perhaps the best work in this area has been done by E. R. Curtius,[2] who devoted a major part of his scholar-

[2] "Dante und das lateinische Mittelalter," *Romanische Forschungen*, LVII (1943), 153-185. And see his *Gesammelte Aufsätze zur romanischen Philologie*, Bern, 1960, pp. 305-345; as well as *European Literature and the Latin Middle Ages, passim*. See also Paget Toynbee, "The Bearing of the *Cursus* on the Text of Dante's *De vulgari eloquentia*," *Proceedings of the British Academy*, 1921-1923, pp. 359-377. One of the best treatments written in English of Dante's rhetorical sources is still James E. Shaw, *The Lady "Philosophy" in the Convivio*, Cambridge, Mass., 1938. August Buck's recent work shows that he is of all *dantisti* the most concerned with this subject. The centenary year saw the publication of his "Gli studi sulla poetica e sulla retorica di Dante e del suo tempo," both in *Cultura e Scuola*, IV (1965), 143-

ship to show forth the complexities of rhetorical consciousness in the varied and yet contiguous consciousnesses of
the Latin Middle Ages. As Curtius points out,[3] citing
Dante's curious passage in *Convivio* I, ii ("Non si concede
per li retorici alcuno di sè medesimo sanza necessaria
cagione parlar"—"the rhetoricians do not grant it to anyone to speak of himself without necessary cause"): "When
Dante referred to 'li retorici,' he certainly did not mean
Aquinas by it [as supposed by Busnelli and Vandelli], but
an *ars dictaminis* that we cannot yet identify."[4] Whatever
the sources of Dante's rhetorical tradition, they were likely
to include what Isidore put forth as a definition of allegory:
alieniloquium (*Etymologiae* I, xxxvii, 22): "This trope
is of various kinds, but the principal ones are the seven following: irony, antiphrasis, enigma, charientismos [dis-
simulated irony], paroemia, sarcasm, and astysmos ['ur-
banity without wrath']," terms which he goes on to define.
What is important to see here is that for Isidore allegory
is a trope, that it has to do with how something is said and
its resultant effect upon the hearer or reader. Today this
sense of the word is no longer current. Yet, in Dante's
time Isidore's wonderful word, *alieniloquium*, would seem
to have had resonance even unto Dante's own formulation

166, and in *Atti del Congresso Internazionale di Studi Danteschi*,
Florence, 1965, pp. 249-278. His notes contain the single most complete
bibliography available on the subject of Dante's rhetoric; see also his
article, "Dantes Selbstverständnis," *DDJb*, XLIII (1965), 7-24.

[3] *European Literature and the Latin Middle Ages*, p. 518.

[4] It is to this rhetorical rule that Dante certainly adverts in *Purg.*
xxx, 63, when he claims that necessity compels him to record the fact
that Beatrice spoke his own name—"Dante." John Freccero's recent
study on Dante's sense of Augustine's *Confessions* in the *Commedia*
(see Ch. IV, note 36, and note 13 below) begins with an analysis of
Purg. xxx, 61-64 in terms of its correspondence with *Conv.* I, ii, 12-14,
where Dante discusses the two main occasions when an author may
speak of himself, and uses as one his *exempla* Augustine's *Confessions*.

of a definition of allegory, for he says in the Letter to Can Grande that the word derives from the Greek *alleon* and the Latin *alienum*, which certainly brings the Isidorean "otherspeech" to mind.

To simplify again, we might divide Dante's three major works after the *Vita Nuova*, and excluding *Monarchia*, into three areas of allegorical interest: *Convivio*, the allegory of the poets; *Commedia*, the allegory of the theologians; *De Vulgari Eloquentia*, the allegory of the rhetoricians. I do not intend by this division to give the impression that Dante himself thought of the three works in any such schematic way. However, I do believe that his concerns, in so far as they are "allegorical" in these works, do more or less correspond to the divisions.

De Vulgari Eloquentia begins (1, i, 3), like Isidore's *Etymologiae* (1, ii, 1; 1, v, 1-4), with a discussion of *gramatica*.[5] Without stopping over the import of Dante's various references to classical rhetoric and its compilation in Isidore,[6] we can nevertheless see that his concern in *De Vulgari Eloquentia*, in so far as it applies to allegory at all, applies to the rhetorical concerns that Isidore identified with allegory, and not either to the allegory of the theologians or to that of the poets. We are free to speculate about the possible greater clarity and depth of Dante's treatment of Isidore and others that might have resulted

[5] For a study of Dante's understanding of the relationship between the vulgar tongue and the Latin art of grammar, see Karl D. Uitti's contribution, "Linguistics and Literary Theory" in the *Linguistics* volume of the Princeton Studies of Humanistic Scholarship in America, Richard Schlatter, general ed., Englewood Cliffs, N.J. [1968].

[6] Who is cited three more times: *D.V.E.* II, i, 1; II, vii, 5; III, xix, 6; by A. G. Ferrers Howell, ed., Temple Classics edition of *The Latin Works of Dante Alighieri*, London, 1914. It is perhaps noteworthy that the first of these citations follows hard upon Isidore's definition of allegory, which occurs some fourteen paragraphs earlier.

had he completed the treatise. He did not, however. Nevertheless, some further sense of Dante as *rhetor* is readily to hand, and in a familiar place: The Letter to Can Grande.

Of all Dante's writing, the thirty-three paragraphs of literary criticism of the *Epistola* are the most densely populated with the rhetorical *topoi* of the Middle Ages, as Curtius has demonstrated.[7] After Dante's proem in praise of Can Grande (1-4), he begins his explication of his own work by quoting Aristotle (5), and then moves on to the "sex . . . inquirenda" which have puzzled so many commentators, from the earliest to the present, and which both Wicksteed[8] and, more recently and with greater depth, Mazzoni[9] have pointed out as being in concord with the literary critical practice of Dante's day. The six things which should be inquired after are "subiectum, agens, forma, finis, libri titulus, et genus phylosophie" (6). Here Dante is the medieval rhetorician in full cry. He is about to become the poetic theologian at the seventh paragraph, where he advances the fourfold technique required for the understanding of his poem, and which we have earlier inspected. Having finished with the allegory of the theologians in the next paragraph, he proceeds with his rhetorical analysis in paragraph 9, with his rather problematic division of his *forma* into two groups, one of three, and one of ten, members.[10] "This curious list" is Moore's[11] reaction to Dante's *forma sive modus tractandi*, which, the

---

[7] "Dante und das lateinische Mittelalter," pp. 163-171.

[8] In the Temple Classics *Latin Works*, p. 364.

[9] F. Mazzoni, "L'Epistola a Cangrande," *Rendiconti dell'Accademia Nazionale dei Lincei*, x, fasc. 3-4 (1955), 191. But see Chapter I, note 33.

[10] For a modern reading see R. P. Blackmur, "Dante's Ten Terms for the Treatment of the Treatise," *Kenyon Review*, XIV (1952), 286-300.

[11] *Studies in Dante*, III, 288.

Epistola says, is "poetic, fictive, descriptive, digressive, transumptive, and also proceeds by definition, division, proof, refutation, and the setting forth of examples." Curtius quotes from similar statements of an anonymous Latin poet who wrote long before Dante; from Abelard; from Alexander of Hales, in whose work (*S. th.* 1, i) he finds five of Dante's ten terms; from Albertus Magnus, saying (*S. T.*, 1, q. 5, *membrum* 1) that theology has another mode from that of *scientia* and *ars*; and finally from Thomas in the same vein. He concludes that of Dante's two groups of five terms—and his lengthy argument is far more convincing than this brief recension—the first group issues, reflecting several sources, from Dante's sense of the rhetorical characteristics of poetry, and the second group from the rhetorical characteristics of philosophy, and even theology. Thus Curtius demonstrates, from still another angle of approach, that Dante's attitude toward Aquinas' distinction between poetry and Scripture was often not one of agreement.[12] "My poem," Curtius would have Dante say, "is, to be sure, a poem; but it is a poem that contains truth, and not mere fictions."

The rest of the *Epistola* is filled with Dante's rhetorical knowledge: in paragraph ten he alludes to Seneca's tragedies and Terence's comedies, as well as to Horace's *Ars Poetica* once again; in paragraphs sixteen and eighteen, to Aristotle; in paragraph nineteen, to Cicero's *Rhetorica*; and twice in paragraph twenty and again in paragraph twenty-one, to Aristotle. And then, bolstering the wisdom of his ancients, he moves to Scripture, for, as he says, "Similiter etiam et scientius facit auctoritas"—"And authority does the same as science." He cites from Scripture: Jeremiah, Wisdom, and Ecclesiasticus, but crowns the

[12] "Dante und das lateinische Mittelalter," pp. 167-171.

passage with the following from Lucan: "Iuppiter est quodcunque vides, quocunque moveris"—"Jupiter is whatever thou seest, wherever thou goest." (The passage is of particular interest to this study. Dante calls Scripture "authority," as we have observed earlier, and then goes on to cite from Lucan, describing "il sommo Giove," and calls the passage *scriptura paganorum*, which may mean merely the writing of the pagans, and may also mean, as I have previously argued, that writing of the pagans which, like Virgil's, Dante's *autore's, scrittura*, speaks *volumi*, and thus is, as it is in this passage, as authoritative in its way as Holy Writ.)

As the *Epistola* draws toward its conclusion, Dante again adverts to Aristotle (25), and then to Aristotle and St. Paul in the same breath (27), to the Bible and Richard of St. Victor, Bernard, and Augustine (28), to Plato's use of metaphor (29), and then to Boethius and John's Apocalypse (33). This cursory glance at the *Epistola* gives us some sense of Dante's knowledge and use of rhetorical tradition.

DANTE'S USE of personification allegory, "the allegory of the poets," is easier to document in the body of the poem. Two passages in the poem, to which I have frequently alluded, give us, when taken together, a natural occasion for the initiation of any such discussion. Each asks the reader to look beneath the veil of the literal words. The first occurs in *Inferno* IX, 61-63. As Dante and Virgil approach the city of Dis, and thus a significant intensification of their experience of sinfulness, they come upon the three Furies (the juxtaposition of the Furies and the walls of Dis was probably suggested to Dante by appearance of the Furies on the shield of Aeneas, *Aen.* VIII, 669, two lines after the phrase "alta ostia Ditis"—"the high gates of Dis"). The Furies, who rend themselves while crying loudly, call for Medusa to come and turn Dante to stone, thinking he is Theseus (*Inf.* ix, 54). This passage also has its counterpart in Virgil: *Aeneid* vi, 389-403. There Charon challenges Aeneas, led by the Sybil, and tries to prevent his access to the underworld, believing him to be either Alcides, come to steal away Cerberus a second time, or Theseus or Pirithous, come again to kidnap the bride of Dis, Proserpina. Dante telescopes the two Virgilian scenes to place the Furies and Medusa as watchdogs of Dis, as it were. And, just as the Furies think Dante is the old Theseus, so did Charon think Aeneas was the same. In each case the true guide gets the pilgrim by the keepers of the gate, although in the *Commedia* this is only finally effectuated by the advent of Grace in the form of an angel. The figuralism is evident: as Theseus, the conqueror of the Labyrinth, once descended into the underworld to kidnap Proserpina, failed, and had to be rescued by Heracles; as Aeneas, descending on even a higher mission, is momentarily checked, but goes on when the Sybil makes his identity and high purpose known; so does Dante, the new Theseus, the new Aeneas, aided by Virgil and one sent from God (line 85), get past Dante's second version of the obstructing Charon (we see Charon himself in *Inf.* iii).

All of this is clear enough. Indeed, so far there is not much question of personification allegory. Once again we see Dante treating pagan literature as though it were history, carefully forming a figural pattern between prior event and what he causes to transpire now. However, when Virgil warns Dante that he must not see the Gorgon or he will never leave Inferno, he does a strange thing. He does not trust Dante's own forces against sin apparently, for he turns Dante around, and not trusting to Dante's own hands, with which the Pilgrim has covered his own eyes, Virgil lends his hands to make sure Dante will not see. The moment certainly invites a moral interpretation, something like, "Stoic restraint is not enough." The passage reminds me—I am not at all sure that it reminded Dante—of the scene in Augustine's *Confessions* (VI, viii) in which Augustine's friend Alypius was lost to the study of the laws by his incurable passion for the gladiatorial combats at the Colosseum.[13] Alypius detested, Augustine

[13] At the conclusion of his brief treatment of Dante's knowledge and use of Augustine, Moore (*Studies in Dante*, I, 294) admits: "I must confess, in conclusion, that I have not been able as yet to investigate the question of Dante's probable acquaintance with the works of St. Augustine nearly as fully as the subject seems to deserve. I am continually coming on fresh points of resemblance." As the reader will remember, this study has several times turned to the *Confessions* as a source for a particular passage in the *Commedia*. Although Dante surely knew some of Augustine's more theological writings, especially *The City of God*, it is also more than likely that the *Confessions* would have seemed to him one of the prime documents which would justify his own use of autobiography (see note 4 above). My own superficial investigations had turned up enough evidence to make Moore's concluding remark seem all the more promising, when John Freccero's recently published study came to my attention: "Dante's Prologue Scene," *Dante Studies* [the new title of the *Annual Report of the Dante Society*], LXXXIV (1966), 1-25. What Freccero does for the first time is to demonstrate Dante's deliberate and conspicuous (once it is conceived—it has gone unconceived for some 650 years) summoning up of the seventh book of the *Confessions*, that part of the work which concerns Augustine's wanderings of the flesh and of the spirit, in the opening cantos of *Inferno*, which concern his own wanderings (see Ch. IV, n. 36). If the *Confessions* serve as the model for the description of the Pilgrim's sinful inner condition which necessitates his extraordinary journey, the *Aeneid*, as I have suggested to Professor Freccero since reading his piece, would seem to be the model for the journey he is about to take. My only major argument with Freccero, both in response to this excellent recent piece and to his earlier studies of Dante, is that he thoroughly scants Dante's knowledge and use of the classical Latin poets. For he is another who prefers to see Bernardus Silvestris where he might better see Virgil.

tells us, the notion of such barbarous spectacles. When his friends dragged him by force to see the games, he decided not to open his eyes, hoping thus to be absent while present. Then, with the roar of the crowd at the fall of a fighter, his stoic reserve fell away, and he was lost to the passive practice of barbarism for some time, until God's merciful hand eventually plucked him out. Augustine's comment upon the story is of interest:

"Which noise entered through his ears, and unlocked his eyes, to make way for the striking and beating down of his soul, which was bold rather than valiant heretofore; and so much weaker, for that it had trusted on itself, which ought only to have trusted on thee. For so soon as he saw the blood, he at the very instant drunk down a kind of savageness; nor did he turn away his head, but fixed his eye upon it, drinking up unawares the very Furies themselves; being much taken with the barbarousness of the sword-fight, and even drunk again with the blood-thirsty joy. Nor was he now the man he was when he came first thither, but became one of the throng he came unto; yea, an entire companion of theirs that brought him thither. What shall I say more? He looked on, he cried out for company, he was inflamed with it, carried home such a measure of madness as spurred him on to come another time: and that not only in their company who first haled him on, but to run before them too, yea, and hale on others also. Yet out of all this didst thou with a most strong and merciful hand pluck him notwithstanding, and taughtest him to repose no more confidence in himself, but upon thee only. But this was not till a great while after." (William Watts' translation in the Loeb Classical Library edition)

There are enough significant similarities between the two texts for us to attempt to "prove" the presence of an Augustinian echo here, especially since Dante's Furies, when they are first mentioned (line 38), are "tre furie infernal di sangue tinte"—"three hellish Furies, stained with blood," a phrase which could conceivably reflect Augustine's "et hauriebat furias . . . et cruenta voluptate inebriabatur"—"and he drank in the Furies . . . and became drunk with bloodstained pleasure." To be sure, Augustine's *furias* is not capitalized, and Watt's translation may play the literal sense false. Nevertheless, the word itself may have found a suggestive lodging in Dante's mind, whether or not Augustine intended a Classical allusion. In addition, there is the common and central potentiality of losing one's soul forever if the gaze become fixed, a situation which in both cases can only be remedied by Grace. And there is the similar moral lesson, illustrating the difference between boldness and strength, and asserting that only in God, and not in ourselves, can our confidence be placed.

To return to our passage in Dante: after Virgil has turned Dante around and covered Dante's face with his hands, the Poet interrupts to make the following address to the reader:[14]

> O voi ch'avete li 'ntelletti sani,
>   mirate la dottrina che s'asconde
>   sotto il velame de li versi strani.

> [O ye who are of good intelligence,
>   regard the doctrine which conceals itself
>   behind the veil of the strange lines.]
>   (*Inf.* IX, 61-63)

[14] The three major studies of Dante's use of apostrophe, explicitly the address to the reader, are Hermann Gmelin, "Die Anrede an den Leser in der Göttlichen Komödie," *DDJb*, XXX (1951), 130-140; Erich Auerbach, "Dante's Addresses to the Reader," *Romance Philology*, VII (1954), 268-278; Leo Spitzer, "The Addresses to the Reader in the 'Commedia,'" *Italica*, XXXII (1955), 143-166.

Our first question must be, in light of the critical perplexity caused by Dante's directive,[15] which "strange lines"? To be brief, I would argue that Dante did not consider the classical references difficult here, especially since he deals with them as "historical" event. But most of the commentators try to deal with this passage as they do with most of the *Commedia*; that is, they turn the whole thing into an extended piece of personification allegory, which, although it does yield some meaning, misses the best meaning. What Dante calls our attention to here, in my opinion, is the strange action of Virgil. To repeat, the mythic material reprocessed through Dante's memory of the *Aeneid* is clear enough: as the agents of Hell would have stopped and destroyed Theseus (Dante will again use Theseus as a type of himself when he confronts the Minotaur in *Inferno* XII, 17) and Aeneas, so now do they threaten Dante, who will, like them, be able to proceed only with divine sanction. It is Virgil's covering of an already covered pair of eyes which is strange; and thus the three lines *which immediately precede* the address to the reader, and which thus are the more likely candidates to prompt it, and which describe Virgil's behavior, are what is at stake.

The usefulness of the passage cited from Augustine is that it suggests not so much a source as a way of reading. And I believe the moral message is the same for both passages, even if they have no relation in terms of Dantesque reminiscence. *La dottrina* is, and many have pointed this out, that man may not have confidence in himself, for his powers are weak. And even the powers of the best

---

[15] For a recent summary of conflicting views, see Sapegno's commentary, vol. I, pp. 105-106. Most of the commentators believe that the phrase "li versi strani" refers to the Furies or Medusa rather than to Virgil's actions.

men, or of that most reasoning of men, Virgil, must in turn depend upon the Grace of God.

And so here, in a very clear example of Dante's use of the allegory of the poets,[16] we find that the technique is combined with the allegory of the theologians, a literal sense that is to be treated as historical, with the exception of Virgil's actions, which are not. They, although they are enacted, are enacted to show a hidden doctrine; they are not so much efficacious within the literal sense of the poem as they are emblematic of a general moral truth. That is precisely the characteristic of personification or philological allegory, which has only to be true *in verbis*, not *in facto*. And it is also important to observe that this kind of allegory comes in all respects as an interruption of the usual

[16] To remind the reader of the excesses of the commentators who read nothing but personification allegory in the *Commedia*, I cite the following passage: ". . . divine mercy (the Virgin) sends its illuminating grace (Lucy), to light Dante's reason (Virgil) back to the principles of right living and true believing as defined by Christian moral philosophy (Matilda) and theology (Beatrice)"—Jefferson Butler Fletcher, *Dante*, New York, 1916, p. 80. It is only fair to point out, however, that excessive belief in the omnipresence of the literal-historical is similarly unfortunate. Such is surely the case when we find a follower of Charles Singleton denying that Dante ever uses personification allegory, as when Rocco Montano, *Storia della poesia di Dante*, vol. II, Naples, p. 72, in discussing the passage in *Purg.* VIII which we are about to put into conjunction with *Inf.* IX, 61-63, denies that Dante even there uses "Greek" allegory. Karl Maurer, "Personifikation und visionäre Persönlichkeitssteigerung in Dantes *Divina commedia*," DDJb, XLIII (1965), 112-137, speaks to the mixture of the two kinds of treatment: "Eine Gruppe wie Paolo und Francesca, die nicht zufällig mit einem Paar zum Nest strebenden Tauben (!) verglichen werden, eine Gestalt wie die Belacquas, dessen Pose der leibhaftigen Faulheit verschwistert scheint (*più negligente/ che se pigrizia fosse sua serocchia*), stehen in der Mitte zwischen bedeutungsreicher Allegorie und ganz persönlichem Portrait" (p. 119). Maurer's discussion of Fortuna (p. 121), whom I shall discuss briefly below, is similarly perceptive about the mixture of poetic ingredients in her being.

technique of the poem, which is to take its literal sense literally or historically.

> Aguzza qui, lettor, ben li occhi al vero,
> ché 'l velo è ora ben tanto sottile,
> certo che 'l trapassar dentro è leggiero.

[Reader, here sharpen well thine eyes to the truth,
  for the veil is now indeed so thin
  that to penetrate within it now is easy.]

(Purg. VIII, 19-21)

The passage that follows this second appeal to the reader to penetrate the veil concerns the coming of the two angels with blunted swords who shall stand guard over the Valley of the Princes during the night against the serpent that comes there every evening (*Purg.* VIII, 22-42). What Dante accomplishes by the reference to his veiled speech here is to serve notice that this action, involving both angel and serpent, is a parable being acted out for the benefit of the denizens of the Valley of Princes, which place is a sort of Eden after the Fall but in suspense, out of history, as it were. What we have here is a pageant, a briefer version of the sort of allegorical procession we shall see in *Purgatorio* XXIX, XXXI and XXXII. The words that warn us to sharpen our eyes serve to remind us, as in the similar passage in *Inferno* IX, not to take the following action literally, but allegorically. And this kind of allegory is the allegory of the poets, not that of the theologians. To be sure, the points of reference here are "historical": first to the Fall and the subsequent guarding of Eden by the Cherubim and flaming sword (Genesis 3:24), and second to the return to Eden in *Purgatorio* XXVIII-XXXIII. However, this nightly event in the Valley of the Princes "happens" on another level, which is further demonstrated by the fact that when the snake appears here, Sordello, the temporary guide, says it is *perhaps* the snake which gave to Eve the bitter food ("forse qual diede ad Eva il cibo amaro"—line 99). My friend and colleague A. B. Giamatti has written well of this moment in the poem:

"That 'forse' sets the tone: perhaps it is the same snake that tempted Eve, perhaps not. The point is that the snake slithers into view and Eden comes to the poet's lips. The snake is pursued by the angels, and we feel that it came as if in a ritual and that the angels with their blunted swords were simply performing their part of the play. The effect is that in the simulacrum of Eden the old dream is enacted for the new souls to remind them not to procrastinate in those spiritual things but to be alert to the needs of the spirit; to remind them that beyond the Valley, whose similarity to Eden has been stressed for two cantos, lies the real garden."[17]

Giamatti's observation continues[18] by pointing out the echo of Limbo which is gained by Dante's use of the words "sommo smalto" in line 114 reflecting the "verde smalto" of *Inferno* IV, 118, and thus bringing together the Elysian fields of the poets and philosophers in Limbo, the Valley of the Princes, and the Garden of Eden, that highest bright spot which is pointed toward by both earlier "gardens."[19]

[17] *The Earthly Paradise and the Renaissance Epic*, Princeton, 1966, p. 100.   [18] *Ibid.*, p. 101n.

[19] The appearance of Giamatti's work removed the necessity of my including in this study my own deliberations on the figural uses of the garden in the *Commedia*. I have included some of my own ideas on this subject, but not in the programmatic form I had originally intend-ed, since I had planned to give the garden, from its first form as the *selva* of *Inf.* I to its last as the Paradisal rose, a chapter of its own.

The two passages which alert us to meanings hidden under veils have much in common. In each case we are asked to analyze the moral sense of a verbal configuration which is presented as philological allegory. In each case the action is either unlikely or "unhistorical" in a way that sets it off from most of the other actions described in the poem. Additionally, in each case, the Pilgrim has come to a barrier (the wall of Dis, the Gate of Purgatory) which can only be broached by the agency of prevenient grace (the angel from God in *Inferno*, and Lucia in *Purgatorio* IX). Thus both passages, behind their literal meanings, hold out parabolic significance: man is nothing without Grace. The double covering laid on by Virgil's hands and the ceremonial defeat of sin by the green angels of hope are, thus, two outstanding examples of the way in which Dante makes use of that earlier kind of allegory, in which words are used to describe actions that are patently, within the conventions of the fiction, "unreal," and thus may have only parabolic or metaphoric meaning. Ciacco, Ulysses, Cato—they and their actions are treated as genuine. The action of these two passages reverts to another mode. It is like the device of the play within the

---

The intermediate *foci* were to have been the green fields of *Inf.* IV, the barren trees of suicide in XIII, the humble vegetation of the shore of Purgatory, the Valley of the Princes, Eden, and then the various permutations of garden we find in *Paradiso*. Giamatti's chapter on Dante, although it does not share my enthusiasm for the nomenclature or for the concepts of medieval exegesis, stops at all these points in a way so suggestive that I find I have only this dimension to add. That would not be enough to justify a treatment of some forty or fifty pages. Furthermore, although I am not at all certain that Professor Giamatti will assent, I would like to suggest to him that it is precisely the figural principle of composition in the *Commedia* that peeks out from behind the excellent perceptions of his study. For another study of this topic, see Julius Wilhelm, "Zum Problem der schönen Landschaft in der Divina Commedia," *DDJb*, XXXIX (1961), 63-79.

play, which reinforces the reality of what we see happening under a proscenium arch by putting a second proscenium behind it, or by sending Marcello Mastroianni to the movies to watch Marcello Mastroianni.

These two passages are a good place to begin because they both call our attention to Dante's use of the language of personification allegory. Yet the *Commedia* contains several personifications. For instance, the goddess Fortuna in *Inferno* vii, 61-96. Is she "real"—"actual" is perhaps the more telling word—or merely the embodiment of a concept? Geryon (*Inf.* xvii) is certainly the embodiment of fraud, but he is treated as actual; he is both actual and a personification, as it were. And in him, and in the other monsters of *Inferno*, we see how Dante joins two techniques of allegory, for the actions Geryon performs take on meaning in light of "history," while what he is is a figuration of moral qualities alone. Indeed, the difference between *figural* and *figurative* is precisely the difference between the two kinds of allegory. Geryon's flight with Dante is figurally related to the flight of Phaethon (*Inf.* xvii, 107) and to that of Icarus (109); but the creature himself is treated as a figurative embodiment of fraud. Geryon only seems to have been made by the poet, and not by God; yet he performs actions which are exactly of the same order as those performed by those who were made by God. And so he, and the other monsters of *Inferno* have, poetically at least, a dual nature. That is, they both exist and do not exist in the order of the actual world with its actual history. An attempt to sort out the degrees of their complex beings is probably doomed either to hairsplitting or to failure. Let us return to Fortuna for a slightly clearer example of pure personification allegory, although even it turns out to be tainted.

Throughout the entire passage in which Dante discusses

her (*Inf.* VII, 61-96), as Virgil explains, following and adding to Boethius, that it is a happy thing that man's affairs on this earth are governed by one who is in fact just; Fortuna would seem to be no other or no more than an abstraction. She is the principle in human affairs which sees to it that the avaricious and the prodigal are always under her ministry and guidance (79), although they are not aware of this.[20] However, at the conclusion of Virgil's speech a strange thing happens: he tells Dante that Fortuna is in bliss among the other angels ("con l'altre prime creature lieta"—line 95) wheeling her sphere, joyful in her blessedness ("volve sua spera e beata si gode"—96). To be sure, we will not see her there among the ranks of angels in *Paradiso* XXVIII. Nevertheless, Dante has Virgil say explicitly that that is where she is, although it would certainly be presumptuous of him to say, on his own authority, that she is in fact there, and so he lets the matter drop.

The interesting problem here is that, even with such a patently philological figuration, Dante ends up treating her as though she were actual and had an actual existence, although from her "action" in the world, as it is described in the poem, we readily enough understand that she is to be taken only as an abstraction. Perhaps all we can say is that Dante sometimes goes to excess in his concreting imaginations. The same might be said of the wonderful

[20] A stockbroker friend once, without thinking of her, gave me my first feeling for Fortuna's ministry of human affairs. He said with a sigh, one twilight cocktail hour, "Imagine that one of your ancestors had invested a dollar, at compound interest rates, in the time of the Caesars, and that you were the sole heir. You would have all the money in the world." That delineates the tragic boundaries of capitalism rather well, I think. And it serves as a sour contemporary comment on Dante's Christian and sunny version of Fortuna.

figuration of the Old Man of Crete[21] in *Inferno* xiv, 94-
120; appropriated by Dante from Daniel 2:32f, Nebu-
chadnezzar's dream, he is patently a personification of the
degeneracy of man. Yet, mixed with Ovid, Virgil, and St.
Paul he becomes more and more "actual," his tears being
the source of the rivers of Inferno, until he is figurally
all those who are outside Grace, Paul's "Old Man." Thus,
he is historically all those since Adam and before Christ
who are without the Christian dispensation; he grieves
for his own fall and for the degeneracy of Rome, which
should not fall. Perhaps even more, he is the type of every
sinner in Hell. And so the Old Man also begins as an
allegorical personification of a moral principle, yet gradually takes on a tangible life of his own, like Antony's
fanciful crocodile in Shakespeare's *Antony and Cleopatra*,
whose tears are likewise real and wet. Thus, even in these
examples of Dante's personifications, we can see that they
have a way of eliding the difference between two kinds
of poetry, two theories of allegory. To a degree, this is
also true for the "historical" creatures of the poem. It
cannot be solely the fault of the commentators that they
have so long read the poem as personification allegory.
Beatrice may quite easily be understood as Theology,
Virgil as Reason. Indeed, the mixture of the two kinds
of allegory is not peculiar to Dante. For the exegetes of
his time, for instance, the Song of Solomon was to be
understood as parable, not as event. And yet, from parable
they extracted figural relationships: Solomon is the type
of Christ, the *sponsa*, his Bride, is the Church. Once again

[21] Some of the important studies are: G. Busnelli, *Il Virgilio dantesco
e il Gran Veglio di Creta*, Rome, 1919; H. T. Silverstein, "The Weeping Statue of Dante's 'Gran Veglio'," *Harvard Studies and Notes in
Philology and Literature*, XIII (1931), 165-184; R. M. Dawkins,
"The 'Gran Veglio' of *Inf.* xiv," *Medium Aevum*, II (1933), 95-107.

Migne's *Index Figurarum*[22] offers a quick way of seeing how various were the practices of exegesis. We know that the rules of the fourfold were essentially agreed upon, and we know that there was substantial agreement that the relationship between literal/historical and allegorical senses was to be seen in terms of historical promise and fulfilment. And this is what we expect to find when we see that Tertullian and nineteen exegetes after him (col. 246) agree that "Joseph . . . per omnes vitae suae eventus Christum Salvatorem mundi exprimebat." Or when we find that Tertullian and thirteen who came after insist that Adam is a type of Christ (col. 243). But we do not expect to find Peter Lombard, who consents in the above, saying elsewhere (in agreement with Richard of St. Victor —col. 250) that Adam is "typus rationis," or Adam Scot telling us that Naaman is "hominis superbi et luxuriosi figura" (col. 258). *Typus* and *figura* are supposed to be used (they usually are) to signify historical allegory. But we find often enough that the exegete—reversing the process we examined above when we saw that some exegetical proceedings move from parabolic literal sense to *figura* (which is "against the rules"), as in the Song of Solomon—also moves from historical literal sense to moralized personification. It would not be difficult to give hundreds of examples of each kind of eclectic practice. This should not suggest that we may be content to say that all there is is eclecticism, for we can find also a continuous adherence to orthodoxy as well. There is a great deal of eclecticism, to be sure. There is even more orthodoxy. Nonetheless, the ability of some exegetes to move so freely between two differing kinds of literal and allegorical senses is, in some respects, dismaying to a modern reader, although it should not be, as we have seen from Dante's

[22] *P.L.* CCXIX, col. 241-264 (see Ch. I, note 14).

own intermingling of the two kinds of allegory in *Convivio* II, i.

We may, in retrospect, think of the Medusa as a personification of that which turns hard the will of man in sin, the Furies as a personification of that in man which despairs and turns against his very being or of that impulse, perhaps, which leads to heresy. That is, we may read the passage in *Inferno* IX, indeed, the entire *Commedia*, as an extended and extensive *Psychomachia*. It "works" when we read it that way, as the *Aeneid* "works" similarly. The only problem in doing so is that when we interiorize the entire poem we make it less meaningful and less interesting, and we end up with an abstractionist, reductionist simplism which turns literature into a dead branch of moral philosophy. The briefest consultation of the moral explications of all the commentators who function primarily in this mode—and that means most of them—will prove that point readily enough. When we make all the actions in the poem stand for something else, and thus prevent them from being themselves, making them only signs of their meanings, we lose the poem, which becomes mere discardable *fabula*. In that sense, the majority of Dante's commentators are not *dantisti* at all.

If then there is a reciprocity between Dante's two primary kinds of allegory, I would certainly argue for the primacy of figuralism, of his adaptation of the fourfold Biblical exegetical tradition; for through this we get the stuff of the poem, and may if we wish also have the other, which treats the stuff as dross and lovingly flies to abstraction. But if we begin with abstraction, we will rarely if ever get at or care about the stuff.

There are many passages in the poem which involve personification allegory. Notably, and first of all, there are the scenes of the first two cantos which take place "nowhere." And then there are the lengthy processions of the Purgatorial pageants in xxix, xxxi, and xxxii. In both places personification is miraculously capped by figuralism. In the first the actual Virgil walks into the totally unreal world of Dante's *psychomachia*; in the second the actual Beatrice appears on the car which is preceded by the most full-blown personification allegory in the entire work. And so I would argue that whatever the extent of Dante's use of personification allegory, it is always subordinate both in purpose and in interest to his essential method of giving his poem form and meaning, that it is an employable though partial technique, while the other lies at the very core of his imagination.

To be sure, almost all allegorical fiction before and after Dante behaves differently from his. In Classical, late Classical, early medieval, and late medieval criticism allegory is either understood tropically as being the general device of saying one thing but meaning another (Isidore's *alieniloquium* comes to mind again); or, if we are dealing with a slightly more sophisticated critical apparatus, allegory is the more pointed device by which an author hides his *sententia* beneath the veil of the fictive words. Here its name may be one of many: *integumentum, involucrum, velum, cortex*.[23] A particularly clear and pleasing formulation of this kind of allegory is found in Bernardus Silvestris: "This kind of showing forth is truly a covering that conceals [*integumentum*], wrapping up the sense [*involvens intellectum*] beneath a fabulous telling of the truth, whence it is called an envelope [*involucrum*]."[24] Lubac's description is to the point here: "Pour ce genre

---

[23] See Robertson, "Some Medieval Literary Terminology," *Studies in Philology*, XLVIII (1951), 692, for "a little glossary" containing some further equivalents of two of these words.

[24] Riedel, p. 3. Quoted and discussed at the close of Chapter II.

d'explication des poètes et des philosophes,—et d'abord
pour leur mode même de présenter leur propre pensée,—
Guillaume de Conches use d'un terme technique: *integumentum*. C'était, comme son équivalent *involcrum*, un mot
cicéronien. Il correspond assez exactement à l'*allegoria*
classique."[25] What if this kind of allegorist wanted to
intermingle historical characters with his fictional allegorical ones. What are we to call them? For instance, in
Psychomachia Prudentius goes out of his way to include at
least one historical person, or reference to one, in each of the
episodes of a work that is otherwise almost pure personification allegory. As a single example I cite the appearance of
Job in the train of Patientia during her struggle with Ira
(line 163). What is the actual Job doing in the train of
the palpably unreal Patientia? To paraphrase Marianne
Moore, we here confront an imaginary battlefield with a
real Job in it. Curtius is helpful on this point: "*Exemplum
(paradeigma) is a technical term of antique rhetoric from
Aristotle onwards and means 'an interpolated anecdote
serving as an example.*' A different form of rhetorical
exemplum was added later (*ca.* 100 B.C.), one which was
of great importance for after times: the 'exemplary figure'
(*eikon, imago*) i.e., 'the incarnation of a quality.' "[26]

In almost all "straight" personification we are, in fact,
likely to find traces of this kind of exemplification, either
direct or indirect. It is one of the main techniques by which
arrant fictiveness attaches itself to the real world. Are these
"exemplary figures" *figurae*? Usually not. In other words,
in the case of the example of an *exemplum* drawn from
Prudentius, Job is not a *figura* of this lady Patientia: He
is an embodiment of the characteristic(s) she also represents. They are related exemplarily, not figurally.

[25] *Exégèse médiévale*, vol. IV, 189-190.
[26] *EL&LMA*, pp. 59-60.

In Dante, however, "exemplary figures" may also be
figurae. In *Purgatorio* each terrace shows us exemplary
figures of the sin that is purged thereon. Perhaps these
are the most obvious and best known *exempla* in the
Commedia. Yet *Inferno* also makes use of the technique.
The listing of the minor, non-speaking characters who
surround the dramatic actors in each area, if not offering
as pure a use of the technique, comes very close to doing
so. For instance, Dido in *Inferno* v is used as an *exemplum*
of lust when we first hear her name, but shortly thereafter
she becomes a *figura* of Francesca when we feel her presence in Dante's quotation of Aeneas' speech to her at the
beginning of *Aeneid* II, which is put into Francesca's
mouth. The *exempla* of personification allegory and those
used in Dante's appropriation of fourfold allegory are essentially the same in nature. It is the nature of the characters with whom they interact that tells us of the large
distance separating the different kinds of allegory which
contain them.

In order to point out further the difference between
Dante's kind of allegory and the more usual literary practice, it is instructive to return to early examples of literary
attention to the differing orders of literal sense. For the
differing kinds of, or modes of, meaning can surely be
best understood as they in turn devolve from the literal.
Whoever it was who wrote the *Rhetorica ad Herennium*
(*ca.* 85 B.C.) followed, as Curtius suggests,[27] the sort of
distinctions among varying literal senses made by Cicero.
This work, known to Dante as the *Nova Rhetorica* of

[27] *Ibid.*, p. 455: "Cicero (*De legibus*, 1, 5) teaches that history is
subject to other laws than poetry: the former is concerned with real
events, the latter with entertainment (*delectatio*)."

Cicero,[28] contains a passage which kept alive the spirit of Aristotle's concern for *mimesis*:

"Id quod in negotiorum expositione positum est tres habet partes: fabulam, historiam, argumentum. Fabula est quae neque veras neque veri similes continet res, ut eae sunt quae tragoediis traditae sunt. Historia est gesta res, sed ab aetatis nostrae memoria remota. Argumentum est ficta res quae tamen fieri potuit, velut argumenta comoediarum."

["The kind of narrative based on the exposition of the facts presents three forms: legendary, historical, and realistic. The legendary tale comprises events neither true nor probable, like those transmitted by tragedies. The historical narrative is an account of exploits actually performed, but removed in time from the recollection of our age. Realistic narrative recounts imaginary events, which yet could have occurred, like the plots of comedies."] (tr. Caplan)[29]

This tripartite distinction among literal senses, which apparently found its way to, among others, Servius, Macrobius, Martianus Capella, and Isidore,[30] may help us to

[28] It is cited in *Epistola* XIII, 19. The work was generally supposed to have been written by Cicero until the fifteenth century, when Valla was the first to doubt its authenticity.

[29] *Ad C. Herennium de ratione dicendi*, ed. and tr. Harry Caplan, London, 1954 (in the Loeb Classical Library), I, viii, 13 (pp. 22-24). The distinction is originally Cicero's—see *De Inventione* I, xix, 27: "argumentum est ficta res, quae tamen fieri potuit."

[30] Servius (E. K. Rand, vol. II, p. 128), on *Aen.* I, 235: "et sciendum est inter fabulam et argumentum, hoc est, historiam, hoc interesse, quod fabula est dicta res contra naturam, sive facta sive non facta, ut de Pasiphae, historia est quicquid secundum naturam dicitur, sive factum sive non factum, ut de Phaedra." Macrobius (*Commentariorum in Somnium Scipionis*, ed. F. Eyssenhardt, p. 481) spends I, ii, 7-21

see that the sort of distinctions I have made in this study were also made by writers in Dante's acquaintance. I am not claiming influence here, though surely Dante knew at least the passage in Isidore. What I do claim is that it is of use to us to consider Dante's *Commedia* in the light of *argumentum*, for it is a poem and not a history; yet it is a poem in which the events may not have actually happened but are to be understood and treated *as though* they had actually happened (all five of our rhetors use a version of the phrase "ficta res quae tamen fieri potuit").[31]

Dante's poem, as I said at the beginning of this chapter, contains various kinds of allegory. As I hope the passages we have hitherto examined demonstrate, he sometimes

---

discussing the three terms, making a distinction similar to that of Servius at I, ii, 9: "in quibusdam enim et argumentum ex ficto locatur, et per mendacia ipse relationis ordo contexitur, ut sunt illae Aesopi fabulae elegantia fictionis illustres, at in aliis argumentum quidem fundatur ueri soliditate, sed haec ipsa ueritas per quaedam composita et ficta profertur, et hoc iam uocatur narratio fabulosa, non fabula, ut sunt cerimoniarum sacra, ut Hesiodi et Orphei, quae de deorum progenie actuue narrantur, ut mystica Pythagoreorum sensa referuntur." Martianus Capella (*De nuptiis*, ed. F. Eyssenhardt, p. 185) differentiates between the three types as follows (v, 550): "Historia est ut Liuii. Fabula neque uera est neque ueri similis ut 'Daphnen in arborem uersam.' Argumentum est, quod non facta sed quae fieri potuerunt continet, ut in comoediis 'patrem timeri' et 'amari meretricem.'" Isidore (*Etymologiae*, *P.L.* LXXXII, col. 124) concludes Book I with the following (I, xliv, 5): "Inter historiam, et argumentum, et fabulam interest. Nam historiae sunt res uerae, quae factae sunt. Argumenta sunt quae, etsi facta non sunt, fieri tamen possunt. Fabulae uero sunt quae nec facta sunt, nec fieri possunt, quia contra naturam sunt."

[31] G. Paparelli, "*Fictio*. La definizione dantesca della poesia," *Filologia romanza*, VII, fasc. 3-4 (1960), 1-83, while not availing himself of the above-cited documents, presents a strong case, going back to Cicero, for the notion that fiction for Dante did not preclude the evidence of the senses, against F. Di Capua, *Insegnamenti retorici medievali e dottrine estetiche moderne nel 'D. v. e.' di Dante*, Napoli, 1947, p. 118n.: "*Fictio* e *fingere* hanno in Dante il significato d'immaginare."

mixes the two major kinds of allegory, making figural and moralized structures of the same moment. In concluding this study, I should like to return to the beginning of Dante's poem in order to make a further suggestion about the significance of those epitomizing first two cantos in light of this research. For Cantos I and II have usually been understood, even by those who propose an essentially figural or even fourfold reading of the poem, to be basically, if not totally, in the mode of personification allegory. I do not dispute this, but am myself becoming more and more convinced that even there Dante has figural extensions in mind for what seems to be pure personification. (I have, in my second chapter, discussed the Virgilian analogues at some length.) The remarks that follow are intended to be taken experimentally.

The narrator-character whom we encounter in the second line of the poem, coming to himself in the dark wood, is first Everyman, and only then himself. I do not here propose to consider any precise allegorical formulation of the general meaning of the cantos: Mankind, lost in sin, requires the aid of Reason, sent to him by Divine Grace, in order to face and defeat sin—that is perhaps a shorter and cruder version of the relatively obvious moral allegorizing which this part of the poem certainly seems to call for and has so often and tediously received. Let us consider more closely the landscape and the figures in the landscape. First there is the dark wood where the way is lost; a hill stands above, its top clothed in light. The poem moves to the interior condition of the Pilgrim: it shows us the Pilgrim looking back at the place of death, the *lago del cor*, from the dangerous waters of which he has just now pulled himself. Now he takes his way again, on the desert slope, climbing back up the hill. He meets the three beasts and retreats. Virgil comes to his aid and (in

Canto II) tells him of the three ladies in Heaven who care for his salvation, the one named Beatrice having remarked that death has embattled him "su la fiumana ove 'l mar non ha vanto" (II, 108). Finally, he begins again his journey.

I have already discussed the Adamic correspondence which I believe ties this most particular Everyman to the first acts of human history after the Fall.[32] Dante is the new Adam, looking up at the place from which he fell (for surely that is the hill which has Eden at its top). And then he becomes Noah surviving the Flood which indeed left no one else alive. Charles Singleton, for the river of *Inferno* II, has cited Hugh of St. Victor on the Ark. "And now let us understand the concupiscence of the world that is *in the heart of man* as *the waters of the flood*" (italics mine). The citation, it seems to me, works even better for the *lago del cor* of *Inferno* I than the *fiumana* of *Inferno* II. And if Dante is the seed of Adam here, barely escaping total destruction, he is also the new Aeneas, whose story we suddenly join at the moment of his wreck upon the coast of Libya. The Pilgrim has now two figural counterparts, one Hebrew, one Trojan. He begins to move along the *piaggia deserta*, having escaped the *pelago*. Thus did the Hebrews cross the Red Sea, led by Moses, and go on across the desert; thus did Aeneas survive his apparent disaster and proceed into Libya's desert. The three beasts would not seem to have any but a playful and verbal relationship to the next adventure of Aeneas.[33] In Jeremiah (5:1-6), however, they refer to the unfaithful Jews in Jerusalem whose backslidings and transgressions they oppose. Dante in the desert is analogous

[32] See Chapter II, note 25.
[33] See Chapter II, note 29.

to the Jews moving back to Jerusalem.[34] And then, in the desert, he meets Virgil (as Aeneas met his goddess mother, who told him his course). Is there a Biblical parallel here? I believe there may be. And although the previous Biblical parallels have been observed by some, this one has not been. Virgil is Virgil, and Virgil is figurally related to John the Baptist, whose desert voice leads to Christ, and who performs the first baptism. What are Dante's first words in describing Virgil? "Quella fonte/ che spandi di parlar sì largo fiume" (lines 79-80). Virgil is a fountain which pours forth a river of speech. Is his "water" figurally related to the baptism in Jordan (Mark 1:5; John 1:28) given by John the Baptist, the first baptism which is then completed in the baptism offered by Jesus in that same river? The last words of Dante to Virgil (*Purgatorio* xxx, 51) are these: "Virgilio a cui per mia salute die' mi" ("Virgil, to whom I gave myself up for my salvation"). And, contained in Dante's last words to Beatrice are these: "O donna . . . che soffristi per la mia salute/ in inferno lasciar le tue vestige" ("O lady . . . who for the sake of my salvation bore the leaving of thy footprints in Hell"—*Paradiso* xxxi, 79-81). At Dante's beginnings we do well to have in mind his endings, and vice versa. It is Beatrice, the figure of Christ, who brings Dante to salvation; it is Virgil who brings Dante to Beatrice. Dante does not (and did not in the *Vita Nuova*) use the word *salute* lightly. His last words to Virgil give him the highest function any one less than Christ may perform, and that is to bring another to Christ. Dante's last words to Virgil assert no less than this, and we have no license to take them other than at face value. The figuralism which results is, I claim, clear in *Purgatorio* xxx. Looking backward, per-

---

[34] As John Freccero has pointed out; I shall discuss his findings shortly.

haps we will more easily see what kind of a river flows behind the metaphor of the river of speech: Jordan. And finally we come to the *fiumana*, which is also, as John Freccero has been almost alone in seeing quite clearly, Jordan,[35]

[35] Recent reinterpretation of the first two cantos, involving close attention particularly to the water images, was initiated by Charles Singleton's first published work on Dante, " 'Sulla fiumana ove 'l mar non ha vanto,' " *RR*, XXXIX (1948), 269-277. The leading expositor of this subject is, in my opinion, John Freccero, many of whose studies have been involved with the "prologue" of the poem. Most to the point here is his recent "The River of Death: *Inf.* II, 108," in *The World of Dante*, ed. S. B. Chandler and J. A. Molinaro, Toronto, 1966, pp. 25-42. My own analysis of the Biblical analogues to the Pilgrim's journey is indebted to his analysis to a large degree, despite the fact that I have differing reasons for agreement on certain particulars. His basic sense of the figural movement, in Cantos I and II, from the crossing of the Red Sea, through the desert, to Jordan, seems to me entirely just. However, had Professor Freccero taken into account the commentary of Filippo Villani, he would have found an early understanding of the *fiumana* exactly like his own: " 'Non uedi tu la morte' (id est Dyabolo), 'che 'l combatte/Su la riuera' (scilicet Jordanis fluminis, qui ponitur pro Sacramento baptismatis). . . ." This is part of Villani's exegesis of *Inferno* II, 107-108. It continues by explaining why the sea "has no vaunt" over Jordan in ways that are simpler and more to the point than Freccero's discussion of Jordan as Oceanus: "Et ad licteram, Jordanis fluuius mare non ingreditur, sed desinit in lacum nitidum et amenum." His distinctions among kinds of bodies of water may reflect those of Isidore (*Etymologiae* XIII, xiv-xix), and might remind the reader that the Dead Sea (into which Jordan flows) is *not* a *mare* but a *lacus* or a *stagnum*. Villani's solution seems to me the best. It is intriguing to see, indeed, how much of Freccero's work has been anticipated by Villani. For instance, that famous *piè fermo* of *Inferno* I, 30 draws from Villani the following comment: "Id est, pede, nostre uoluntatis executio figuratur"—a formulation nearly identical with Freccero's own in "Dante's Firm Foot and the Journey without a Guide," *Harvard Theological Review*, LII (1959), 245-282. Further, Villani even points to the equivalence between the wandering Dante and the wandering young Augustine, the partial subject of Freccero's recent and excellent piece, "Dante's Prologue Scene," *Dante Studies*, LXXXIV (1966), 1-25: Villani makes the equivalence between Dante's state in the *piaggia deserta* and the *status* "gentilis populi ante conuersionem ad fidem Chripsti, et de bello animi

now under the gaze of Beatrice, who is *figura Christi*, and who will in fact be in charge of Dante's final baptism, in *Purgatorio* xxxiii, thus balancing the baptism overseen by Virgil in *Purgatorio* i—both of these later watery scenes prepared for by the "two Jordans" of *Inferno* i and ii.[36]

This tentative sketching of the dense figural pattern which I believe lies beneath the more usually discussed personification allegory of the first two cantos will, I hope, be taken as experimentally as it is offered. My own considerations aside, it is clear from the work of others, especially that of John Freccero, that Dante has mingled here the two kinds of allegory even when, as I have previously

---

ipsius in conuersione, ut accidit in beato Augustino, qui longe stetit cathecuminus." Freccero and Villani share the same excellences, and shortcomings: they both fail to grasp, in my opinion, the centrality of the text of the *Aeneid* to Dante's poem, insisting instead that Dante read Virgil through a veil, as Villani says in his introduction: "Poete uero, quibus proprium est inuenta philosophye sub figmentis occulere, et integumentis inuoluere et uelare." However, he will later insist, when explicating the line (*Inf.* i, 84) in which Dante proclaims his debt to Virgil, that Dante did not take his *allegorias* on Virgil from the allegorists, but drew them out himself ("allegorias de profundo effodit") from the depths of the poem. Of all the critics of the *Commedia* during the past six and one-half centuries, Villani is the closest to Freccero, the new Villani, a figural correspondence which is reinforced when we consider that, where the bulk of Freccero's work has been concerned with the first canto of the poem, all that Villani left us in his commentary on that very canto. There almost seems to be a design in things.

[36] Dante's response to the Apostle John in *Par.* xxvi, 62, in which the Pilgrim summarizes his conversion to the Good in a watery metaphor that certainly seems to reflect "la fiumana ove 'l mar non ha vanto" of *Inf.* ii, 108, serves as a further commentary within the poem on the waters of the opening cantos. For now Dante says that he was drawn forth "from the sea of wrongful love" ("del mar de l'amor torto"), and placed on the shore of rightful love. Seen in this light (which was shown to me by my student, Robin McAllister) the sea of *Inf.* ii "has no vaunt" over the river because wrongful love has no power against baptism.

attempted to demonstrate, he most surely seems to be using only personification allegory.

THIS STUDY has occupied itself with four aspects of Dante's figuralism. The first, which, as noted, has gradually received increased attention and acceptance, is Dante's involvement with the theory of the allegory of the theologians. The second, which has received hardly any study at all, concerns his rather straightforward adaptation of Christian allegoresis in his own poem, the creation of a universal history which begins with Genesis and ends with the counterpart of Revelation, *sub specie aeternitatis*. The third concerns his sense of other literature, a sense which made of Ovid and Virgil in addition to the Bible the compendia of that universal history.[37] The fourth involves a more loosely connected subject which I have called, with some hesitation, "verbal figuralism," arguing that Dante treated the very words of his own poem as things, the meanings of which (like the meaning of Moses) only become clear when we arrive at later contexts which complete the meaning.

Thus, although the title of the work is *Allegory in Dante's* Commedia, its treatment violates the usual sense of the word allegory, and attempts to restore to our critical sense of the poem the primacy of the literal, without which, as Dante says, it is impossible to attend to the other senses.[38]

[37] The only study I have seen which makes any concerted use of these first three techniques in a combination that, to my way of reading, gets at the essential givens of Dante's poem is the unpublished dissertation of Sister Marie Catherine Pohndorf, to which I must advert this final time.

[38] *Convivio* II, i, 8. Appended here is St. Augustine's defense of the historicity of the first three chapters of Genesis against the Greek allegorists of his own day, which also expounds upon the importance

of the literal, and discusses the same distinctions which are at stake in this study of the *Commedia*, or at least in the pretext of Dante's poem as this study sees that pretext. It is from *De Genesi ad litteram*, the great work of Augustine's "middle period," ca. 401-415: "In fact, the narrative of these texts is not in the mode of figurative speech, as is found in the Canticle of Canticles, but is entirely a record of events, as is found in the Books of Kings and others like them. Because these texts report events as our common experience of human life reflects them, it is not difficult, it is even extremely simple, to accept them first of all literally and then to explain the future things which they have signified. However, because here in Genesis there are told things which do not concur with our intuitions of the course of our habitual experience, some do not wish to understand these things as events in themselves, but as figurative speech. And such as these claim that history, that is, the narration of actual events, begins only in that place in the text where Adam and Eve, sent out of Paradise, come together and generate. As though it would be ordinary in our experience either that Adam and Eve lived so many years, or that Enoch was carried up to Heaven, or that an old and sterile woman bore a child, or other things of this kind" (VIII, i, 2). Similarly, we might understand a historical view, "a record of events," behind the letters of Dante's "Genesis," in which the three opening historical analogues to the Pilgrim are Adam sent forth from Eden, Aeneas shipwrecked, and Augustine in his errancy. Did Dante knowingly begin his poem, which moves from Alpha to Omega, with three "Alphas"—Adam, Aeneas, Augustine? Perhaps he did.

APPENDIX I

THE FOURTEENTH-CENTURY
COMMENTATORS
ON FOURFOLD ALLEGORY

The Letter to Can Grande left its mark, whether directly or indirectly, on almost all of Dante's earliest critics. This fact in itself is of little critical import, since the commentators themselves make extraordinarily little use of theological allegory, preferring to pursue a more congenial form of explication, namely, that of personification allegory. Nevertheless, it is historically important and significant that almost all of them, at the outset of their investigations, feel compelled to make obeisance to a theological allegorical principle, even if it is one which they either do not understand in relationship to the text of the poem, or do not choose to employ in any broad or meaningful way.[1] Their statements occupy a place in the proem of their respective commentaries, or, if not there, sometimes in their discussions of *Inferno* I.

As for the mode of transmission of the *Epistola*'s fourfold distinctions, nothing will be said here. The subject is complex and necessarily confused, especially when with Francesco Mazzoni, we consider that the first fourteenth-century commentator to cite Dante explicitly as the author of the *Epistola* is also the last one, Filippo Villani, and

[1] For a discussion of the figural awareness of nine of the eleven commentators dealt with here (it does not consider Guido da Pisa or the Anonimo), see Andrea Ciotti, "Il concetto della 'figura' e la poetica della 'visione' nei commentatori trecentischi della 'Commedia,' " *Convivium*, xxx (1962), 264-292, 399-415.

that only a few of the other commentators, it would seem, have even read the document themselves.[2]

What is offered here, then, is evidence that the first readers of the *Commedia* did take seriously the exegetical claims expressed more cogently by the *Epistola*, even if their critical practice usually belies their understanding of the *Epistola's* precepts. For their essential exegetical technique corresponds very closely to Dante's own technique in *Convivio*. That is, although he there claims that four senses are in play (*Conv.* II, i), his actual practice is almost always to divide his *canzoni* into literal (which is *bella menzogna*) and allegorical (which is the meaning hidden under the veil of the fictive words). To be sure, like some of his commentators,[3] he does on occasion invoke the concepts and techniques of Scriptural exegesis.[4] Nevertheless, in both *Convivio* and the fourteenth-century commentaries, the predominant mode is to treat the poem— despite the opening assertion of an allegorical principle modeled on that of the Biblical commentators—as *bella*

[2] See F. Mazzoni, "L'Epistola a Cangrande," *Rendiconti dell'Accademia Nazionale dei Lincei*, X, fasc. 3-4 (1955), 157-198. The first to make these observations was G. Boffito, "L'Epistola di Dante Alighieri a Cangrande della Scala: saggio d'edizione critica e di commento," *Memorie della Reale Accademia delle Scienze di Torino*, s. 2a, LVIII (1907), I. A work I should have liked to consult has just come to my attention. I have ordered but not yet seen B. Sandkühler, *Die frühen Dante-Kommentare und ihr Verhältnis zur mittelalterlichen Kommentartradition*, Munich, 1967.

[3] See Ciotti's study (note I above) for discussions of specific texts in the various commentators which show an awareness of the figural tradition and a sense that the text of Dante's poem has a significant relationship to the literal sense of Scripture. My only quarrel with Ciotti is that he does not make it clear that the passages he cites do not reflect the dominant critical method of the commentators, who, as I have said above, apply personification allegory to the text of the poem while espousing, to some degree at least, theological allegory.

[4] See Chapter I, note 26.

menzogna, dividing it carefully into "letter" and "allegory," and by "allegory" almost always signifying personification allegory. In other words, the essential mode of the commentators contradicts their own claims that the poem contains the four Biblical senses. This is not especially surprising, since that mode of reading the poem has persevered through six centuries. The initial confusions, as well as the later ones, are perhaps traceable to the single honorable supposition that "only God can write that way." And all the commentators have the excuse that no other secular work they might have known had ever shown that God's way of writing could be adapted to the purposes of secular fiction, that they had no exemplary model against which to judge Dante's work. Thus they see it against the models they do know in which allegory is "Greek" allegory, the "this *for* that," the truth hidden beneath a veil, the literal sense being mere discardable fable.

It is important to know how little actual use of fourfold interpretation the commentators make (although there are many more particular instances, or at least attempts, in the fourteenth century than there will be until our own), for their opening salvos would seem to promise a great deal of such analysis. I offer these opening statements below, following the brief listing of all the signed or identified commentaries as well as one of the four anonymous interpretations cited by Toynbee.[5] The most interesting statement (excepting Villani's) seems to me that of Pietro

---

[5] Whose datings I follow, sometimes adjusting them to Mazzoni's more recent investigation. See Paget Toynbee, *Dante Alighieri, His Life and Works*, New York, 1965. This is Charles Singleton's updating of the 1910 edition, and contains, in Appendix D, pp. 272-275, a chronological listing of the commentaries which were written from the fourteenth to the sixteenth centuries. However, despite the usefulness of this listing, I must point out its serious scholarly shortcomings: at least four of the fourteenth-century entries describe critical texts which have long since been superseded. In addition, the commentary of Villani is not even mentioned.

Alighieri. His attempt to distinguish four kinds of literal sense is especially arresting.[6] The anonymous commentor, it would surely seem, was influenced by Pietro's formulation, and I include him primarily in order to give Pietro's longer and more involved discussion of the sevenfold senses he finds in the poem some further, and possibly clearer, expression.

The reader will see that my own treatment of Dante's allegory corresponds to some degree with Pietro's, at least in that his first four senses involve distinctions about the kinds of literal sense the poem employs, and in that his last three are the classical exegetical "spiritual senses." Pietro's first four divisions, however, seem to me confused and even self-contradictory: his third sense (*apologeticus*—what would seem to correspond to Cicero's and to Augustine's "middle style," that is, the style of instruction) and his fourth sense (*metaphoricus*—both Cicero and Augustine say that metaphors and other figurative speech are the earmark of the "middle style") are actually describing the same phenomenon. This phenomenon, furthermore, is primarily the same as what he describes by his first sense, the "*literal*, superficial, or parabolic," which points to such phenomena as Biblical parable, which, I claim, is precisely *metaphoricus* and *apologeticus*. I must admit that I cannot judge whether Pietro is confused or whether I am. Nevertheless, what is clear is that his desire to make distinctions about degrees of literalness is of major importance, at least as it encourages others to do so also, even if few have tried.

1. Graziolo de' Bambaglioli (Latin, 1324)
2. Jacopo di Dante (Italian, before 1325)
3. Guido da Pisa (Latin, ca. 1324)

[6] See John Paul Bowden, *An Analysis of Pietro Alighieri's Commentary on the Divine Comedy*, New York, 1951.

4. Jacopo della Lana (Italian, ca. 1328)
5. *L'Ottimo Commento* (Italian, 1333)
6. Pietro di Dante (Latin, ca. 1340)
7. Giovanni Boccaccio (Italian, 1373)
8. Benvenuto da Imola (Latin, 1373-1380)
9. Francesco da Buti (Italian, 1385-1395)
10. Anonimo (Italian, ca. 1400)
11. Filippo Villani (Latin, ca. 1400)

1. *Comento alla cantica dell'Inferno di D. Allighieri, di autore anonimo* (pub. W. W. Vernon, Florence, 1848). This is the Italian translation of Graziolo de' Bambaglioli's *commento* (see Moore, *Studies in Dante*, III, p. 345). The standard Latin text, which I have not seen, is to be found in *Il commento dantesco del "Colombino" di Siviglia*, ed. A. Fiammazzo, Savona, 1915. The brief *proemio* does not refer to the Letter to Can Grande, but does establish the straightforward use of personification allegory which is the earmark of the body of the work. In these two respects, it has a great deal in common with the commentary of Jacopo Alighieri. Graziolo's possible gnostic tendencies are displayed in his frequent assertions that the poem is most concerned with "Wisdom" (the word *sapienza* is the key word of his *proemio*). This notion is further supported when we consider his treatment of the Veltro (p. 21), who, claims Graziolo, will bring "sapienza" to the world, which is without it. In the *proemio* he also displays his predilection for personification allegory when he is the first to equate Virgil with personified Reason (p. 3): "quello sommo poeta Vergilio sicome la vera ragione medesima."

2. *Chiose alla Cantica dell'Inferno di Dante Alighieri scritte da Jacopo Alighieri* (ed. Jarro [G. Piccini], Florence, 1915). In his very brief introduction (pp. 43-45) Jacopo speaks with great brevity about allegory (p. 44),

and not in such a way as to be of great interest to a student of his father's work. Of the two sons—if the works that bear their names are truly their own—Pietro was either more naturally gifted in the direction of literary criticism or had, as is possible, better training. Jacopo's commentary on *Inferno* is a rather miserable performance in the elaboration of the obvious and in the obfuscation of the clear. His continual mode is flat-footed allegorization, and his work is mainly of interest for its historical notes. His remarks on the subject of allegory are as follow:

" . . . per questo proemio dichiarerò parte de' suoi principii per abbreviarmi più nelle seguenti cose, dicendo ch'il principio delle intenzioni del presente autore è di dimostrare di sotto alegorico colore le tre qualitadi dell'umana generazione."

["... in this proem I shall explain his principles in order to be less lengthy in what follows. I say that the guiding principle of the author's intention is to show, beneath an allegorical guise, the three characteristics of the human race (those moral propensities which are treated in turn by each of the three *cantiche*)."]

3. All that is available in print of the commentary of Guido da Pisa is to be found in *Bull. Soc. Dant.*, n.s. VIII (1901), 150-157. There are strong similarities between this work and Jacopo della Lana's *proemio*. As his remarks near their conclusion, Guido speaks of allegory as follows (p. 156):

"Primus namque intellectus, sive sensus, quem continet Comedia, dicitur hystoricus; secundus allegoricus; tertius tropologicus; quartus vero et ultimus dicitur anagogicus. Primus, dico, intellectus est hystoricus: iste intellectus non se extendit nisi ad literam, sicut quando accipimus

'Minorem' [sic] judicem et assessorem inferni, qui disiudi-
cat animas descendentes. Secundus intellectus est allegoricus, per quem intelligo quod litera, sive historia, unum
significat in cortice et aliud in medulla; et secundum istum
intellectum allegoricum Minos tenet figuram divine
iustitie. Tertius intellectus est tropologicus, sive moralis,
per quem intelligo quomodo me ipsum debeo iudicare; et
secundum istum intellectum Minos tenet figuram rationis
humane, que debet regere totum hominem, sive remorsus
conscientie, qui debet mala facta corrigere. Quartus vero
et ultimus intellectus est anagogicus, per quem sperare
debeo digna recipere pro commissis; et secundum istum
intellectum Minos tenet figuram spei, qua mediante penam
pro peccatis et gloriam pro virtutibus sperare debemus."

["For the first discernment, or sense, which the *Commedia*
contains is called historical; the second, allegorical; the
third, tropological; and the fourth and last is called anagogical. I say the first sense is historical: this sense does
not extend beyond the letter, as when we understand that
Minos is the judge and jury of Hell, who passes judgment on the souls as they come down. The second sense
is the allegorical, by which I understand how the literal,
or historical, means one thing on its shell, and another in
its kernel; and according to the allegorical sense Minos
contains the figure of divine justice. The third is the
tropological, or moral, by which I understand how I ought
to sit in judgment on myself; and according to this sense
Minos contains the figure of human reason—which ought
to rule the whole man—and of remorseful conscience,
which ought to regulate evil deeds. And the fourth and
last is called the anagogical, by which I ought to hope
to be returned good desert for good practice; and according to this sense Minos contains the figure of what we

should hope for, rendering punishment for our sins and eternal life for our goodness."]

4. *Comedia di Dante degli Allagherii col commento di Jacopo della Lana Bolognese* (ed. Luciano Scarabelli, Bologna, 1866). There is a more recent edition by F. Schmidt-Knatz, Frankfurt am Main, 1939, which I have not seen. Jacopo's treatment of fourfold allegory would seem to be indebted to Guido's, or Guido's to Jacopo's, as each uses Minos as its example. Here, in his *proemio*, Jacopo is following the usual distinction, also made in the Letter to Can Grande, and here somewhat garbled, between the form of the treatise and the form of the treatment (p. 98):

". . . la forma poetica, la qual' è fittiva ed esemplipositiva ave IIII intendimenti; lo primo si è lo *letterale* o vero storiale, lo quale non si stende più innanti che sia la lettera, nè oltre lo termine, in ch' ella è posta, siccome quando elli pone Minos nell'Inferno per uno demonio iudicatore delle anime. Lo secondo si è *allegorico*, per lo quale lo termine della litteratura uno suona e altro intende, siccome è interpretare lo detto Minos per la giustizia, la qual giudica le anime secondo lor condizione. Lo terzo è detto *tropo* cioè morale, per lo quale s'interpreta il detto Minos primo re, che fu in Creta, giusto, donando al vizioso pena, e a li virtuosi merito; così moralmente si pone per giudice in Inferno, che dicerna per la condizione delle anime a ciascuna il luogo, e la pena che a lei si avviene. Lo quarto è detto *anagogico*, per lo qual s'interpreta spiritualmente gli esempli a similitudine della detta Comedia, siccome quando fa menzione d'alcune singolari persone, come quivi: *Ell' è Semiramis* ecc., che non si deve intendere che quella persona sia posta in inferno o altrove in luogo determinativamente qui posta; imperochè questo è occulto e segreto alli mondani: ma spiritualmente s'intende che quel vizio che è attribuito a colui overo virtù per tal modo si è punito o purgato o rimunerato per la giustizia di Dio, salvo di quelli de' quali Santa Chiesa scrive; non in quanto l'autore d'essi scrive, ma in quanto la Chiesa li canonizza e per santi tiene, siamo certi che ivi sono."

[". . . the form of the poetry, which is fictional and example-giving, has four meanings; the first is the *literal*, or historical, and it does not extend beyond the letter, nor beyond the intention the letter implies, as when the author puts Minos in *Inferno* as the demon who judges the souls. The second is *allegorical*, by which the intention of the letter is to say one thing and mean another, as when this same Minos is to be interpreted as justice, which judges the souls according as to their quality. The third is called *tropological*, or moral, by which Minos is to be interpreted the first king, who lived in Crete, just, rendering punishment to the sinful man, reward to the virtuous; thus, morally, he has his place as judge in *Inferno*, discerning by the quality of each soul its proper place and proper punishment. The fourth is called *anagogical*, by which we may interpret the spiritual meaning of similar examples in this same *Commedia*, as when any particular person is mentioned, for instance: "That is Semiramis," etc. (*Inf.* v, 58), which should not be understood to mean that this person was put in *Inferno*, or any other place which we may ascertain; rather, such matters are occult, hidden from earthly eyes. Spiritually, nevertheless, we are to understand that the sin attributed to one, or indeed the virtue, similarly, is punished or purged or rewarded by God's justice. However, when the author writes of those of whom the Holy Church has written, and when the Church has canonized them, holding them as saints, we may then be sure that where he says they are they are."]

5. *L'Ottimo commento della Divina Commedia: testo inedito d'un contemporaneo di Dante* (ed. Alessandro Torri, Pisa, 1827-1829) begins with a most brief *proemio*, given in full below. Although it makes no reference to fourfold exegesis at the outset, it is still interesting in that it initially commits itself to the processes of personification allegory, as is immediately apparent (p. 1):

"Ad aprire l'intenzione dell' Autore, è da sapere delle figure, ch'ei usa in questo suo volume: ed è da notare, che Dante pone sé in forma comune d'uomo, nel quale è l'anima ragionevole, e la potenza sensibile, e la potenza vegetabile, e lo libero arbitrio: e d'uomo, dico, intento nelle sensualitadi di questo mondo, inclinato ad esse; o vero sè in forma del libero arbitrio, inchinante alle sensualitadi: Virgilio per la ragione sensuale, dirizzante lo libero arbitrio alla cognizione de' vizj e delle virtudi: Beatrice per la Teologia della Divina Scritture: la gentile Donna, che si compiange nel Cielo, per la Grazia preveniente ed impetrante da Dio, che per l'amore, che l'Autore porta alla Divina Scrittura, gli sia mandato lo suo soccorso: Lucia per la Grazia cooperante ed ausiliante; senza le quali non era sufficiente la salute. E così comincia:"

["To lay bare the intention of the author, and to come to know the figures of speech which he employs in this his volume, we must take note that Dante takes on the common form of man, who has a rational soul as well as a sensitive and a vegetative potency, and also freedom of the will. And, I say, he takes on himself the form of the man who is concerned with the sensory aspects of this world, and is even inclined to them. Indeed, he presents himself as free will leaning toward sensuality; Virgil as worldly reason directing the free will toward the cognizance of the vices and the virtues; Beatrice as the Theology of Holy Scripture; the kind Lady, who pities him in Heaven, as the prevenient and rogatory Grace of God, which, by the love the author bears for Holy Scripture, sent him aid; Lucy as cooperating and auxiliary Grace, without which his salvation in Heaven were not enough. And the poem begins:"]

6. *Petri Allegherii super Dantis ipsius genitoris comoediam, Commentarium* (pub. W. W. Vernon, ed. V. Nannucci, Florence, 1846) contains the longest and possibly the most interesting discussion of Dante's, his father's, allegory. The sevenfold division is curious. It is probably fair to say that the first four senses represent an attempt to define, or at least analyze, varying degrees of literalness, while the last three are the conventional second, third, and fourth senses. Despite this ingenious and complex (and perhaps confusing) introduction, Pietro's actual commentary is hardly ever concerned with any kind of rigorous application of the principles he enunciates here, preferring the safer, or at least more usual, techniques of personification allegory, as is evident, for example, within his treatment of *brachium Dei* in the final paragraph below. The passage occurs in the introductory statement which precedes the text of the poem (pp. 4-8):

"Causa formalis duplex est, scilicet, forma tractatus, et forma tractandi. Forma tractatus est divisio ipsius libri, qui dividitur et partitur per tres libros; qui libri postea dividuntur per centum capitula; quae capitula postea dividuntur per suas partes et rhythmos. Forma tractandi est septemcuplex, prout septemcuplex est sensus, quo utitur in hoc poemate noster auctor.

"Nam primo utitur quodam sensu, qui dicitur *literalis*, sive superficialis et parabolicus: hoc est, quod scribit quaedam, quae non importabunt aliud intellectum nisi ut litera sola sonabit; nam non omnia hic scripta includunt sententiam, sed propter verba sententiam et figuram importantia inseruntur. Unde Augustinus in 15.° de civitate Dei ait: *non omnia, quae gesta narrantur, significare aliquid putanda sunt, sed propter illa, quae aliquid significant, attexuntur. Solo vomere terra perscinditur, sed ut hoc fieri possit, etiam cetera alia membra aratri sunt necessaria.* Et ut scribitur in Decretis: *licet in veteri lege multa sub figura ponantur, tamen quaedam ad literam sunt solum intelligenda, ut in praecepto illo*: non occides, non moechaberis etc.

"Secundo utitur quodam sensu, qui dicitur *historicus*, dictus ab *historia*: quae historia dicitur ab *historin*, quod est *videre*, ex eo quod ea quae in historia narrantur, ac si essent subjecta visui declarantur: et continet res veras et verisimiles. Nam haec vox *Hierusalem* historice intelligitur ipsa civitas terrestris, quae est in Syria, in illa parte quae dicitur Palestina etc., idest gesta.

"Tertio utitur quodam sensu, qui dicitur *apologeticus*, ab *apologus*, qui est oratio, quae nec veras nec verisimiles res continet, est tamen inventa ad instructionem transumptivam hominum. Unde Philosophus: *transferentes secundum aliquam similitudinem.* De quo stylo ait Horatius sic in poetria:

> *Scribendi recte sapere est et principium et fons.*
> *Ficta voluptatis causa sint proxima veris,*
> *Nec quodcumque velit poscat sibi fabula credi.*
> *Omne tulit punctum qui miscuit utile dulci,*
> *Nam prodesse volunt, aut delectare poetae.*

Ut etiam facit iste auctor, reducendo fabulas tales ad nostram informationem. Et differt a fabula, quae dicitur a *fando*, quae nihil informationis habet nisi vocem. Tamen poeta eis fabulis utitur aut delectationis causa, aut rerum naturam ostendendo, aut propter mores informandos, secundum Isidorum Ethimolog.: de cujus speciebus vide Macrobium de Somnio Scipionis circa principium.

"Quarto utitur alio sensu, qui dicitur *metaphoricus*, qui dicitur a *meta*, quod est *extra*, et *fora* naturam, unde *metaphora*, quasi sermo, sive oratio extra naturam: ut cum auctor noster fingit lignum loqui, prout facit infra in XIII.° Capitulo Inferni.

"Quinto utitur alio sensu, qui dicitur *allegoricus*, quod idem est quam alienum; nam allegoria dicitur ab *alleon*, quod est *alienum*. Et differt a metaphorico superdicto, quod allegoricus loquitur intra se, metaphoricus extra se, ut ecce: haec vox *Hierusalem*, quae historice, ut dixi, pro terrestri civitate accipitur, allegorice pro civitate Dei militante. Et scribitur allegorice, quando per id quod factum est intelligitur aliud quod factum sit, ut ecce de duello David cum Golia, quod significat bellum commissum per Christum cum Diabolo in ara crucis. Sic et cum auctor iste dicit se descendisse in Infernum per phantasiam intellectualiter, non personaliter, prout fecit, intelligit se descendisse ad infimum statum vitiorum, et inde exisse etc.

"Sexto utitur alio sensu, qui dicitur *tropologicus*, unde *tropologia* dicitur, quasi moralis intellectus, et dicitur a *tropos*, quasi *conversio*; ut cum verba nostra convertimur ad mores informandos. Et scribitur tropologice, quoniam per id quod factum est datur intelligi quod faciendum sit; ut haec vox *Hierusalem* tropologice accipitur pro anima fideli.

"Septimo utitur quodam alio sensu, qui dicitur *anagogicus*, unde *anagogia*, idest spiritualis intellectus, sive superior; unde dicta vox *Hierusalem* anagogice intelligitur coelestis et triumphans Ecclesia. Nam anagogice quis loquitur, cum datur intelligi quod desideratum est, et cum per terrena dantur intelligi coelestia; unde dicitur ab *ana*, quod est *supra*, et *goge*, quod est *ducere*. Ad quae praedicta facit quod dicit Gregorius in Moralibus: *quaedam historica expositione transcurrimus, et per allegoriam typica investigatione perscrutamur: quaedam per sola allegoricae moralitatis instructa discutimus*. Nam aliqua juxta literam intelligi nequeunt; nam literaliter talia accepta non instructionem, sed errorem inducerent. Nam si ad literam intelligeremus illum sanctum virum Job, ubi dicit: *eligit suspendium anima mea, et mortem ossa mea*, quid erroneum esset. Igitur ipse Job et alii scribentes sub talibus superdictis sensibus intelligi debent; et etiam auctor noster. Nam quis sani intellectus crederet ipsum ita descendisse, et talia vidisse, nisi cum distinctione dictorum modorum loquendi ad figuram? Nam non est ipse literalis sensus ipsa figura, sed id quod est figuratum; nam et cum scribitur *brachium Dei*, ut in Joan. 22. ex dicto Isaiae, non est sensus quod brachium Deo sit, sed id quod per brachium significatur, scilicet virtus operativa. Amodo cum auctor loquitur et describit talem et talem in Inferno, Purgatorio, et Paradiso, cum dictis sensibus diversimode intelligatur, ut poeta, cujus officium est ut, ea quae vere gesta sunt, in alias species obliquis figurationibus cum decore aliquo conversa traducat, secundum Isidorum."

["The formal cause is twofold, to wit, the form of the treatise and the form of the treatment. The form of the treatise is the division of the work, which is divided in parts corresponding to the three books; these books are in turn divided into one hundred chapters; and the chapters are in turn divided into smaller parts and rhythmic feet.

The form of the treatment is sevenfold, as our author makes use in this poem of seven senses.

"Now the first sense he employs is called *literal*, or superficial and parabolic: that is, according as he writes certain things which have no meaning except as the letter alone is meaningful; for not everything written here contains significance, but is put into the poem alongside of words which carry with themselves significance and figure. Augustine speaks to this point in the fifteenth book of the City of God: *Not all things narrated as fact are to be thought of as signifying something else. Some things are woven in among others which do have further signification. The earth is rent asunder by the ploughshare alone, but in order to accomplish this result, certain other parts of the plough are also necessary.* And as is written in the Decretals: *It is fitting that in the Old Law many things are set down as figures, while certain others are only to be understood literally, as in the Commandments,* 'Thou shalt not kill,' 'Thou shalt not commit adultery,' *etc.*

"The second sense he uses is called *historical*, from *historia*, which derives from *historin*, that is, *to see*, because in this sense things are narrated as history, or else, if they are presented as things seen, declared to be history. And this sense contains things true and things true-seeming.[7] For by the word *Jerusalem* is understood, historically, that terrestrial city which is in Syria, in that area which is called Palestine, etc., and it is a fact.

"The third sense he uses is called *apologetic*, from *moral tale* [the word is frequently used to describe Aesop's fables], a discourse which contains things neither true nor true-seeming, yet which are, nonetheless, devised for the uplifting instruction of man. Whence Aristotle: *transposing*

---

[7] It is pleasing to find Pietro rehearsing here the attributes usually lent to *argumentum*. See Chapter VI, note 30.

in accord with some similarity. Of which mode of expression Horace discourses in verse:

> *Of writing well is wisdom source and font.*
> *Fictions that would please should pass for true.*
> *Let your tale not beg us to believe in what it pleases,*
> *For he wins every point who with pleasure blends*
>   *instruction,*
> *And to be of use or else delight is every poet's aim.*

And in this way also our author composes, shaping such tales to our conception. And they differ from the usual tale, a word deriving from the word *hearsay*, which contains no ideas but only words. Moreover, the poet employs these tales either to delight, or to expose to view the nature of things, or to shape morals, as Isidore says in his *Etymologies*: concerning whose views see the *Dream of Scipio*, by Macrobius, near the beginning.

"The fourth sense he uses is called *metaphorical*, which derives from *meta*, which means *apart from*, or *beyond*, nature, whence the word *metaphor*, which means discourse or use of language departing from nature: as when our author makes the tree speak, which he does in the thirteenth chapter of *Inferno*, below.

"The fifth sense he uses is called *allegorical*, because itself is as another [compare Horace, 'tamquam alter idem']; for allegory is derived from *alleon*, which means *other*. And this differs from the metaphorical sense discussed above because the allegorical has meaning within itself, the metaphorical beyond itself, as the following example makes plain: this word *Jerusalem*, by which historically, as I have said, is understood the terrestrial city, is allegorically understood as the Militant City of God. And writing is allegorical, when by what is understood to have happened something else that has happened is also understood, as in the example of the battle of David with Goliath, which signifies the war undertaken by Christ against the Devil on the altar of the cross. And thus, when the author says that he descended into Hell, in his imagination, intellectually, not personally—as he had done—he discerns that he had gone down to the lowest state of sin, and then had come back up, etc.

"The sixth sense he uses is called *tropological*, or moral sense, and derives from *tropos*, or *a turning toward*; as when words turn us toward the shaping of our moral lives. And writing is tropological when by what is understood as having happened what should be done is given to be understood; as by this word *Jerusalem* is tropologically understood the faithful soul.

"The seventh sense is called *anagogical*, from which word comes *anagoge*, the spiritual, or higher, sense; whence by the aforementioned word *Jerusalem* is anagogically understood the celestial Church Triumphant. For we understand anagogically when what is longed for is given to be understood, when heavenly things are given to be understood by earthly ones; whence the word derives from *ana*, which means *above*, and *goge*, which means *to lead*. And in these premises he follows what Gregory says in his *Moralia*: *We pass over certain historical matters in our exposition, while we scrutinize the types by means of allegory; we discuss certain other instructive matters only in light of their moral sense.* For some things may not be understood literally, and such are the things which, when taken literally, lead not to instruction, but to error. For if we take literally the words of that holy man Job, when he says: *My soul chooseth strangling, and death my bones* [Job 7:15], how misleading it might be. Therefore, Job and the other writers must be understood in such senses as I have described above. And the same is true of our author. For who of sane mind would believe he himself made such a descent, or himself saw such things, unless enjoining the distinction concerning the modes of things said in figurative speech? For the literal sense is not itself a figure; but it is what is figured.[8] And when the words *the arm of God* [probably a reference to Isaiah 51:9] are written, as in chapter 22 of John, quoting Isaiah, the meaning is not that God has an arm, but what is signified by 'arm,' that is, the power of action. And it is just so when our author speaks, describing this or that in *Inferno*, *Purgatorio*, and *Paradiso*, since it should be understood that, in diverse ways, by means of the senses I have discussed, it is the office of the poet to transpose those things which have truly happened into other appearances by means of indirect figurations, and with some decorum, as Isidore says."]

7. *Esposizioni sopra la Comedia di Dante* (ed. Giorgio Padoan, Milan, 1965) by Giovanni Boccaccio offer a sharp contrast to the highly developed sense of Scriptural exegesis to be found in Pietro. Boccaccio deals perfunctorily with allegory in his *accessus* (p. 2). However, in his lengthy commentary on *Inferno* 1, 73—Virgil's phrase "poeta fui"—he will return at greater length to the subject when he cites the Psalm "In exitu Israel de Aegypto" (p. 57). That passage is for the most part a fairly faithful reproduction of the key paragraphs of the Letter to Can Grande. Thus, although it is important to know that Boccaccio seems to have been acquainted with the text of that document, in whatever form and under whatever auspices, there is little reason to reproduce it in turn here, and only one of its sentences shall detain us. Summarizing

[8] Pietro probably here recites Aquinas' definition of the *sensus parabolicus* (*S.T.* I, i, 10): "Nam per voces significatur aliquid proprie vel figurative; nec est litteralis sensus ipsa figura sed id quod est figuratum. . . ."

the distinction between the literal and the other senses, and before he goes on to cite the *Epistola* with some exactitude, Boccaccio would seem to recapitulate his own exegetical method rather than Dante's. The literal sense, he says, is that signified by the letter, as you have heard him expound above. The allegorical sense, consonant with Boccaccio's own non-"historical" literal sense, is described as follows: "Il secondo senso è 'allegorico,' o vero 'morale.' " As Padoan's note points out, Boccaccio has omitted the third spiritual sense here. Or has he? It is difficult to be sure, but I believe that Boccaccio has merely kept to his own definition of allegory, which, though paying lip service to four senses, essentially operates in only two: literal and allegorical/moral. He has not, it is my opinion, pointed to sense two and sense three of theological allegory, but only to the generalized allegorical sense of the allegory of the poets, which is often enough called the "allegorico ovvero morale" by any number of medieval personification allegorists. Immediately after this sentence, Boccaccio slips into the *Epistola*'s clear distinctions among the four senses. I realize that it seems at first foolish to maintain that Boccaccio quotes faithfully a document he did not comprehend. Yet we have seen that others before (and after) him have also done so. The practice of his commentary is thoroughly to do without the distinctions he has copied into his text. The theoretical basis for his allegorical practice is clearly enunciated in the *accessus*, which, as I have said, deals not with fourfold, but with twofold "allegory of the poets."

"Le cause di questo libro son quatro: la materiale, la formale, la efficiente e la finale. La materiale è, nella presente opera, doppia, così come è doppio il suggetto, il quale è colla materia una medesima cosa: per ciò che altro suggetto è quello del senso litterale e altro quello del senso allegorico, li quali nel presente libro amenduni sono, sì come manifestamente aparirà nel processo. È adunque il suggetto, secondo il senso litterale, lo stato dell'anime dopo la morte de' corpi semplicemente preso, per ciò che di quello, e intorno a quello, tutto il processo della presente opera intende; il suggetto secondo il senso allegorico è: come l'uomo, per lo libero arbitrio meritando e dismeritando, è alla giustizia di guiderdonare e di punire obligato."

To be sure, Boccaccio's language would suggest at least indirect, and probably direct, acquaintance with the *Epistola*. Yet what is also true is that this section of it can, and often has been, read as a plea on Dante's part merely for a twofold interpretation. And that, at any rate, is precisely what he gets from Boccaccio's reading, with its strict delineation of each canto into "esposizione litterale" and "esposizione allegorica."

["The causes of the work are four in number: material, formal, efficient and final. The matter is, in the present work, twofold, since the subject—which is the same as the matter—is twofold; the one subject, thus, is that of the literal sense, the other that of the allegorical sense, both of which are to be found in the present work, as shall be clear from what follows. The subject, according to the literal sense, is then, simply understood, the state of the souls after the death of the body; the entire process of the present work is understood from this and around this. According to the allegorical sense the subject is man, as by his free will he is worthy and unworthy, is liable to compensatory or punishing justice."]

8. *Benevenuti de Rambaldis de Imola, Comentum super Dantis Aldigherij Comoediam* (ed. J. P. Lacaita, pub. W.

W. Vernon, Florence, 1887) contains, once again in the *Introductio*, the briefest of allusions to the four Biblical senses (pp. 7-8). And I must point out that the authority of later editors does not support the genuineness of the passage I offer here as a matter of interest, and which is absent from the edition of Promis and Negroni (Milan, 1888) of the commentary of Stefano Talice da Ricaldone, which, following Barbi, many scholars now believe to be a better version of Benvenuto's actual commentary than Vernon's edition, which bears his name, although it was written about 1475:

"Hic namque poeta peritissimus, omnium coelestium, terrestrium, et infernorum profunda speculabiliter contemplatus, singula quaeque descripsit historice, allegorice, tropologice, et anagogice, ut merito de ejus opere totius sapientiae et eloquentiae plenissime dicere posset. . . ."

["For he, the most skilled poet, having gazed upon the depths of all heaven, earth, and hell, has written down each thing he saw historically, allegorically, morally, and anagogically, so that one may say that his great work is most full of all wisdom and eloquence. . . ."]

9. The *Commento di Francesco da Buti sopra la Divina Comedia di Dante Allighieri* (ed. Crescentino Giannini, Pisa, 1858-1862) also contains a *proemio*, one which frequently refers to the "senso allegorico, ovvero morale," and which concludes with the following statement (pp. 14-15):

"Et inanzi che si cominci la esposizione, si dee notare che tutte le esposizioni si fanno in uno di questi quattro modi; cioè o secondo la lettera, com' io ò ora sposta la storia litterale; o secondo la nostra fede, e questa si chiama sposizione allegorica; o secondo la moralità delle virtù e del modo del vivere, e questa si chiama morale; o secondo l'eterna vita, che da noi si spera, e questa si chiama esposizione anagogica. . . ."

It then goes on to give illustration of the above by giving an analysis, which closely corresponds to the one offered in the Letter to Can Grande, of Psalm 114 (113 in the Vulgate), "In Israel de Aegypto," finally concluding with the following explanation of the familiar distich, one that clearly displays the writer's misunderstanding of fourfold allegory by turning it into twofold personification allegory:

"E di queste esposizioni dicono li versi: *Littera gesta refert, quid credas allegoria, moralis quid agas, quid speres anagogia.* E però esporremo prima la lettera et appresso secondo l'allegoria o vero moralità, secondo ch' io crederò che sia stata intenzione dell' autore."

Once again the essential tactic within the commentary is to "explain" the literal, that is, to paraphrase it, and then to go on to the "allegorical, or moral" meaning, which is consistently expressed as though only personification allegory were at stake.

["And before I begin my exposition, it should be noted that all the expositions are made in one of these four ways: that is, either according to the letter, as I have just now explained the literal story; or according to our faith, and that is called allegorical exposition; or according to the moral sense of the virtues and of our way of life, and that is called moral; or according to eternal life, for which we hope, and that is called anagogical exposition. . . .

"And of these expositions tell the verses: *The literal reports deeds; what you should believe, the allegorical; the moral, what you should do; what you should hope for,* the anagoge. And therefore we shall expound first the letter, and then second according to the allegory or moral sense, according as I believe it was the intention of the author."]

10. *Commento alla Divina Commedia d'anonimo fiorentino del secolo XIV* (ed. Pietro Fanfani, Bologna, 1866-1874). This commentary follows that of Pietro di Dante in its seven-part division of the *forma tractandi,* as is readily apparent. The prefatory matter given below appears within the commentary to Canto 1, rather than in a *proemio* (pp. 9-10):

"La forma del trattare è di sette guise, siccome di sette guise lo intendimento che usa il nostro Autore in questa sua poesia, cioè litterale, superficiale e parabolico, cioè, che scrive alcune cose che non importono altro intendimento, se non come suona la lettera; et secondariamente usa senso storico, et contiene cose vere et verisimili: siccome dice storialmente *Jerusalem,* s'intende quella Città ch' è in Sorìa. In terzo luogo usa senso apologico quando non contiene verità nè simile a verità; ma è trovato a amaestramento transuntivo degli uomini; però che l'Autore, inducendo le favole a nostra informazione, o vuogli fare utile, o dilettare, o mostrare la natura delle cose o pur costumi. Il quarto è senso metaforico. Metafora è uno detto quasi fuori di natura, come quando l'Autore finge uno legno parlare, siccome nel xiij° canto d'Inferno. Il quinto è allegorico: l'allegorico favella infra sè; il metaforico fuori di sè: Jerusalem storialmente è la Città di Sorìa; allegoricamente è la Chiesa di Dio militante. Scrivesi allegoricamente quando per quello ch' è fatto s'intende un'altra cosa fatta, siccome per la battaglia fatta fra Davit et Golia s'intende la battaglia che Cristo fece col diavolo in sulla croce: et così quando l'Autore dice sè essere sceso in Inferno per fantasía et non personalmente, ma essere disceso allo 'nferno allo strazio de' vizj, et quindi essere uscito. Il sesto senso è tropologico. Tropología è detta quasi Morale intendimento, quando le nostre parole convertiamo a informare costumi: et scrivesi tropologicamente, quando per quello ch' è fatto si dà a intendere quello ch' è da fare, come questa voce *Jerusalem* s'intende per l'Anima fedele. Il vij° luogo usa senso anagogico. Anagogico ciò è Spirituale intendimento, overo soprano, siccome la detta voce *Jerusalem* anagogicamente s'intende la celestiale et triunfante ecclesia. Anagogicamente si favella quando si dànno a intendere cose celestiali."

Since the debt this commentary owes to that of Pietro di Dante approaches the debt a translator owes his author, it is not surprising that this introductory statement of allegorical principles, like Pietro's, shows a greater familiarity with the actual techniques of fourfold exegesis than almost any other.

["The form of the treatment is of seven modes, as is the intention of our author in this poem, that is, literal, superficial and parabolic, that is, writing certain things which have no other meaning, except for the literal; and secondly he employs the historical sense, and it contains things true and true-seeming, as *Jerusalem* means, historically, that City which is in Syria. Third, he uses the apologetic sense, which does not contain things true or true-seeming, but is devised for the uplifting instruction of man; moreover, the author, shaping such tales to our conception, wants to make them be of profit or delight, or to expose to view the nature of things, or of morals. The fourth is the metaphorical sense. Metaphor is something said beyond nature, as when the author makes a tree speak, as in the thirteenth canto of *Inferno*. The fifth is allegorical: the allegorical has meaning within itself, the metaphorical beyond itself: Jerusalem is historically the City in Syria; allegorically it is the Militant City of God. Writing is allegorical when by what has happened is understood something else that has happened, as the battle of David with Goliath signifies the battle made by Christ against the Devil on the cross. And thus, when the author says that he descended into Hell, in his imagination, and not personally, he means to say that he went down to the hell that is the torture of sin, and then came back up again. The sixth sense is tropological. Tropology signifies Moral meaning, as when words turn us toward the shaping of morals; and writing is tropological when by what has happened is understood what should be done, as by this word *Jerusalem* is understood the faithful Soul. Seventh, he uses the anagogical sense. The anagogical is the Spiritual, or higher, sense, as when by the aforementioned word *Jerusalem* is anagogically understood the celestial Church Triumphant. We understand anagogically when we are given to understand things heavenly."]

11. *Il comento al primo canto dell'Inferno pubblicato e annotato da Giuseppe Cugnoni* (Città di Castello, 1896) of Filippo Villani is, of all the commentaries, the most involved with fourfold allegory, not only in its relatively clear statement of principles at the outset, but in its handling of the text of *Inferno* 1, where Villani frequently looks into Christian history in order to find analogues to the poetic action. It is unfortunate that all we have from Villani is his critical insight into a single canto. Nevertheless, even this commentary makes the usual critical neglect of his work in favor of the better known and more complete fourteenth-century commentaries a cause for dismay.

The passage below is to be found in Villani's *prefatio*, pp. 25-28:

". . . nostri theologi quatuor dumtaxat in sacris licteris posuerunt theotoricos intellectus, videlicet hystoricum, allegoricum, moralem, et anagogicum: quos in expositione uersus prophete dicentis: 'In exitu Israel de Egypto, domus Iacob "de populo barbaro,' exemplariter ostendunt. Nam, si simplicis hystorie ueritatem uelimus agnoscere, liberatio ebrayci populi de seruitute Pharaonis facta per Moysem apparebit. Huic ei persimilem licteralem poterimus applicare, qui nichil affert significati citra uerborum sonum; de quo dicit Aurelius Augustinus 'Non enim omnia, que in complexione orationis, costructionis gratia, inseruntur, significare aliquid morale putanda sunt; sed procter ea que aliquid significant attexuntur.' Si uero de licterali hystoricoque allegoriam uelimus elicere, tropum intelligemus, quo aliquid nobis dicitur, et aliud significatur; iuxta illud: Eua fabricata est de latere Ade dormientis; hoc est Ecclesia producta est de latere Christi pendentis in cruce. Similiter in uersu nostro figuratur nostra redemptio facta per Christum. Ceterum allegorie species, secundum gramaticos, septem sunt: videlicet yronia, enigma, anthifrasis, carientismos, paroemia, sarchasmos, et antismos. Sed horum uestigationem peritis gramatice derelinquo, cum non sit intentionis poete vulgariter docere gramaticam; sed moralem tradere philosophyam. Audi Gregorium, romanum pontificem, de se dicentem, dum Iob exponit: 'Non miotacismi collisionem fugio, non barbarismi confusionem deuito, situs motusque etiam propositionum casus seruare contempno, quia indignum uehementer existimo, ut uerba celestis oraculi restringam sub regulis Donati.' Ego intellectum potius considerans, quam exquisitam gramaticam, sicubi error inueniretur gramatice discipline in scripturis

meis, si uerborum intellectum uerum capiant, oro pios
lectores ne curent. Et, prosequendo, dico, quod grecum
nomen allegoria est, compositum ab *allon*, quod alienum
seu diuersum latine sonat, et *gore*, quod est intellectus. Et
sub isto generali nomine omnes sensus, ab hystorico lic-
teralique differentes, allegorici nuncupantur. Post allegoricum, in specie sua, subsequitur moralis, in quo, in uersu
prophete, ostenditur anime conuerse ymago de luctu
miseriaque peccati ad statum gratie. Verumtamen huic
poterimus sotiare apologicum, hoc est fabulosum, qualem
efferunt elegantes Esopi fabule, quo transumptiue ad instructionem nostram, irrationabilium nature, collocutiones
gestaque trasferuntur. Hiis duobus adicitur tropologicus,
id est conuersiuus, in quo, per illud quod factum est, quod
fieri debet datur intelligi; et sic resoluitur in moralem. Nam
dum inuehit poeta in peccatores, ad instructionem nostram
sermo conuertitur. Post moralem theologi anagogicum
posuerunt, id est spiritualem, pro quo versus prophete
nobis significat, exitum anime sancte, exute corpore, a cor-
ruptionis seruitute, ad eterne glorie libertatem. Hinc motus,
dicebat apostolus: 'Cupio dissolui, et esse cum Christo.'
Super istos quatuor theotoricos intellectus principales, per
prudentes, uersus editi sunt, qui dicunt: 'Lictera gesta
refert; quid credas allegoria;—Moralis quid agas; quid
speres anagogia.' Ex istis colligere possumus, in hoc opere
duplex fore subiectum, circa quod alterni sensus isti decur-
runt. Nam, si spectemus ad licteram, erit pro materia et
subiecto status animarum exutarum corpore simpliciter
sumptus; nam circa ipsum totius operis processus uersatur:
si uero ad allegoriam mentis oculos inflectamus; subiectum
atque materia erit homo uiator, pro ut, merendo uel
demerendo per arbitrii libertatem, iustitie premiandi et
puniendi erit obnoxius."

["... our theologians have set down precisely four theological senses for Scripture, and they are these: historical, allegorical, moral, and anagogical. They are seen exemplified in the following prophetic verse, 'When Israel went out of Egypt, the house of Jacob from a people of strange language.' And, if we wish to know simply the historical truth of these lines, the liberation of the Hebrew people from their slavery under Pharoah, which was wrought by Moses, will be apparent. We may also understand that a similar literal sense at times conveys nothing of significance beyond the literal meaning of the words, concerning which fact Aurelius Augustine says: 'For not all things which, in the complexity of discourse are introduced for the sake of arrangement, are to be thought of as having some moral significance; for some are merely woven in among those things which do have such significance.' If from the literal and historical we wish to draw out the allegory, we must understand the trope by which one thing is told us and another is meant along with it: Eve was created from the side of sleeping Adam; thus was the Church brought out of the side of Christ hanging on the cross. Similarly, in our verse is figured our redemption wrought by Christ. The various kinds of allegory, according to the grammarians, are seven: to wit, irony, enigma, antiphrasis, carientismos, paroemia, sarcasm, and antismos.[9] But I leave the investigation of these to those skilled in grammar, since it is not the intention of the poet to teach rhetoric in the vernacular, but to transmit moral philosophy. Hear Gregory, bishop of Rome, speaking of himself while he expounds Job: 'I do not flee a confrontation with metacism, nor do I shun other confounding improprieties of

---

[9] The grammarian Filippo has in mind is surely either Isidore, or one of the many who borrowed from Isidore—see *Etymologiae*, I, xxxvii, 22.

speech, but I do disdain service in the cause of the proper placement and cases of prepositions, because I urgently believe it unworthy of me to subjugate the words of heavenly prophecy to the rules of Donatus.' Paying more attention to what should be discerned than to exquisite considerations of grammar, I entreat my pious readers not to mind if in any place an error should be found in the rhetorical technique of my writings, so long as they understand the true meaning of the words. And, continuing, I say that the word *allegory* is from the Greek, made up of *allon*, which means *other* or *different*, and *gore*, which means *sense*. And by this generic name all the senses which depart from the historical and literal are called *allegorical*. After the allegorical, and in its own respect, follows the moral, by which, in the prophetic verse, is revealed the representation of the conversion of the soul from the misery of sin to the state of grace. Furthermore, to this sense we are able to add the apological, which is fictitious, that which may be drawn with good judgment from Aesop's fables in order to draw forth from them, despite their irrational nature, sayings and deeds for our uplifting instruction. Superadded to these two is the tropological, or 'conversionary,' where because of what has happened, what we ought to do is given to be understood; and thus this sense flows into the moral. For while the poet inveighs against sinners, his discourse is turned toward our instruction. After the moral sense the theologians put the anagogical, or spiritual, as where the prophetic verse points to the escape of the holy soul, having put off its flesh, from the slavery of corruption to the liberty of eternal glory. Thus moved, the Apostle said: 'I desire to depart, and to be with Christ' [Philippians 1:23]. Of these four theological senses tell those verses which were made known by the wise: 'The letter reports facts; the allegory, what you should believe; the moral, what you should do; what you should hope for, the anagoge.' From all this, we may gather that the subject of this work, around which the various senses play, is twofold. For, if we inspect the letter, taken simply, its subject or matter will be the state of the souls which have left behind the flesh, for the process of the whole work turns about this. If we turn the eyes of our mind to the allegory, the subject matter will be *homo viator*, according as, in the freedom of his will, by good or ill deserts, he becomes liable to rewarding or punishing justice."]

To recapitulate briefly what may be the most precise and useful complex statement of fourfold allegory ever put down by a secular man of letters, Filippo identifies and distinguishes among the senses as follows:

1. further-signifying literal/historical: Israel out of Egypt; distinct from
1a. *non* further-signifying literal/historical (following Augustine);
2. allegorical (*not* that of the grammarians) is typology: Israel = our redemption;
3. moral: Israel, type of us, urges our conversion; based on literal/historical;
3a. moral developed from fictional tales, like Aesop's, called apological;
3b. tropological, which is part of the moral; as opposed to apological, it depends on actual events; the kind of moral sense you find depends on the kind of literal sense it comes from: further-signifying literal/historical or *fabula*.
4. anagogical, again based on literal/historical: Israel points to Glory.

Although I confess I do not understand why Filippo should have attempted to distinguish between moral (3) and tropological (3b), since he ends up admitting that they flow into one another, I still do not know a single critic of Dante's poem who has put the theory so succinctly. His commentary, once it sets to the work of explication, while it is lacking in the classical learning we find in Pietro (his father's son on that score), is far more effective in pointing to the Biblical analogues that lie beneath the poem's literal sense.[10] I am aware that my championing of Filippo Villani is self-serving. Perhaps if *dantisti* had been reading him all these years this book would have been written long ago by someone else.

[10] See Chapter VI, note 35.

GOD'S "VISIBLE SPEECH"

One of the results of a figural approach to Dante's *Commedia* is that the reader begins to attain a firmer sense of the formative principles of the work. The following discovery, made recently by one of my students, Gregory Curfman, is an example of the results that occur when a reader sees the *Commedia's* parts in relation to its whole. I feel a certain discomfort in appropriating Mr. Curfman's work for my own, and I do so only because there is a possibility that his short paper "*Giustizia* in Dante's 'Visible Speech'"[1] may not find its way into print, although I hope that one day it shall. However, since two of the suggestions that surround his discovery are my own, I offer his findings here in brief, combined with my own additions.

The essential point of Curfman's paper is one that probably should have been seen long ago: in three moments of the poem, one in each *cantica*, Dante deliberately puts before the reader's eye what he himself calls "visibile parlare" (*Purg.* x, 95), in each case attaching the phenomenon to a common thematic concern. The passages in question are: the writing over Hell Gate (*Inf.* iii, 1-9); the encounter between Trajan and the widow which is sculpted on the wall of the Terrace of Pride (*Purg.* x, 73-96); and the "sky writing" of the eagle in the sphere of Jupiter, "DILIGITE IUSTITIAM . . . QUI IUDICATIS TERRAM" (*Par.* xviii, 91-93). The first and the last have one thing in common which is immediately striking: each consists of monumentally hieratic inscription written by God Himself. The first, the

[1] Curfman's argument is fuller than my brief recapitulation of it.

inscription over Hell Gate, tells us that God made it;[2] the last is the first sentence of the Book of Wisdom. The common denominator also applies, if not quite so immediately, to the passage in *Purgatorio* x. For there we are concerned again with God's art, this time with a mimetic perfection which is capable of rendering human figures so realistically that we can hear them speak. It is of this art that Dante uses the phrase "visibile parlare," which also applies, tangentially at least, to the "visible speech" we find over Hell Gate and in the sphere of Jupiter.

To see this much is pleasing if we are merely interested in finding in Dante a non-directional compulsion to form. Yet, as Mr. Curfman points out, there is a thematic bearing to this elegant decoration, for each of the passages contains a central word, and that word is *giustizia* (*Inf.* iii, 4; *Purg.* x, 93; *Par.* xviii, 91—this last in its Latin form). Thus God's art is concerned with justice, human and divine, in the writing over Hell Gate; in the exemplum of the humility of Trajan, expressed in his just behavior to the widow;[3] and in the heavenly sign flashed by the eagle.

Again, to see this much more would also be pleasing. Mr. Curfman, however, has seen further, suggesting that the Emperor Trajan might be a third common element in the configuration. It is Trajan who is depicted in *Purgatorio* x. And who is there, in the eyebrow of the speaking eagle in *Paradiso* xx, 43-45, signaling God's Grace and

---

[2] In most texts, including the standard critical text of the Società Dantesca Italiana (1960), the inscription is in capital letters. However, in Giorgio Petrocchi's new critical text, which I have only recently received (Società Dantesca Italiana, Edizione Nazionale, Milan, 1966), I find that the first nine lines of Canto iii are *not* capitalized. I also find no explanation or justification for this departure from recent format.

[3] Curtius, *EL&LMA*, p. 364, cites John of Salisbury, *Policraticus*, i, 317, 6f (ed. Webb) for a literary source of the scene.

therefore Divine Justice? Trajan. Mr. Curfman wanted
to find Trajan also present in or behind the writing over
Hell Gate. A. C. Charity's recent work *Events and Their
Afterlife*,[4] yields the trace of Trajan, even if the path to
the Emperor is not a direct one. Charity points out the
relevance of Dante's situation, "nel mezzo del cammin,"
at the opening of the poem to Isaiah 38:10, the words of
Hezekiah: "In dimidio dierum meorum vadam ad portas
inferi" (". . . in the cutting off of my days, I shall go to
the gates of the grave"). Clearly, Hezekiah, sick unto
death in the midst of life (Isa. 38:1), as Charity points
out, is a *figura* of Dante.[5] I second his thought, especially
as the heading of Chapter 38 in the Vulgate is "Canticum
Ezechiae a morte liberati," words that apply with rigorous
exactitude to Dante's situation in *Inferno* I and II. Now
Hezekiah also appears in the *Commedia*, and when he
does so he is to be found in *Paradiso* xx, 49-54, in the
eyebrow of the eagle right next to Trajan, "who would
also appear to be a sort of 'type' of Dante, in that he descended to hell and yet was ultimately saved."[6] Hezekiah
and Trajan are figures of Dante in that each was saved
from death by Grace. I confess that this is a roundabout
way of making Trajan a poetic common denominator for
each of the three "visible speech" passages, but I think
Dante himself might have been pleased to make the con-

[4] Cambridge, 1966, p. 230.

[5] The phrase "ad portas inferi" may have seemed particularly appropriate to Dante, since the Pilgrim is headed toward the Gate of
Hell, or *ad portam Inferni*. Recently two others have also seen Hezekiah as *figura Dantis*: André Pézard, "Ce qui gronde en l'éternel (*Inf.*
VI, 94-115)," *Studi danteschi*, XLII (1965), 207-233: ". . . une leçon
d'Isaïe: celle que Dante a savamment inscrite au fronton de sa *Comédie*,
comme une annonciation et comme un symbole . . ." (p. 224); Giorgio
Petrocchi, "Appunti per una conversazione sull'esordio del poema,"
L'Alighieri, VII, I (1966), 29.

[6] Charity, p. 230n.

nection, perhaps because it is such a quiet one. It is the sort of detail that perhaps was not primarily meant to be discovered, one put into the poem in the joy of harmonious composition.

Yet I think there is another good reason for thinking that Dante thought of Trajan—or at least of the Imperium and its justice, of which Trajan is one of the main *exempla* for Dante—when he made Hell Gate. In all the many commentaries on that imposing structure, no one, to my knowledge, has yet seen that upon which it is modeled: the Gate of Hell is a representation of a Roman triumphal arch. Every one of these that has been preserved stands with its central portal showing above it several lines of capital letters sculpted in stone, beginning with the traditional formula

IMP · CAESARI · DIVI

and going on to name and enumerate the hero in whose honor it is erected. Thus each sinner comes to Hell through an archway which reminds him of the perfection of justice, human and divine, which rules the world he sinned in. The words sculpted in stone in capital letters with which the visionary part of the *Commedia* begins serve not only to remind us that the words of this poem are "real," but also that the poem begins by invoking the memory of that shape which for a Roman poet most mocks opposers and most celebrates true justice as well as the hand of God, which made this arch in triumphant display of divine justice. It is also fitting that the visionary part of the poem begins with the very words of God, sculpted in stone as on the tablets of the Law, for this is the poem which has taken as its model God's way of writing.

APPENDIX III

FEAR, PITY, AND
FIRMNESS IN *INFERNO*

When we consider the task Dante had to face in keeping his vast poem in motion for one hundred cantos, we do not often enough see clearly that one of his prime means of locomotion is the record he offers of his own development. Francis Fergusson has frequently alluded to the striking resemblance between Dante's poetic and that of Aristotle, which Dante almost certainly did not know in any direct light.[1] I mention the *Poetics* because we find—or should have found—that the essential process by which the Pilgrim's soul moves forward is very close to the Aristotelian notion of the katharsis of pity and fear. That is, we are able to document the fact that as Dante moves from Canto III to Canto XXXIV he passes through five cycles,[2] each of which finds him experiencing fear, pity, and firmness in turn, although not always in that order. These five cycles correspond more or less exactly to the divisions of sin made in Canto XI, and may be described as follows:

1. The sins of incontinence. Cantos III-VIII
2. The sins of violence. Cantos VIII-XVII

[1] See his *Dante's Drama of the Mind* and his *Dante, passim.*

[2] Joan M. Ferrante's recent study, "*Malebolge* (*Inf.* XVIII-XXX) as the Key to the Structure of Dante's *Inferno*," *Romance Philology*, XX (1967), 456-466, which argues with considerable force and evidence for a fivefold division of the moral plan of Hell, gives my argument support, since her divisions and mine are almost precisely the same, while our two "systems" were arrived at independently, and do not depend upon similar approaches or upon similar evidence within the poem.

301

3. The sins of fraud (*bolge* 1-4).   Cantos XVII-XX
4. The sins of fraud (*bolge* 5-10).   Cantos XXI-XXIX
5. The sins of treachery.   Cantos XXXI-XXXIII

Each of these five divisions shows us Dante moving among three states of response to what he sees: in the first two, the movement is from fear to pity to firmness; in the last three, for reasons we will examine shortly, from fear to firmness to pity and its purgation.

1. Once he begins his descent, Dante is first accosted by fear ("spavento"—III, 131), when the earthquake shakes the plain before he crosses Acheron—so much so that he faints. In the following canto, Dante takes Virgil's pallor for fear, while it is actually the sign of pity (IV, 21). The exchange readies us for Dante's own emotional reaction to Paolo and Francesca in the following canto, at the conclusion of which he will faint again, this time for pity ("pietade"—V, 140). In Canto VI Dante sees Ciacco, whose situation "invites him to weep" (VI, 59). Significantly enough, he does not. Thus, though feeling pity for his fellow Florentine, his fellow-feeling is not as strong as it was for those two lost to lust, mainly because he does not share Ciacco's sin as he had shared theirs, and possibly because his expression of pity for them had purged him of the bulk of his pity for the incontinent. Again, when he first sees the avaricious and the prodigal, he feels some emergent pity ("lo cor quasi compunto"—VII, 36), which is quickly stifled when Virgil tells him about the sinners he regards. In Canto VIII, the canto of anger, and the last of the area of incontinence, Dante becomes seized by the righteous indignation which so pleases Virgil, when he sees his teacher push Filippo Argenti back into the muddy Styx (VIII, 44). His "course" in incontinence is complete— Virgil for the first time can leave him alone (VIII, 109f)—

now that he can scorn a sin of that area, and by implication, all sins of that area. His satisfaction is necessarily
short-lived, for he must proceed to another zone.

2. The first sight of Dis with its angry defending devils
causes Dante to think he will never make it back to this
world (VIII, 96). He is undone ("disfatto"—100), and
Virgil must tell him not to fear ("Non temer"—104).
The staunch Christian in incontinence has become the fearful visitor to violence. At the beginning of Canto IX he is
pale again with *viltà* (line 1), and feels fear ("paura"—13),
only to feel the same again at the advent of the Furies
(51). However, if the Pilgrim is fearful at the beginning
of his experience in this area, at least he does not faint.
He is starting to show the effects of his education in sin
which is, naturally, cumulative to some degree, even
though in another respect he must start out fresh in each
new realm of sin. As usual, Dante has things both ways,
as he wants them. His fear is continued in the next canto
when Farinata rears up from his "monument" and addresses his countryman ("temendo"—line 30). Dante's
pity makes a tentative appearance in this area when he
feels sorry for his words to Cavalcante ("di mia colpa compunto"—X, 109). Before it can develop, he feels fear one
more time when Pier della Vigna, tree that he is, gives
out his bloody words while asking for pity (XIII, 36, 45).
Finally, in line 84, he feels *pietà* for Pier. This *moto
spiritale* is developed further in his interview with Brunetto Latini in Canto XV. However, although Brunetto
does draw sympathy from Dante, it is important to notice
that the pupil's courtesy to his "teacher" takes no explicitly pitying form. He expresses his gratitude for Brunetto's
teaching, his surprise at finding him here, but no pity for
him. He is similarly courteous, only more reserved, among
the Florentine homosexuals of Canto XVI; and finally, in

Canto xvii, he is once again firm as he comes to the limit of the second great area of Inferno. The sign of his staunchness against violence is to be seen in the fact that Virgil can allow him to go off alone to survey the usurers, the last sinners of this area. He observes them with cold contempt in his new-found strength. It is the first time he has gone anywhere alone in Hell, and he passes the test without difficulty, as he "passed the test" of being left alone briefly in Canto viii. The episodes are in parallel position, each occurring at the close of one of the first two great areas of sin. In a moment, however, he is to be attacked once more by fear.

3. Virgil welcomes Dante back to the descent upon the back of Geryon with the words "Or sie forte e ardito" ("Now be strong and bold"—xvii, 81). Dante's response is to tremble with fear (line 87), although he masters his cowardice out of shame. Nevertheless, his fear continues to be felt when it is compared to that of Phaethon in a similar situation (107), and to that of the falling Icarus (109); finally, he is afraid ("timido"—121) of what he will find upon landing, and trembles (123).

Until now the progression has been identical in each area, and so we might expect that Dante will next move to pity, and then to staunchness. However, now a change occurs in the order of his responses, one which makes a certain amount of sense. First of all, having undergone two areas of sin the reader has begun to have some idea of what to expect, and Dante probably wanted to vary the pattern a bit. More functionally, the area Dante has entered is that of fraud, a sin which can work against and involve even good men, if they are unwary. And so, after the expected fearful introduction to fraud, the Pilgrim is strangely staunch. He is unmoved at the pickle the panders and seducers, and then the flatterers, are in (Canto xviii). And then in Canto xix he is given a full twenty-eight lines of invective against Popes Nicholas III, Boniface VIII, and Clement V (lines 90-117) which seems greatly to please Virgil (121), a sure sign that the pupil is behaving with proper Christian firmness. This condition gives way to pity at the sight of the diviners in Canto xx. Dante weeps (line 25), but stops when he is rebuked by Virgil for his *pietà* (28).

4. *Paura* begins the next area with Canto xxi, 27, when Dante sees the barrators, and continues in line 133, when Virgil tells him to stop being fearful ("paventi"), although Dante continues to be so in Canto xxiii ("Maestro . . . i' ho pavento"—21-22) until Virgil picks him up and carries him like a baby (40). Upon reaching the sixth of the Malebolge Dante is staunch once more. He begins a denunciation of the hypocrites ("O frati, i vostri mali . . ."— xxiii, 109), a sure sign of firmness in *Inferno*, but is distracted when he catches sight of the crucified Caiaphas. His own righteous indignation is mirrored in that of Virgil at the end of the canto (146). Continuing his firmness, Dante in the next canto informs Virgil that he is "forte e ardito" (xxiv, 60). And upon seeing Vanni Fucci among the thieves, entwined by serpents, he continues to show his staunchness by being pleased at the sight (xxv, 4). That emotion suddenly gives way to pity in his grief for lost Ulysses ("Allor mi dolsi, e ora mi ridoglio"—xxvi, 19). His sympathy for Ulysses is also mirrored by the fall he almost takes in his eagerness to see the great adventurer (line 45). This emotion remains with Dante despite a momentary harshness to Mosca (xxviii, 109), which is swept away by his desire to weep at all he has seen among the schismatics of that canto in the opening lines of the next one (xxix, 1-3), and is furthered by the pity he feels

for Geri del Bello (xxix, 36, 44) among the falsiners. But here he covers his ears against the piteous shouts.

5. Again as he is about to leave one area to proceed to another, he feels fear: now it is the sight of the giants who stand over the pit of Hell who inspire it (xxxi, 39). It is intensified when Ephialtes shakes himself (109), and felt again when Antaeus bends down to pick up Dante and Virgil and deposit them below (141). Once again Dante becomes staunch, here when he threatens to pull out Bocca's hair if the traitor fails to tell him his tale. (xxxii, 99). This staunchness continues now through the most pitiful canto in the *Inferno*. Throughout Ugolino's speech, which employs the words *pianger, lacrimar, dolor*, and their derivatives eleven times in sixty-seven lines (xxxiii, 9-75), although the reader surely feels pity, Dante does not weep (Ugolino points this out when he asks Dante, in line 42, "If thou dost not weep at this, at what dost thou weep?"). And so here, for the first time, Dante expresses no pity, although he is more forcefully invited to do so than ever before. Thus, here, firmness does not graduate to pity, although the action observed is surely pitiful. The firmness, now specifically against pity, is continued in the last scene of the canto when Dante does not open Fra Alberigo's iced-over eyes as he has promised to do, dismissing his apparent cruelty with the magnificently illiberal line (150), "e cortesia fu lui esser villano" ("and it was courtesy to be a churl to that man").

The five cycles completed, the Pilgrim must undergo his final test in Canto xxxiv when he faces Satan. At the first sight of Satan Dante draws back to Virgil for shelter (9), and then turns chill and feeble with fear (22) as though suspended between life and death—the same condition that was his in the prologue of the poem. That fear will be forgotten in the sight of the stars that ends the *cantica.* Canto xxxiv, as fearful epilogue, balances the fearful prologue of *Inferno* i and ii.

That these five cycles of emotional response seem to be arranged fairly programmatically is of less interest to me than the fact that they exist, for even without programmatic disposition they help us discover another aspect of Dante's compositional scheme. Yet it is perhaps informative to discover that the Poet makes the Pilgrim's encounters with Francesca, Cavalcante, Pier della Vigna, Brunetto, Ulysses, and Ugolino—the encounters which have always drawn forth the sympathetic admiration of romantic critics—take place in their appointed order, which is precisely at each stage in his development when the Pilgrim must harden himself against pity for the damned.

THE MORAL SYSTEM OF THE
COMMEDIA AND THE
SEVEN CAPITAL SINS

Dante divides Hell into Aristotelian-Ciceronian compartments (as he himself tells us in *Inferno* xi), and Paradise into three Ptolemaic angelic triads (as he tells us in *Paradiso* xxviii). Purgatory, on the other hand, is clearly and naturally ordered by the Seven Sins, corresponding to the seven terraces of the Mount. For various and good reasons, a few of Dante's commentators have wondered whether or not there is a common scheme of moral order which unites the three *cantiche*. The most recent (and partially successful) attempt to defy Dante's own statements about *Inferno* and *Paradiso* is that made by T. K. Swing in his often acute study, *The Fragile Leaves of the Sibyl: Dante's Master Plan*.[1] Swing's work, which refers to only six critics of Dante in its bibliography, does not take into account probably the most convincing of all attempts to make a unitary system for the moral plan of the three realms. This work is Luigi Valli's restatement and adumbration of his master's theories *L'allegoria di Dante secondo Giovanni Pascoli*.[2] Valli follows Pascoli in finding that Dante has organized the entire poem in accord with the Seven Sins in order to harmonize the Christian doctrine of Original Sin, the tripartite Aristotelian classification of evil, the Catholic doctrine of the Seven Sins, and the Ptolemaic system of nine spheres. Thus Pascoli, according to Valli, sees the opening of *Inferno*

---

[1] Westminster, Md., 1962.   [2] Bologna [1922], pp. 7-35.

as a picture of "peccato originale non o invano redento (Selva Oscura)."[3] My own conclusion is that Dante did, albeit in small ways that are far from self-evident, pull the poem together in his use of the Seven Sins, but that he did so in a way that is of decorational importance rather than of primary structural significance. In this I oppose both Pascoli/Valli and Swing, all of whom argue for the revelation of a major secret in the poem's composition. Since Dante has told us clearly that he has organized *Inferno* in accord with Aristotle/Cicero and *Paradiso* in accord with the nine celestial spheres of Ptolemaic astronomy and the medieval hierarchy of angels, I see no way that we may look beyond his claims and find them intentionally misleading, which is the inevitable result of Swing's thesis; and I hesitate at the prospect of arid schematization which seems to me the result of Valli's approach.

Swing claims that he works backward from the plan of *Paradiso* to find the Seven Sins as the structural backbone of the entire poem. His work belies his claim. First of all, a quick glance will reveal that his treatments of the corresponding moments of *Purgatorio* and *Inferno* are quite long and detailed, while those of what he claims to be the corresponding parts of *Paradiso* are extremely brief and often forced. Had he consulted Valli he would probably have found that he had turned the Seven Sins, as they occur in *Paradiso*, precisely upside down. This is eventually rather damaging to his argument.

Since the Seven Sins are clearly enunciated only in *Purgatorio*, and since four of the seven give their names

[3] In the diagram facing p. 32. Of *Inf.* I and II as corresponding to Eden after the Fall, see Chapter II of this study where I draw a similar conclusion for different reasons.

to four of the areas of *Inferno*, it is simplest to begin with the correlations between these two *cantiche*.

Inferno, once we get past the Neutrals and the Virtuous Pagans, starts out with the sins in the proper order. Canto v is Lust; vi, Gluttony; vii should then be Avarice, and it is. The fourth sin is Sloth, or *accidia*. Where is it? In the next canto, although it often goes unnoticed. As Virgil prepares Dante for the vision of the Wrathful, he tells his pupil that he is about to see those who were sad in the sweet air that is joyful in the sun, carrying within themselves an *accidioso* smoke, now saddened in the black slime of the Styx ("Tristi fummo/ ne l'aere dolce che dal sol s'allegra,/ portando dentro accidioso fummo:/ or ci attristiam nella belleta negra"—*Inf.* vii, 121-124). Together, the word *accidioso* and the posture, attitude, and behavior of those in Canto viii spell not so much Wrath as Sloth. It is not clear to me whether Dante in Canto viii wants us to think that all who practiced *ira* were essentially slothful, or that only some of them were. What does seem important is that he wanted to include the fourth sin at the appropriate juncture. For the fifth one is Wrath, and it is either described as the sin of Filippo Argenti, thus intermingled with *accidia*, or it gets its turn in the next large division of the poem, which is that of Violence.

This area of the poem is subdivided into three categories: Violence is carried out against others, self, and God. As we approach the area we first see its guardian demon, the Minotaur, who is described as "ira bestial"—"bestial wrath" (*Inf.* xii, 33), and who guards the place where "ira folle"—"mad wrath" (line 49) is punished. That Dante thought of what he calls Wrath as at least to some degree including *accidia*, and of what he calls Violence as being principally the result of Wrath, is buttressed by a nice detail in *Purgatorio* xvii, among the Wrathful.[4] There the *exempla* of the sin which is to be purged on that terrace are three in number. Procne, Haman, and Amata are, respectively, if we think about it only a moment, *exempla* of each of the three categories of Violence we examined in Cantos xii through xvii of *Inferno*: Procne, of violence against others in that she slew her own son Itys in a frenzy of wrath (*Meta.* vi, 412f); Haman, of violence against God in that he, wrathful against Mordecai (Esther 3:5), wanted to slay all the Jews, God's chosen people; Amata, of violence against self in that she hanged herself when she thought Turnus was dead (*Aen.* xii, 595f).

The next great area of *Inferno* goes correctly by the name of Fraud. Did Dante think of it also as Envy, the sixth sin? If he did, he probably thought of Fraud as issuing from the passion of Envy, that is, thought of the Christian root of the pagan sin. This is far from certain, but the case is helped considerably because Dante twice uses the word for Envy, *invidia*, in its verb form, in the area (*Inf.* xxv, 99 and xxvi, 24).

This tentative argument is also bolstered when we consider that there is little doubt that the last area, Treachery, is seen in major respects to be the same sin as, or at least to issue from, Pride. For any Christian, Pride is Lucifer's other name; and it is the fallen angel who is the first *exemplum*, followed by the giants we also see at the bottom of Hell, and who is figured on the pavement of Pride in *Purgatorio* xii (25-36).

To review, we are certain that Dante uses the first three sins in their proper order in *Inferno*; we are almost positive that he refers to Sloth, Wrath, and Pride in the appropriate places; and then we can almost surely argue

[4] Lines 18-39.

that he must have had Envy in mind for Fraud, thus supporting the relatively meager evidence we find within the poem at that point.

Although I disagree strongly with T. K. Swing about the moral order of *Paradiso*, my findings, though they are sometimes the result of a different way of thinking, are extremely close to his concerning *Inferno*. Again, however, I must emphasize a major distinction. I do not believe that Dante's careful ticking off of the Seven Sins in *Inferno* does away with the actual Classical division of sins which is put into Virgil's mouth in Canto xi, as Swing is wont to believe. Dante as usual has it both, indeed many, ways. Doctrinally, however, he must guarantee his vision with Christian doctrine, and so the Seven Sins should be somewhere, and in the right order, in *Inferno*. Secondly, as a poet, and as the kind of symmetry-loving and detail-conscious poet that he is, Dante enjoys small architectonic detail. The two instincts are not incompatible, as the whole work attests; speculation on which of them is stronger here is perhaps irrelevant and certainly beyond the possibilities of proof. A Christian reader today, like Professor Swing, may be most moved to celebrate the hidden doctrine. Another will be most pleased by the decorational detail, the compulsion to form *in parva*. They are both right.

If relatively little imagination is required to discover the way in which Dante hinges the broad and clear moral outline of *Purgatorio* to the complexities of the moral system of *Inferno*, what of the apparently antithetic moral structure of *Paradiso*? Since that part of the poem is to celebrate the virtues, where does it have room for the vices? One part of each celestial area is devoted not to the joy of blessedness but to the sinfulness of Earth. In each sphere someone makes a violent denunciation of sublunar behavior. These denunciations, then, are the logical places to look for traces of the Seven Sins. After the first two spheres, Moon and Mercury,[5] four of the seven heavens (the first three and the last) contain denunciations of earthly behavior which connect with the Seven Sins, each in its proper place, all adhering to the proper order. The fourth, fifth, and sixth are less clearly identified or not referred to.[6] And yet even then, in the surrounding detail of each sphere, we find some supporting detail which might point to Dante's concern to include the Seven Sins even in *Paradiso*. The fact that the four spheres that almost certainly contain references to the Seven Sins also use subordinate detail to clarify the sins referred to in the denunciations helps to bolster the argument.

Why Dante chose to omit Moon and Mercury from the system is not particularly puzzling. He had nine spheres and seven sins, and he chose to omit the first two spheres. Venus, then, must be Lust. That is not surprising after all. This planet is believed by earthlings to ray forth "il folle amore" ("mad love"—*Par.* VIII, 2). Carlo Martello, Cunizza, and Folco all loved the world too much, and Cunizza even confesses to Lust, "because the light of this star overcame me" ("perché mi vinse il lume d'esta stella" —*Par.* IX, 33). These details certainly set the atmosphere for a correspondence between the Heavenly Venus and Earthly Lust. The inclusion of the reference to the presence in this sphere of Rahab the whore (IX, 115) adds to the overtone of the lust that typified life below for all present here. Then Folco concludes the canto and the

[5] Pascoli/Valli also exempt these two spheres. Their order, arrived at otherwise than mine, is in substance precisely the same.

[6] A pleasing parallel to the relative hiddenness of the corresponding sins of *Inferno*. In that *cantica* the first three are named, while in *Paradiso* the first three are more easily discovered than the fourth, fifth, and sixth. The seventh sin in each, Pride, is to be recognized emblematically in the references to Lucifer.

sphere with his denunciation of Florence (127-142) for her coinage of the florin, which has turned the shepherd into the wolf. Thus it would seem to be only Avarice, and not Lust, which is the topic of his angry sermon—until we come to its final word, one that summarizes the sixteen lines that precede it, which is "l'adultero." To think of the coinage of, and the trading in of, money as fornication, as any reader of *Inferno* xvii will remember, was not strange to Dante or to his time. As usury was a form of fornication there, so cupidity seen from here is adultery. And thus, in this single word, which now attaches to the details of lust that were present in the souls we meet who recall their past lives, Dante ties together the sin of Lust and the continuing malefaction in the world below. Once again, as was frequently the case in *Inferno*, the detail is small, calling no great attention to itself.

Almost all of *Paradiso* xi is taken up by Thomas' thoroughly characteristic exposition of a phrase he has used previously, "u' ben s'impingua, se non si vaneggia" ("where there is good fattening if they do not stray"— *Par.* x, 96 and xi, 139). The image of sheep being properly fed and led follows from the previous similar shepherd-into-wolf image in *Paradiso* ix, 131-132, to which I have referred. Here the appropriate sin that should be referred to is gluttony. And, in Thomas' denunciation of the corruption of the Dominican order, bad shepherds now whereas their leader and founder had been a good one, the expression of their peculiar sinfulness is related to gluttony: Dominic's flock has grown so greedy for new foods that it can only stray through various wild pastures ("Ma 'l suo peculio di nova vivenda/ è fatto ghiotto, sì ch'esser non puote/ che per diversi salti non si spanda"—*Par.* xi, 124-126). The world has been understood to hunger (*gola*) for the news of Solomon's Song (*Par.* x, 111), thus also setting the stage for the metaphoric equivalence of bad shepherding and gluttony in the denunciation. And so here, as in the sphere of Venus, the denunciation of bad conduct on earth is expressed with a striking metaphor which associates what would ordinarily be an unrelated sin to one of the Seven Sins. That this is the case is reinforced when we turn to the second denunciation in the Sun, that of degenerate Franciscans by Bonaventura. As the central action of this sphere has been the mutual and reciprocal praise of Franciscans by a Dominican and of Dominicans by a Franciscan, so each praiser once turns to blame those of his own order who have failed where the path was so clearly marked. Bonaventura's language of blame is parallel to that of Thomas' denunciation. The orbit of true faith and deed which circled about St. Francis is compared, in its degeneracy, to a loaf of bread turned to mold ("sì ch'è la muffa dov'era la gromma"—*Par.* xii, 114). The result of this turning from the true way is again compared to bad food: lines 119-120 refer to the parable in Matthew 13:24-30, 36-43, concerning the wheat and the tares. The degenerate Franciscans have given over the "verace manna" (line 84) for this rotten food, or accepted tares instead of wheat. Thus, throughout the three cantos in the Sun, the images of true food are contrasted with improper hunger; and Dante is able through metaphor to assert the less than immediately meaningful, although eventually telling, appropriateness of Gluttony.

In Mars, Cacciaguida denounces the current behavior of Florentines, invoking the woes of overzealous commercial life (*Par.* xvi, 52-84) and capping his description with the comparison of the ebb and flow of wealth to the instability of Moon-pulled tides; "così fa di Fiorenza la

Fortuna" ("thus Fortune does with Florence"—line 84).
We should remember the goddess Fortuna from *Inferno*
VII, the canto of Avarice and Prodigality, where she is associated with the third of the Seven Sins, Avarice, which is
the one we expect to find referred to here. The avarice of
Florentines, treated as "adultery" when it is denounced
in Venus (*Par.* IX, 142), is treated here as Avarice and
Prodigality proper. To underline the point in the following canto, Dante has Cacciaguida say of Florence that there
Christ Himself is bought and sold every day ("Cristo
tutto dì si merca"—*Par.* XVII, 51), behavior which surely
betokens the height of Avarice and Prodigality.

In Jupiter Dante himself makes a denunciation for the
only time in *Paradiso*. It concerns the Papal Court at
Avignon. Against the bright star of Justice rises a smoke
that vitiates its ray ("il fummo che 'l tuo raggio vizia"—
Par. XVIII, 120). The passage continues by attacking the
buying and selling in the temple that would seem to be
connected with Avarice. However, the following *terzina*
takes a second tack, scolding the Avignonian clergy for its
withholding of communion and its sale of canceled excommunications in such a way that Sloth may be seen behind
the words. Where the Crusaders fought with swords (line
127), these men merely withhold communion. Where
Peter and Paul labored for Christ and wrote the Bible,
these men write only to cancel excommunications for their
own profit (130-131). In the final four lines of the canto
Dante lets them speak for themselves, and we hear plainly
the voices of self-absorbed, witty men, exemplars of *accidia*,
condensed into this single imitation which would seem to
be modeled from life. (The closest thing to it in the entire
Commedia is probably the negligent, witty, self-absorbed
speech of Belacqua, the very emblem of the slothful life.)

... "I' ho fermo 'l disiro
sì a colui che volle viver solo
e che per salti fu tratto al martiro,
ch'io non conosco il pescator né Polo."

[... "I have so set my longing
on him who wished to live solitary
and was dragged to martyrdom by dancing feet
that I do not know the Fisherman nor Paul."]
(*Par.* xviii, 133-136)

The imaginary churchman who utters these words is, it seems to me, the picture of the physically comfortable and spiritually negligent creature who for Dante embodies Sloth. He cares only for the florin now being minted in Avignon that bears the picture of John the Baptist, who is represented, in the eyes of the lazy cleric of Avignon, merely as being a rather effete solitary who was sold for a dance of Salome. The jest, so distasteful and yet so perfectly realized, indicts the teller in such a way that the smoke we saw at the opening of Dante's denunciation may have now become associated in our minds with the first smoke we saw in the poem: that "accidioso fummo" of *Inferno* vii, 123, which there was the sign of *accidia*. The substance here certainly seems to fit Avarice better than Sloth. Yet I would argue for the tone of the entire passage, in conjunction with the possibly "loaded" word *fummo*, as indicating that it is Sloth which is on Dante's mind, embodied in his representation of the intellectually able but thoroughly lazy clergy he must have often encountered. In stark contrast to this scene of clerical misbehavior in *Paradiso* xviii is the scene we found in the eighteenth canto of *Purgatorio*. There the zealous Abbot of San Zeno at Verona paid back his slothful days on earth by racing along the Terrace of Sloth. It is possible that Dante had *Purga-*

317

torio xviii in mind for *Paradiso* xviii. And if the word for sloth is absent here, its manner does seem to be present.

As a place, as Valli points out, Saturn, "the mild" planet, is naturally opposed to anger. And in that place, denouncing the corrupt clergy, Peter Damian's contemplative patience gives way to righteous anger as he attacks "li moderni pastori" (*Par.* xxi, 130-135), who are, however, in no way associated with Wrath by Peter's words. The spirits who surround him end the canto with a shout of support for his denunciation which sound to Dante like thunder (142), the traditional sign of God's angry displeasure with man. And in the following canto Beatrice explains to Dante that what he has heard promises that God's vengeance ("la vendetta"—*Par.* xxii, 14) is soon to come. Similarly, at the conclusion of this canto Benedict, angry at clerical malfeasance, is joined by the spirits who surround him, and all go upward like a whirlwind ("come turbo"—*Par.* xxii, 99), that other natural sign of God's angry displeasure. These vestiges of anger—righteous anger—appear to be all we shall find here. For once there would seem to be no correlation whatsoever between the sin denounced and the appropriate one of the Seven Sins, unless in Dante's vision of Earth as the "threshing-floor which makes us so fierce" ("L'aiuola che ci fa tanto feroci" —*Par.* xxii, 151) human ferocity is to be understood as being synonymous with Wrath.[7]

In the sphere of the Fixed Stars, which Dante enters in the sign of Gemini (the Twins who themselves are a sign of concord) he encounters the cooperative spirit exemplified in the relationship revealed among Peter, James, and John, themselves representative of the communal accomplishments of the twelve Apostles. More impressive as proof that Dante is thinking of Envy here is the temporary

---

[7] For this suggestion I am indebted to Peter Schäffer.

blindness he undergoes (*Par.* xxv, 136-139), and which is figurally related to the blindness of Saul of Tarsus that was taken away by Ananias' hand (*Par.* xxvi, 12; Acts 9:10-18). For blindness has been the central image of Envy in *Purgatorio* xiii-xv, where Dante made use of the medieval etymology of the Latin *invidia* to see in Envy a form of blindness. His blindness here is fairly likely to be intended to remind us of that earlier version of the sin, which is countered there as here by images of fraternal love. Even in this high sphere of fraternal bliss we come upon a denunciation of earthly failings. Again it is directed against the corrupt clergy (as are all but two of the Paradisal outcries, the ones reserved for Florence). This time Peter holds forth against those who have usurped his place (*Par.* xxvii, 22), those ravening wolves in shepherds' clothing (55). Thus here the image which describes the procedures of covetousness is that of fraud. As we saw earlier, there seems to exist, for Dante, a correlation between fraudulence and Envy in *Inferno*, and my argument must rely on that thread to make the connection to Envy here. Again, as in the sphere of Saturn, the surrounding details must be primarily relied on in order to make the connection, although here there may be a little more justification in finding the trace of Envy in Peter's speech, the main purport of which is to assail the fraudulent practice of simony (xxvii, 40-60).

The *Primo Mobile*, where Dante is acquainted with the angels and their ranks, contains three denunciations, all made by Beatrice. The first, continuing that of Peter in the same canto (xxvii), attacks *cupidigia*, that radical sin which seems to be cognate with Pride ("Radix malorum est cupiditas") in the medieval imagination.[8] The second con-

[8] James E. Shaw's " 'And the Evening and the Morning Were One Day' (*Paradiso*, xxvii, 136-138)," *Modern Philology*, xviii (1921),

cerns the fallen angels (xxix), and the third attacks puffed
up preachers. This last (xxix, 85-126) denounces false
philosophy that is practised out of vanity, and thus bookish
pride that cares only for applause and nothing for the
truth. That Pride lies close beneath the surface of the first
and third attacks is probably made certain by the middle
one, in which Beatrice takes us back to *Inferno* xxxiv:

> Principio del cader fu il maladetto
> superbir di colui che tu vedesti
> da tutti i pesi del mondo costretto.

> [The beginning of the Fall was the cursed
> pride of him whom thou didst see
> constrained by every universal weight.]
> (Par. xxix, 55-57)

This reminiscence of Satan, with its specific reference to his
pride against God, leaves little room for argument against
the notion that in *Primo Mobile* Dante draws a clear line
of opposition between proud Lucifer and the humble
("modesti"—line 58) angels he has just now seen.

Some of the evidence presented here is thin. Nevertheless, I believe there is enough that is solid to make it more
than a likely possibility that Dante planned to reflect each
of the Seven Sins, in programmatic fashion, in each of the
three *cantiche* of the *Commedia*.

580-581, describes *cupidigia* as follows: ". . . that general sin which
includes all others, which is the common disease of the whole world,
which is the same as St. Augustine's 'amor privatus,' love of self. This
is the sin that caused Lucifer to fall; the sin that, in his case, is often
called pride."

ALLEGORY

Apollonio, Mario, *Dante: Storia della Commedia*, 3rd. ed., 2 vols., Milan, 1965.

Arensberg, Walter, *The Cryptography of Dante*, New York, 1921.

Auerbach, Erich, *Dante: Poet of the Secular World*, tr. Ralph Manheim, Chicago, 1961 [1929, *Dante als Dichter der irdischen Welt*].

————, *Scenes from the Drama of European Literature: Six Essays*, tr. Ralph Manheim, Catherine Garvin, and Erich Auerbach, New York, 1959. Contains: "Figura" [1944], 11-76, and "St. Francis of Assisi in Dante's *Commedia*" [1944], 79-98.

————, "Figurative Texts Illustrating Certain Passages of Dante's *Commedia*," *Speculum*, XXI (1946), 474-489. [A continuation of "Figura."]

————, "Dante's Prayer to the Virgin (*Paradiso*, XXXIII) and Earlier Eulogies," *Romance Philology*, III (1949), 1-26.

————, "Typological Symbolism in Medieval Literature," *Yale French Studies*, no. 9 (1952), 3-10.

————, *Literary Language and Its Public in Late Latin Antiquity and in the Middle Ages*, tr. Ralph Manheim, New York, 1965.

Baker, Susan, "The Analogy of a Poem: Dante's Dream," *Sewanee Review*, LXXIV (1966), 438-449.

————, "The Crowned Knot of Fire: A Study of the Influence of Medieval Symbolism on Modern Poetry," unpub. diss. (Univ. of Minn., 1966).

Barbi, Michele, "Allegoria e lettera sulla 'Divina Commedia,'" in *Problemi fondamentali per un nuovo com-*

mento della Divina Commedia, Florence, 1955, 115-140.

Barelli, Vincenzo, *L'allegoria della Divina Commedia*, Florence, 1864.

Beichner, Paul E., "The Allegorical Interpretation of Medieval Literature," *PMLA*, LXXXII (1967), 33-38.

Bergin, Thomas G., *Dante*, Boston, 1965, esp. 250-264.

——, "Dante's 'Comedy'—Letter and Spirit," *Virginia Quarterly Review*, XLI (1965), 525-541.

Bernardo, Aldo S., "Petrarch's Attitude toward Dante," *PMLA*, LXX (1955), 488-517.

——, "The Three Beasts and Perspective in the *Divine Comedy*," *PMLA*, LXXVIII (1963), 14-24.

——, "Flesh, Spirit, and Rebirth at the Center of Dante's *Comedy*," *Symposium*, XIX (1965), 335-351.

Bethurum, Dorothy, ed., *Critical Approaches to Medieval Literature: Selected Papers from the English Institute*, 1958-1959, New York, 1960. [Contains three papers on the topic "Patristic Exegesis in the Criticism of Medieval Literature," by E. Talbot Donaldson, R. E. Kaske, and Charles Donahue.]

Bezanker, Abraham, "An Introduction to the Problem of Allegory in Literary Criticism," unpub. diss. Univ. of Mich., 1954).

Bietenholtz, Peter G., "Clio and Thalia: The Place of History in Dante's *Comedy*," *Canadian Journal of History*, I, 2 (1966), 1-25.

Blackmur, R. P., "Dante's Ten Terms for the Treatment of the Treatise," *Kenyon Review*, XIV (1952), 286-300.

Bloom, Edward A., "The Allegorical Principle," *ELH*, XVIII (1951), 163-190.

Bloomfield, M. W., "Symbolism in Mediaeval Literature," *Modern Philology*, LVI (1958), 73-81.

————, *Piers Plowman as a Fourteenth-century Apocalypse*, New Brunswick, 1961, esp. 30-31.

Boffito, G., "L'Epistola di Dante Alighieri a Cangrande della Scala: saggio d'edizione critica e di commento," *Memorie della Reale Accademia delle Scienze di Torino*, s. 2a, LVIII (1907), 1-39.

Born, L. K., "Ovid and Allegory," *Speculum*, IX (1934), 362-379.

Bowden, John Paul, *An Analysis of Pietro Alighieri's Commentary on the Divine Comedy*, New York, 1951.

Brandeis, Irma, *The Ladder of Vision*, New York, 1960.

de Bruyne, Edgar, *Études d'esthétique médiévale*, Bruges, 1946 [pub. in *Rijksuniversiteit te Gent*, vols. 97-99].

Buck, August, "Gli studi sulla poetica e sulla retorica di Dante e del suo tempo," in *Atti del Congresso Internazionale di Studi Danteschi*, Florence, 1965, 249-278. [Also in *Cultura e Scuola*, IV (1965), 143-166.]

————, "Dantes Selbstverständnis," *DDJb*, XLIII (1965), 7-24.

Busnelli, G., and G. Vandelli, eds. *Il convivio*, vol. I, Florence, 1934, 240-242, Appendice I to *Convivio* II, "Sopra i quattro sensi delle scritture."

Camilli, A., "Le figurazioni allegoriche," *Studi danteschi*, XXVIII (1959), 197-215.

Caplan, Harry, "The Four Senses of Scriptural Interpretation and the Mediaeval Theory of Preaching," *Speculum*, IV (1929), 282-290.

Casciola, Brizio, *L'enimma dantesco*, Bergamo, 1950.

Charity, A. C., *Events and Their Afterlife: The Dialectics of Christian Typology in the Bible and Dante*, Cambridge, 1966, esp. 167-261.

Chistoni, Paride, *La seconda fase del pensiero dantesco*, Leghorn, 1903, esp. Ch. VI.

Chydenius, Johan, *The Typological Problem in Dante*, in *Societas Scientiarum Fennica Commentationes Humanarum Litterarum*, xxv, Helsingfors, 1958, 1-159.

———, "The Theory of Mediaeval Symbolism," *CHL*, xxvii, Helsingfors, 1960, 1-42.

Cian, Vittorio, *Oltre l'enigma dantesco del Veltro*, Turin, 1945.

Ciotti, Andrea, "Il concetto della 'figura' e la poetica della 'visione' nei commentatori trecenteschi della 'Commedia'," *Convivium*, xxx (1962), 264-292, 399-415.

———, "Alcune citazioni di Alano di Lilla nei commenti trecenteschi della *Commedia*," *L'Alighieri*, iii, 1 (1962), 35-42.

———, "Isidoro di Siviglia e i commentatori trecenteschi della *Commedia*," *L'Alighieri*, v, 2 (1964), 36-44.

Cook, Albert, *The Classic Line: A Study in Epic Poetry*, Bloomington, Ind., 1966, esp. 211-245.

Croce, Benedetto, *La poesia di Dante*, Bari, 1921.

Curtius, Ernst Robert, "Das Buch als Symbol in der Divina Commedia," in *Festschrift zum sechzigsten Geburtstag von Paul Clemen*, Bonn, 1926, 44-54.

———, "Dante und das lateinische Mittelalter," *Romanische Forschungen*, lvii (1943), 153-185.

———, "Neue Dantestudien" [1947], in *Gesammelte Aufsätze zur romanischen Philologie*, Bern, 1960, 305-345.

———, *European Literature and the Latin Middle Ages*, tr. Willard R. Trask, New York, 1963 [1948].

Damon, Phillip W., "The Two Modes of Allegory in Dante's *Convivio*," *Philological Quarterly*, xl (1961), 144-149.

———, *Modes of Analogy in Ancient and Medieval Verse*, Berkeley, 1961.

Daniélou, Jean, *Sacrementum Futuri: Études sur les origines de la typologie biblique*, Paris, 1950.

——, "The Problem of Symbolism," *Thought*, xxv (1950), 423-440.

——, *Études d'exégèse judéo-chrétienne: Les Testimonia*, Paris, 1966.

Dunbar, H. Flanders, *Symbolism in Medieval Thought and Its Consummation in the Divine Comedy*, New Haven, 1929, esp. 243-330.

Durling, Robert M., *The Figure of the Poet in Renaissance Epic*, Cambridge, Mass., 1965.

Fallani, Giovanni, *Poesia e teologia nella Divina Commedia*, 2 vols., Milan, 1959-1961.

Faral, Edmond, *Les arts poétiques du XIIe et du XIIIe siècle*, Paris, 1924.

Fergusson, Francis, *Dante's Drama of the Mind*, Princeton, 1953.

——, *Dante*, New York, 1966.

Ferrall, Rose Nolan, *The D. X. V. Prophecy: Dante and the Sabbatum Fidelium: An Introductory Study in the Allegorical Interpretation of the Divine Comedy*, Oxford, 1938.

Flamini, Francesco, *I significati reconditi della Commedia di Dante*, 2 vols., Leghorn, 1903, esp. vol. i, 36-40.

Fletcher, Angus, *Allegory: The Theory of a Symbolic Mode*, Ithaca, 1964.

Fletcher, Jefferson Butler, *Dante*, New York, 1916.

——, *Symbolism of the Divine Comedy*, New York, 1921.

Foster, David William, "The Misunderstanding of Dante in Fifteenth-Century Spanish Poetry," *Comparative Literature*, xvi (1964), 338-347.

——, "Figural Interpretation and the *Auto de los Reyes Magos*," *Romanic Review*, lviii (1967), 3-11.

——, *"De Maria Egyptiaca* and the Medieval Figural Tradition," *Italica*, XLIV (1967), 135-143.

——, "Calderón's 'La Torre De Babilonia' and Christian Allegory," *Criticism*, IX (1967), 142-154.

Foster, Kenelm, *God's Tree*, London, 1957, esp. Ch. I, "Dante as a Christian Poet."

Frank, Robert Worth, Jr., "The Art of Reading Medieval Personification-Allegory," *ELH*, XX (1953), 237-250.

Freccero, John, "Dante's Firm Foot and the Journey without a Guide," *Harvard Theological Review*, LII (1959), 245-282.

——, "Dante's Pilgrim in a Gyre," *PMLA*, LXXVI (1961), 168-181.

——, "Infernal Inversion and Christian Conversion," *Italica*, XLII (1965), 35-41.

——, "The Sign of Satan," *Modern Language Notes*, LXXX (1965), 11-26.

——, "The River of Death: *Inferno* II, 108," in *The World of Dante*, ed. S. B. Chandler and J. A. Molinaro, Toronto, 1966, 25-42.

——, "Dante's Prologue Scene," *Dante Studies*, LXXXIV (1966), 1-25.

Frye, Northrop, "Allegory," in *Encyclopedia of Poetry and Poetics*, ed. Alex Preminger, Princeton, 1965, 12-14.

Geffcken, J., "Allegory, Allegorical Interpretation," in *Encyclopedia of Religion and Ethics*, ed. James Hastings, New York, 1913, 327-331.

Getto, Giovanni, "Poesia e teologia nel *Paradiso* di Dante," in *Aspetti della poesia di Dante*, Florence, 1947, 119-188.

Giamatti, A. Bartlett, *The Earthly Paradise and the Renaissance Epic*, Princeton, 1966, esp. 94-119.

Gilbert, Allan H., *Dante and His Comedy*, New York, 1963, esp. 29-42.

326

————, "Did Dante Dedicate the *Paradiso* to Can Grande della Scala?" *Italica*, XLIII (1966), 100-124.

Gillet, Louis, *Dante*, Paris, 1965, esp. 115-122.

Gilson, Étienne, *Dante et la philosophie*, 2nd ed., Paris, 1953.

————, "Poésie et vérité dans la 'Genealogia' de Boccace," in *Studi sul Boccaccio*, vol. II, 1964, 253-282.

————, "Poésie et théologie dans la 'Divine Comédie,'" in *Atti del Congresso Internazionale di Studi Danteschi*, Florence, 1965, 197-223.

Grana, Gianni, "La poesia teologica di Dante in una sintesi di G. Fallani," *L'Alighieri*, III, 1 (1962), 51-58.

Grant, Robert M., *A Short History of the Interpretation of the Bible*, rev. ed., New York, 1963.

Greene, R. H., "Dante's 'Allegory of the Poets' and the Mediaeval Theory of Poetic Fiction," *Comparative Literature*, IX (1957), 118-128.

Greene, T. M., "Dramas of Selfhood in the *Comedy*," in *From Time to Eternity*, ed. T. G. Bergin, New Haven, 1967, 103-136.

Guerri, Domenico, *Il commento del Boccaccio a Dante*, Bari, 1926.

Hanson, R. P. C., *Allegory and Event: A Study of the Sources and Significance of Origen's Interpretation of Scripture*, London, 1959.

Hardie, C. G., "The Epistle to Cangrande Again," *DDJb*, XXXVIII (1960), 51-74.

————, "Beatrice's Chariot in Dante's Earthly Paradise," *DDJb*, XXXIX (1961), 137-172.

Hatzfeld, H., "The Problem of Literary Interpretation Reconsidered," *Orbis Litterarum*, XIX (1964), 66-76.

Huizinga, J., *The Waning of the Middle Ages*, New York, 1956 [1924], esp. Ch. XV, "Symbolism in Its Decline."

Jaeger, Werner, *Early Christianity and Greek Paideia*, Cambridge, Mass., 1961.

Jauss, H. R., "Form und Auffassung der Allegorie in der Tradition der Psychomachia," in *Medium Aevum Vivum: Festschrift für Walther Bulst*, ed. H. R. Jauss and Dieter Schaller, Heidelberg, 1960, 179-206.

————, *Genèse de la poésie allégorique au moyen âge*, Heidelberg, 1962.

Kantorowicz, E., *The King's Two Bodies: A Study in Medieval Political Theology*, Princeton, 1957.

Kaske, R. E., "Dante's 'DXV' and 'Veltro'," *Traditio*, xvii (1961), 185-254. [Reprinted in shorter form in *Dante: A Collection of Critical Essays*, ed. John Freccero, Englewood Cliffs, N.J., 122-140.]

Katzenellenbogen, Adolf, *Allegories of the Virtues and Vices in Mediaeval Art*, New York, 1964.

Kelly, J. N. D., *Early Christian Doctrines*, New York, 1958, esp. 69-78.

Kuhn, Hugo, *Dichtung und Welt im Mittelalter*, Stuttgart, 1959.

Lampe, G. W. H., and K. J. Woollcombe, *Essays on Typology*, London, 1957.

Leclercq, Jean, *The Love of Learning and the Desire for God*, tr. Catherine Misrahi, New York, 1961.

Leo, Ulrich, *Sehen und Wirklichkeit bei Dante*, Frankfurt am Main, 1957.

————, "Vorrede zu einer Lectura Dantis," *DDJb*, xxxviii (1960), 18-50.

Lewis, C. S., *The Allegory of Love: A Study in Medieval Tradition*, Oxford, 1936.

————, *The Discarded Image: An Introduction to Medieval and Renaissance Literature*, Cambridge, 1964.

————, "Imagery in the Last Eleven Cantos of Dante's

'Comedy'," in *Studies in Medieval and Renaissance Literature*, Cambridge, 1966, 83-84.

Locke, F. W., "The Gate of Hell (*Inferno* iii, 1-69)," *Neophilologus*, xlv (1961), 199-210.

Lubac, Henri de, *Histoire et esprit: l'intelligence de l'Écriture d'après Origène*, Paris, 1950.

———, *Exégèse médiévale: les quatre sens de l'Écriture*, 4 vols., Paris, 1959-1964.

Malagoli, L., *Linguaggio e poesia nella Divina Commedia*, Genoa, 1949, esp. Ch. v, "La concretezza di Dante e il metafisicismo critico."

———, *Saggio sulla Divina Commedia*, Florence, 1962, esp. 128-139.

Marzot, Giulio, "Dante e la Bibbia," *Cultura e Scuola*, iv (1965), 180-193.

Maurer, Karl, "Personifikation und visionäre Persönlichkeitssteigerung in Dantes *Divina commedia*," *DDJb*, xliii (1965), 112-137.

Mazzeo, Joseph Anthony, *Structure and Thought in the Paradiso*, Ithaca, 1958, esp. Ch. ii, "Dante's Conception of Poetic Expression."

———, *Medieval Cultural Tradition in Dante's Comedy*, Ithaca, 1960.

Mazzoni, Francesco, "L'Epistola a Cangrande," *Rendiconti dell'Accademia Nazionale dei Lincei*, x, fasc. 3-4 (1955), 157-198.

———, "Per l'Epistola a Cangrande," in *Studi in onore di Angelo Monteverdi*, vol. ii, Modena, 1959, 498-516.

———, "Pietro Alighieri interprete di Danti," *Studi danteschi*, xl (1963), 279-360.

———, "La critica dantesca del secolo xiv," *Cultura e Scuola*, iv (1965), 285-297.

McNair, Philip, "The Poetry of the 'Comedy,'" in *The*

Mind of Dante, ed. U. Limentani, Cambridge, 1965, 17-46.

Meersseman, G. G., "Dante come teologo," in *Atti del Congresso Internazionale di Studi Danteschi*, Florence, 1965, 177-195.

————, "Erich Auerbach e la scoperta del realismo in Dante e in Boccaccio," *Convivium*, XXVI (1958), 16-26.

Montano, Rocco, *Storia della poesia di Dante*, 2 vols., Naples, 1962, esp. vol. I, 304-332.

Montgomery, Robert L., "Allegory and the Incredible Fable: The Italian View from Dante to Tasso," *PMLA*, LXXXI (1966), 45-55.

Moore, Edward, *Studies in Dante*, 3rd Series, Oxford, 1903, esp. 284-374.

Nardi, Bruno, "Le figurazioni allegoriche e l'allegoria della 'donna gentile'," in *Nel mondo di Dante*, Rome, 1944, 23-40.

————, "I sensi delle scritture (*Conv.* II, i, 2 sgg.)," in *Nel mondo di Dante*, 55-61.

————, "Dante profeta," in *Dante e la cultura medievale*, Bari, 1949, 336-416.

————, *Dal "Convivio" alla "Commedia,"* Rome, 1960.

————, "Il punto sull'Epistola a Cangrande," *Lectura Dantis Scaligera*, Florence, 1960.

————, "Filosofia e teologia ai tempi di Dante in rapporto al pensiero del poeta," in *Atti del Congresso Internazionale di Studi Danteschi*, Florence, 1965, 79-175. [Reprinted in *Saggi e note*—see below—3-109.]

————, "Sull' interpretazione allegorica e sulla struttura della *Commedia* di Dante," in *Saggi e note di critica dantesca*, Milano, 1966, 146-157.

————, "Osservazioni sul medievale 'accessus ad auctores' in rapporto all' *Epistola a Cangrande*," in *Saggi e note*, 268-305.

Nemetz, A., "Literalness and the 'Sensus litteralis'," *Speculum*, XXXIV (1959), 76-89.

Olschki, Leonardo, *Dante 'Poeta Veltro,'* Florence, 1953.

Osgood, Charles G., *Boccaccio on Poetry*, Princeton, 1930, xi-xlix.

d'Ovidio, F., "L'Epistola a Cangrande," in *Studii sulla Divina Commedia*, Milan-Palermo, 1901, 448-485.

Ozanam, A.-F., *Dante et la philosophie catholique au treizième siècle*, Paris, 1839.

Padoan, Giorgio, "Introduzione" to Boccaccio's *Esposizioni sopra la Comedia di Dante*, Milano, 1965, esp. xxvi-xxxi.

Pagliaro, Antonino, "Simbolo e allegoria nella Divina Commedia," *L'Alighieri*, IV, 2 (1963), 3-35.

Paparelli, G. "*Fictio*. La definizione dantesca della poesia," *Filologia romanza*, VII, fasc. 3-4 (1960), 1-83.

Parodi, E. G., *Poesia e storia nella "Divina Commedia,"* Naples, 1920.

Pascoli, Giovanni, *Sotto il velame*, Messina, 1900.

——, *La mirabile visione*, 3rd ed., Bologna, 1923.

Patch, H. R., "The Symbolism of the Supernatural in the *Divine Comedy*," *Romance Philology*, X (1957), 204-209.

Petronio, Giuseppe, "*L'Inferno* (problemi di metodo)," *Cultura e Scuola*, IV (1965), 362-378.

Pézard, André, *Le 'Convivio' de Dante, sa lettre, son esprit*, Paris, 1940.

——, *Dante sous la pluie de feu (Enfer, chant* XV*)*, Paris, 1950, esp. 247-254 and Appendice VIII, "Les quatre sens de l'Ecriture," 372-400.

Pietrobono, Luigi, "Per l'allegoria di Dante," in *Saggi danteschi*, Rome, 1936, 221-231.

——, "L'allegorismo e Dante," in *Nuovi saggi danteschi*, Turin [1954], 37-54.

——, "L'Epistola a Can Grande," in *Nuovi saggi danteschi*, 199-244.

——, "Struttura, allegoria e poesia nella *Divina Commedia*," *Nuovi saggi danteschi*, 245-277.

——, "Appunti e lezioni: l'allegoria," *L'Alighieri*, i, 2 (1960), 15-18.

Pohndorf, Sister Marie Catherine, "Conceptual Imagery Related to the Journey Theme in Dante's *Commedia* Interpreted in Light of the Medieval Exegetical Method," unpub. diss. (Denver Univ., 1965).

Pollmann, Leo, "Vom *Convivio* zur *Epistola a Can Grande*," *Cultura neolatina*, xxiv (1964), 39-53.

Post, Chandler Rathfon, *Mediaeval Spanish Allegory*, Cambridge, Mass., 1915.

Ralphs, Sheila, "Dante, Poet of the Exodus," *Theology*, lxviii (1965), 479-485.

Renucci, Paul, "Dantismo esoterico nel secolo presente," in *Atti del Congresso Internazionale di Studi Danteschi*, Florence, 1965, 305-332.

Robertson, D. W., Jr., "Some Medieval Literary Terminology, with Special Reference to Chrétien de Troyes," *Studies in Philology*, xlviii (1951), 669-692.

——, *A Preface to Chaucer: Studies in Medieval Perspectives*, Princeton, 1962, esp. 286-317, 348-352.

Rossi, L. R., "Dante and the Poetic Tradition in the Commentary of Benvenuto da Imola," *Italica*, xxxii (1955), 215-223.

Sandkühler, B., *Die frühen Dante-Kommentare und ihr Verhältnis zur mittelalterlichen Kommentartradition*, Munich, 1967.

Santi, Antonio, *L'ordinamento morale e l'allegoria della Divina Commedia*, 2 vols., Palermo, 1923-1924.

Sapegno, Natalino, *Il trecento*, Milan, 1934, esp. Ch. iii,

"La fortuna di Dante e la letteratura allegorica e didattica."

————, "Introduzione alla *Commedia*" [1957], in *Pagine di storia letteraria*, Palermo, 1960, 29-49.

Sarolli, Gian Roberto, "Dante 'scriba Dei'," *Convivium*, XXXI (1963), 385-422, 513-544, 641-671.

————, "Dante's Katabasis and Mission," in *The World of Dante*, ed. S. B. Chandler and J. A. Molinaro, Toronto, 1966, 80-116.

————, "Prolegomena alla 'Commedia'," *Convivium*, XXXIV (1966), 77-112.

Sayers, Dorothy L., *Introductory Papers on Dante*, New York, 1954.

Scott, J. A., "Allegory in the *Purgatorio*," *Italica*, XXXVII (1960), 167-184.

Shaw, James E., *The Lady "Philosophy" in the Convivio*, Cambridge, Mass., 1938.

Silverstein, H. T., "Allegory and Literary Form," *PMLA*, LXXXII (1967), 28-32.

Singleton, Charles S., " 'Sulla fiumana ove 'l mar non ha vanto'," *Romanic Review*, XXXIX (1948), 269-277.

————, *An Essay on the Vita Nuova*, Cambridge, Mass., 1949.

————, *Dante Studies 1: Commedia: Elements of Structure*, Cambridge, Mass., 1954.

————, "The Irreducible Dove," *Comparative Literature*, IX (1957), 129-135.

————, *Dante Studies 2: Journey to Beatrice*, Cambridge Mass., 1958.

————, " 'In exitu Israel de Aegypto'," *78th Annual Report of the Dante Society* (1960), 1-24.

————, "*Inferno* x: Guido's Disdain," *Modern Language Notes*, LXXVII (1962), 49-65.

————, "The Poet's Number at the Center," *Modern Language Notes*, LXXX (1965), 1-10.

————, "The Vistas in Retrospect," in *Atti del Congresso Internazionale di Studi Danteschi*, Florence, 1965, 279-304. [Reprinted in *Modern Language Notes*, LXXXI (1966), 55-80.]

Smalley, Beryl, *The Study of the Bible in the Middle Ages*, Oxford, 1952.

Spicq, C., *Esquisse d'une histoire de l'exégèse latine au moyen âge*, Paris, 1944.

Stambler, Bernard, *Dante's Other World: The 'Purgatorio' as Guide to the 'Divine Comedy,'* New York, 1957, esp. 54-78.

————, "Three Dreams," *Books Abroad* [Special Dante Issue] (May 1965), 81-92, esp. 89-92.

Stewart, J. A., *The Myths of Plato*, London, 1905, esp. the "Excursus on Allegory," 230-258.

Swing, T. K., *The Fragile Leaves of the Sibyl: Dante's Master Plan*, Westminster, Md., 1962.

Synave, P., "La Doctrine de Saint-Thomas d'Aquin sur le sens littéral des Écritures," *Revue Biblique*, XXXV (1926), 40-65.

Tate, Allen, "The Symbolic Imagination: A Meditation on Dante's Three Mirrors," in *Discussions of the Divine Comedy*, ed. Irma Brandeis, Boston, 1961, 102-111.

————, "The Unliteral Imagination; Or, I, too, Dislike It," *Southern Review*, I (1965), 530-542.

Toynbee, Paget, "Rahab's Place in Dante's Paradise," in *Dante Studies and Researches*, London, 1902, 287-288.

————, "Boccaccio's Commentary on the *Divina Commedia*," in *Dante Studies*, Oxford, 1921, 53-81.

————, "The Bearing of the *Cursus* on the Text of Dante's *De vulgari eloquentia*," *Proceedings of the British Academy* (1912-1923), 359-377.

Tuve, Rosemond, *Allegorical Imagery*, Princeton, 1966.

Udny, S., "The Interpretation of Dante," *Living Age*, ccxxxvii (1903), 735-744.

Valensin, Auguste, *Le Christianisme de Dante*, Paris, 1954, esp. 15-18.

Valli, Luigi, *L'allegoria di Dante secondo Giovanni Pascoli*, Bologna [1922].

Vallone, Aldo, "Personificazione simbolo e allegoria nel Medio Evo dinanzi a Dante," *Filologia e Letteratura*, x (1964), 189-224.

Vasoli, Cesare, "Filosofia e teologia in Dante," *Cultura e Scuola*, iv (1965), 47-71, esp. 62-71.

Weinberg, Bernard, *A History of Literary Criticism in the Italian Renaissance*, vol. i, Chicago, 1961.

Wellek, René, "The Concept of Realism in Literary Scholarship," in *Concepts of Criticism*, ed. Stephen G. Nichols, Jr., New Haven, 1963, 222-255.

Westermann, Claus, ed., *Essays on Old Testament Hermeneutics*, tr. J. L. Mays, Richmond, Va., 1963. [Contains two essays of particular interest to the literary scholar: Gerhard von Rad, "Typological Interpretation of the Old Testament," 17-39; Walther Eichrodt, "Is Typological Exegesis an Appropriate Method?" 224-245.]

Wicksteed, Philip H., *Dante and Aquinas*, London, 1913.

Williams, Charles, *The Figure of Beatrice*, London, 1943.

DANTE AS READER

Auerbach, Erich, "Dante und Virgil," *Das Humanistische Gymnasium*, XLII (1931), 136-144.

Austin, H. D., " 'Black But Comely' (*Par.* XXVII, 136-8)," *Philological Quarterly*, XV (1936), 352-357.

Bacchelli, Riccardo, " 'Per te poeta fui,' " *Studi danteschi*, XLII (1965), 5-28.

Battaglia, Salvatore, "Introduzione alla teoria del poeta teologo," *Cultura e Scuola*, IV (1965), 72-86.

Berrigan, J. R., "*Vinculum Pacis*: Vergil and Dante," *Classical Bulletin*, XLVIII (1967), 49-53.

Bezzola, Reto R., "L'opera di Dante, sintesi poetica dell'antichità e del medioevo cristiano," in *Atti del Congresso Internazionale di Studi Danteschi*, Florence, 1965, 379-395.

Bickersteth, Geoffrey L., *Dante's Virgil: A Poet's Poet*, [Glasgow], 1951.

Bolgar, R. R., *The Classical Heritage and Its Beneficiaries*, New York, 1964 [1954].

Bonfanti, Nicolina, *Fonti virgiliane dell'oltretomba dantesco*, Messina, 1918.

Brugnoli, Giorgio, "Dante *Inferno* 30, 13 sgg.," *L'Alighieri*, VII, 1 (1966), 98-99.

Busnelli, Giovanni, *Il Virgilio dantesco e il gran veglio di Creta*, 2nd ed., Rome, 1919.

Comparetti, Domenico, *Vergil in the Middle Ages*, tr. E. F. M. Benecke [reprint of 2nd ed., 1908], Hamden, Conn., 1966.

Consoli, Domenico, *Significato del Virgilio dantesco*, Florence, 1967.

Contini, Gianfranco, "Dante come poeta popolare e come autore classico," *Acta Litteraria Academiae Scientiarum Hungaricae*, VIII (1966), 155-168.

Curtius, Ernst Robert, "Das Schiff der Argonauten," in *Kritische Essays zur europäischen Literatur*, Bern, 1950.

Damon, Phillip W., "Dante's Ulysses and the Mythic Tradition," in *Medieval Secular Literature: Four Essays*, ed. Wm. Matthews, Berkeley and Los Angeles, 1965, 24-45.

Davis, Charles Till, *Dante and the Idea of Rome*, Oxford, 1957.

Dawkins, R. M., "The 'Gran Veglio' of *Inferno* XIV," *Medium Aevum*, II (1933), 95-107.

Drew, D. L. M., *The Allegory of the Aeneid*, Oxford, 1927.

Esposito, Enzo, "Dante traduttore di Virgilio," *L'Italia che scrive*, XLVIII (1965) 335-336.

Fitzgerald, Robert, "The Style That Does Honor," *Kenyon Review*, XIV (1952), 278-285.

———, "Generations of Leaves," *Perspectives USA*, no. 8 (1954), 68-85.

Franz, A., "Dante zitiert: II," *DDJb*, XXIX-XXX (1951), 41-105, esp. 92-105.

Gardner, E. G., *Virgil in Italian Poetry*, London, 1931.

Gargano Cosenza, G., "*Lo bello stile*," Messina, 1901.

Georgii, Heinrich, *Die antike Äneiskritik*, Stuttgart, 1891.

Ghisalberti, Fausto, "Arnolfo d'Orléans: un cultore di Ovidio nel secolo XII," *Memorie del Reale Istituto Lombardo, Cl. lett.*, XXIV (1932), 157-230.

———, "L'enigma delle Naiadi," *Studi danteschi*, XVI (1932), 105-125.

———, "Giovanni del Virgilio espositore delle 'Metamorfosi,'" *Giornale dantesco*, XXXIV (1933), 3-107, esp. 14-19.

———, " 'L'Ovidius Moralizatus' di Pierre Bersuire," *Studi romanzi*, XXIII (1933), 5-32.

———, "La quadriga del sole nel 'Convivio,' " *Studi danteschi*, XVIII (1934), 69-77.

———, "Il commentario medioevale all'*Ovidius maior* consultato da Dante," *Rendiconti dell'Istituto Lombardo, Accademia di scienze e lettere*, C (1966), 267-275.

Gilson, Étienne, "Qu'est-ce qu'une ombre? (Dante, *Purg.* XXV)," *Archives d'Histoire Doctrinale et Littéraire du Moyen Age*, XL (1965), 71-93.

Gmelin, H., "Dante und die römischen Dichter," *DDJb*, XXXI-XXXII (1953), 42-65.

Goldstein, Harvey D., "*Enea e Paolo*: A Reading of the 26th Canto of Dante's *Inferno*," *Symposium*, XIX (1965), 316-327.

Graf, Arturo, *Roma nella memoria e nelle immaginazioni del medio evo*, 2 vols., Turin, 1882-1883.

Hollander, Robert, "Dante's Use of *Aeneid* I in *Inferno* I and II," *Comparative Literature*, XX (1968), 142-156.

Inguagiato, Vincenzina, "Come Dante col Poema rinnovelli l'azione d'Enea e di s. Paolo," *Giornale dantesco*, XVIII (1900), 193-199.

Kardos, Tibor, "L'umanesimo di Dante fra il Medioevo ed il Rinascimento," *Acta Litteraria Academiae Scientiarum Hungaricae*, VIII (1966), 1-60.

Lenkeith, Nancy, *Dante and the Legend of Rome*, London, 1952.

Leo, Ulrich, "The Unfinished Convivio and Dante's Rereading of the Aeneid," *Mediaeval Studies*, XIII (1951), 41-64.

Logan, Terence P., "The Characterization of Ulysses in Homer, Virgil and Dante: A Study in Sources and

Analogues," *82nd Annual Report of the Dante Society* (1964), 19-46.

Mackail, J. W., *Virgil*, London, 1931.

Martellotti, Guido, "Dante e i classici," *Cultura e Scuola*, IV (1965), 125-137.

Masera, Giovanni, "Come Dante abbia fantasiosamente derivato dall'Eneide virgiliana," *Giornale dantesco*, XXXII (1931), 121-131.

Mazzoni, Francesco, "Saggio di un nuovo commento alla 'Commedia': il canto IV dell' 'Inferno,' " *Studi danteschi*, XLII (1965), 29-204.

Mazzoni, Guido, "Dante e Virgilio," in *Almae luces malae cruces*, Bologna, 1941, 1-21.

McKenzie, K., "Virgil and Dante," in *The Tradition of Virgil*, Princeton, 1930, 11-21.

Moore, C. H., "Prophecy in the Ancient Epic," *Harvard Studies in Classical Philology*, XXXII (1921), 99-175.

Moore, Edward, *Studies in Dante, First Series, Scripture and Classical Authors in Dante*, Oxford, 1896.

Müller-Bochat, E., "Der allegorische Äneas und die Auslegung des Danteschen Jenseits im 14. Jahrhundert," *DDJb*, XLIV-XLV (1966-1967), 59-81.

Nardi, Bruno, "Tre momenti dell'incontro di Dante con Virgilio," in *Saggi e note di critica dantesca*, Milano, 1966 [reprinted from *L'Alighieri*, VI, 2 (1965), 42-53].

d'Ovidio, F., "Non soltanto lo bello stile tolse da lui," *Atene e Roma*, I (1898), 15-25.

Padoan, Giorgio, "Il mito di Teseo e il cristianesimo di Stazio," *Lettere italiane*, XI (1959), 432-457.

———, "Ulisse 'fandi fictor' e le vie della Sapienza," *Studi danteschi*, XXXVII (1960), 21-61.

———, "Tradizione e fortuna del commento all' 'Eneide'

di Bernardo Silvestre," *Italia medioevale e umanistica*, III (1960), 227-240.

Palgen, Rudolf, "Die Virgilsage in der Göttlichen Komö-die," *DDJb*, XIV (1932), 1-26.

———, "La Légende virgilienne dans la *Divine Comé-die*," *Romania*, LXXIII (1952), 332-390.

———, "Dantes Vergil-Gestalt," in *Werden und Wesen der Komödie Dantes*, Graz, 1955, 126-172.

Paratore, Ettore, "Lucano e Dante," *L'Alighieri*, II, 2 (1961), 3-25.

Pézard, André, *Dante sous la pluie de feu*, Paris, 1950, esp. Appendice IV, "Donat, Virgile et Dante," 339-354.

Pöschl, Viktor, *The Art of Virgil: Image and Symbol in the Aeneid*, tr. Gerda Seligson, Ann Arbor, 1962.

Raby, F. J. E., "Some Notes on Dante and Macrobius," *Medium Aevum*, XXXV (1966), 117-121.

Rand, E. K., *Ovid and His Influence*, Boston, 1925, esp. 143-145.

Renaudet, Augustin, *Dante humaniste*, Paris, 1952, esp. 88-100, 459-475.

Renucci, Paul, *Dante, disciple et juge du monde gréco-latin*, Paris, 1954, esp. 282-291.

von Richthofen, Erich, *Veltro und Diana: Dantes mittelal-terliche und antike Gleichnisse nebst einer Darstellung ihren Ausdrucksformen*, Tübingen, 1956.

Robson, C. A., "Dante's Use in the *Divina Commedia* of the Medieval Allegories on Ovid," in *Centenary Essays on Dante by Members of the Oxford Dante Society*, Oxford, 1965, 1-38.

Ronconi, Alessandro, "Per Dante interprete dei poeti latini," *Studi danteschi*, XLI (1964), 5-44.

Rossi, Mario, "Il Virgilio allegorico ed il Virgilio poetico," in *Gusto filologico e gusto poetico*, Bari, 1942, 112-128.

Santoro, Mario, "Virgilio personaggio della 'Divina Commedia,'" *Cultura e Scuola*, IV (1965), 343-355.

Schelkle, Karl Hermann, *Virgil in der Deutung Augustins*, Stuttgart-Berlin, 1939.

Silverstein, H. T., "The Weeping Statue and Dante's *Gran Veglio*," *Harvard Studies and Notes in Philology and Literature*, XIII (1931), 165-184.

———, "Dante and Vergil the Mystic," *Harvard Studies and Notes in Philology and Literature*, XIV (1932), 51-82.

Sirago, Vito, "Dante e gli autori latini," *Lettere italiane*, III (1951), 99-134.

Toynbee, Paget, "Dante and the Lancelot Romance," in *Dante Studies and Researches*, London, 1902, 1-37.

Vaccaluzzo, Nunzio, "Le fonti del Catone dantesco," *Giornale storico della letteratura italiana*, XL (1902), 140-150.

———, *Dal lungo silenzio*, Messina, 1903.

Vossler, Karl, *Mediaeval Culture*, tr. W. C. Lawton, vol. II, New York, 1929.

Weiss, Roberto, "Dante e l'umanesimo del suo tempo," *Lettere italiane*, XIX (1967), 279-290.

Whitfield, J. H., *Dante and Virgil*, Oxford, 1949.

———, "Dante's Virgil," *Books Abroad* [Special Dante Issue] (May 1965), 136-140.

Wilhelm, Julius, "Dantes Führer durch die Jenseitsreiche," *DDJb*, XXIX-XXX (1951), 106-129.

———, "Zum Problem der schönen Landschaft in der Divina Commedia. Mit besonderer Berücksichtigung des locus amoenus-Topos," *DDJb*, XXXIX (1961), 63-79.

Zabughin, V., *Virgilio nel rinascimento italiano*, 2 vols., Bologna, 1921, esp. vol. I, 3-16.

INDEX

Abelard, 157n, 238

accommodative metaphor, 192n, 196n, 201

Acedia, 136n, 140

Achilles, 147

Adam, 140, 145, 189; as *"typus rationis,"* 252; rib figure of Church, 25, 293; prefiguring Dante, 80-83, 154, 260, 265n

Adam Scot, 252

addresses to the reader, 243n

Aeneas as prefiguration of Dante, 81, 105, 222-23, 260, 265n

Aesop, 258n, 280

Alanus de Insulis, 54, 196n, 226

Albertus Magnus, 238

Alexander of Hales, 238

Alexandria, 4

Alighieri, Pietro, *see* Pietro di Dante

allegoria, synonyms of, 28, 58, 60

allegoria, various meanings of, 28-29

"allegory of the rhetoricians," 234, 236

Alpha and Omega, 231 and n

Anchises, 222

Andreas Capellanus, 108n

Apollo as Christ, 207

Apollonius Rhodos, 227

Aquinas, St. Thomas, 32, 71, 132, 200n, 235, 238; *Quodlibet* VII, a, 16, 18n; *S.T.* I, i, 10, 15-24, 37n, 283n

Arensberg, W., 129n

argumentum, see fabula

Aristotle, 9, 10, 43, 52, 226, 234, 237, 238, 239, 255, 257, 280, 301, 308-309

Arnulf of Orléans, 202, 210-12, 214

Astraea, 152n

Auerbach, E., 20, 28n, 48-49, 52, 57, 59, 77n, 128n, 147n, 177n, 201n, 243n

Augustine, St., 5, 71, 99, 133, 234, 239, 269, 293, 320n; as prefiguration of Dante, 262n, 265n; *Confessions*, 165n, 179, 235n; four senses in, 15-17n; parallels between *Confs.* and *Aeneid*, 12 and n; reaction to schools of rhetoric, 11n; reaction to Virgil, 11-12, 99; passages discussed or referred to: *Confs I, xiii,* 11n, 99; *I, xvii,* 11n; *VI, viii,* 241-43; *VIII, xi,* 144n; *VIII, xii,* 7, 112-14; *De Civ. Dei XV,* 280; *XVI, ii,* 23, 64n; *XVIII, xv-xxi,* 99; *De Gen ad litt. VIII, i,* 265n; *XII,* 200n; *De Gen ad litt. (imper. liber) II, 5,* 15n; *De Trinitate XV, ix, 15,* 17n, 18n, 21; *De Util. cred. III, 5 & 8,* 16n

Augustus Caesar, 182, 184n, 189

Aurora, 176, 193

Austin, H. D., 177n, 179n

autore, Virgil as, 78

balba and associated words, 169, 174

baptism, adult, 196n

Barbi, M., 159n, 164n, 286

Barone, G., 125n

Batard, Y., 74n

Benvenuto da Imola, 83, 87n, 92n, 181, 190, 285-86

Bergin, T., 233

Bernard of Clairvaux, 199n, 239

Bernardo, A. S., 80n, 90n

Bernardus Silvestris, 19, 84, 94n, 102, 116n, 202n, 241n, 254

Berretta, G., 181n

343